M O V I N G   U P !

A Guidebook for Women in Educational Administration

Second Edition

Judith Thompson Witmer

Published in partnership with the
American Association of School Administrators

Rowman & Littlefield Education
Lanham, Maryland • Toronto • Oxford
2006

Published in partnership with the
American Association of School Administrators

Published in the United States of America
by Rowman & Littlefield Education
A Division of Rowman & Littlefield Publishers, Inc.
A wholly owned subsidiary of The Rowman & Littlefield Publishing Group, Inc.
4501 Forbes Boulevard, Suite 200, Lanham, Maryland 20706
www.rowmaneducation.com

PO Box 317
Oxford
OX2 9RU, UK

Copyright © 2006 by Judith Thompson Witmer
First edition © 1995 published by Technomic Publishing Co., ISBN
1566762359

British Library Cataloguing in Publication Information Available

Library of Congress Cataloging-in-Publication Data

Witmer, Judith T.
  Moving up! : a guidebook for women in educational administration / Judith
Thompson Witmer. — 2nd ed.
      p. cm.
  Includes bibliographical references.
  ISBN 1-57886-361-9 (hardback : alk. paper) — ISBN 1-57886-362-7 (pbk. :
alk. paper)
  1. Women school administrators—United States. 2. Women college admin-
istrators—United States. 3. Educational leadership—United States. I. Title.
  LB2831.82.W58 2006
  371.2'011'082—dc22

                                                            2005022396

∞™ The paper used in this publication meets the minimum requirements of
American National Standard for Information Sciences—Permanence of Paper
for Printed Library Materials, ANSI/NISO Z39.48-1992.
Manufactured in the United States of America.

CONTENTS

①

PREPARING FOR TOMORROW

We all are the sum total of our experiences. We cannot change who we are at this given moment because we cannot change the past. However, we do have control over who we will become tomorrow. Knowing that, you can begin to build your own future. You have freedom of choice. It is you who must decide either "This is what I want" or "I do not feel strongly enough about my situation to make a change in my life at this time." This fundamental decision may appear to be oversimplified, but it is the elemental choice you yourself must make. No one can make the decision for you. If you are not sure whether you are ready to make a change, you need to carefully consider the guidance in this chapter to help you clarify your own situation and to make the decision that is right for *you*.

DO I NEED A CHANGE?

The catalyst that will help you determine if you need a change can come from a variety of situations or for any number of reasons; for example, (1) you may be weary of the same routine, day after day, year after year; (2) you may be tired of being "just a teacher" (I am not questioning the

honorableness of the profession, but am repeating the attitudinal comments made in that certain tone of voice that we all recognize as being
condescending); (3) you may be angry that you have so little control over
your own day-to-day routine; or (4) you may be annoyed that everything
you have done and are continuing to do in the classroom (and extracurricular duties as well) is taken for granted.

You'll also find many reasons—or excuses—why a job change (and
advancement) cannot be in your immediate future: (1) in your present
situation, you at least know what to expect, and even the surprises are
predictable; therefore, you are safe; (2) the salary schedule is guaran-
teed and your job is secure; (3) your classroom (or office) has been
freshly painted; (4) the next class (or the one that is two years hence) is
said to be a top-notch group; (5) you promised your best friend you
would be there when her child comes through the system; (6) you receive your share of accolades and that gives you the professional satisfaction you need; (7) you hate to give up directing the play or coaching
the team or advising the student council (who would do those things if
you left?).

If you are already in a supervisory or administrative position, you also
can think of many reasons for not seeking advancement: (1) you like
what you are doing; (2) you already know the things they teach in the
preparation programs for educational administration, so why should you
waste your time and money? (3) the person to whom you report said he
or she would "keep an eye out" on your behalf; (4) you feel an obligation
to the institution since you would be hard to replace in your present position; or (5) you don't want to travel any farther to work.

Your decision to seek a change also will have an effect on your family,
and it is not easy to disregard these factors: (1) your children are too
young, and/or they need you to drive them to their lessons and events;
(2) your elderly father counts on you; (3) who would manage the home
responsibilities while you are off busily pursuing a career that might itself result in even more time away from home? (4) you don't want to
think about the possibility of having to ask the family to relocate; and (5)
what if you fail?

Stop right there! Do you see what is happening? Look back and carefully note the list of reasons you have made for pursuing a change in
your career. Then look at the list of reasons why a career change appears

so formidable and, perhaps, in your mind, impossible. Before you too readily dismiss your desire for change and advancement, ask yourself if you just might be looking for easy reasons to back out, reasons that later you will regret.

Take another look above at the reasons people usually give for making a career change and you will note that they all stem from dissatisfaction with the status quo. They have their roots in anger, frustration, and annoyance, or in guilt over family obligations. This reasoning and these negative responses are reactionary, and are, for the most part, pure rationalization as to why you think you cannot possibly consider a career change and the effort it requires.

Most women do not think beyond these two reasons: (1) dissatisfaction with the current position and (2) reasons they cannot make a change. They fail to take the next step to ask, "What would a career move do for me?" That is the question on which you need to focus. The reasons of "why not" need to be replaced with "Reasons Why I Want to Be Moving Up the Career Ladder."

DISSATISFACTION: THE MAIN FACTOR

Dissatisfaction, even though reactionary and emotional, is the main reason people begin to think in terms of change. In making my own personal list of reasons to move into administration, the dissatisfaction reasons provided most of the impetus I needed. There I was, at forty-five, deciding to leave the classroom. Like many others, I periodically had thought about a move for many years, but I was successful in what I was doing; I liked teaching and was very involved in the life of the school. In fact, there were some colleagues who kidded me about being "married to the school." I laughed at their jibes, knowing what they said was so, and I took a kind of delight in my narrow-focused "status." My teaching assignments were college-prep students, and I was directing and producing the spring musicals as well as creating student-centered, full-blown performances for baccalaureate and commencement ceremonies. My younger child was a sophomore in the high school, and I was attending all of the band competitions, football games, and wrestling matches (most of the senior players were in my classes).

Yet there was an increasingly nagging urge to do something else, to fulfill a desire, to keep a promise to R. J. Lantz, the college supervisor of my student teaching, and, perhaps most of all, to prove that I could succeed in another capacity. In addition, the comments that were meant as compliments were beginning to strike me as being patronizing. I didn't want to hear—even one more time—someone say to me, "Are you *still* teaching?" or "You should be teaching in college." (Is this sounding familiar to you?) And, I must admit, the final impetus was the action of a new principal who arbitrarily and single-handedly decided that the "best teachers" should be assigned the "intellectually disadvantaged" sections.

I vividly recall the first day of the school year that was the turning point of my professional life. At the end of the day, I came home, telephoned the local extension center of a major university, asked what courses were being offered, left the house, and signed up for a supervision course that began within the hour. I left a note for my husband: "Went to University Center. Am enrolling in a program for principal certification." What appeared to my friends and family as a rash action actually had roots that were very deep and rankling. This sudden action, I have since discovered, is not at all unusual for women.

LET'S BE RATIONAL

While I certainly am not the only teacher to make such a dramatic and seemingly impulsive move, I must recommend that you give your own decision more clearly defined attention. A more rational approach in deciding on a career plan is to generate a list of advantages and disadvantages and to put in writing your own reasons for wanting to make a change for career advancement. You need to ask yourself:

- What do I want to do?
- What kind of position do I want?
- Do I see myself moving in small steps or can I take a giant leap?
- In two to five years, what do I want to be doing in my current profession or in another profession?

These are the beginning questions and should be answered before you make any definite plans. It is necessary for you to make such a list because, if you do not, it will be too easy for you to lose sight of your goal.

PRELIMINARY PLANS: HOW CAN I GET STARTED?

Once you have decided to at least explore the possibility of a change, you should ask yourself, "What do I need to do to get where I want to go?" To answer this will require you to list your assets:

- What skills do I already have?
- What skills are needed in the job I want to prepare for?
- Which of these skills are transferable to my career goal?

It isn't enough to say, "I want to be a principal or a director of curriculum." You need to find out what those jobs entail. There are several ways to do this:

1. Apply and get hired; you'll get firsthand experience immediately! (Just kidding, although in rare cases this does happen, so don't totally overlook such an opportunity.)
2. The next best thing, and far more realistic, is to arrange to "shadow" someone who is in a position in which you may be interested. This is sometimes possible as part of your course work (more about preparation programs later), or perhaps you can simply ask the person in your district if you can spend a day with her or him, shadowing.
3. Most people are very flattered to be asked to share their day and their job experiences, so also ask for time to sit and chat about the person's job responsibilities. You'll find that most administrators are pleased to help anyone who is aspiring to follow in their footsteps. Many people make the mistake of thinking that those established in their professions are jealously guarding their positions. Quite the contrary. Most will go out of their way to help you.
4. Another way to familiarize yourself with various administrative positions is to read the job descriptions in your district's policy manual.

The duties should be listed there. (If your district doesn't have job descriptions, the National School Boards Association does, and your district may have a copy of their manual.) If you can arrange for an appointment with the director of personnel, you can discuss the job expectations and how closely the reality meets the expectation.

5. If neither shadowing nor becoming informed about job positions in your local organization is feasible, then you might contact the state and national professional associations for assistance. Perhaps your own professional organization can provide resources as well. You also can find job descriptions on the Internet.

6. Additional printed source material is available in college libraries in the Educational (or School) Administration section. These books should provide the names of professional organizations in each specialty as well as the names of major professional organizations for the field of educational administration, in both public education and higher education. These also can be found on the Internet.

7. Another suggestion is to subscribe to the journal published by the professional specialty in which you are interested. If you cannot find the name of the journal, check with the public or school librarian for a catalog of journal publications or search the Internet. (Also see chapter 15.)

NEEDED SKILLS AND CERTIFICATION

Once you know what the expectations are for each position, you need to match your skills against the job. Make a list of the tasks of the positions in which you are most interested, followed by a list of the skills required for each task. Then, place a check mark on the skills that you have. The result will show the areas in which you need to develop or improve your skills.

A special certification is required for most educational administrative positions in public schools. This certification usually is granted by each state's department of education and is based on criteria that include specialized training, usually at the university level. Not all administrative positions require a specialized certification, however. For example, in many states the director of personnel does not have state certification. A principal, an assistant superintendent, a person with a general business background, or even a classroom teacher might be considered to be qualified by any given school district. Also, the titles for positions may not be the same among the various states. For specific information, check with the certification bureau in your state department of education.

To meet the criteria for required certification, you must enroll in a formal program at a university. Usually a certification program will include courses that qualify for more than one administrative position. It is wise to apply for admission to a program before or soon after you begin to take courses, so that all of your course work counts toward certification. It is also both prudent and politic to do this course work through only one university; for example, if you complete the requirements for a principal's certificate, you can continue to accumulate credits toward superintendency certification, using the earlier credits as a base.

WHY EDUCATIONAL ADMINISTRATION?

Make sure you are very clear in your own mind as to why you want to become an administrator before you pursue such a career path. Altruistic goals are admirable, but be sure you have a clear sense of purpose before you invest time and money. Also note that very few persons have ever found administration to be easier than teaching, so if your expectation is that your hours will be shorter because you won't have papers to correct, don't leave the classroom.

Most women choose administration for the same reason that men do: more money, more autonomy, more status, and more power. (Women's view of power, however, differs from that of men. The male culture often views power as power-in-itself and for themselves, while women view it as limitless, tending to empower others as they themselves acquire power.) In addition to power, there is a desire for personal growth, expression of creativity, and a broader range of influence (empowering others).

KEEP DANCING

Remember when you were in dancing school? The parallels to school administration are worth considering. Just as there are very few "born dancers," so there are very few "born administrators." Both dancing and administration are learned arts and practiced crafts, with a bit of flair and costuming. Remember feeling wonderful in that sparkling costume, the matching hair accessory, the shiny patent shoes or luxurious pink satin *en pointe* toe shoes? That moment on stage is indelible and leaves most of us wanting to recapture the moment in the spotlight. You could not perform with confidence, though, unless you had learned not only the dance steps but also the hand movements and the finesse of the whole performance.

Training to become an administrator is a lot like those dancing lessons you endured before you were considered a performer worthy of the stage, and finesse is considered a key quality of a successful administrator. Just as there was the frustration of learning new steps, the drudgery of practice, and the perseverance of attending class every week (even when there were other things you also wanted to do), so is there frustration, drudgery, and perseverance in preparing to become an educational administrator. Being the neophyte in an introductory course is not much different from being the novice in leotards. And the lessons learned in dancing school are the same as the ones you will need in graduate school: persistence, practice, and performance.

FROM DANCING SCHOOL TO CAREER PATH

The example of dancing school is used here to emphasize that men and women do not approach career paths in the same way. Studies show that the pattern of men's careers does not provide a good fit for those of women because women face a different set of opportunities and problems than men do.

Men tend to plan in advance, more carefully, and at an earlier age than women do. They map out a skill development plan, either formally or informally, anticipating their career steps. They are more definite about what position they want next, and they know where they want to be by a specific age.

On the other hand, women tend to be constantly trying to prove themselves by doing a good job. Women generally have had the attitude that if you work hard, you will be rewarded for your efforts. Women believe that if they work long, hard hours, they'll be promoted. It may come as a surprise to many, but research suggests that this probably is not true.

WHAT'S A WOMAN TO DO?

Traditionally women have been left to their own devices. They have tried to copy men's strategies, while remaining feminine in appearance. Women have had few role models to follow, and, as a result, find themselves changing tactics with every new article they read or with each person they talk to. Notably, in a given school district, a woman does not have as wide a choice of role models as men do.

It is a known fact that mentors play a very important role in the development of their protégés, and most chief executives (be they of corporations or school districts) have had mentors who played a very large part in their success. Yet finding a mentor—one of the most successfully demonstrated ways to build a career—is difficult for most women. Because they usually begin their administrative careers later in life, they are not in a position to seek a mentor, as mentors are almost by definition older than their protégés.

The other obvious hindrance to finding a mentor is that of gender. A mentoring relationship, being voluntary, is established in the same way a friendship is; therefore, it cannot be imposed from without. Most men are reluctant to serve as mentors to women, not only because of the risk of having their motives questioned, but also because of the difference in administrative style. Men and women do not do things in the same way, so for a man to mentor a woman would not be as effective as his serving as mentor to another man. This is not a gender stereotype statement; it is just a basic fact of professional life. It is an instance of people gravitating to others who are like them.

Throughout this book you will be advised to network and to act as a mentor as well as to seek a mentor. However, the reality is that finding or being a mentor may not be easy. Therefore, to devise your own career path, you may need to consider other strategies for career planning over which you personally have more control.

HOW WELL DO YOU FIT THE PROFILE?

For the most part, women administrators in public education (K–12) are older than women in higher education. They also often are firstborn or only children and, as such, are usually higher achievers. They tend to have higher IQs and higher levels of academic achievement, and are more likely to hold the doctorate than men (Schuster and Foote in Kowalski, 2003). Women in general are more likely to attain the education level of their mothers and achieve higher educational levels than their fathers (just as their mothers had more education than their husbands). Women administrators are more likely to be married than not, and the majority are married to college graduates, a number of whom have advanced degrees.

BARRIERS TO CAREER PATHS

Nationwide, the culture of educational administration is dominated by white males and their orientations. The U.S. Department of Labor has described the superintendency as the most gender-stratified executive position in the country (Bjork in Skrla, 2003). And while the percentage of female superintendents rose from 6.6 percent in 1992 to nearly 14 percent in 2000, the disparity between male and female superintendents is disheartening, especially since approximately 73 percent of teachers are female. According to the American Association of School Administrators (AASA), the lack of female superintendents is a major issue, particularly in light of the fact that school boards increasingly receive fewer and fewer applications from women when a superintendent position opens (Vail, 2001). With more than 50 percent of graduates in educational administration doctoral programs being women, something about the job or the hiring process must be eliminating female candidates.

Male superintendents are usually younger than their female counterparts. The same holds true for principals, with men attaining principalships in their mid-to-late twenties while women begin to consider the same positions in their thirties. Women who enter school administration are more likely to be risk takers and are more likely to take risks in their administrative positions than men and to rock the boat to accomplish their goals. Because it appears that the only females who enter the field are highly skilled, highly motivated, and persistent, the quality of the women administrators is excellent. Women also are more likely to be members of professional organizations, which is just one more instance of women doing what they think is expected as well as trying to learn as much as they can.

Superintendents are not usually hired from within the system where they are working in another position, and they typically hold three superintendencies during their career of some fifteen to seventeen years. This means the superintendent's family will be making possibly four moves, an action less likely to be easy for women.

Data from the AASA's newest ten-year examination of the profession provides some insight on the lack of representation of women (Glass, 2000). (Bear in mind, however, that these responses are from those in the positions, not those aspiring to the positions, and that of the 2,262 superintendents who responded, only 297 were women.)

1. Women are not in positions that normally lead to the superintendency.
2. Women are not gaining superintendent's credentials in preparation programs.
3. Women are not as experienced nor as interested in district-wide fiscal management.
4. Women are not interested in the superintendency for personal reasons.
5. School boards are reluctant to hire women superintendents.
6. Women enter the field of education for different purposes.
7. Women enter too late.

The typical career path of men in school administration is from coach or athletic director to assistant secondary principal to principal, assistant superintendent, and superintendent. Women rarely achieve the superintendency by this route. With men, it's cut and dried. They go right from teacher to principal. Women are required to prove themselves again and again, and when they do reach the central office, they often are in their early fifties and, with retirement in their near future, often don't want to proceed further. Despite this, we know and have seen that women make good, excellent, and even outstanding educational administrators; therefore, we must encourage more to take a deliberate and planned career path to these positions. It can be done.

On an encouraging note, more recently a significant amount of attention has been focused on the role of women in the superintendency and the principalship. The effect of Title IX (1972) was that school board members are now reminded of the federal guideline concerning the promotion of women and minorities. In addition, superintendent search firms have been more aggressive in identifying women candidates, while the gender composition of school boards gradually has shifted toward a more even distribution between women and men (Glass, 2000).

A SLOW SHIFT

The AASA study of superintendents mentioned above also offered strategies to address the lack of women in administrative positions:

1. The nature of the superintendency should be changed by lessening the oppressive workload.
2. Boards should make it possible for women superintendents to excel in what they like to do (what they do best). This suggestion would have women superintendents spending a greater degree of working time in curriculum and instruction, with day-to-day budget and fiscal management shifted to an assistant superintendent.
3. States and higher education institutions should provide incentives to women to gain the superintendent's certificate. Yearlong superintendency internships and a system of mentoring are suggested.
4. Districts and search firms should be rewarded (financially) by states for hiring women or minority superintendents.

Some years ago a similar plan was suggested by *Academe* (reprinted in Kaplan and Tinsley, 1989) for moving women in higher education out of dead-end positions into senior management:

1. CEOs and governing boards of higher institutions must become actively involved in affirmative action by supporting the advancement of women and minorities in a publicly stated personal and institutional commitment. Search procedures must insist that qualified women and minorities be interviewed. Communication networks must be established and professional development programs implemented.
2. Women themselves must commit to their own advancement by attaining appropriate degrees and credentials, by working through the political processes and organizational structures of the institutions, by supporting the requisite changes, and by taking risks.
3. Women need to support other women.

YOUR OWN CAREER PATH

Realizing that there are both formal and informal movements to encourage broader consideration of women candidates, now is the time to begin your plans for career advancement. Some of the steps are easy; in fact, you already may be taking them. Others you may need to work on, but you can begin to chart your own educational administration career path now:

1. **Continue your education.** Pursue and attain the degree or certification expected for the position or positions you are seeking. There are many ways to do this. An ever-increasing number of universities are offering off-site or branch campus programs for advanced degrees and program certification. Some medium-sized cities have established education or university centers that are conglomerates or cooperatives among a number of universities. Even in rural areas, there are extension programs available. Another possibility is to do home study through distance learning, increasingly being offered by larger universities. The possibilities are endless, so find out what will work best for you.
2. **Join professional associations** in your current field and in the area(s) to which you aspire. You will learn the names of experts in

the field and become familiar with the terminology and trends in the field. The journals published by these associations may list job postings and certainly will advertise conferences sponsored by the specialty. Often these journals publish articles that give helpful information on moving up the career ladder. If there are state organizations, attend their conferences and, if at all possible, volunteer for committees. In addition, learn about what services these organizations offer to their members.

3. **Join major action groups** so that people get to know you and you get to know the "movers and shakers." There are many institutions and organizations that you can join. Don't limit your activities to educational groups. Search your own community or region for such organizations as the Council for Public Education, advisory boards for nonprofit organizations, corporations, and cultural institutions.

4. **Attend training sessions** and avail yourself of any staff development opportunities offered by your present institution. Volunteer to represent your department or specialty at regional, state, or national conferences.

5. **Develop skills** so that people will notice you. Offer to help with the newsletter. Get appointed to school-community committees. Offer to help in an area other than your own specialty. For example, if you are a building-level administrator, volunteer to serve on district-wide committees. If you are in higher education, offer to help plan an event or to serve as a mentor to new faculty or even students. If there are areas that are potentially advantageous to your career plans, educate yourself so that you can be of service to leaders in those areas. Get out there and make yourself useful (and, in turn, *noticed*). And, remember to introduce yourself to people who may not know you.

6. **Do your best to avoid positions with built-in failure.** If a certain job has a track record of failure, don't take it unless you are positive you can succeed. Apply only for those jobs for which there is a high rate of success. Do not get into a situation doomed to failure. It is a widely accepted perception that when men fail, there is an external reason, but that when women fail, it is their own fault. Don't get caught in this.

7. **Don't be limited** by the job responsibilities listed for your position. Accept any opportunities that come your way, even if they call for extra work or longer hours (to a point). This is not to advise you to be taken advantage of. Look at programs that are important to your institution. Learn about these programs and become involved in them.

8. **Take any opportunity** to represent the institution, locally or on a broader scale. Offer to be part of a panel or presentation team for public meetings. Be an active promoter for your institution, always speaking of it in positive terms.

9. **Offer to establish community or parent advisory groups** or establish an advocacy office, or an information "clearinghouse" through your office.

10. **Subscribe to and read broadly** in the educational journals, both at the level of your current position and in the area to which you aspire. (See also number 2 above.)

11. **Write articles** for publication. You have an area of expertise. That, combined with your own research or practical experience, can provide the basis for journal articles. If you are hesitant about this, enroll in a workshop or a course on report writing, or writing for publication. If you are currently enrolled in a graduate program, you may be able to base an article on an assignment you have completed for one of your courses.

12. **Occasionally offer to record the minutes** or to write the report for a committee on which you serve. Don't hesitate to volunteer; just don't allow the expectation that as a female it is your place to serve as recording secretary. If you make it clear that you are volunteering for a particular instance, and you do this with a smile, you could earn a lot of respect.

13. **Be willing to be considered a recognized "expert"** or "specialist" in at least two areas. This may mean extra study on your part, but it will be worth it. Being considered an expert may occur of its own accord if you become published. (One particular incident comes to mind in my own experience. I was asked to write a book chapter on a particularly controversial topic of statewide interest. Even before the book was published, I was being invited to serve on panels on the topic. I don't consider

myself expert on the subject at all, and can name at least a dozen people locally whom I would consider experts, but I was the one called to present.) So be ready.

14. **Apply to be a presenter** at selected conferences. There are usually open invitations posted in journals, asking for interested parties to submit proposals for consideration. Having a good knowledge base usually is enough to allow you to write an appealing proposal. If you are accepted, you can do more preparation. One word of advice: Choose a topic with high interest appeal.

15. **Don't ever have a headache.** If you are prone to headaches, don't admit it. A headache is a sign of weakness, particularly for females. As one with a history of migraines, I can empathize and, in fact, can completely understand someone's inability to perform well under duress; however, you may end up, as I did, with a male supervisor who never in his life had had a headache, and, therefore, headaches to him were not real, nor were they a valid reason for absence. If you have a headache, call it something else—eye strain, neuralgia, a pulled neck muscle, even an ulcer, but never a headache.

16. **Hone your "rainmaking" skills.** In business this refers specifically to increasing revenues by generating new clients or discovering new customers' needs. In educational organizations, rainmaking skills might be such things as strategic planning in particular and risk taking in general. Rainmakers make things happen.

17. **Follow the precepts of business and entrepreneurship.** There are many more similarities than differences between business and education and between administration and entrepreneurship. Being familiar with business theories and practices can give you an edge.

18. **Start mentoring.** Even though this point was addressed in an earlier section, the importance of having and being a mentor cannot be overemphasized.

LOOKING AND ACTING LIKE A FEMALE ADMINISTRATOR

A major focus of marketing is on packaging, the appearance of a product. You, in essence, are packaging yourself to act like, talk like, and look like an administrator. There is no trickery or façade involved. It is just smart business to dress like those in the job position to which you aspire. This dressing for the next desired job is easy advice to follow, provided (1) you can find a woman to emulate and (2) the members of your institution dress conservatively. It will be a bit more difficult for you to look like the others and yet look professional, however, if your male counterpart doesn't wear (or appears not to own) a jacket, or if your superior's idea of style is Hush Puppies and an unbuttoned shirt. In such cases, you should still opt for the professional look, a cut above the aforementioned counterpart. This will be acceptable because you are female, and will certainly put you in a favorable light when you meet others outside the immediate office.

Choosing a Wardrobe

Like most other aspects of entering a profession dominated by men, dressing for the position is not as easy for women. A man needs only well-pressed suits or slacks and a jacket, crisp shirts, and good leather shoes. The only personal choice he might have to make is whether or not to grow facial hair. On the other hand, women have many decisions to make regarding a personal wardrobe and hairstyle. A man can rotate ten suits (or sport coats and jackets) in any given season, but a woman who wears the same suit (or any other ensemble) within a two-week period risks raised eyebrows. As an administrator, you can't wear things too short, too revealing, too bright, too trendy, or too youthful. A suit signals authority and is always safe in any situation.

Flat heels may make you look too casual, but very high heels are neither practical nor conservative enough to befit an executive position; you should opt for medium-high, unless you are very tall, in which case a low-medium might be a better choice. A word of advice: Your shoes should match or be darker than the darkest color you are wearing.

Professionally manicured nails by today's trends are said to be the mark of a professional woman, yet they may also indicate a lack of seriousness, especially if the nails are long and the color bright. Jewelry is also part of the packaging: Is large equated with gaudy or with panache? Should you wear rings on more than two fingers? Should you avoid extra-large earrings? Or jangling bracelets? Or should you stay with pearls and gold? The answer to any of these questions is, of course, not

absolute in every circumstance. The best advice is that old axiom, usually applied to one's conduct, "When in doubt, don't."

Even better than following the advice of caution, however, is to be observant. Watch what business and professional women are wearing. If
you are isolated and rarely have an opportunity to observe colleagues of
equal rank, then subscribe to tradition. Take notice of what women news
commentators wear, or take time to page through some of the better
shop-by-mail specialty catalogs, such as Barrie Pace, Talbots, or Jos. A.
Bank. These offer both high-quality merchandise and good customer
service. You can also consult a dressing guide such as the one found in
Letitia Baldrige's book *New Manners for New Times* or her earlier best
seller, *New Complete Guide to Executive Manners*. Another good practice is to find a specialty shop and identify a salesclerk who will take the
time to learn what you like and will even shop for you through special
ordering. Another possibility is to use a personal shopper. Such services
are readily found in medium-to-large-sized cities.

When it comes to selecting a wardrobe, use common sense and ask
yourself the following questions:

1. Is this item appropriate to the image I wish to convey? Is it the
   best fabric I can afford?
2. Is it appropriate to the position I hold?
3. Will what I am wearing call undue personal attention to me? Have
   I considered that a monochromatic color scheme is considered to
   be more sophisticated and professional than an outfit with more
   than one color?
4. Is what I am considering for purchase basic enough in cut and fabric and color so that it does not appear faddish, and is it something
   that I can wear for several seasons?
5. Is the cut and fit flattering to my body shape and size?

Women in administrative posts should adapt the unwritten rules followed by successful men. Long sleeves should be the rule, whether you
are wearing a dress (with its jacket close by) or a blouse. Even if your
arms have been described as "willowy" or in other flattering terms, keep
them covered while on the job. If you have removed your jacket in your
office, keep it close by so that you can quickly put it on if you leave your

office. You should also, of course, put your jacket on if anyone (other than your secretary, a very good friend, or a family member) enters your office to speak with you. Wearing your jacket (1) is a sign of respect to your guest and (2) gives you a professional demeanor. Also, don't forget to rise from your desk if a visitor comes into your office.

You should keep grooming items in your office, briefcase, or purse to use to freshen up during the day or prior to an evening engagement. If at all possible, however, go home to change into a fresh dark dinner dress. This will make you stand out in a most positive way among all of those in their rumpled suits. If the social event you are attending is a reception or other occasion of less than two hours' duration, you may want to consider leaving your purse (sans valuables, since you have had an opportunity to go home) in the car. Or carry a very small purse with a narrow shoulder strap. This will leave your hands free for exchanging handshakes and for carrying a small plate or glass. You will appear more polished and not encumbered with anything extraneous.

For daily use, a purse should be no larger than it needs to be to contain what you absolutely need. Regardless of the size, however, it should be well organized. A purse with compartments works best. Makeup and other grooming aids can be put into a zippered toiletries case in one compartment of the purse; keys, billfold or money purse, and glasses case in another; and any business materials you might need, such as pens, notebook or PDA, cell phone, and business cards, in a third. A head scarf is also a handy item to have with you, as is a spare pair of stockings.

Wear a hairstyle that you like. Most advisors suggest that you wear short or short-to-medium length as that length is usually easier to care for, but do not be restricted if you are more comfortable otherwise. Personally, I like longer hair, and although I believe a shorter style might be more flattering to a woman "of a certain age," I do not like the feel of short hair on myself. However, to offset the full head of hair and the image it may convey, I dress very conservatively.

One way to rotate your wardrobe is to line up your suits in the closet, take each morning's suit out from the right end of the closet, and at the end of the day, after brushing and airing it, replace it in your closet at the left end. Label your shoe boxes and store them by color. The quickest way to scan and select your jewelry is to keep it in jewelry chests to avoid having to open a number of little boxes every morning. To avoid wearing the same suit to the same event or meeting with the same people, keep a small notebook in your dressing room and every day jot down what you are wearing. Above all, remember that you want to be recognized as an administrator, and dressing like an executive makes that point.

As a public school or higher education professional, you have a certain stature in the community and, as an authority figure, you are expected to maintain a particular comportment of appearance and action. For example, you should always dress appropriately. While I live in blue jeans at home, I would not wear them into the community, even to run errands. Patronizing the local pub is more a matter of community norm and varies from one area to another. Make sure you know what the expectations are, however, and err on the side of caution.

CAREER ASSESSMENT

Once you are enrolled in an administrative preparation program, you should consider a formal assessment of your potential for being a successful administrator. There are credible assessment centers located throughout the nation that are worth your consideration. Through interviews, simulations, and problem-solving processes, your job skills and potential for administrative positions are evaluated by practicing administrators who have received specialized training. The National Association of Secondary School Principals (NASSP) Assessment Center is one such assessment program that uses a team of assessors who observe and record the behavior of the participants. This program measures leadership potential in skill areas essential to successful school leadership.

The NASSP offers a contemporary assessment tool, Selecting and Developing the 21st Century Principal, to help identify and/or develop effective school leaders. It is designed to measure leadership potential by diagnosing the behavior strengths and development needs of prospective and practicing principals in skills identified as critical for success in the principalship. There are four identified behavior strengths:

• Be an effective instructional leader (Setting Instructional Direction, Teamwork, Sensitivity)

- Resolve complex problems (Judgment, Results Orientation, Organizational Ability)
- Communicate effectively (Oral Communication, Written Communication)
- Develop self and others (Development of Others, Understanding Own Strengths and Weaknesses)

Participants engage in a series of authentic, interrelated activities for one day (these activities simulate the work of a school principal) while they are observed by trained assessors. Each participant receives an assessment report that is reviewed individually with the participant by the center director.

The centers make it clear that participating in the assessment is the collective judgment of the assessor group and that the results are not intended to be so comprehensive that other facets of professional development, educational training, or professional experiences would eliminate a candidate for any administrative position.

The assessment is just one more tool that may help those who are hiring to have a more complete appraisal of you and that may be even more helpful for the person being assessed as to areas perhaps needing improvement or areas of strength. For many women, an assessment can serve as a validation as well as a guide for improvement.

As a participant in an independent assessment center, I found the process to be valuable, even though my superintendent mocked the results, as I had scored higher than anyone else to date at the time I was evaluated. (I say this only to emphasize the importance of these assessments whether or not your present employer supports them.) Even though the results of a study of assessment centers found that men receive preferential treatment regardless of their level of skill (Schneider and Wallich, 1990), involving yourself in a formal assessment shows potential employers that you are interested in self-improvement and that you have a professional attitude and a serious intent.

MARKETING SUMMARY

Most studies show that there is no one way to the top, the near top, or even the middle level of administration. Boards are whimsical, and agendas (both open and hidden) change with each election. Still, however, it is almost mandatory to take all of the steps outlined above. The credentials and politics are requisite. Following these steps is a necessary part of the process. You increase your chances to a large extent by following the advice given herein. You can always take some consolation in the fact that, without all of the hoops to jump through, you would have less chance to be given any consideration.

Do not apologize for following these suggestions in marketing yourself. No one can promote your skills and qualifications as well as you yourself can. If you are doing a good job in your present position and no one knows about it, you can't expect the job searchers to find you. You need to have visibility. Inform the local paper as to special programs you are operating. Write the article(s) yourself if that will help the paper publish the events. Get in the public and the professional eye. And remember the advice given above on rainmaking.

YOUR SHELF LIFE: A WORD TO THE "OVER THIRTY-FIVES"

Age is an issue, no matter how much we choose to discount its impact on career plans. In addition to all of the figures cited as to the earlier age at which men enter administration, there is also a definite age bias.

Most people will be tactful about the age issue, but it is real. If you begin your career tracking in your thirties, your colleagues will be rather neutral in their comments about your plans. As you enter an advanced degree or certification program as a "thirtysomething," you will be welcomed, touted, and feted by the university departmental resident faculty. If you don't begin to plan for a move up the career ladder until your forties, your colleagues will be polite but the question, either voiced or unspoken, will be "Why?" Your closest friends or family members may pose the question outright. The graduate program faculty will accept your application with welcoming smiles because you no doubt will be a well-above-average student, diligent and dedicated. You also have much practical experience and many life skills that will add to class discussions. The professors will be able to identify with you because you are closer in age to them and share a common social heritage.

There will, however, come a day when, no matter how much they enjoy your interest in your studies, at least one of your kindly professors will take you aside and ask you if you are aware of the odds you face in your administrative goals. She or he will be ever so polite and diplomatic. Be prepared. This will happen, if not with a professor, then definitely with a senior administrator in your institution. If you can face this avuncular "heart-to-heart" talk with a bit of humor, the conversation will be easier for both of you.

My standard answer to anyone who has had the temerity to ask why I began a doctoral program in my mid-forties is not an original reply, but rather something I read many years ago and tucked away in the recesses of my response system: "I'm going to be fifty anyhow. I decided that I would be fifty with a doctorate rather than fifty without it." Your fiftieth birthday, too, will arrive someday. Don't let that fact deter you from your goal.

I was also realistic in knowing when I entered the doctoral program that chances of attaining a superintendency were slim, but I was willing to take that chance because I knew that I was pursuing the doctoral degree for me and not really for any other reason. The bumpy road was made smoother because I met a woman the first night of the first class, and we knew by the end of that initial course that we were committed to completing our doctorates and that we would supply emotional support to each other through the program. I can only wish that each of you find the same kind of friend that I found in Jean. We were each other's lifeline for six years. I know that she and I could have made it alone, but how much better to have each other to discuss the course material and our career goals. I shall never forget the girlish laughter as we had our "senior formals" taken for the college yearbook, and the overwhelming pride and giddiness we felt as we marched side by side at the graduation ceremony.

Beyond Passages

In 2000, 42 percent of all adult women were over fifty. Use this fact as a reaffirmation of your own decision to carve a new career and as a confirmation that it is, indeed, your turn to take charge of the world, or at least of an educational institution.

THE PRESENTATION PACKAGE

Surprisingly, many aspiring administrators do not realize the importance of resumes and vitae, particularly if they have not been in the job market for a period of time. With the ever-increasing number of governmental regulations, most notably those addressing equal opportunity, educational institutions no longer can be cavalier in their hiring procedures. They must follow certain guidelines so that their procedures do not come into question, let alone result in a lawsuit because of unfair hiring practices. While some of these regulations have opened more doors to women and minorities, the negative effect is that much time is spent in advertising positions and holding interviews when, in some instances, the institution already knows whom it plans to hire, yet must go through the interviewing process just to be in compliance. As a result, many applicants find themselves getting their hopes up during the process, only to be disappointed not to be hired because the institution had the position promised to someone or at least knew whom they wanted to hire.

You need to know the reality of these practices so that you can resist taking rejections personally. Moreover, because women often are naive about the realities of the job market, they find themselves up against candidates who are more savvy, even though they may not necessarily be better qualified. Rather than lose your self-confidence, take the advice in this chapter and follow the steps suggested. As a result, you should greatly increase your chances of achieving the position for which you are qualified.

The most essential talent in a job search is being able to communicate your skills to a prospective employer. You must be able to express yourself well in writing and speaking because both the resume and the interview are an extension of your administrative skills. You will be judged on those skills by those who read your resume and conduct your interview. Be ready to be your best.

JOB SEARCH READINESS

As you near the time to begin your own job search, start to collect standard (and not-so-standard, if you can get them) job application forms (see appendix A). Complete the forms as though you were going to apply. The areas in which you are weak will immediately become apparent. If there are sections you are leaving blank (aside from military service), then get to work and improve in those areas.

The section asking applicants to list publications is a typical concern for many first-time applicants. You, however, are starting your career plan well in advance, so you have time to fill that gap, as well as others in which you sense a need for improvement. If this is your first attempt at writing for publication, begin small. Because there are numerous regional or statewide professional newsletters that would welcome articles, this is a good place to begin. It's better to have your articles published in a small, limited-audience publication than to send your manuscript to a national journal and (1) wait months for acceptance and publication or (2) face possible rejection (a common fate of novice writers).

Allow yourself sufficient time to prepare your credentials before you begin to apply for administrative positions. As a preliminary overview, you should consider the following:

1. Decide if you are willing to relocate or under what conditions you would be willing to move. If you should be made a good offer, you

may find yourself negotiating with a spouse and children at a time
when the pressure of interviewing is in itself enough.

2. Think about matching your personal and professional style with
the needs and expectations of the school district or college/university.
Do not apply to an institution in which your leadership style would
not fit. While you may be flexible, you cannot adjust your style to
the point of becoming someone other than yourself.

3. Do not apply for a position that has a "no-win" situation, either because it may be beyond your present capabilities and experience or
because there are problems in the institution that would defeat
even the most experienced administrator.

POWER RESUMES

To present yourself in the best possible way, you should seek professional assistance in creating a top-notch resume,[1] vita,[2] or curriculum vitae.[3] There is a skill to crafting a resume/vita that most people do not
have the time or inclination to hone. Professional resume writing services are available in cities and in many larger communities; however, be
very discriminating in your search for a service that has a great deal of
experience in preparing documents for educators and that does not use
a resume software template. Making the mistake of going to a "resume
factory" will result in a style not at all distinctive for an administrative
position in an educational setting. Check the *Chronicle of Higher Education* for services specializing in resumes and curriculum vitae for educators (and also for job postings). If you believe you have the skill to
prepare your own resume, the same caution is given to not use a form
(perhaps downloaded from the Internet) that looks like every other one
the search committee sees.

In order to have the best possible document, you should begin collecting any material that might be even remotely helpful to the service
(or to you) in preparing your resume/vita. Draw up an accurate listing of
your educational preparation, with dates of graduation, the name and
address of each institution, the kind of degree, the specialty, and your
dissertation or thesis topic. Of course, you'll also need a record of all administrative and teaching experiences: titles, dates, institutions.

You should also prepare a list of accomplishments you achieved at each post, as well as a listing of responsibilities for each. Include any innovations you instituted or programs you designed or implemented. Do this over a period of two or three weeks, unless you are very organized and have all of this material in a file. Also, make a listing of all honors and awards you have received, presentations you have made, and publications. (Your dissertation or thesis does not count as a publication unless it was actually *published* and not just printed for the dissertation archives.)

If you have additional data that you believe to be pertinent, include it. The more information you begin with and the better organized your materials are, the better the final product will be.

If you prefer to write your own resume or vita, purchase a guidebook. Follow the example closest to your particular situation, as you will find very few, if any, samples of resumes/vitae specifically for educational administrators. Once you have composed your document, give your final draft to someone you trust to proofread, for you will not find your own mistakes or typographical errors. Be sure your proofreader is experienced not only in locating errors but also in checking for consistency of style. She or he should also be very familiar with the field of educational administration. You cannot afford to have errors of either format or fact.

A resume in the field of educational administration should be two pages. A curriculum vitae can be as many pages as are necessary to include publications, presentations, awards, honors, professional association memberships, civic activities, and (for higher education applicants) courses taught. Even a curriculum vitae, however, should provide the most important information in the first three pages. Page arrangement is also very important. Again, if you are not skilled in page design, it is better to leave this to the experts.

Your resume should focus on where you want to go, not where you have been. For example, if you are applying for a position as an elementary principal, focus on those skills and accomplishments that highlight your ability to be an educational leader on that level. The fact that you taught second grade is very nice, but what innovative programs did you implement? What curriculum committees did you chair? How did you get the parents or community involved? Emphasize skills that will aid you as an administrator.

Remember to include skills such as team building, morale development, or the fact that you were able to mobilize all the staff and students in a campaign to clean up a stream. Stress your leadership skills, especially in areas where you actually *led*, such as "Developed and implemented the first . . ." or "Led the committee that . . ." In seeking a management position, be selective in listing your union activities. Do not neglect mentioning them, if you held a leadership position, but be careful in your choice of words.

In emphasizing your major achievements, be clear, even if you are applying to the organization in which you have served for many years. Others will not remember what you did, unless you remind them. If you can include quantitative data, do so. For example, in listing such items as cost-cutting measures, grants awarded to the district, budget reduction, or staff retrenchment, use actual amounts.

If your background includes strong skills, you may want to list these prior to your work record under a heading such as "Skills" or "Proficiencies" or "Profile."

Sample 1

Highly effective in the organizing/scheduling of faculty, conferences, and development of progressive learning programs

Outstanding skills in the fields of training, lecturing, university relations, and collaborative working experiences

Demonstrated leadership in **coordinating comprehensive marketing plans** through entrepreneurial processes

Very successful in designing, developing, and presenting **customer-driven educational programs**

Skilled in organizing and leading a **team effort** within an academic environment

Sample 2

Excellent time-management skills, thorough planner, highly organized

Skilled administrator with a special interest in the legal environment surrounding education

Highly motivated, self-directed administrator with demonstrated organizational and interpersonal skills

Proficient in management techniques leading to the creation of a strong work environment

While it is not necessary to list every function you have performed, every month of work, or every job you ever held, do have all of the years covered. Do not leave gaps in your work history that might suggest you were let go from a position. If you took time off for child rearing or a family crisis, in your cover letter state something positive that you learned from those years (without mentioning those years specifically), or in the interview make a reference to your chairmanship of the Red Cross for the county during the years you were not employed.

Do not include personal data such as your age, marital status, and number of children. In listing credentials, memberships, outside activities, and academic awards, be careful to select the ones that identify professional interests or management skills. Omit such items as "Enjoy reading and travel." This marks you as a lightweight. On the other hand, if you have an unusual hobby or interest that might intrigue the reader or interviewer, you may want to list it. Make sure it makes you sound adventuresome or willing to take risks, but not too unusual.

Finally, you should consider what the end product should look like. What color and style of paper will make the best showing for the kind of position you are seeking? As trends in colors and papers have a tendency to vary every two or three years, you should check with someone who works with writing or reading resumes for advice on the best choice for you. Purchase a heavier weight paper (25 lb.) and use black ink, perhaps with a dark blue for the header on the first page. It is likely that copies will be made of your materials, and if you use colored paper and/or colored ink, the copies will not be attractive to the readers. Remember that your vita is the first impression you are making. It will determine to a great extent whether or not you will be considered for an interview.

REFERENCES

Many people are at a loss when it comes to compiling a list of references. This confusion stems from a less-than-clear understanding of the purpose of references, a reluctance to ask people to serve as references, and an unwillingness to tell people that a job search for another position is on your agenda.

It is not always comfortable asking persons to serve as references, so you must make clear in your own mind that you are choosing a new career path and that preparing a list of references is part of that process. Most people are pleased to be asked to be a reference for you, so don't feel any hesitation in making your request.

Your references are not character witnesses; they are persons who are able to attest to your suitability to the position sought. Begin with a long list of possibilities—at least as many as twenty-five; then hone this list of names to the best twelve, based on (1) the kind of position you are seeking, (2) the business or profession of each reference, and (3) what you need from each person.

Of those twelve best names, only four to six (unless a different number is specifically requested) will ever appear on any individual list of references, as you will be selecting from your list of twelve for each position you seek. For example, you may hold the qualifications for several possible areas of employment, and you will want the most appropriate references for each of these positions as you apply for them.

It is also a good practice to use personalized letterhead that matches the paper of your resume and cover letter. If you use a professional writing service, that service should be able to prepare this matching letterhead.

Good manners dictate that you ask a person to serve as a reference. Do not assume that you have any person's permission. If possible, all references should have a surname different from yours, even if they are not related to you. (If, however, the reference is truly important and its absence could affect your being hired, then place the following after the name: [No relation].) Your references should also be available to take calls during business hours and have privacy to speak confidentially.

Each reference should be a successful professional person. She or he should be self-confident, upbeat, and outgoing, as well as having good oral and written communication skills. It also helps if the reference has a desire to help you succeed.

Most employers prefer to call the references and speak to them, rather than receive letters of reference. This change has come about through today's freedom of information rule, which resulted in persons writing only glowing letters of recommendation. As a result, prospective employers prefer to talk directly to your references and ask them specific questions. Some positions still require formal letters of reference, but these instances are becoming fewer.

Getting the most out of your references is a skill, and if you take the time to follow these steps, you will end up with more effective references:

1. Make an initial telephone call to each prospective reference. Following a brief greeting and exchange of pleasantries, explain that you are seeking a new position. Explain how you have been preparing, and what kind of position you are pursuing. Ask if she or he would be willing to serve as a reference. Be specific as to whether you need a letter or if she or he will be listed in your resume or application with the likelihood of being interviewed by telephone. Tell your references that you will send information that should make either task easier.

2. Send these persons a copy of your resume and other pertinent information; this should include a summary of work you might have done with the person, or similar work you did alone but in which both of you share an interest. The packet of information should also include a list of questions you expect the reference to be asked in a telephone call from the prospective employer. You might also send an outline or summary of your accomplishments and work traits, as well as an example or summary suitable for that particular individual to include in his or her recommendation of you. Make sure you send your material within a day or two of your initial telephone conversation. By supplying this information, you are making it easier for the reference to write the letter or respond to questions; in addition, then, to some extent you can direct the content. Don't be embarrassed by this unabashed sales pitch; most references will be glad for the help.

3. Follow up. Telephone each reference within a week to discuss the materials you sent and to answer any questions.

Once you have a specific position for which you are applying, call your selected references with the information of the name of the person to whom they should write or from whom they should be hearing. Also take this opportunity to have a practice discussion of the possible questions if the person welcomes the suggestion.

Remember to write thank-you notes to each person who has agreed to serve as a reference for you. Your note will be a reminder to your references of your consideration of their time, for it does take time to write a good letter of reference and to prepare for a possible telephone interview.

WHERE THE JOBS ARE

For someone new in the field of educational administration, finding job postings can be a formidable task. You must make it your business to check all possible sources at hand as well as through the informal network. As in most businesses and professions, those who are in the positions are most likely to know where the openings are, simply because they have a broader network and they keep in touch with people in their own field and in related areas. Let your colleagues know that you are looking. Enlist the aid of your superordinate, if that is possible in your individual situation. Also speak to the director of personnel for your institution. Most people are willing to help.

There are also more systematic ways in which to search for positions. The first place I would recommend for those in or aspiring to positions in higher education is the *Chronicle of Higher Education*. If you are serious in your search, subscribe to this publication. Even if you are not sure whether you are interested in seeking a position in higher education, I still would recommend that you subscribe to this publication. The *Chronicle* is published weekly and is the best source for information on events in higher education as well the best source for job postings. Other publications to follow include *Education Week* and *Teacher Magazine*, as well as their job posting service at www.agentk-12.org. You might also want to look at www.careers.org and www.worktree.com.

In addition, you should subscribe to the job postings of your university's career services office; you often can receive these listings gratis for a year following graduation from any degree program. Some state organizations affiliated with the American School Boards Association also publish journals that carry job listings. Other professional journals list job openings either in their publications or on their websites.

There are several commercial publications, such as *Career Opportunity News* (also available online), "Current Jobs Bulletin" (which can be ordered at the online site www.graduatejobs.com), and others that can be accessed online with any combination of words including *jobs, careers*, and *education*. Don't neglect city newspapers, as some schools and universities do prefer to use the classifieds! You may also want to check the websites of various search firms (see appendix B).

THE COVER LETTER

A common mistake made by many applicants is to not give the cover letter the attention it deserves. Don't approach the cover letter as a chore; rather, it is an opportunity to summarize or highlight your qualifications and to arouse the reader's interest. The letter must be flawless in every way; it should be attention-getting, yet dignified. If you want to make a very professional impression, have the letter written by a professional or a good friend who knows how to write with distinction and finesse, yet will produce a letter that reads as if it had been written by you.

If you are confident in your own writing ability and want to compose your own cover letter, make sure to include these five essential parts:

1. In the first paragraph, state the position for which you are applying and note your interest in the position. Tell how you heard about the opening. Was it posted in the *Chronicle of Higher Education*? In a local or city newspaper? In a professional journal? On a website? Did you learn about it from a job listing service? From a colleague? Or were you invited to apply?
2. Tell why this institution (or district) interests you by citing its reputation or by acknowledging two or three of its accomplishments and how your own background (interest or experience) complements these.
3. Briefly summarize your experiences.
4. Briefly highlight your qualifications, taking care to mention the qualifications you possess that match those they are seeking. Your objective is to interest the reader—and the committee—in meeting you and in talking with you.

5. In the concluding paragraph, make a summary statement and include an ending sentence stating that you are looking forward to meeting with the committee to discuss your qualifications and/or what you can do to serve the institution.

Always use the highest quality paper, and avoid textured paper because printer ink will not adhere well. The cover letter should not exceed one page unless your experience and credentials allow for expansion.

Address your letter to a specific person with a specific title. If you are uncertain to whom the letter should be addressed, call the institution and ask. If you are told that it is a committee, or if the person cannot or will not give you a specific name, use the address as given in the advertisement. Your salutation would then be "Dear Members of the Search Committee."

As noted above, the cover letter should be targeted to the specific position for which you are applying. Never send a standard form letter. If possible, the cover letter should match your resume, both in paper and in font style, preferably Times Roman or a similar serif style. This letter should be written on your own letterhead. If you are using a resume or career service, they can provide you with sheets of matching letterhead. Do *not* use stationery from your place of employment.

ADDITIONAL APPLICATION MATERIALS

Be sure you include in your packet of materials all requested credentials and supporting documents. If there will be a delay in your receiving, for example, a current transcript or a criminal clearance form (required in some states), send copies of earlier records with a note of explanation that current documents will be forthcoming.

The application form itself (more common in public schools than in institutions of higher education) must also be completed in full. If an area, such as military service, does not apply to you, fill in the blank with "NA" (not applicable) or a dash to indicate that not answering the question is deliberate and not a careless oversight. Type the application responses; try scanning it if you can do so and if the result appears exactly like the original. If using a typewriter, it is a good idea to make a few copies of the blank application to use as practice copies.

Mail your application packet in a clean, new envelope with both the receiver's and the sender's names and addresses typed clearly. Special envelopes with the message "Resume Enclosed—Please Do Not Bend" are available from many resume writing services. You might also ask about special presentation folders. These presentation folders should be used only in applying for executive positions; otherwise, you risk appearing pretentious.

RESPONSES TO APPLICATIONS

Once the institution receives your materials, they should send you an acknowledgment. If you do not hear from someone a week past the closing date for applying, it is acceptable for you to call to ask if your materials were received. It is also acceptable for you to call to ask their projected timeline (for interviewing and for the subsequent selection of the successful candidate). Do not ask further questions. If, on the other hand, you do receive a letter (or postcard) acknowledging receipt of your packet of materials, it is not necessary to reply. It is appropriate to reply, however, if the letter contains further information regarding the timeline and any other pertinent facts. Send a brief note thanking the writer for sending you the information and close by stating that you look forward to meeting with the search committee.

You may receive either a telephone call or a letter inviting you for an interview. (Unsuccessful applicants should receive a letter, even if it is only a form letter, but frequently an institution does not reply at all.) Once you have been invited to interview, try to find out how many applicants are being interviewed. Ask the interviewing process and time line. Find out if there will be a screening interview followed by interviews of the finalists. If there will be a large number of applicants, ask for an early interview time. If this is a second round, ask for the last time slot. Whether the interviewers are aware of it or not, they often use a strong last or next-to-last interview as a yardstick against which to measure the field. There is also a theory that a strong first candidate will set the criteria by which others are measured. I would suggest that if there are six or fewer candidates, ask for the final slot. If that is not available, try for the first one.

PREPARING FOR THE INTERVIEW

The interview is all. No matter who is the best person for the job, she who does best in the interview most likely will land the position. This is true unless the position is "wired," meaning the committee already knows whom they want and/or the position has been promised. When this circumstance happens, you have three choices: (1) choose not to apply or not to interview for the position; (2) interview anyhow, particularly if it is the kind of position to which you aspire; the interview will serve as a practice for you; or (3) interview as well as you can; the committee may be so impressed that they will reconsider their previous commitment, and you may be offered the position. The other positive possibility is that, while you are not selected for this position, you may be considered for a similar position or for the next opening.

Another prospect is that someone will remember you and pass your name on to someone else. That happened to me on two occasions, when I received calls from the search consultant who asked me to apply for other positions; in both instances, I was told that the inside candidate had been selected, as the committee felt an obligation to him. Calls inviting me to interview were also precipitated by the impression I made in the interview process. Other administrators have told me of similar experiences.

Do Your Homework!

Approach an invitation to interview as a major project you have been assigned. If you are well prepared, you will increase your confidence and ease your anxiety. You will also be better prepared to emphasize your own skills, experiences, and capabilities as they relate to the institutional needs.

If you have enough advance notice, subscribe to the local newspaper, or the metropolitan newspaper that services the area. It will help acclimate you to the area and its culture. Make a trip to your state department of education and ask to read the reports of the district or institution. For example, in many states, school districts are required to submit strategic plans or school improvement plans. These are a matter of public record, and you have a right to read them. Materials cannot, of course, be taken from the building, so plan to have enough time to make notes.

Contact anyone you know in the area, or people who might know people living in the area. This is part of networking. Here is where your serving on state or national committees, speaking at conferences, or being published pays off. In fact, if you have been published in a state or national journal, call the editor who worked with you to see if she or he can suggest people you should contact to learn more about the position or the area.

Make a visit to the town—in advance, if at all possible. Learn what you can about the area and the people. Have breakfast or lunch, and strike up a conversation with the waitress or any friendly person in the restaurant, news agency, or any other retail store. Ask these people for their general views on the institution as well as specifics such as: Who are the power brokers? Is there harmony between the faculty and the administration? Is the professional association strong? What do they see as the strengths of the institution? The problems?

Visit the local library and read back issues of the newspaper. Go to the administration building and ask for newsletters or brochures; request copies of any materials given to prospective residents. You can identify yourself, but do not walk beyond the reception desk. To go further might be misconstrued as being pushy.

If there is a search consultant for the position, call and ask who will be on the interview committee. If you are provided names, pay particular attention to them as you find them in the print material you have collected from the institution. Be matter-of-fact and businesslike in talking with the consultant. Chances are you will learn more if you are neither nervous-sounding nor apologetic. It is also appropriate for you to ask the consultant if it would be allowable for you to visit the schools in the district or the campus in advance.

Read everything carefully and take notes. Remember, you are prepping for a major exam. Familiarize yourself with the names of the administrators, the buildings, and the board of directors. Learn the annual budget figure, whether or not there are new facilities being built, the demographics, number of staff and students, educational priorities, standardized test scores, rankings, strengths, weaknesses, hidden agendas, tax base, and so forth. How do you fit?

Prepare a Portfolio

Take time to prepare a portfolio of materials to take with you to the interview. This portfolio should be of good quality leather with interior plastic sleeves in which to insert materials. Include copies of the following:

1. Resume or curriculum vitae
2. Application
3. List and samples of your publications
4. List of major committees on which you have actively served and/or that you have chaired
5. Replies to the narrative questions asked on the application
6. Reports of any major projects you designed or developed
7. Brochures you have designed or that show your involvement in a project
8. News releases
9. Speeches you have made
10. List of questions to ask during the interview

This portfolio is for your use. Prior to the interview, review these documents so that you are very familiar with their contents. Carry the portfolio with you to the interview so that you can, if necessary, call attention to any of these materials.

In addition to your portfolio, prepare individual portfolios for the interview committee members. The materials for the committee members should be briefer and in slim file folders or pocket folders. Make sure these folders appear put together with care, but expendable. As you distribute these folders, say something like this: "I've prepared some material that, I hope, will give you a better idea of who I am, the kinds of experiences I've had, and the kind of work I do. These are only copies, so you can feel free to dispose of them once you are finished with them."

These paper portfolios can be distributed at the beginning of your interview, during the interview in response to a question that may give you a good opening, or as a part of your closing remarks. (Usually, it is best to distribute the materials at the beginning of the interview, as the contents may arouse interest to ask you further questions—questions that you can answer well!)

You might want to ask the person who greets you and who will escort you to a waiting area how structured the interview will be. Explain that you have materials to distribute and would like to decide when the best moment would be to do this. If she or he seems confused or put off by this question, just smile and don't pursue further discussion. Of the items in your personal portfolio, I would suggest you include the following in the packets for the committee:

1. Copies of articles you've published (If you have published a number of articles, select the two or three best, plus a list of all publications.)
2. Selected press releases
3. Copies of speeches (no more than two)
4. Sample of a curriculum unit you have developed, or a financial report, or an annual report—whatever is appropriate to the position
5. Brochures you have designed or that show results of your work
6. Information on any specialized or innovative programs or processes you have developed and/or implemented

Practice

Remember all of the work that went into your final dance recital performance? The same kind of intense preparation is required for a good interview. Practice, practice, practice! Ask others who have interviewed for similar positions for help in compiling questions you may be asked. In addition to reviewing the questions, use a tape recorder or video camera, with someone else posing the questions and you answering them. After listening to your answers, try them again, this time using the most confident tone you can enlist. Compare the two responses. Following this, and if you are not too self-conscious, practice in front of a mirror.

There are also consulting services that can help you, particularly if you are not comfortable discussing your situation with others or if you want objective, professional assistance.

What to Wear

Stick with a basic, conservative look. A gray or navy suit of worsted wool is best. If you have several suits from which to choose, wear what you look best in and, more importantly, what you feel comfortable in. For example, don't wear a straight skirt if you are going to be tugging at it. A gored or pleated skirt will be far more comfortable and is less apt to show wrinkles. Medium heels are best, in a dark color: black or navy. Avoid large or gaudy jewelry, or anything that makes a statement, including ribbons pinned to your lapel whose colors denote a political message or a cause. Do not wear heavy makeup or cologne (unless it is *very* light). Cologne, especially in a small room, gives some people a headache.

The main point to dressing for an interview is to not call attention to your appearance. You want to be judged by what you know and not by how you look, so be understated in your attire.

Arrival and Waiting Time

Arrive on time for the interview, no more than ten minutes in advance. If you are traveling a distance, allow yourself plenty of time to reach your destination, and stop somewhere to check your grooming from head to foot. While you are waiting for your appointed time, do not be writing; instead, take these waiting minutes to compose yourself and to concentrate on the task at hand. Mentally review your notes, or look at the publications on the table in the waiting area; these may provide current information to the materials you picked up on your earlier visit. Think of something complimentary you can say about the building—note its design, cleanliness, general appearance, or displays, especially if there are awards displayed.

First Impressions

Smile, look the interviewer(s) in the eye, and extend a firm, enthusiastic handshake to each person, unless the tight quarters of the room and/or the table prohibit contact. If you are nervous to the point that your hands become clammy, wipe them with a tissue before entering the room. If your hands are particularly cold, rub them together. If you are carrying your portfolios in a briefcase (suggested method), do not also carry a purse. Any emergency needs, such as tissues, pen, and paper, plus your car keys, can be kept in your briefcase. Place your briefcase on the table only long enough to retrieve your portfolio and the packets, then place it, closed, on the floor beside you.

Remind yourself that the committee is interested in you or you wouldn't be there. Even if you are the token female, at least you are being interviewed. Make them remember you.

Being Interviewed by One Interviewer

If you are interviewed in an office by one person, scan the room for a place to sit other than across the desk from the interviewer. After a smile, a warm handshake, and stating your name, you might say, "Mind if we sit here?" indicating two chairs, preferably at right angles. You should try to position yourself side-by-side with the interviewer. If you are right-handed, your best side usually is the right side. Watch the body language of the interviewer and respond in kind. If she or he has a leg crossed over the other toward you and is leaning toward you, then cross your legs (at the ankle only) in her or his direction. Lean toward the interviewer to indicate interest and to give that person your full attention.

Look for a topic in common for opening small talk—photos, ornaments, a paperweight on the desk. If you do not know how long the interview is to last, you might say something like this: "Mr. Jordan, I want to be sensitive to your time. I realize you probably have other appointments, and I do not want to infringe on them. How much time do we have for our interview?" If the interviewer uses your first name, still refer to her or him by title, unless asked to do otherwise.

Interview Questions

Bear in mind that in an interview you are proving yourself on two levels, as a fine *person* and as someone who can do the best *job*. The people hiring you want to be assured that you are like them and will reflect their views and values, and that you know how to do the job they want accomplished.

Very likely, the first question will be along the lines of "Tell us about yourself." They do not really want to know about your background, except that it is respectable and preferably middle-class. They care little about where you were born, where you went to school, if you are married or have children, how you spent your summer vacation. What they really want to know is how you will fit in, how you will get along with them, and how you will make them look good. You can achieve this by preparing a narrative summary of your experiences in a way that tells the story of where you have been and what experiences made you who you have become. When possible, describe experiences that demonstrate the skill set you have listed on your vita. If you know that there is a sensitive issue in the district, you might want to tell about a time you successfully handled a similar issue or resolved a conflict.

The interviewers may ask, "How will you help the institution?" but they really mean "How easy will you be to work with?" Be prepared for this question, even if it is stated in different terms. Be ready to relate experiences similar to what their institution is facing (or has faced) and tell about how you handled those situations. For example, if their concern is inclusion or gifted students or school security, include references to these issues. If they say, "Tell us about yourself," you can give a brief review of your educational experiences and neatly hit the issues important to them. This is why it is so important to research the institution. This entire second part of the answer should not exceed half a page if it were written.

Another likely question you will be asked is "What would you say are your weak points?" Your answer is to tie your "weakness" to a strength; for example, "I usually finish jobs ahead of schedule, which may be misconstrued as rushing, but the truth is that I like to get right at a task and not procrastinate." In response to a question such as "They say you're the first in and the last to leave every day. Why?" you might respond with one of the following:

1. "I enjoy my work!"
2. "There are areas in which I wish to expand my experience, so I requested the extra assignment."
3. "My superintendent relies on me and I don't wish to disappoint her, as she has given me the opportunity to learn so much."

Another favorite interview question you might also be asked is "Where do you see yourself in five years?" The following are possible replies:

1. Contributing to making _____ (name the institution) or another school district/university the best in the state/nation.

2. Taking on the task of _____ (whatever you think the district needs).
3. As the best _____ (name of position for which you are being interviewed) in the state.

Some questions may be asked just to see how sensitive you are about certain issues—personal, educational, or political. There is a legal consequence to asking certain questions, such as "Do you plan to have a family?" or "How do your children (or husband) feel about relocating?" or "What do you do in your leisure time?" or even, as a friend of mine was asked, "How is your health?" These questions need to be answered very tactfully. While there is a natural temptation to remind the questioner that these questions aren't allowable, you do not want to antagonize the committee. It is best to answer such questions with a bit of humor. For example, in response to the question on leisure time, which is more likely to be asked of a single woman, you might say something along the lines of, "I use some of my leisure time for reading educational journals so that I can keep current with the research, and I'm working hard on my golf game to break 80."

Be ready for "problem" questions as well, such as the following:

- Give me an example of a time you worked under heavy stress and the sacrifices you made to achieve an important work goal.
- What would you intend to accomplish within the first year that suggests I should hire you?
- How do you deal with someone who disagrees with you?

If someone on the committee persists in *not* using your academic title (Doctor), it may be a deliberate move to see if that is a sensitive issue with you. Again, try a little levity, such as the answer I sometimes give when I am asked, "Shall we call you Dr. Witmer?" My response is something along the lines of the following, which, incidentally, is one of the real, though minor, reasons I pursued the degree: "Well, my husband always said I attained my doctorate just to avoid being referred to as Ms."

Occasionally, unusual questions will be asked. Two come to mind from my own experiences. One district posed this question to me: "We are caught in a situation where we have two elementary principals and one new elementary building ready to open this fall. Both gentlemen are held in high regard in the community and we do not want to demote either of them to the position of assistant principal. One of them holds a superintendent's certificate. We are being strongly advised by some members of the community to appoint this person superintendent to solve the problem of having two elementary principals. What would you advise us?" Given more experience, I would now answer the question differently than I did then. I answered honestly, only to be told later by the person advising the board behind the scenes that the board was so impressed by my interview that they would have hired me, except that because they felt I answered with such expertise and confidence, they followed the advice I gave them and appointed one of the principals as their superintendent! The other question came from another interview when I was asked, "If we opened your veins, what color would your blood be?" I suppose that is some psychological profile question, but, again, I answered as honestly as I could and said, "White and blue," which were the school's colors.

More recently, boards are being advised to ask "situation" questions, posing a scenario or dilemma and asking the candidate how she or he would handle it. The best preparation for this is experience; second is to be well read in order to have suggestions to draw on; and third is to answer with common sense. One of the things you can always say is that you would first make sure you have as much information on the situation as possible, you would be respectful of confidentiality, you would regard the law, and you would deliberate and not make a hasty decision.

A favorite question, usually asked near the end of the interview, is "Why should we hire you?" What is meant is "What can you do that the other candidates can't?" This is a question that you can prepare for in advance. Even if it is not specifically asked during the interview, you can use your prepared answer as a part of your closing remarks. Base your answer on matching your qualifications to what the institution wants. Remember, answer in terms of what you can do for the institution, not what it can do for you.

Listen attentively. You will be able to determine the interviewers' opinions and philosophies, and possibly their own personal agendas. Their personal views will be even more discernible when they ask their own questions rather than following a script prepared by a consultant or the chief administrator.

Look directly at the interviewers. As each individual asks you a question, give her or him your full attention. As you reply, look directly at this person for the first third of your answer. Then look at others at the table as you continue with your answer, returning to the questioner for your conclusion.

Be precise in your choice of words. Beware of loading your answers with educational jargon, yet do answer with correct terminology. Be prepared to use the words in context and to discuss the underlying concepts of such terms as standards, assessment, systemic change, site-based management, equity, problem-based learning, school safety, or whatever initiatives they are dealing with.

Incorporate in your answers words that help to reinforce your integrity, loyalty, commitment, and effectiveness. Examples of operative word choices are *analyze, assess, capable, democratic, develop, efficient, empower, enthusiastic, excellence, improve, initiate, lead, listen, mission, motivate, participate, productive, professional, reliable, research, responsible, results, strengths,* and *thorough*.

Asking Questions

Prepare questions to ask in your interview. Your questions should serve two purposes: to show your own knowledge of the institution and to find out if you and the organization will be a match. The following are suggestions for questions that may be appropriate. You can build on these to fit your particular situation:

1. Why is the person presently in the position leaving?
2. What are the expectations for this position?
3. If I were the person selected for the position, what evidence would you use to determine whether I am successful?
4. (For higher education) What is the organizational structure of the Board of Trustees? How often do they meet? Who sets the agenda?
5. How would you assess parent involvement in the institution?
6. What avenues do the students have to bring issues to the administration?
7. What are the community expectations for this position?
8. What is it that you are most proud of about the institution? What would you like to see changed?

Closing the Interview

In general people remember only about 10 percent of what they hear. In the case of an interview where the committee members are intent on the proceedings, it is estimated that 15 percent of what you say will be remembered an hour after you have gone. (This is another reason for being the final one interviewed. What you say will remain with the committee for a bit longer.) If you want to be remembered as enthusiastic, confident, energetic, honest, and dependable, make a strong closing impact.

If you are asked if you would like to add anything at the end of the interview, take the opportunity to say that you believe you would be a good match for the institution, that you are even more interested in the position now that you have met the board (or whoever does the interviewing), and that you would devote your energies to the organization. Leave with a smile, direct eye contact to each interviewer, and a handshake to as many as you can. Add a comment or two, such as "This sounds like a great opportunity," or "I would very much enjoy working with you," or even "I look forward to hearing from you." Thank the interviewers. Thank the person who greeted and tended to you and/or who scheduled the interview, then leave. Do not linger.

Within twenty-four hours, write a thank-you note, either handwritten on professional-quality notepaper or typewritten on the same paper and letterhead as your cover letter. The letter should highlight your interview discussion and reiterate your qualifications and continuing interest. Keep it to one short page.

In the unfortunate circumstance when you are not the successful candidate, you should still write a letter of response. Express your gratitude for being considered for the position, mention something positive about the experience, and wish the successful candidate well.

THINGS TO REMEMBER ABOUT INTERVIEWING

1. Practice answering the questions aloud at home for at least a week in advance.
2. Emphasize your successes, not your job responsibilities.

3. Remember, one of the major things you are selling is your personality.

4. Focus your answers on *children* and the education of children, but don't refer to them as "my children," as in "I would want the best for all of my children."

5. Use an administrative point of view; do not use teacher talk, expressions, or point of view.

6. Use "When I get the position (or job) I want," not "If I get this position."

7. Do not dwell on your former educational institution. If you must use phrases to make references to work you have accomplished, use "a university in which I once worked," "my former district," "in my present position," "a neighboring district," "an out-of-state district," and so forth.

8. If there is a period of silence, wait about fifteen to twenty seconds, then ask a question.

9. Make the interviewers feel glad they invited you. Make them feel good about themselves.

10. Smile. This interview is a good experience for you, regardless of the outcome.

11. Have your list of questions ready.

12. Answer in brief, decisive statements.

13. Do not speak negatively about your present organization or anyone in it.

14. If the situation arises, compliment your present institution as well as the one for which you are being interviewed.

15. Convey your own sincere belief in the profession you are practicing and always be honest and true to your own philosophy of education.

NEGOTIATING YOUR CONTRACT

So, they want you! Aren't you glad you didn't scare them off initially by responding to the board's hints about not expecting as high a salary "being a first-year superintendent"? Aren't you glad you knew that you get the best contract when they've looked at everybody else and decided they want you?

Many women are not comfortable negotiating because they lack the experience and confidence that comes with experience, but remember that bargaining is a key business skill you need to have. Make an effort as soon as possible in your preparation to sit in on negotiations or attend seminars, or read books such as *Getting to Yes* (by Roger Fisher and William Ury) and other guides on negotiation techniques.

While all employment contracts need to meet the basic elements of contract formation in order to be valid (see appendix C for a sample contract) and may need to meet specific state statutory requirements, the core of the agreement is the compensation and benefits. Therefore, you need to know the going rate of compensation for superintendents in your state, in your area, and in schools with similar demographics. You also need to be very aware that salary is only part of the story of compensation. Among items that you might want to consider in lieu of salary are the following:

- Tax-deferred annuities
- Contributions to an IRA
- The right to perform work outside the district and engage in professional activities
- Membership dues for professional and community organizations
- Conference registration and travel expenses
- Refund of unused vacation and sick leave upon termination of employment
- Payment for an annual physical examination
- Life and health insurance
- Tuition reimbursement
- A home office
- A professional library
- A personal trainer
- Payment of personal auto insurance premiums
- Swing loans to allow purchase of a new home (if moving into the district) while the previous home is on the market, and moving expenses (Holmes, 1999)

Contracts also should include language about the length of employment, provisions for fixed annual increases or a method to determine annual salary for the length of the contract, and terms of, as well as procedures to be followed in the event of, early termination or discharge.

Lastly, never sign a contract without having your attorney read through it. Enter into your partnership with the board with your eyes open and your hand extended for a handshake.

NOTES

1. A resume is a one- or two-page summary listing personal, educational, and professional experiences, qualifications intended to demonstrate suitability for a particular position. It focuses attention on an individual's strongest qualifications.

2. A vita is more comprehensive than a resume. It emphasizes professional qualifications and activities. A vita is at least three pages in length.

3. A curriculum vitae is more comprehensive than either a resume or a vita. It is multipaged and includes publications, research studies, presentations, papers, and other supporting facts that give a "life of your studies." A curriculum vitae (CV) is usually most appropriate for higher education and for high-level administrative positions in basic education (school districts).

SYSTEMS AND FUNCTIONS

Everything operates by systems and functions. From our bodies to world government and from genes to the universe, there are operations and functions that occur within a system. Education is no different. No matter at what level of educational institution or on what level of administration in that institution, the position functions within a system.

SYSTEMS

Even though education has long had a reputation as not being organized as a business, it is still a system. Therefore, as an aspiring administrator, you should make it your concern to understand the systems operating in an educational setting and to make those systems work for you.

Educational institutions are a part of a complex, interdependent system in which everything influences and plays against everything else. Just as one thing cannot be *changed* in isolation from all other things, so nothing can be *understood* in isolation. This interrelationship of all things has always been the foundation of public education as well as businesses, but it was Ludwig von Bertalanffy who brought to deliberate attention the idea that there are certain common principles that can serve as unifying principles in organizations.

Understanding Systems

Getzels and Guba (best known for their work in the study of organizational behavior) introduced social systems theory to education, and it was their view of the complex interaction between the individual and the institution that has stimulated research in this field. Their research shows that satisfaction on the part of both the individual and the institution will occur only if the needs and the expectations of each are *not* in conflict, and only if long-range goals can be met—sometimes at the sacrifice of short-term needs.

An educational institution is viewed and operated as a social or sociopolitical system made up of a collection of groups that collaborate both to (1) achieve system goals and (2) accomplish the goals of their own group. To take schools-as-a-system one step further, educational institutions are considered "open systems," as they are made up of interrelated parts that interact with and are influenced by their surrounding environments.

As an administrator, thinking in terms of systems provides a practical as well as intellectual way of dealing with issues and problems. Adopting a systems viewpoint helps you to focus on both wholes and parts, recognize the dynamic interrelationships among various aspects of a situation, and be goal oriented. An example of these dynamic interrelationships can be seen in the following situation:

> A middle school boy missed an assigned detention because of a firm order from his mother (who had not known of his detention assignment) that he not miss his after-school music lesson. Two weeks later, upon the boy's return to school following the school's being closed because of vacation followed by unusually severe weather conditions, the boy was reassigned to detention, again, as fate would have it, on the day of his private music lesson. The mother wrote a note to the principal asking that the detention assignment be scheduled on an alternate day as her son had also missed several music lessons because of the impassability of the roads. The principal was adamant in refusing to consider the mother's request (which was not to forgive the detention, but to reschedule it). "I'm making the decisions here," were his words.

Every step of this situation shows that the systems worked, yet did not resolve the problem. The principal's decision supported the organizational and student behavior system, but we are left asking what impact this had on the communication and the parent support system.

Everyone can agree that it is necessary for student behavior policy and guidelines (organizational system) to be followed if there is to be any structure in the organization. Therefore, disciplinary action is an appropriate response to the infraction of the student who had the music lesson conflict. However, the need of the student and his parent also should have been addressed. A better communication system could have prevented much of the misunderstanding. Instead, much annoyance on the part of everyone involved created unnecessary anxiety and the irreparable damage of several systems.

Unfortunately, organizational environments are not always clear since one system cannot be separated from another and elements in each of them cannot be defined in isolation. Schools are complex behemoths, and perhaps the best we can hope for is that not all of the systems are in turmoil at the same time.

A brief example of a principal using a systems approach in planning is in making teaching assignments. To be effective in an educational system, the instructional leader must consider (1) what is best for the organization (what courses should be offered in a given year or semester); (2) what is best for the students (which instructors are best for a particular class or section); and (3) what is best for the faculty (what their specialties and/or their preferences are). Realistically, however, it may not be possible to meet the needs of all three (organization, students, faculty) with one solution or decision. Which system, then, should come into play here? Who should decide what? And how can the impact of each decision be aligned to every other system?

Can You Work Your Way through the System?

To find your own way through the morass of system after system and the interaction of all systems, you must first understand the educational system in which you currently operate. Once you understand it, learn to work in it. Only then can you begin to think about changing it. Don't ever go into a new position with the main goal of "tearing down the system and starting all over again." Even if you are a hired gun, do not attempt to make any changes until you understand everything you can about that particular system, beginning with its culture.

You need to understand as thoroughly as possible how things work and who makes them work. This is more difficult than it first appears because an organizational culture is fluid and changes with every new political or social issue and with any change in the organization's demographics. This constant change is the reason why you must continue to study the organization and the people in it. Attitudes and loyalties change quickly, and what worked last year, particularly in another place, will not necessarily be successful this year or in a different institution. You must always keep on top of what is happening. Listen to what others say about the organization and its constituents—staff, students, parents, community, businesses—and synthesize all of that information, adding that to your own observations.

Political Savvy

You can acquire political savvy by understanding how systems work, being observant, carefully thinking things through, and planning your moves. Following are a series of specific behaviors you need to master in order to be politically savvy, to work within the educational career system, to promote your career, and, most of all, to be a highly successful educational administrator:

1. Mingle with the movers. If you are the CEO, have lunch with the board president. (Pick up your own check.) If you are an administrator in a line position, extend an invitation for coffee to the person to whom you report. Attend conferences, meetings, and social events that are attended by the movers in the educational community and the local social community.

2. Build a network and don't ally yourself with only one person. You could suddenly be left alone. (Techniques for networking can be found in chapter 11.) Establish friendships with those on the ladder below you as well as those above. You never know who might be able to help you or who might move to another district or university and keep you in mind for openings there. In addition, good friends will support you in your successes as well as your missteps. These friends will also be your cheerleaders to the community.

3. Make sure people know what you are doing. Promote your ideas yourself; don't rely on someone else to make your presentations,

either to a superior, to the board of trustees, or to the public. (More on this can be found below, under the heading "Promoting Yourself.")

4. Be very cautious in becoming involved in internal politics; know when to get in and when to keep out. Be careful not to discuss personalities with anyone. Do not criticize to others either your superiors or the people who report to you. Invariably, the person spoken about will hear about it. Be sensitive to material that is confidential and do not discuss it. Do not answer questions if what you say could be harmful to anyone.

5. Take part in community activities. If you are not currently active in community affairs, find at least one organization or project in which to become involved. Be selective, but try to assume the chairmanship of a special committee in the organization.

Promoting Yourself

No one can advance your cause better than you can, and the ways suggested here are typical promotional techniques. Nothing is contrived, for to be obvious about promoting yourself would do more harm than good. Think of these techniques as a way to be your own goodwill ambassador.

Keep Your Word

This may not seem like self-promotion, but it is very important that if you say you will do something, you will do it. If you are to attend a meeting, be there. Pay attention to what may seem to be trivial details, for they are the very things that reflect your reliability and integrity. *Return all telephone calls*. This is a matter of courtesy and to not do this can be far more harmful than many people realize.

Use Business Cards

Make sure you always have business cards available. If your institution does not provide them, purchase your own. Select a conservative style, but with something distinctive, using either colored ink or colored card stock paper. Protocol dictates that academic titles such as PhD, EdD, or DEd follow the names, as in Robert L. Walter, Ph.D. However, if you go into private practice or consulting, you may want to have a second set of cards with "Dr. Jean S. Jones" to use in instances where you are dealing with a public that is not familiar with the academic titles or when you need to reinforce the fact that you are degreed. I advise this because the public's first perception is that women are *not* titled, and you will be addressed either as "Ms." or by your first name, even by complete strangers. Using your title as a preface to your name is more likely to avoid this unsolicited familiarity.

Keep cards in card cases so they do not become dog-eared. In a social situation in which you want to give someone your home telephone number, use the back of your card to write the number. Remember also to always carry a pen.

Tell People What You Do

Make sure everyone you are associated with knows what you do. This is particularly important for women administrators. If you identify yourself only as being "with _____ College" or "with _____ School District," it may be assumed that you are either teaching or working in an office. While this assumption is changing, until the perception for both sexes is equal, you need to say, "Carolyn Cameron, Provost for Mid-Academe College." Even if you are greeting someone you have met before, as you extend your hand, state your name and affiliation. Then you should add, "We met at the South Central Comptrollers Meeting last month in Center City." Whether or not that person remembers, the individual will be relieved to be reminded.

Offer Your Services

Another way to self-promote is to offer a seminar or to serve as a speaker for programs of various organizations. Again, you are an expert in an area that not all others are. Among members of local civic or service organizations, you likely are the expert on education. Be willing to provide an overview of what is happening in the field of education or about a particular event in your institution, such as a building program, a change in curriculum, or even a controversial bond issue. A word of caution here: Unless you are the CEO, always check with your superior to make sure you understand both the issue and the board's stand on it. Regardless of any disclaimers you make to the contrary, you will be looked upon as officially speaking for the institution in whatever you say. By virtue of your being on the dais, you are imbued with authority.

Send Notes and Letters

Send appropriate messages to colleagues: letters of congratulations, thank-you notes, and news clippings or copies of articles on items of interest. Not everybody takes the time to do this, but it will pay off. If you are a building-level administrator, send notes to staff and students alike.

Have postcard-size cards printed for these in-house notes, with the emblem or logo of the school and in the school colors. Send these with a handwritten message for every honor or achievement of staff or students. While this is time-consuming, it is well worth the effort. And when someone makes a presentation to your organization, always send a thank-you note.

Share Information

Share information with colleagues, both internal and external. If you are involved in a project, help someone who is doing something similar. Some states have an electronic bulletin board through which general postings can be sent to all colleges and universities, or to all school districts in the state. Occasionally there will be calls for assistance in gathering data or for information of a more general nature. If you can respond or help in any way, do so. If you are the one gathering information, send a thank-you note, as well as a copy of the results of your study, to everyone who responded.

Aid a Competitor

As an indication of your own self-confidence, lend a hand to a competitor. Invite her or him to speak at an event. When you come upon information you think may be of interest, send it. Attach to this information a note, such as "I heard you were working in this area and thought this might be helpful." Such courtesies are disarming but will place you in good stead.

Set Aside Self-Modesty

Don't be falsely modest. It is not a virtue to let others take the credit for work that you do. Certainly you want to share credit if the project or event is a joint effort, but do not neglect yourself. If an event is scheduled, arrange for photographs to be taken of everyone. If there is a printed program, make sure that everyone's name is included. If you have been an important contributor to the program, project, or event, it is important to promote this.

Ask for Commendations in Writing

If you have been praised for a particularly outstanding project, you might mention that a letter would be appreciated. Whether it is from your superior or the president of the alumni board or the parents' council, your response to the verbal compliment could be something like "I'm pleased things went so well and that I could help. I would very much appreciate it if you could put that in writing for me, and perhaps you could send a copy to _____ (your superior)." If you are not comfortable doing this, you might later ask if you may use the person as a reference.

Enhance the Appearance of Your Office

The appearance of your office can also add to self-promotion. Even though you may have standard-issue furniture, you can add a personal touch with a few well-placed objects that can serve not only as a reflection of your good taste, but also as conversation openers, especially for those you may be meeting for the first time. Don't be afraid to display your credentials framed on a wall, but if you have more than a dozen, be selective. Consider adding your own comfortable pair of chairs so that one-on-one meetings do not have to be held across a desk. Attractive desk or table lamps can also add to the comfort and attractiveness of your office. An area rug can enhance the space as well. A mix of family pictures and photos of colleagues in tasteful frames is good, but do not prop unframed snapshots against the wall or any other place, and do not tape anything to the wall. Remember, your office reflects you, your tastes, and your professional attitude.

Publish

As mentioned earlier, writing is a very effective way to build or enhance your reputation as a knowledgeable person. This is a more crucial factor in higher education than in basic education, but it can be important in advancing your career at all levels. There are hundreds of educational journals, thus providing many opportunities for publication. Even an article in the local or regional newspaper can be a start.

Keep in mind that everything printed becomes permanent, so select your topics carefully. Don't write anything that could later embarrass you or harm your reputation. And remember that if you choose to address a controversial issue, you risk alienating at least half of the readers.

Notify the Public Media

Don't forget to prepare a press release when you are promoted, are elected to serve on a board or prestigious committee, or have been honored in some way. Send the release to the newspaper, along with a black-and-white photograph. Make sure to use a formal business photograph taken by a professional and not a candid of you standing against the wall.

Call the education editor if you are involved in a project that is newsworthy. Offer to be interviewed, or invite the newspaper to send a reporter and photographer to cover an event. Stay in contact through an occasional letter, card, or e-mail, perhaps by sending an idea for an article. Be accessible (without soliciting) and chances are you will be the one they call when they need a person to quote in your area of expertise.

Overall, be accessible to your public, your colleagues, and your staff. Show everyone respect and courtesy. Education is a people business, and the most effective way to serve your clients is to deal directly with the people involved at every step.

FUNCTIONS

There are key administrative functions that are the foundation of any organization. While no administrator would be expected to have either the time or the expertise to perform all the details of all the tasks, the chief executive or administrator would be expected to have an understanding and working knowledge of all areas. For purposes of this guidebook, we'll view these general functions from the point of view of a school superintendent, as that view will provide the most comprehensive one. Most other administrative positions, in both basic and higher education, follow, to a lesser or greater degree, the tasks and functions of a school superintendent.

Understanding Functions

Key administrative functions are tasks, duties, processes, or actions for which an administrator is employed. Functions are what makes an organization operate, and the chief administrator has the responsibility to make decisions about purposes and procedures, provide leadership, secure compliance from subordinates, deal with conflict, manage change, relate to the culture of the organization, plan, organize, communicate, and control or oversee. The typical functions of school administration include (1) organizational structure, (2) board–superintendent relations, (3) business management and finance, (4) personnel administration, (5) curriculum and instruction, (6) support services, (7) extracurricular activities, (8) educational facilities, (9) community relations, (10) state and federal relations, (11) strategic planning, and (12) research, evaluation, and accountability.

Superintendent as the Key

The superintendent is the key to the success of a school district, and selecting a superintendent is the most important decision faced by a board of school directors. She or he serves as an extension of the board, and will be the most public and visible person in the local school district. She or he, therefore, must perpetuate what is best in the district while preparing for its future success. The superintendent is expected to honor past achievements and build upon them for the future. Just as a family or a nation cherishes its forebears, so must a successful school district maintain pride in its history as it excels today and plans for tomorrow.

Planning for Action

As you begin your tenure as superintendent, the first question you need to address is "What kind of school district do we wish to be?" The answer to that question, when discussed, refined, and agreed upon by the board, administration, teachers, parents, community, and students, will become the basis for the district's mission statement, which may or may not change with a new superintendent. Whether new or retained, the mission statement is the driving force behind all other decisions.

Once the mission statement is agreed upon, the district should define its goals. These should be written in practical terms and be student-centered. You and your administrative staff should then outline an action plan, placing the district goals on a matrix of short-range and long-range goals with specified target dates determined by joint planning of the board and administration. The superintendent is responsible for the implementation of the plan, supported by the administrative team. (See the section titled "An Entry Plan" in chapter 10 for more detail.)

Organization Structure

There are many ways to organize and structure an organization. Once the purpose of the institution, under your direction, has been established through the mission statement and district goals, you can turn to structuring the organization so that it can best carry out the goals and mission of the institution.

As superintendent, you should take care not to appear threatening to the staff. Be cautious in making any statements that could be misconstrued. While a staff has hopes that you will clean up _____ (whatever the main concern happens to be), that same staff will not welcome any change that affects them personally. Do not, therefore, announce, "There'll be a lot of changes made around here." Tuck into the back of your head this axiom: "Everyone wants reform, but no one wants change."

Currently, the most popular organizational style can be termed colle-gial, cooperative, committee-based, site-based, shared decision making, or any other combination of terms that imply that everyone has a say. This kind of organizational structure may be closest to the democratic ideal, but it can be difficult to administer in the face of the increasing strength of teachers' unions. It may be complex trying to plan as equals knowing that there is an adversarial relationship in the background by virtue of collective bargaining. However, with careful planning, a con-certed effort toward respecting all points of view, and a well-designed, broad-based communications system, you can make this work.

Board–Superintendent Relations

As superintendent, one of your major functions is to promote trust between the board and the administration. You are the spokesperson for the board to the administrative staff, yet you also represent the admin-istrative team to the board as well as the public. Just remember that your first duty is to the board, even though that will sometimes place you in an uncomfortable position with your administrative staff. While you can express the administrative concerns to the board and speak on their behalf, you personally are directly responsible to the board.

The board's role is to oversee the functioning of the school district by setting policy and direction. The superintendent's role is to lead the op-eration of the institution. However, in reality the board and the super-intendent need to work as a team. When the partnership is not clear about the different responsibilities, the board may jump in where it shouldn't, resulting in micromanagement on the part of the board, or the superintendent may not check with or communicate to the board, doing things that the board members themselves think *they* should do (Schouten, 2002). To avoid this kind of misunderstanding and potential conflict, you should have a clear strategic vision and definite goals.

Suggestions to make your working relationship with the board run more smoothly include the following:

- Meet with the board president to plan the board agenda and to determine which items are informational and which warrant dis-cussion.

- Come prepared to meetings with presentations of items in an organized manner, listing options and their impact.
- Respond promptly and accurately to requests for information.
- Support the board's decisions once they are made.
- Communicate regularly with the board members on recurring issues and communicate immediately on unpredictable issues and events.
- Promote openness with all board members by meeting with any board member on any issue, plan, or program he or she wishes to discuss. However, do not hold secret meetings with individual board members.
- Develop a support base for the board among the administrative team and the public through advisory committees. (See the section on community advisory committees below.)

Your objective is to have a professional relationship with the board members. While this relationship should be cordial, it is first and foremost a business relationship. A relaxed atmosphere is appropriate during work sessions, but the public board meetings should be conducted in a formal, businesslike way.

Your relationship with the board is of primary importance, for it will determine the smooth operation of the institution as well as your future. However, there will be times when you will not be in agreement with the board's actions. You may state the reasons why you do not recommend a particular action be taken by the board, and you may raise objections to their decision. Regardless of your differences, however, never become openly confrontational in a public meeting. Discuss strong differences of opinion in informal sessions, or privately with the person with whom you may have a disagreement.

Business Management and Finance

Your best action here is to demonstrate to the board your keen understanding of the functions of business management and finance. It is still difficult for some people to realize the competency of women in financial matters, so you may have to tolerate a bit of kidding in this area until everyone becomes comfortable with your understanding of, and perhaps expertise in, fiscal matters. Your best tactic may be to make a review of the budget your first priority. Among your initial actions, you should consider one or more of the following:

- Review all procedures with the business manager and make it clear that the manager and you will develop a partnership relationship.
- Review the current accounting system for possible streamlining.
- Review the organization of the business office.
- Design an organizational structure and financial flowchart to be distributed to every administrative office and to board members.
- Demystify the budgeting process by actively involving all administrators and the board finance committee in the ongoing process.
- In-service the board on the budgetary process and plan the process together.
- Employ systems analysis as part of the budgeting process.
- Consider all possible budgeting methods and select or adapt, by consensus, the method best for your district.
- Collaborate with the principals who, working with the teachers in their buildings, will determine allocation of resources within their respective buildings.
- Predetermine fixed dates, in structuring each year's budget, for completion of specified actions.
- Seek community input by going into the community and holding informal budget meetings throughout the district.
- Conduct a continuous review of the effectiveness of the current budget, noting any imbalances created between programs that are overfinanced compared with those that are underfinanced.
- Assess educational programs to include monetary impact, both short-term and long-range.
- Issue, on a regular basis, financial reports, showing total expenditures to date and balances in the chief accounts.
- Initiate creative, accepted methods to maximize investment earnings.

Taking the initiative in addressing business management and finances early in your tenure will immediately signal that you are comfortable in this area.

Personnel

Depending upon the size of the school district, you may or may not be the person with first-line responsibility for personnel. Regardless, you will want to have a plan to make it very clear that this function is an important one that will operate very smoothly. The well-being of all employees is essential to the successful operation of your school district; therefore, you need to have procedures established to assure fair and equitable treatment of all concerned. Your personnel program should, at minimum, reflect all of the following:

- A comprehensive system for dealing with all district personnel in a fair and equitable manner
- A positive work ethic for all personnel through a program of personal and professional accountability
- A system of personnel records for all school employees in order to provide a comprehensive, efficient, accurate, and current record of all matters pertinent to employment, transfer, tenure, retirement, leave, benefits, promotion, and certification
- A district hiring procedure
- A close working relationship with the principals in planning and anticipating personnel needs of the school program
- A job analysis to provide information needed to make administrative decisions based on facts, including job title, number of positions for each title, salary ranges within job titles, and listing of duties, education, certification, licensing, and experience requirements (skills, aptitudes, abilities)
- A job classification system including categories such as managerial, professional, supervisory, paraprofessional, secretarial or clerical, technical, and maintenance or custodial
- Job descriptions, with a consistent format, including title, qualifications, reporting hierarchy, line of supervision, job goals, performance responsibilities, terms of employment, and evaluation

You may find that the function of personnel will be one of the more difficult because most women are found to be more accommodating of the individual, yet are more likely to be accused of not being considerate of the home responsibilities of staff members. Any woman administrator, therefore, faces more dilemmas in personnel areas than men do, as she struggles among objective decisions, subjective attitudes, and second-guessing as to what she is being expected to do.

Curriculum and Instruction

If you have been in education for any length of time, you most likely hold a definite and clear view as to what should be taught and how it should be taught. As you began your administrative training you probably retained these views, but soon began to realize that it is not necessarily the leader who decides the content of the curriculum and the method of instruction. Paradoxically, the closer you come to being the instructional leader, the more you realize that it isn't you who will make the classroom choices in curriculum.

Curriculum should be based on the educational goals of the organization. It is not determined in isolation by you, but is a reflection of the beliefs of the community (local and state) tempered by research and practical experience. Your role is to make sure that the very best curriculum is provided.

In collaboration with the curriculum specialists, principals, teachers, students, and parents, you should assure that the following steps are taken:

- Set the standard for high expectations, policies, and procedures to support excellence in student performance, monitoring of student performance, monitoring and support of improvement efforts, recognition of student achievement, curriculum continuity, and positive school climate.
- Conduct a curriculum audit to determine what the district does well and what needs to be improved: Are teachers following the established curriculum? Are students learning what we want them to learn? Should we be offering all of the courses that we do? What is the impact of each subject discipline upon all other subjects?
- Establish broad, general goals upon which objectives of each program can be based. The goals should include ones that relate to the *individual* learners and their talents, needs, interests, and abilities and ones that relate to the *society* and its values.

- Determine, through team management, learning outcomes based on what the district wants students to know and to be able to do, and establish basic competencies that all students should master.
- Aim for mental, ethical, aesthetic, and personal growth of each child by educating all students to take their places as productive, enfranchised citizens.
- Prepare students to earn a living by acquiring information and organized knowledge, developing intellectual skills, and enlarging understanding.
- Prepare students for postsecondary education, making sure they have the skills and knowledge to successfully complete a program.
- Prepare students for lifetime learning.
- Evaluate, through a survey instrument, the effectiveness of the curriculum for the post–high school needs of the graduates.

School Reform

The advent of school reform is forcing schools and communities to ask a very basic question: *What is it that we want our children to know and to be able to do?* Many states and many school communities are struggling with how to answer this question because there are probably as many answers as there are people to provide them. What you as the educational leader must do is to understand that the educational decisions cannot be made by one person and that reform cannot be imposed from your office. Regardless of how knowledgeable you are in matters of curriculum, you cannot force your ideas upon others. You can educate your committee and show them why your suggestions have merit, but if change does not begin "from the bottom up," with everyone having a voice in the choices, the reforms will not work. It is the responsibility of the superintendent to provide the resources and to maintain the integrity of the purpose of school change.

Prepare yourself before you begin any planning strategy. Change is messy. The staff feels powerless. Whatever the current reform initiative is, teachers say they are "going around in circles." On the other hand, the schools that are not as rudderless are those in which the administration has spent a great deal of time learning *processes* and how *systems* operate. That may not seem like curriculum development, but it is the key to leadership in curriculum development. An administrator who knows how to get from point A to point B is the one whose curriculum planning will be successful.

Support Services

Without support services, the institution would not function well. You must pay close attention to these areas, for the superintendent who gains insight into the infrastructure of the organization will be appreciated for having a finger on the pulse of the institution. While it is not expected that the superintendent will personally serve in the following tasks, these are important functions that you should oversee.

Guidance Services

Through the use of surveys, interviews, and research of the latest materials outlining job trends and employer requirements, as well as effective educational methods, guidance services should address the following: (1) identification of the guidance services' functions that are perceived as necessary and desirable by students, graduates, parents, and colleagues; (2) identification of the needs and requirements of colleges, other post–high school institutions, and the military and employers; and (3) establishment of consistent policies and procedures for the services, with the goal of achieving optimum utilization of resources, in order to provide to every student the maximum appropriate guidance services possible.

Transportation Services

These services should conduct annual cost analyses, both for school-day transportation and for extracurricular activities. Other functions that should be the responsibility of transportation services include auditing for efficiency and effectiveness; conducting periodic needs assessments; and surveying students, parents, coaches, and advisors of extracurricular activities.

Food Services

Food services should conduct an annual cost analysis and determine if the needs of the students are being met in the best possible way. School menus have long been criticized (with many exceptions, of course), with complaints ranging from limited menus and bland offerings to blame for the rising obesity rates in schoolchildren. Some schools are looking at breakfast programs and nutrition policies that include reducing the amount of fatty foods, eliminating soft drinks, increasing fruit and salad offerings, and filling vending machines with nutritious alternatives to sodas and candy.

Environmental Management

Environmental management goes beyond routine cleaning and maintenance, addressed in the section on educational facilities. Environmental management implies a comprehensive plan to focus attention of all persons who work in or attend the school on (1) developing a sense of ownership and care for the buildings and grounds, and for all supplies and equipment, and (2) recognizing that all resources are limited.

Extracurricular Activities

Too often extracurricular activities do not come under the purview of the superintendent. As they are an important part of the school in educating the whole child, extracurricular activities should be given your close attention. They are a budget item and are an area by which the school is known to the community. The general public may not know the scores on standardized tests, but they are aware of a winning sports season and the spring musical. You should know what these activities are, what they cost, and what impact they have on the educational goals of the school district.

As superintendent, you should work with the building principals to monitor and improve extracurricular activities through the following means: (1) annual evaluation of each program, including time spent, outcomes, problems, total cost, and recommendations; (2) annual evaluation of each extracurricular advisor by the principal, of each head coach by the principal and the athletic director, and of each assistant coach by the head coach and athletic director, followed by review by the principal; (3) annual review of all extracurricular activities in order to determine which to recommend for continued funding, which should be replaced, and which should be eliminated; (4) annual report to the board on the number of students, total cost of each activity, and recommendations; (5) a concerted effort to reach out to students who traditionally do not participate and encourage them to become involved in extracurricular activities; and (6) an active effort to gain financial and volunteer support of parents, community, and alumni.

Educational Facilities

Overseeing facilities is not one of the more interesting functions of an educational administrator, unless there are unlimited funds or plans for a new campus to be designed by a prominent architect. Because schools are not known for their aesthetics and sometimes not even their cleanliness, comfort, or basic function, the educational leader who can make facilities a high-priority item will be viewed by some as a miracle worker. In today's economy and in states where 75–80 percent of the taxpayers do not have children in the school system, it becomes more and more difficult to maintain the public's support for the school's daily operations, let alone renovations or building programs. It requires much creativity on the part of the superintendent to convince the community and sometimes even the board that money spent on facilities is a wise use of resources.

As superintendent, you should pay close attention to the following needs associated with educational facilities: (1) a preventive maintenance plan, (2) a planned equipment replacement program, (3) job descriptions and job responsibility charts, (4) a trained, experienced supervisor, (5) work schedules according to building use and need, (6) appropriate use of maintenance equipment and cleaning supplies, (7) uniforms for custodial and maintenance staff to foster dignity and develop an identity, (8) pride in the appearance of each building, (9) energy-saving measures, (10) a hiring system, (11) ongoing evaluation of the security system, (12) guidelines for use of school facilities by the community, and (13) related work orders.

The primary aim in operating buildings is to provide for teachers and students an optimum environment for learning. When the existing structures no longer are cost-effective or no longer can provide even minimum amenities, it becomes the responsibility of the superintendent to form a community-school committee to initiate a study on the feasibility of renovations or a new building. As superintendent you should become informed about the impact of new curriculum programming on facilities, especially in uncertain economic times when most of the citizenry are unresponsive to the needs of schools.

School–Community Relations

It is the wise administrator who understands the importance of community involvement and who works toward building a positive and active relationship between the school and its community through the following actions:

- Personal community involvement through community-superintendent meetings
- Use of special-occasion communication and acknowledgments such as follow-up notes to recap major points of a meeting with a parent or teacher; memos to the staff congratulating a member who has won special recognition; congratulatory notes to students, teachers, and other employees; surveys of the public; thank-you notes, as appropriate, to businesses; thank-you notes for press coverage; open thank-you notes, in the local newspaper, to the public following their support on a school-related issue
- Formation of a network of key communicators from the community who can give accurate information to the public and aid in rumor control
- Implementation of a public relations plan using marketplace strategies to better inform the community
- Encouragement of a system of community involvement for both building and district concerns
- "Image-building" such as articles written for the press; a quarterly newsletter; "Dear Superintendent" letters (an invitation to the public to write to the superintendent); and open forums on specific educational topics

- In-servicing of all staff on how to be good ambassadors to the community through a system of keeping the staff informed and involved
- Publication of a booklet giving an overview of the school district and providing details that would promote the district (This also could be useful in attracting home buyers to the district.)
- Invitations to the public to visit the schools
- Making all buildings more appealing and welcoming to visitors, by using signs, bright colors, attractive displays, and a designated greeter in each building
- Partnerships with businesses
- Solicitation of graduates (alumni) to become involved in sponsoring activities, projects, or internships
- Community service projects conducted by students through their service clubs

Community Advisory Committees

Probably the single most effective method for building good school–community relations is to inaugurate a community advisory board that can serve in an advisory capacity to the board. Not only will you gain appreciation for opening a path for community members to be heard directly without appearing confrontational in a public meeting of the board, but also you and your board will find many practical advantages in having a good sounding board. In today's complicated and volatile world of court rulings, textbook selections, state curriculum mandates, drug and alcohol policies, security concerns, teacher contracts, angry parents, and taxes, it is helpful to have a way to extend the knowledge of your board members by calling on the expertise of interested members of the school community.

Ask yourself, "Could the board make even better decisions if they had more facts, and information supplied by members of the community willing to do the research? Would decisions be more readily reached if the board had a better idea of what the school community would more willingly accept? Would there be more support for the board if more members of the community were involved in the schools and understood what they are trying to accomplish? And would it be helpful to have an established and organized system through which the board of school directors could tap the specialized information base some of the citizens possess?"

A community advisory committee can give you this, and more. The purpose of such a committee is to provide input, information, and suggestions to the school board from interested members of the school community. Its function is advisory, and the board is not bound by its advice. An advisory committee is established by the board and serves at the pleasure of the board. It most certainly does not replace the deliberations and ultimate decision-making responsibility that is the province of school directors.

Typically, board members carefully read, research, question, and discuss each agenda item as it comes before the board. Through this process, they become reasonably comfortable with their decisions. However, what often is overlooked in this process is the fact that no board can know or learn everything about every issue. With the kinds of decisions faced by school boards today, it is prudent to look beyond the membership of the official board to the support provided by an advisory committee.

Such a committee would be, first of all, very helpful in offering voices from the various subgroups in the community. Second, a broader base of knowledge can be tapped through a community advisory system. A third reason for establishing advisory committees is to allow special-interest groups to be heard in committee rather than in a full-fledged board meeting. Not only does this approach allow for a smoother public meeting, but it also affords an opportunity for those with single-issue agendas to present their positions much earlier in the decision-making process.

An important point often overlooked by boards is the fourth reason for maintaining advisory groups. Open committee meetings provide a means of rumor control, particularly if the board encourages the key communicators in the school community to participate on these committees. The final reason for operating community advisory committees is to establish accountability and credibility for the board of school directors, the district, and the superintendent. Because many citizens have no idea of the enormity of school-district operations, through such committees more people will see firsthand how complicated many school issues are. Better still, some will begin to understand the impact of decisions and the effect of those decisions on *all* systems.

Reinforce with your board that establishing community advisory committees is not a sign of weakness, of indecisiveness, or of lessening authority. If anything, opening the school board to community input very well could be the most important step taken by a board and superintendent wise enough to realize the positive impact such a move would make on the business of the board and on the public view of the board.

Representative Small Group Participation

Either in addition, or as an alternative, to a community advisory committee is the practice of convening small groups instead of holding large public hearings on issues affecting the school community. These small groups can be effective by encouraging broad-based, large-scale participation through a coalition of organizations that represent many different segments of the community. The leaders of these organizations should be asked to recruit people from their networks to participate in these groups. (This provides a much better balance of interests than sending out an "all-call" announcement inviting "anyone" to attend.)

Limiting the discussion groups to eight to twelve people per group allows everyone to contribute, as does providing an impartial and well-trained facilitator and asking participants to set ground rules. As superintendent and convener, you can make it clear that the groups will meet several times *on this particular issue,* with an initial session that focuses on their experiences and concerns, a subsequent session on the critical decision facing the district, and a final session that helps the group decide how each member of the group can contribute to the success of their decision. You can encourage a successful outcome by providing the groups with basic information about the situation, as well as a fair and candid restatement of the main argument about what should be done. These materials should establish a framework for the sessions.

The participants should be told at the outset that, in addition to making recommendations, they will be asked to take action and to be thinking about what they can do on a number of levels: as individuals, as members of new or existing organizations, and as a community. A large group meeting at the conclusion of the small group meetings can move the participants to the action stage (Leighninger, 2003).

Agency Relationships

You also should make plans to establish a good relationship with state and federal agencies. As the involvement of outside agencies in educational institutions becomes even more prevalent, it is increasingly important to develop cooperative linkages with typically noneducational agencies on all levels of government. The school no longer stands by itself, as education takes on broader and farther-reaching implications, from providing breakfast to establishing health centers and day care for the children of students. These auxiliary programs require school districts to become involved with agencies heretofore not considered by educational institutions as being relevant to the educational system. It would be politic to become familiar with these agencies, their programs, and their operational procedures.

Research, Evaluation, and Accountability

Many published lists of administrative tasks do not include research, evaluation, and accountability. However, with the increased clamor from the public, special interest groups, and governmental agencies, schools must be better prepared to answer to public scrutiny.

Research should be an ongoing process in every school district, but because it is a task easily placed to the side, it is often the last thing to receive the attention of administrators. It is necessary, then, for you, as the superintendent, to serve as the role model and to make the research component an expectation of the job responsibilities of all administrators. You can structure your administrative cabinet meetings to allow for discussion of current trends and issues in education, occasionally assigning a particular topic for discussion and expecting all administrators to formally prepare for the discussion. This provides an excellent professional development opportunity as well. In addition, you can arrange for administrative seminars through continuing education services of a nearby university.

Your district also should be conducting its own research in order to develop information leading to solutions to problems faced by the district itself. You should encourage basic research that might involve testing of ideas by a number of cooperating school districts. Another research opportunity would be to offer your district as a site for a doctoral dissertation study. By doing so, not only would you advance the knowledge in the field, but, also, you would directly benefit by having a study conducted on one of your own programs. You might also lead your school district in cooperating with and providing support for the development of state and federally funded research centers for basic research.

An evaluation component should be built into every program of the school, both curricular and extracurricular. No program should operate, year after year, without your understanding of the benefits and the drawbacks. Just because a particular program is traditional is not reason enough to continue it. Take the lead in developing a formal system of evaluation, if one is not presently in place.

Evaluations are undertaken for a variety of reasons: to judge ongoing programs and estimate the usefulness of attempts to improve them; to assess new programs and initiatives; to increase the effectiveness of program management and administration; and to satisfy accountability requirements of program sponsors, typically the state departments of education. Because of increased government mandates on accountability, the role and structure of evaluation is taking on a new look that, in turn, is determining curriculum decisions with a stronger emphasis on meeting state standards.

In summary, you, as superintendent, must take the lead in establishing cooperative participation in the development of educational goals and objectives and a system by which these can be attained. You also need to develop professional performance expectations for all employees and programs. Basic research and development programs should be established. Criteria for accountability also must be specified, and responsibility must be fixed: Who is going to be held accountable for what?

As the chief educational leader, the responsibility is ultimately yours. You must determine who should be doing what in order for the organization to perform at optimal efficiency and effectiveness, so that the public knows the value of its schools and knows of your commitment, accountability, and leadership.

4

HIERARCHY HIGHS AND LOWS

Those who believe that collegial management is the wave of the future might very well contend that the construct of hierarchy should be viewed only in historical perspective. Traditional views, however, maintain that as long as there is an organization, there will be tracks, levels, layers, and some kind of strata. Even what is termed a flat organization has a structure, a system of who is responsible for what and who is accountable to whom.

Organizations of equal partners also maintain a structure, for even while the responsibilities of each partner may be *equal*, they are different. For example, if Partner A is responsible for a particular task in the partnership, she is accountable to Partner B for the task being done; conversely, Partner B is accountable to Partner A for the tasks for which he is responsible.

The true pyramid model, in which authority is invested in the person at the top, is not as prevalent in today's organizational structure, yet this general pyramid paradigm will change very slowly because someone ultimately has to be accountable. Today's administrator must be prepared to operate in various structures as they evolve, keeping an eye on participatory models, but keeping a foot on the rungs of the hierarchy model as used by most educational institutions.

POWER, AUTHORITY, AND INFLUENCE

Power, authority, and influence are inherent in a hierarchical structure and are important to its operation. They are, however, three separate and distinct qualities that can come into play either individually or collectively. While with power or authority you can exert influence, and with influence you may be imbued with power or authority as well, possessing one is no guarantee that the other two will follow. Many influential people prefer not to be powerful in the traditional sense of the word, and there are also many in power or with authority who have very little influence on others.

Power

Power usually implies the ability to use force—not necessarily *using* the force, but having the *ability* to use the force if one so chooses. Power has also been defined as control, and this control might be of information, personal affection, prestige, or behavior. While generally viewed as negative, power can also be positive, as in "the power of healing."

Both personal power and power of position are used in work relationships. An example of personal power is in sharing information with a favored few. The "old boys' club" that stands together in the hallway, or meets for coffee with the department chairman every Wednesday morning, or goes to hunting camp together, is a reflection of personal power. Power of position can be used in evaluating personnel and may determine such factors as salary, preferential assignment of classes, and recommendations for promotion. Political favors are another example of positional power.

Power plays a large role in a hierarchy. For example, first-line supervisors may have power because of their influence with even more powerful leaders higher up the chain of command. This friendship and influence with their superiors gives the supervisors a better position with their subordinates because these favored supervisors are able to get rewards (or favors) for their subordinates.

Any position in the hierarchy provides a person with various sources of power—mobility, flextime, decisions on who may attend conferences, provision of direct information, and, in some cases, protection of subordinates.

One of the popular ways of defining power is to categorize it in three ways:

1. *Power over* is the ability to create intended effects on other people through coercion, inducement, or influence over opinion.
2. *Power within* is the spirit of life in which each person discovers or expands his or her own inherent value.
3. *Power with* is the human interconnectedness in community, such as showing mutual respect, being willing to listen, developing the capacity of people to act and do together, and allowing for infinite differing (Desmond, 1993).

Authority

Authority in the traditional sense is thought of as "the right to command." A person with authority is legitimized by virtue of the position held. Authority provides this legitimate power that depends on the expectations of the group; for example, those in an academic department know what is expected of them and what is expected of the department chairman in their working relationship. Authority also specifies the area of freedom of action and interaction, for example, that of a building principal who has restricted authority within the building. The principal's authority is clearly defined as being "everything that happens in this building."

Authority, however, is not power. As part of its definition or understanding, authority does not have the force and coercion that power does. It can, however, be made legitimate through tradition, religion, and law. Authority holds status, but a status that can be revoked either by those who appointed the person invoked with the authority or by subordinates who refuse to obey the commands. Thus, authority, to be effective, depends upon *acknowledgment by others* of that authority. As an example, an educational leader initially gains authority because of the position held; however, if either subordinates or superordinates ignore the authority, it is lost.

We all have seen examples of this loss of authority in the classroom. Once a teacher is no longer viewed by the students as having authority and the students observe that this teacher is not receiving the support of the principal, the students can, if they so choose, decide to make the classroom unmanageable. As we have also seen, the teacher whose authority is not supported does not usually remain in education. A principal can also lose authority: either the teachers ignore suggestions and directives, or the superintendent begins to deal directly with the teaching staff, reversing decisions of the principal.

If you ever find yourself in a position in which you sense your authority is eroding, immediately start looking for the cause. Ask yourself these questions: Are you being inconsistent in your dealings with the staff? Is there someone on staff trying to undermine you? Is there a problem with the union? Is there an underlying problem that you cannot possibly know about?

To get to the root of the possible cause, start documenting everything that happens. In addition, if there is someone on the staff who is absolutely discreet and whom you totally trust, talk to this person, but listen more than you speak. Don't reveal your fears; just ask if something is troubling the staff. Don't mention that you sense any loss of authority, and be very careful what you do say, for unless the person is exceptional (and there are some who are, but not many), what you discuss will be shared with at least one other staff member, and that staff member may not be as trustworthy as your initial confidante.

If you suspect the superintendent is working against you, either deliberately or unwittingly, make an appointment to discuss your view of what is happening. Do not be confrontational and do not make any accusations; just express that you are sensing roadblocks. Ask for assistance in trying to locate the trouble spots. If, after six months, you are still not getting the superintendent's backing, it might be time to ask for her or his help in finding another principalship in another district. Again, do not be either defensive or accusatory. Strive to remain collegial. Say nothing that sounds final. By the close of this conversation, you should know where you stand.

Influence

Influence is the strongest kind of leadership quality, as it implies a reciprocal relationship between a leader and followers, a relationship that is willingly offered by both sides. The leader who holds leadership through influence often has the ability to move subordinates toward the acceptance of his or her goals so that they become the goals of both the leader and the followers. The followers will remain loyal until the direction or ideas change to those with which they do not agree. At that point the influence is lost.

As a woman, you need to remember that, in general, expectations for how a *person* holding power and authority should behave are at odds with expectations for how a *woman* should behave. If you talk in ways expected of women, you are more likely to be liked than respected. If you talk in ways expected of men, you are more likely to be respected than liked. Therein lies the dilemma: everything you do to enhance your assertiveness risks undercutting your femininity in the eyes of many. And everything you do to fit the expectation of how you (as a woman) should talk risks undercutting the impression of competence.

WHO'S IN CHARGE?

While the question "Who's in charge?" is frequently asked in jest, the intent of the question is quite serious. Most people in any situation want to know who has the last say, who has the power of veto, who is ultimately responsible or accountable, and who will give them the answer they want to hear.

Women in positions of leadership hear the question "Who's in charge?" being asked of them more often than men do because the questioner often assumes that a woman in any position is not the person who has the final say. Particularly in instances of student discipline, male parents are more likely not to accept the authority of a female administrator. During my tenure as a high school principal, when a male parent disagreed with a disciplinary action, he would invariably ask, "Who's in charge?" When he wouldn't like my plain and simple response, "I am," he would rephrase the question, "I mean, who's *really* in charge?"

Being in charge implies more than dealing with discipline, although disciplining students is always a major concern of the school board that hires a female principal. Disciplining students may be a nuisance, but it is less difficult if you have an established process of "being in charge."

Try to view handling discipline as an opportunity to display your leadership. These daily discipline skills will help prepare you for larger issues that will present even broader leadership opportunities. For example, if a situation arises on a building level and you can handle it, do so. Don't look around for help from the athletic director or call in a panic to the district office. Deal with the situation and, if conditions warrant, keep the superintendent informed of what is happening and how you have handled (or are handling) the problem. Stay calm, take charge, and keep everyone informed.

I remember clearly one morning when, after I had broadcast the daily announcements, I was told, "Something is happening in the halls. You had better see what is going on." After surveying the situation to discover approximately two hundred students sitting on the floor and blocking the main hallway, I decided that the most expedient action would be to use the public address system to ask the students to disband. I made an announcement that the students would have ten minutes to clear the halls and return to their classes, after which time they would be charged with class cutting. I also told them that I would meet with those who were directly involved in the incident that had precipitated the sit-in, and that these students should report to the auditorium.

I then called the superintendent and reviewed the events at hand. Shortly after, the media descended with their cameras and microphones. I would not allow them in the building, but I agreed to be interviewed at noon at the edge of the parking lot. I learned through this event, and others that followed, that discipline events and crises were not all that different, once the process was established: (1) take immediate necessary action, (2) gather facts, (3) treat all involved with respect, (4) keep everyone informed, (5) make a decision, and (6) follow through.

School dilemmas are unlike any other because they involve dealing with children in a protected environment. You must be very careful not to make decisions too hastily, yet you must be perceived as decisive. Above all else, remember to remain (at least visibly) calm. Do not make rash decisions or reveal by your body language or facial expression that you are not in control of the situation. Very few others will offer advice for fear of being drawn into any wrong action you may take. If there are other administrators in the building and there is time, certainly you should confer with them, but for immediate reaction to a crisis, react at once, with the best judgment you have.

One thing I learned is always to allow for "saving face," whether that of a student or a teacher. Allow for choice, time for responses, and an opportunity for those involved to keep their dignity (even though they may not be acting in a very dignified manner). Note that during the sit-in, the students were not *ordered* to immediately clear the hall. To do so in such a situation, without the resources to enforce the order, would present a challenge to the students. By offering them a choice, I acknowledged the students' concerns. In all dilemma situations, you must allow time to thoroughly investigate before taking final action. Remember, you are dealing with people's futures as well as with the immediate incident.

SUBORDINATES AND SUPERORDINATES

Let's say you're finally in a position of authority. You have the technical skill you need and some experience as a group leader. You've taught, you've chaired, you've organized, and you've presented. Now you are ready to administrate. That means that, regardless of your position and title, you are going to be dealing with people, both as a superordinate and as a subordinate.

Working with Subordinates

As an administrator in a new position, you must give several functions your immediate consideration. The first is to build trust. This is the most important task and the area that may take the longest. You can begin to build trust by following through on what you say you will do, by listening to people and never inappropriately sharing the information with others, and by always being honest. If you want your subordinates to do something, lead by example. If you are the principal, for instance, pick up paper you see on the floor, return left trays to the cafeteria window, speak to students who pass by, and include yourself in the list for cafeteria or parking lot duty. Not only are you modeling good behavior, you also are setting up opportunities to work side by side with others. Another gain for you is that, by being visible in open areas, you make yourself accessible to people. Serve as an ad hoc member of every committee under your jurisdiction and join these committees on occasion, offering your assistance in answering questions or smoothing a pathway. This gives you an opportunity to build working relationships that are better than personal ones (in your position as a supervisor). Don't give directives; people resent being *told* what to do. "Will you please . . ." can have more power than "Go and do . . . ."

When challenged or criticized, try not to act defensive—at least in front of those who are criticizing. Listen while the critic talks, but don't interrupt (unless the person is overtly rude). A safe response is "I am sorry you feel that way." If the challenge occurs in the presence of others, say, "Would you like to come to the office where we can discuss this?" Don't argue. If he (or she, although more unlikely) responds, "No," you can reply in an even tone, "Then let's talk later." That keeps the option open for discussion and prevents a confrontation. Make sure there are others who hear you make the offer to continue the discussion.

Many new administrators make the mistake of trying to do everything themselves. They are afraid that if they delegate, they will be viewed as not being able to do the job themselves. You must remember that you are not expected to do everything yourself. An administrative position is designed to be one of delegation because the tasks of the position are greater than one single person can possibly do. Thus, you need to assign duties that can be carried out by others but for which you accept ultimate responsibility. For example, you can make the following assignments:

- Ask your secretary to open and sort your mail.
- Supervise special programs by initiating the project, giving general guidance, monitoring, evaluating, and approving the final product. The actual planning and writing should be carried out by the teaching staff and any specialist needed.
- While you may hold the responsibility for major reports, this is another area in which you can assign others to collect the information and compile it.
- Attending meetings can be delegated if they are not meetings for which your attendance is mandatory. Not only will it take less of

your time to hear the report of your subordinate who attends, it also could be a very valuable experience for the person you are sending.

There are many advantages to delegating. Not only does it give you time for more valuable tasks that you personally must handle, but it also helps the employees gain leadership skills and discover talents they may not have known they have.

There are, of course, certain tasks that should not be delegated. These include the following:

- No one else should delegate over another's jurisdiction.
- Performance evaluations should be conducted only by the administrator in charge.
- Administrative action against school employees cannot be delegated to others.
- Planning in the area for which the supervisor is responsible must by done by that person; however, advice and information can be supplied by others.
- An area of confidentiality cannot and must not be delegated.

Working with Superordinates

When you meet in your supervisor's office, do not be seated until you are invited. If you are given a choice of place to sit, if possible choose a chair that places you at eye level with the supervisor. Try to avoid sitting across from her or him at the desk, if only because you will unconsciously assume a posture of being "called to the office." If that is the only chair, at least turn it slightly. If there are two chairs at right angles, choose that spot, or if there is a small conference table, position yourself beside or at a right angle to your supervisor.

If the meeting is held in your office, make sure you have arranged a comfortable area and do whatever is necessary to not meet across your desk. Make sure you are ready in advance—desk in order, jacket donned, things generally tidied. Rise to greet your guest and offer her or him the seat you have designated. If she or he chooses to sit elsewhere, follow the lead and don't make an issue of the seating arrangement. After a brief exchange of pleasantries, get to the purpose of the meeting.

Wherever the site of your meeting, be prepared with whatever materials you may need. Have your papers or presentation organized so that no time is wasted. Stay focused on the task at hand. Speak clearly and forthrightly. Keep a log of meetings and document all that you do. You do not need to keep a detailed journal, but it is wise to keep any written communication or records of work. Particularly if the purpose of the meeting is to determine further action or next steps, be sure that you are clear as to the intent of your supervisor, and do not close the meeting until you have written down and reviewed what was agreed upon.

If you are in a vulnerable or uncertain position, it is a good idea to follow the meeting with a written memo summarizing the points covered and listing agreed-upon action to be followed. Ask for a response if you feel that you may not be completely clear on something. If you think you have it down pat, you could close with a pleasant "Let me know if this isn't the way you see it." And then read or state the main points as you view them.

Always follow through in a timely fashion. Do what is expected and avoid delays. If something unexpected causes a delay, let your supervisor know in advance about the problem(s) you are encountering, and ask for an extension of time. Don't wait until close to the deadline to request or announce a delay. As a female, you don't want to give any opportunity for such comments as "Women are always late," even though research does not bear this out.

GENDER AND SUPERVISION

Women tend to want to improve whatever it is they are charged with doing and are willing to learn how to do it better. That is one of the reasons why women are more comfortable than men with supervision and evaluation. First of all, women come from a background of nurturing and caring. This, combined with the desire to make things better, provides a good basis for the role of supervising. Complimenting also comes easily to women, and they don't mind beginning a dialogue with an informal kind word or two.

Gender cannot be separated from supervision because supervisors and those being supervised are not genderless. There is a certain dynamic between a female supervisor and a female subordinate just as there is between any of the other gender combinations. Add to that the different personalities of each player, and an individual scenario could be written for each pair. However, there are certain generalities that can be made, based on a fundamental principle: People tend to like people like themselves. We immediately identify with people like us. We are comfortable with them. We understand them. We approve of them. We hire them . . . and we rate them higher than we do those who are not so much like us. Total objectivity in supervision is a myth. Therefore, as administrators we should acknowledge that we may be treating some very excellent people unfairly and thus make a conscious effort to be more objective.

The fact that men and women are different, and the fact that they cannot view each other the way they view one of their own gender, is probably the main reason why being evaluated by a person of the opposite sex is so often viewed as unfair. When a male supervisor is doing an evaluation of a female, what he sees is that she is not doing things the way he would; as a result, he does not rate her performance as highly as he rates a male who does things the way the supervisor himself does. While there are many exceptions, in general a man does not look as favorably upon the work of the women he supervises because the style, the process, or the product are not what he is used to. (The reverse is also true. Women usually rate other women more highly because they better identify with what they see being done.)

As a woman administrator, you will find being a supervisor places you in double jeopardy: (1) the men you supervise won't like being *evaluated* by you, even though they may not mind, and may even like, being supervised by a woman, and (2) men are more likely than women to "go over your head" in objecting to your evaluation. Typically men who believe they have been unfairly evaluated will not claim that the woman is biased, but that she is lacking in ability to evaluate. On the other hand, women are more likely to claim gender bias of their supervisor.

To avoid these situations as much as possible, be consistent in your supervisory process, be frequent in your informal evaluations, and keep good records. You need to make a concerted effort to be fair. Below are some specific points to keep in mind:

1. Don't stereotype any person or group, whether by gender, age, culture, or physical appearance.
2. Concentrate on specific, observable behavior tied to the institutional mission and goals.
3. Evaluate performance against previously agreed-upon goals for the person being rated.
4. Limit the evaluation to present, not past, performances. Don't let a previous rating, positive or negative, affect the current one.
5. Strike a balance in looking at performance since the last evaluation. If past performances have not been good, don't overpraise if a very recent task has been carried out well, as this recent one may be an exception. Certainly give praise, but don't let this rule your rating.
6. Give constructive feedback. Make specific suggestions for improvement.
7. Keep personal feelings out of the evaluation process. Accept the fact that not everyone is fond of everyone else.
8. Don't apologize for the evaluation. You can be tactful and even sympathetic to the conditions that resulted in a poor evaluation, or you can express regret that the job performance does not meet expectations, but don't accept the blame for a poor evaluation.
9. Prepare for the meeting. Do not assume you will remember what points you want to make. Have your notes ready.
10. Conclude the performance review by summarizing what has been discussed and by planning the next steps.

POLITICS

Politics is prevalent in any organization, and education is no exception. There are many subgroups and many individual interests or needs at play because most individuals in a school have no access to power. They, therefore, feel the need for being part of a group because groups provide their members with more information—information necessary for political survival—than an individual can have on his or her own.

The reality of politics is that various interest groups must be accommodated in order to avoid irresolvable conflicts. The issues may change, but the struggles are ongoing because politics is based on concern over issues. Politics is very closely tied to power, authority, and influence, and is, in fact, the process that occurs when the person or group who has power, authority, or influence takes action to achieve a goal or to effect a result.

As an administrator, you, too, are political to the extent that you are in a position of authority and influence. The skill comes in learning how to use that authority, and how not to be taken advantage of by those who want to make use of your political power for their own use.

It would be unrealistic to advise new administrators to not become involved in politics, as a person cannot be apolitical in an organization. This does not mean, however, that you need to choose sides, but that you need to learn, as quickly as possible, the intermingling of the politics of the board, the community, and the organization itself. Study the players, the issues, and the background of the organization and its culture, and document your findings. Read articles and books on the subject of organizational politics and the power of politics; there are many to be found in the business management and political science sections of the library or bookstore. As always, your best move is to be prepared, and while there is no substitute for experience, you need to be constantly alert as to what is happening around you. (Also see chapter 12.)

PROMOTION: "UP FROM THE RANKS" OR "OUTSIDER"?

The issue of how to prepare yourself for advancement was addressed in chapter 1. Heed the suggestions given there, whether you are seeking a promotion from within the system or are free to relocate. While your chances for promotion are statistically higher if you are free to move, studies have shown that when women change administrative positions they are more likely to move within their present institution, whereas men are more likely to be recruited from outside the institution. Department chairs, district supervisors, and principals tend to remain in the school district in which they began their administrative career. Assistant principals are most likely to become principals in the school district if they are in a building in which the principal is promoted or retires. If an assistant is in a school where the principal plans to be in the position for at least ten (more) years, the assistant, after three to five years, likely will search elsewhere for a school of her or his own.

The odds of moving up the career ladder from the elementary classroom are even more difficult for three reasons:

1. Even though about two-thirds of the nation's schools are elementary, few have assistant principals and almost none have department chair positions. Elementary classroom teachers must jump straight from the classroom to the principalship—a difficult prospect in most districts (Glass, 2000).
2. More elementary teachers make the move to a principalship after several years in a coordinating position such as in special education or as a team leader in a middle school. And since there are not many opportunities for these coordinating positions, this lessens the chances of a promotion (Glass, 2000).
3. Because most elementary teachers (75 percent) are women, there is a general perception that elementary teachers would not have the "authority" persona to lead a district. In addition, elementary teachers have fewer opportunities to hold highly visible leadership roles in the district in extracurricular activities such as sports or the arts.

Most people will advise you to begin your administrative career anywhere but in the district in which you are a member of the faculty because the adjustment is difficult. You personally may adjust very well, but it is often difficult for the other faculty members in your own institution to adjust to you in another role. No doubt nearly every person who has ever considered an administrative position has been given that same advice, yet very few heed it. The few who strike out on their own are more apt to have a long-range plan. They are viewing their next move, fully aware that their chances to move beyond the first administrative post will increase greatly outside their own institution. The old adage "You're only considered an expert if you're from out of town" didn't become part of folklore without having some substance in truth.

Up through the Ranks

If you do come up through the ranks, there will be an initial honeymoon phase in which you will be surrounded by well-wishers, more than half of whom are very sincere in offering their good wishes. For a while you will be the symbol that there can be life after the classroom, and there may even be a flurry of activity as a few faculty colleagues also decide to pursue credentials for an administrative post. Your supporters will count on you for (their) "truth and justice," and they will believe in their hearts that things (at least for them) will become better under your leadership. And, indeed, things may improve for them. (Recall that people support people like themselves.) Soon a coterie of "your people" will begin to form, and as your authority, power, and influence increase, so will theirs. Those who consider themselves your friends will believe that they do not have to ask for favors because they know you will do things the right way (their way). Those who do not particularly like you personally will lie low for a while and just do their jobs, waiting for you to make a mistake.

Before too long, something controversial will occur. It might be as simple as a classroom observation or a student disciplinary problem, or it could be something as major as a curriculum change or a crisis situation. The battle lines will be drawn. Everything anyone ever knew (or thinks he or she knows) about you or any grudge anyone holds will be thrown out as a criticism of whatever action you are taking on the issue. You probably will survive this skirmish, and if the result is a positive one (especially if you can negotiate a "win-win" result), you will be accepted by more of the staff. However, if you should lose, the defeat will be more difficult for you to cope with. Don't look for sympathy. Pick up the pieces and learn from the experience. You can rise above losing a skirmish or two, but if you sense a real battle at hand, you need to rethink your leadership style and/or look for a position elsewhere.

The Outsider

If, on the other hand, you are new to the district, you arrive with a clean slate. Because you are an unknown, you will be watched closely, and every decision you make will be debated, weighed, and judged in the faculty room. Your advantage is that you know more about yourself than they do, and they cannot know what your moves will be. At the same time, you are at a disadvantage because you have to prove yourself anew every day. You are not riding on your past proven excellence because nobody knows about it. Unless you make a real blunder, however, the general assumption will be that because you are credentialed, you are qualified.

Female, New Kid or Old Hand

Now, if we throw into this equation the fact that you are female, the burden of proof that you can do the job will occur daily. People will watch, not for you to make a decision, but for you to make a mistake. Trust in and loyalty to you will come very slowly, and you cannot let your guard down, ever. Be pleasant, even make occasional jokes at your own expense, but never stop looking over your shoulder. If you find yourself in a dilemma, solve it yourself. Do not go running to your superior or to the top person (unless the dilemma is only short of a catastrophe and has ramifications for the entire operation). Do not ask for favors. If you can't reach the light fixture, in a manner of speaking, get a ladder. If you have a problem with a parent, deal with it yourself. If you have a defiant student, don't lose your temper and don't raise your voice. In all cases, react calmly and be decisive. Use good judgment (remember not to make a final decision on anything until you have all the facts possible), and you should earn the respect of your faculty. Above all, be honest and be fair. With honesty and fairness you will make your mark.

Experienced administrators agree on most of the following advice to all newcomers:

1. Become familiar (prior to your arrival if possible) with policy manuals, regulations, and the teacher contract.
2. Know the kind of student support programs and the staff who are responsible for those programs.
3. Understand the legal processes related to student and staff personnel issues, especially that of due process and discipline procedures—and know where to find additional information quickly. An excellent guide is *A Digest of Supreme Court Decisions Affecting Education* (Zirkel, Nalbone Richardson, and Goldberg, 2001; this guide is updated periodically, and at the time of this printing, the book is in its fourth edition).[1]

4. Be prepared to follow the staff evaluation procedures in relation to your institution's practices (and make sure they are following state school law).
5. Continue to develop your organizational skills.
6. Most important, know when it is time for the next advancement and be prepared to move when that time comes.

SO YOU WANT TO STAY?

The days of moving from the mailroom to the boardroom are long gone. Your chances of moving from faculty member to CEO are just as slim. Do not have any illusions about this. No matter how good you are—and perhaps even because you are good—you will not be viewed as having the right experience, credentials, or personality to do the "big" job. This is especially true if you are a woman. You will always be perceived as a teacher, even if you have performed outstandingly as an administrator.

Most people cannot readjust their perceptions well enough to see you as a credible candidate, regardless of the leadership you have demonstrated, the honors you have garnered, the books or articles you have written, the programs you have implemented, or the improvements you have made in the institution. In your home school, you will always be Mrs. Johnson, the home economics teacher, or that Ms. (Mzzzzz) Stanton who always had a lot of kids hanging around after school. There are some cases where "home boys" (and a few girls) ended their careers at their first educational institutions, but almost without exception they had left and, in some instances, were later invited to return. It seems that a rite of passage must occur, that you must go somewhere else to prove your worth, before you can return as the conquering hero(ine).

If you are aspiring to the top administrative position, be ready to relocate because you are too well-known to be considered CEO material on your home turf. Regardless how unsullied your reputation, there will be people on the search committee who erroneously remember (1) a piece of gossip, (2) the poor grade you gave their child, (3) something you wore, or (4) something you were thought to have said. You will not be able to defend yourself because the doubts these issues raise will not be discussed with you.

Don't discount jealousy. Some of those who were pleased to see you in a middle management position will resent your ascent to anything higher. You are a reminder of what they have not achieved. You are a symbol of what they have not accomplished (whether or not they ever wanted to is beside the point when envy is involved). And they think everything came to you so easily! They would rather not acknowledge the sacrifices you made in your personal life to prepare yourself for promotion. No matter how hard you may have tried to be fair and just, you will have angered some people along the way.

Another source of enmity can come from a fellow administrator. For example, if you are a faculty member whose immediate supervisor would become your subordinate if you attained a certain administrative position, you probably cannot count on that person's support. More likely, she or he would work behind the scenes against your candidacy, particularly if you had had any disagreements when she or he was your supervisor. The person will not forget any difficulty you may have caused and she or he will discount, if not discredit, your achievements.

If you are hoping to be promoted from within, probably the most awkward position you can be in is that of assistant superintendent or vice president. Unless the CEO is (truly and not just tokenly) your mentor and is sincerely and openly grooming you for her or his position, you should actively pursue a position at another institution. If the current chief senses in any way that you are hungry for her or his position, she or he may take perverse delight in pretending to take you into her or his confidence, only to be setting you up for failure. If, in addition, you are good in your position and she or he resents the good press you are receiving, watch yourself. You are in a most precarious position. Your only chance of survival is to find a position elsewhere.

If the jealousy has turned to animosity (either overt or covert), you may want to think twice before you ask for support. Weigh your moves very carefully. You may need to decide which is riskier—to apply for other positions without telling your present chief and risk her or his anger or hurt, which might lead to vindictive action against your candidacy, or to tell and risk her or his sabotaging you by making some well-placed phone calls to the search consultant. These things do happen.

These frightening, but very real, possibilities are mentioned here not to discourage you, but to urge you to use caution. You as a woman are in a vulnerable position, and even if you have the courage to face your superior with your concerns, you risk being labeled a "paranoid female," or worse, being subjected to gender-biased crude epithets.

LETTING GO

Changing positions will affect more than the work you do, the title you hold, and the office in which you are placed. When you move from one position to another, there will be significant changes in tasks, behaviors, norms, and values. Even though you want the change in role, the fact that it is a change will create at least minimal stress and varying degrees of strain. This strain might manifest itself in a range of ways, such as feelings of having lost control, fear of failure, self-doubts about personal competence and ability, impatience and frustration, and increased feelings of uncertainty brought about by significant changes in your professional work life. Letting go of one set of professional functions and identities while learning others can be risky, wearisome, and frustrating, so don't be surprised when you feel let down.

These anxiety expectations may come as a surprise because the excitement of a promotion to a new position is a very positive experience. It is almost always a move by choice and usually is a move that has been a long-range goal, a goal well planned for and painstakingly prepared for. You are not expecting stress or strain, so its appearance is disturbing. While the strain will be less noticeable by those who are eager for an administrative position and who feel confident in their abilities, there is still a lurking fear of the unknown.

Every change incurs risk. You are leaving a position over which you had control. You no doubt devoted a great deal of time and energy, dedication and talent, skills and expertise to building the perfect college preparatory math program, establishing a student assistance program, or writing foolproof proposals. You enjoy the relationships you have established with your colleagues and with the students. Nobody questions you because you are a proven quality. You have control of your area, and you know no one can coach the softball team better than you can.

Fear of failure is another example of strain resulting from role transitions. This fear of failure (and its cousin, fear of success) is tied to self-doubt. "Will this new position be what I expect it to be?" and "Will I be able to meet the expectations of the institution?" are the two main questions in fear of failure. These self-doubts are not an indication that you do not have the skills, but rather are nagging thoughts that lead to second-guessing your decision to make a change in your life. Again, you know you have been successful in the past. Read your list of accomplishments and then match that list to the job description of the new position. This should help ease your anxiety. You know you have the skills to do the job. (See chapter 7 for more on fear of failure.)

Loss of identity is another kind of strain. This process is usually more pronounced and longer lasting than either fear of control or fear of failure. Most professionals very closely identify their *personal* selves with their *professional* selves, and these identities have been built with layer woven into layer. Self-identities are built up gradually over the years by internalizing the meanings and expectations of many roles played, and the greater the centrality of a previous role to individual self-identity, the higher the amount of strain experienced. In other words, for those who most closely identify their personal selves with their professional roles, the greater the strain of leaving that role.

To help avoid some of the strain of changing roles, you need to start projecting yourself into the position you are next seeking rather than continuing to portray your present role. Start by dressing for the position you expect to attain. You will sense some of this change of view of your role as you shift your focus while taking administrative courses in your preparatory program, but additional shifting needs to be consciously made through your own initiative.

For example, my graduate students confirmed my own experience in that as they progressed through the certification program, they found themselves thinking less and less like a classroom teacher and more and more like their principal. One student in particular smiled as he related his once-strong ties to and leadership in the powerful teachers' union in his district. He had been the strident voice in negotiations and in faculty meetings. His colleagues began to wonder why he became silent when controversial issues were raised and criticism of the principal occurred in the faculty room. He shared with his classmates that even though he was not interested in seeking an administrative post at that time, he found himself thinking more like an administrator. The same is true for those who are already administrators and who are seeking deanships or superintendencies. As they prepare for a change of career, they change their perspective and discover that their interests change as well.

Separation Pangs

For some, it is wrenching to reconcile the management and leadership skills being learned in university classrooms with the still-engrained attitudes of current positions. You may find yourself philosophically torn between what you now do and what you expect you will have to do as an administrator or in another administrative position with different responsibilities. It may be that you have found a comfort level, or a commitment to a belief in what you are doing, or you may truly love the tasks and functions of your present position and not be able to imagine yourself doing anything else. Transitions are particularly difficult for those who are not emotionally ready for a role change.

Some in role transitions find it very hard to shift gears on an interpersonal level. Simply stated, they find it very awkward and emotionally stressful to restructure relationships that must change—at least to some degree. This is a problem you will encounter if you are promoted from within. To go from classroom teacher to principal can place a strain on friendships, particularly if the friendships are close and long-standing. When you become the evaluator, a whole new dimension is added to the relationship. As mature, educated, understanding adults, friends should be able to work this out. Some can, but be prepared to lose the friendship of those who cannot.

This separation will have an emotional effect on you as well. There may be a distinct sense of loss as you separate from your peers—the friends and colleagues who over the years became your clique, your lunch partners, and your confidantes.

As an administrator you will find yourself separated. You will have lost your support group and a strong familial bond. Your world has shifted, and you have left "us" and joined "them." The professional and personal intimacy is gone. Do not make the mistake of taking your lunch to the faculty lounge. Conversation will cease, or at least become guarded. Remember what you talked about in the faculty room? That is still the main topic of conversation, only now it is about *you*.

Career experts say that separation pangs are among the hidden costs of taking a career turn. You have changed. Your colleagues have not. Whether out of jealousy or out of fear (of your supervisory position over them), those still in the ranks may not like the comparison of who you are and who they are. If you were, like the graduate student cited above, an activist in the teachers' organization or an outspoken critic of the administration, you may also find your old peer group to be judgmental of your change of allegiance. You and they may both feel betrayed. They may think you are selling out, and you may feel that they are being cold and unsupportive.

Overcoming dependency on your old peer group is one of the most important thresholds to cross professionally and emotionally as you launch your own career track. While it may not be easy, you need to admit that you have changed. Your actions say that you no longer identify with the "old gang," so do not try to deny your change of focus. You are the one who chose to let go of the comfort and close friendship of your colleagues.

New Support Groups and Very Special Friendships

Once you have made your career move, you should broaden your sphere of professional friends (even more than you have been doing as you prepared for this move through networking). You may be fortunate enough to have established reliable and warm friendships with class-mates in your professional degree program. These colleagues share the kind of goals you are pursuing and talk the same talk. They also provide you with the confirmation that you are not alone. Nothing is more com-forting or reassuring than to be able to talk freely with a colleague, ei-ther to talk about a particular problem that is currently bothering you or to have a discussion on a broad educational issue.

There are some rare and very special instances in which a friendship is so secure that a career advancement will have no effect on the rela-tionship. If you have such a relationship, treasure it. Such friends are ir-replaceable and do not occur more than once in a lifetime. Maintain that friendship at all costs. Chances are, that relationship will be your ballast and your link to reality.

If you work at it, you can still remain friends with people you super-vise. After all, if you have worked closely with colleagues for many years, you share many memories and you can't simply shut the door on those experiences. You just must, however, accept the fact that the relationship has changed and go on to build a new relationship of mutual professional respect for and personal consideration of all staff. Later, when your peers retire or you change careers again, throw a party and celebrate the friendships, the joint commitment, and, most of all, the shared experiences.

Saying Good-Bye

Speaking of celebrations and farewells, know when it is time to say good-bye. Whether you leave to take a new position, for retirement, or because of a financial incentive, depart with dignity:

- Accept that you are setting aside an identity you have had for some time and that you are leaving something familiar and secure.
- Seek professional counseling if you are having difficulty in making decisions regarding what to do with the rest of your life.
- Involve your family to discuss the impact that your leaving a public institution will have on them and you. Some people go through a slight initial depression until they readjust, while others bounce right into another career.
- If you leave a position under stress, give yourself some time and space to regroup. Reevaluate your skills. You'll be surprised how marketable you are.
- Throw a party so that friends and colleagues can bid you an honorable and fitting farewell. You need to do this in order to officially close this chapter of your life.
- Organize your day. Keep an appointment calendar and, if you aren't starting another position immediately, schedule other activities. Now may be a good time to do the writing you've not had time for before and to catch up on journal reading.
- Leave while you're ahead. Consider your position in the organization and your projected status. For example, if you are in a vulnerable position such as facing the arrival of a new president when you are the vice president, you may end up with a new assignment. Be aware of these signals and make it your choice to leave if you sense

you will be transferred to a position that means nothing to you. It is time to let go.

NOTE

1. Another example of a law guidebook is *The Pennsylvania School Law Handbook*, the most recent edition being 2001, published by the Pennsylvania School Boards Association. Check with your own state school board association.

⑤

LEADERSHIP

It is helpful to the educational institution that the terms *leader* and *leadership* are genderless words, unencumbered by the commotion surrounding words such as *chairman, chairwoman,* and *chair*.[1] However, leadership as a concept has become a trend of its own, as everyone who writes in any area of work feels compelled to redefine leadership from the viewpoint of a specialized area. Everyone tries to put a spin on the word, with the result that leadership can mean almost anything anyone wants it to mean. Even colleges and some high schools are including a leadership component in their program of study. The positive result should be that more people will have an understanding of the need for leadership in any endeavor involving more than one person, but the negative prospect resulting from all of this is that everyone who completes work for a degree or even a leadership course may feel entitled to a job that guarantees a position of leadership.

There has been a plethora of studies conducted in the past fifty years on the essence of leadership, the qualities of leadership, the tasks of leadership, and any other way in which leadership can be analyzed. Workshops and seminars abound, and books dealing with the subject of leadership could fill a small library, yet we still have not exhausted the subject. Every year more ideas on leadership are generated as our society goes through changes and problems, and as priorities ebb and flow. In addition, as women more and more frequently take on the mantle of leadership, we will find the definition and understanding of leadership further refined to reflect with even more precision the qualities that constitute feminine leadership. This chapter provides a very brief overview of the leadership theories that most education writers agree as being the ones most relevant to educational administration.

LEADERSHIP: A BRIEF HISTORICAL OVERVIEW

The earliest major theory of leadership is the "great man" theory, which is the belief that in every group or tribe or country there is one person who becomes the leader because of certain leadership qualities. Leadership was thought to be determined by destiny. Such luminaries in the "great man" category include Alexander the Great, Hannibal, Julius Caesar, Benjamin Franklin, Napoleon, and Winston Churchill. Major events in history were thought to revolve around these great leaders, and it was further believed that history could best be understood by studying the traits and qualities of its leaders. It was also thought that such people were born with outstanding traits or qualities and that they would be leaders regardless of the time or place in which they lived.

The other side of the debate as to whether history makes the man or the man makes history is the "environmental" or "situational" theory, which is the belief that a great leader emerges as a result of time, place, and circumstance, and that the leader is directed and controlled by the historical environment or situation. The ones who became the leaders were those who possessed the abilities and skills needed to solve the existing social problems at their particular time in history.

What these two general theories overlook, however, is the interactive effects of the individual and the situation. More recent views now see leadership as a combination of the situation itself, the type of specific task to be accomplished, the characteristics of those being led, the characteristics of the leader, and the specific conditions of the situation. It is also generally believed that the traits of the leader must be in some way related to the traits of those being led. (Here again we are reminded that people are drawn to people like themselves and with whom they can identify.)

The Ohio State Studies

Because *traits* are hard to observe and therefore could not easily be quantified, studies conducted at Ohio State University and Michigan State University resulted in viewing leadership as *behavior*, which can be observed. Initially, the phases of the behavioral research seemed as frustrating as the trait approach because the number of behaviors identified was staggering. These studies, still the foundation for the most widely accepted leadership theories, identified four factors that appeared consistently to describe leadership behavior: (1) showing consideration, (2) initiating structure, (3) production emphasis, and (4) social sensitivity (although sometimes different terms are used) (Bass, 1981).

According to the Michigan study, showing consideration for other group members accounted for 50 percent of the leadership functions and initiating structure 30 percent. The findings concluded that there are two basic leadership functions: (1) helping the group to achieve a specific goal and (2) helping to maintain or build the group itself. The Ohio State Leadership Studies, as they became known, concurred and termed these two leadership functions (1) consideration and (2) initiation of structure. "Consideration" refers to the extent to which a leader exhibits concern for the welfare of other members of the group (people-oriented leadership), while "initiation of structure" refers to the extent to which a leader initiates activity in the group, organizes the activity, and defines the way work is to be done (task-oriented leadership).

These studies resulted in the Leadership Behavior Description Questionnaire (LBDQ), which measures leadership behavior. The LBDQ has been used in areas as diverse as industry, the military, education, medicine (hospitals), and government. A variety of investigations using LBDQ have taken place to measure the leadership behavior of college administrators and public school administrators. These results show that in higher education at the level of department chairman, the administrative competence correlated .36 with consideration and .48 with initiation of structure. In public education, superintendents who were rated as effective leaders by both staff and school board members were described as being high in both consideration and initiation of structure. While numerous studies were conducted with school principals, results from those studies varied. As might be expected, consideration and initiation of structure were not solely concerned with internal leadership, but were determined by external factors as well (Halpin, 1957; Murphy, 2003).

Contingency Theory

In the 1970s a concept identified as "contingency theory" began to be used as a tool to facilitate understanding of the effect of "situations" on leadership behavior. Linked with the theory of open systems (chapter 3), contingency theory stresses that variability in needs and demands requires variability in responses from the organization. In other words, contingency theory says that the typical way of doing things is not always appropriate in all kinds of decisions. All factors in the situation should be weighed and information should be gathered before continuing with what always has been done or choosing another (contingency) plan of action. Proponents of the theory believe that even a leader who has strong attributes in both task and consideration cannot be prepared for every eventuality and, therefore, leaders need to be prepared to accept that separate components of the system can respond as the situation requires.

LEADERSHIP ACCORDING TO WARREN BENNIS: THE PLEA FOR LIBERAL ARTS

To date, the leadership studies of Warren Bennis come closest to what will probably be honored as the foundation for feminine leadership. In describing leadership Bennis speaks of the "liberal arts" philosophy as "in part, the process of fully becoming oneself" (quoted in Godfrey, 1992, p. 5). (This concept of "becoming one's self" has the imprint of Virginia Woolf's *A Room of One's Own*, as well as Maslow's theory of self-actualization.) Bennis also celebrates rather than denigrates feelings, and he urges that feelings be used creatively, saying that persons with empathy inspire others more than leaders who do not have empathy. But, above all, he acknowledges that character is the key to leadership and says that effective leaders, as well as effective people, understand that there is no difference between becoming an effective leader and becoming a fully integrated human being (Bennis, 1999). Both Nel

Noddings (who identified and named the "ethic of caring") and Carol Gilligan (*In a Different Voice*) would, I believe, agree with Bennis's view of leadership as being not only more humanistic, but certainly more balanced, as it includes leadership that is guided by "persons" rather than directed by either men or women.

Being viewed as a person seems to be a prerequisite for advancement even in industries where there is a higher percentage of younger employees. According to Mark Ursino, who worked for Bill Gates for nine years, "If you're a woman around there [Microsoft], then you have a hard time. If you become a *person*, then you can get something done" (Illingworth, 1994, p. 96).

An emerging approach to leadership is more dependent on identity development, a belief that the importance of knowing oneself as one ascends to a leadership position is nearly universal. Fullan (2001) in referring to Robert Kegan's work on the evolving self, notes that knowing only the skill sets is not enough; rather, he says, aspiring leaders also need to cultivate personal growth as part of their adult development and professional development.

Sally Helgesen (1990) continues the thought advanced by Carol Gilligan that women have their own (different) voice. She also says that the need to express one's own values within a management style is an essential element in developing one's true voice. Helgesen enhances this idea by citing many successful leaders including Nancy Badore: "[To] be fully me is the only way I can be creative and spark creativity in others" (p. 150). Cantor and Bernay (1992) pick up on this idea of individuality in their popular work *Women in Power*, in which they profile a number of women in leadership positions. Cantor and Bernay quote then Congresswoman Barbara Mikulski (D-Maryland) on leadership: "[A] leader must first have a clear state of mind, her own vision, which energizes her, motivates others, then creates that state of mind in others" (p. 188). Now Senator Mikulski has website with a link to "Senator Barb's Favorite Crab Cake Recipe." (I doubt we would see a male senator's link such as "Senator Bob's Garage Cleaning.") Cantor and Bernay further supply their own definition of leadership (p. 112):

Competent Self + Creative Aggression + Woman Power = Leadership

Returning to his own liberal arts motif, Bennis joins John Gardner in the belief that the best leaders have intuitive and conceptual skills as well as logical and analytical talents. Bennis (1989) calls these leaders "whole brained" (pp. 102–103). Gardner (*Leadership Development*, 1987), in writings that predate the findings of Bennis, states, "At the college level, the best preparation is a liberal arts education. It is essential to broaden and deepen the understanding of those individuals who will have in their hands the future of our communities and our society. That means covering the whole range of the liberal arts, from science to literature, from mathematics to history" (p. 11).

Bennis (1989) reinforces this idea of a "broad-based" education by quoting Jamie Raskin, a Boston prosecutor: "Leadership is based on the ability to see how all humanity is related, how all parts of society are related, and how things move in the same direction" (pp. 91–92). Corday (quoted in Bennis, 1989) connects leadership to success by saying, "People who go to plays, read books, know the classics, have open minds and enjoy experiences are more apt to be successful" (p. 86).

When Bennis, in a different study with coauthor Burt Nanus, interviewed ninety of the top leaders at the corporate and university levels, these leaders talked about persistence and self-knowledge; willingness to take risks and accept losses; commitment, consistency and challenge; and learning. According to these interviews, leaders have a very strong commitment to learning. Some are voracious readers and others surround themselves with bright people. (This is one of the reasons Harry Truman was such an unexpectedly successful leader. He surrounded himself with the best advisors of the time and was not afraid to take their advice. He was also a man who was not afraid to make decisions [based on the advice he sought from others], and who fully accepted the responsibility of the office. As he said, "The buck stops here." And he meant it. Truman was a man "of the people," yet a man who respected history and honored those who knew history, respected it, and learned from it.) From these interviews, Bennis confirms that learning is viewed as "the source of high-octane energy that keeps up the momentum by continually sparking new understanding, new ideas, and new challenges. It is absolutely indispensable under today's conditions of rapid change and complexity" (quoted in Dyer, 1991, p. 2).

John Gardner has always been a very strong advocate of studying the liberal arts as the best preparation for leadership. One of the main points in his treatise "Leadership Development" (1987) is that because today's leaders live in a world that changes more quickly than its leaders can relearn, the *leaders must understand the larger framework in which change occurs.* The only way to know this larger framework is for leaders to understand their own culture and history, so that they can draw on paths already traveled. In addition, Gardner (1987) believes, leaders are constantly in situations that require the weighing of values. It is only by

> absorbing, through religion, literature, psychology, sociology, drama and the like, the hopes, fears, aspirations and dilemmas of their people and of the species, by coming to understand what our ancestors valued and fought for, by coming to know through history and biography the extraordinary outlines of the human story, that they may hope to discharge their leadership duties with wisdom. . . .
>
> Leaders must understand the culture. But much of the culture is latent. It exists in the minds of its members, in their dreams, in their unconscious. It can be discerned in their legends, in the art and drama of the day, in religious themes, in their history as a people, in the seminal documents, [and] in the stories of their heroes. (pp. 12–13)

PERSONAL PREREQUISITES FOR LEADERSHIP

Even with the many leadership theories, an individual still must ask, "What makes a leader?" How can you as an aspiring administrator develop personal prerequisites for leadership? How can you prepare for the role of leader? Hearing Gardner's early response that there are no traits that will guarantee successful leadership in all situations is not very satisfactory.

Ralph Stogdill (whose pertinent research spans forty years) in 1959 summarized more than fifty studies of leadership conducted during a thirty-year period. His findings and summary, while completed three decades ago, still provide the best comprehensive list for aspiring leaders on every level. In fact, most of the leadership theories found in his definitive *Handbook of Leadership* are still referenced today. Stogdill suggested that it is the function of the leader to maintain the group's structure and goal direction and to reconcile conflicting demands that arise within and outside the group. These functions also include defining objectives, providing means for attaining goals, facilitating action and interaction in the group, maintaining the group's cohesiveness and the members' satisfaction, and facilitating the group's performance of the task (Bass, 1990, p. 384).

In 1974 Stogdill provided "functions of an effective leader":

1. Goal Achievement, which includes technical skills, administrative skills, task motivation and application, leadership achievement, and maintaining standards of performance.
2. Group Maintenance, which includes social and interpersonal skills, social nearness or friendliness, group task supportiveness, maintaining cohesive work group, facilitating coordination and teamwork, and intellectual and communication skills (Dimock, 1987, p. 6).

John Gardner ("Attributes and Context," 1987) also devised a list of leadership traits, found in his *Leadership Papers*, prepared for the Leadership Studies Program sponsored by the Independent Sector. Gardner terms these leadership traits *attributes* and qualifies his listing with the reminder that not all attributes are present in every leader and that the importance of the attribute to effective leadership will vary with the situation:

1. Physical vitality and stamina
2. Intelligence and judgment in action
3. Willingness to accept responsibility
4. Task competence
5. Understanding followers and their needs
6. Skill in dealing with people
7. The need to achieve
8. The capacity to motivate
9. Courage, resolution, and steadiness
10. The capacity to win and hold trust
11. The capacity to manage, decide, and set priorities
12. Confidence

13. Ascendance, dominance, and assertiveness
14. Adaptability and flexibility of approach (Gardner, 1990, in Curry, 2000)

Traits, characteristics, and attributes of educational administrators do not differ from the general leadership traits. However, studies conducted by educators of educators are somewhat more specific to the field of educational administration, and the results are offered here for that reason:

1. Being a good problem solver
2. Having strong organizational skills
3. Developing excellent people skills
4. Understanding the nuts and bolts of the school business
5. Demonstrating integrity and honesty
6. Remaining nonjudgmental—both of people and of ideas
7. Having the ability to listen to other people
8. Being committed to the education of all children
9. Recognizing people for good work
10. Being able to work long hours
11. Being a good communicator
12. Being able to take risks and take a stand when necessary
13. Being able to separate what is important from what is not (Mahoney, 1990, p. 26)

Taking a page from her own practical guidebook for women entrepreneurs, Joline Godfrey (1992), currently CEO of her own company, Independent Means Inc., and a popular conference presenter, says that the following leadership traits are needed to be a successful woman in today's way of doing business:

1. Ease in relationships and a drive for connection
2. Whole people—head, heart, and hands
3. Appreciation of complexity and process
4. Desire for balance and self-awareness
5. Sense of artistry, imagination, and playfulness
6. Integrated vision of business and ethics
7. Courage

Importantly, Michael Fullan (2001), a contemporary and popular voice in leadership, has identified five themes of leadership that incorporate the research findings of Godfrey and Noddings, along with the recognition that the more complex society gets, the more sophisticated leadership must become:

1. The **moral purpose** of leadership is to act with the intention of making a positive difference in the lives of employees, customers, and society as a whole.
2. Leaders must **understand the change process**.
3. Leaders must be able to **build relationships**. (The single factor common to every successful change initiative is that relationships improve.)
4. Leaders must commit to constantly **generating and increasing knowledge** inside and outside the organization.
5. Leaders must also commit to **coherence making**.

Fullan also emphasizes the importance of character: "Authentic leaders display character, and character is the defining characteristic of authentic leadership" (p. 14). This supports what Bennis (1999) notes on the importance of character:

For exemplary leaders, character goes beyond ethical behavior. . . . They [the leaders] understand that there is no difference between becoming an effective leader and becoming a fully integrated human being. . . . Character develops throughout life, including work life. . . . [By] examining the kinds of decisions they make and don't make, senior executives and those they manage can develop their own character and cultivate new leadership throughout the organization.

For executive leaders, character is framed by drive, competence, and integrity. Most senior executives have the drive and competence necessary to lead. But too often organizations elevate people who lack the moral compass [integrity] . . . [and by] using resources for no higher purpose than achievement of their own goals, they often diminish the enterprise (p. 22).

To lead an organization requires caring about relationships. Villani (1999) notes that leadership that supports and nurtures is a large part of what builds a strong sense of community, promoting growth. While not exclusively the province of women, certainly there is a shift toward supporting those qualities that are more associated with women, and we can take some optimism from that.

It is particularly noteworthy that the trend in the new guidelines published by the American Association of School Administrators (1993), *Professional Standards for the Superintendency*, is away from charismatic, authoritative school management to flexible, creative, and visionary leadership. This appears to be naturally (but perhaps not intentionally) setting the newer stage for the personal characteristics most found in women.

STYLES OF LEADERSHIP

There are various ways to categorize leadership styles, but most researchers and writers agree on two major divisions, with several subdivisions designated according to the specific interest of the individual studies. Here we take a look at the two major divisions, with a brief view of several of the more common styles. Most readers will be able to identify their leadership styles based on the ones reviewed.

Autocratic and Democratic

The two major divisions of leadership styles are autocratic and democratic. All other styles follow from these two clusters. Both are the result of an attempt to answer the question, prevalent throughout history, "How shall people be governed or guided or led?" The answer has always been based on the belief of the prevailing culture. If a particular historical culture believes in the prevalence of *evil*, it follows in belief that the populace has to be controlled and directed, even *improved*, by some kind of authority. This situation calls for autocratic leadership. If the prevailing belief is that humankind is essentially *good*, then persons would be given the freedom in which to choose, to learn, to grow, and to govern for themselves. In this situation the required leadership style would be democratic.

The major difference between autocratic and democratic leadership styles is that the autocratic leader dictates what is to be done and the democratic leader shares the decision making with subordinates. The autocratic leader is not concerned about group members' needs for their own autonomy and development. The democratic leader shows concern for the needs of subordinates to contribute to the operation and development of the organization. The autocratic leader is personal in praise, but aloof in attitude; the democratic leader is factual in praise and shortens the social distance from the leader to members of the group.

These styles, moreover, are not always absolute. A benevolent autocrat could be dictatorial, yet paternalistic, while the participative, democratic leader could encourage group decision making yet place emphasis on getting the job done more than on the needs of the group. Bear in mind that labels are general and provide only a point of reference.

Autocratic leadership can be based on power or persuasion, and a leader with power can successfully coerce others because of that power. Democratic leadership can mean various things, but is usually found in leaders who have embraced democratic principles through experience as (1) a follower of a successful democratic leader, (2) an active participant in committees practicing consensus, (3) an instructor using cooperative learning, or (4) the product of a professional preparation program that provided training or a strong philosophical grounding in the benefits of democratic leadership.

An authoritarian leadership style is most successful (1) when the leader has more accurate information about the subject and/or controls the resources to support the results and (2) when speed and accuracy are held to be important. Conversely, a democratic leadership style is effective in (1) reducing personnel turnover and absenteeism and (2) achieving higher productivity.

Studies conducted specifically in school systems show that democratic leadership leads to better communication, cooperation, and coordination. The leaders are considered to be more flexible and innovative, as well as overall more effective. Their personnel experience a greater sense of self-actualization and satisfaction from their work and they achieve superior educational results. Likewise, studies in higher education institutions conclude that, with democratic leadership, more favorable outcomes are experienced and faculty are more satisfied with the administrative decision making (Bass, 1981).

Laissez-Faire

Laissez-faire leaders usually come under criticism and are said to hide behind paperwork in their offices, give subordinates too much responsibility, do not set clear goals, and generally let things drift along in the status quo. Usually, employees feel insecure. Left free to their own devices, those under laissez-faire who are involved in problem solving or decision making find their results to be of lower quality, less effective, and less satisfying. Laissez-faire leadership also can lead to less cohesiveness among members of the group, as there is little motivation (unless there is an emerging leader from the group itself).

As a new administrator you should be cautioned that a laissez-faire leadership style can occur in the process of trying to be a democratic manager. There is a danger in believing that if you give subordinates freedom they will do what they are supposed to do. You need to establish structured expectations of followers and a process for achieving these expectations. As a democratic leader, you must take an active part in helping to define both the expectations and the direction of the group or institution. These processes will not happen without specific leadership.

Situational Leadership

As noted in chapter 3, systems theory suggests that what happens outside the organization is likely to affect what takes place inside and will, in turn, determine what kind of leader would be most effective in a particular organization at any given time. Task requirements also affect what kind of leader is needed and what kind of leadership behavior will result in greater productivity and follower satisfaction in the institution.

Not to complicate things for an aspiring administrator who is already trying to match herself or himself to a leadership style or to hone skills that will result in the desired leadership style, there is also the path-goal theory, which posits that the leadership style of an individual varies as situations within an organization change. Path-goal theory states that as a leader faces different problems or circumstances in the organization, that individual adjusts the leadership style accordingly.

The field of education has been receptive to expanding the view of leadership, and, while research in leadership was prevalent in the 1950s and early 1960s, there have since been so many educational issues demanding the attention of both the researchers and the public (teacher militancy, student activism, multiculturalism, literacy, dropout prevention, violence in the schools, and, more recently, overall accountability) that the study of leadership has been quite overshadowed by overriding social issues.

At present, there appears to be a trend toward finding leaders who can help solve these problems in addition to serving as the institution's educational leader. Thus we add to the mix the need for leaders who (1) have the personal characteristics to be a social leader or are capable of shifting styles according to the situation *and* (2) know the field so well as to be the leader of educational programs as well.

As we have emphasized throughout this book, the tactics of leadership are all important. Unfortunately, social scientists have not yet produced a comprehensive theory of leadership. Thus, an individual can only do the best she or he can to prepare all of the skills that are required, in order to be confident in her or his prevailing style and to be ready to adjust to changing situations.

Group Leadership

In essence, all leadership is group leadership because there is no point in being a leader if there is no one to lead. Group leadership as a separate category of style, however, evolved because the word *group* implies that, in every group, there is a leader and that a different style of leadership is needed for each separate group. Thus, group leadership is closest to situational leadership, which, according to Dimock (1987), "assumes that leaders may have certain traits or skills that will increase the probability of their becoming a leader, but these characteristics may be important only in that situation" (p. 4). Dimock also mentions characteristics of emerging group leaders that echo various suggestions offered to aspiring administrators (with practical application suggestions by this author):

1. The person who does the most talking is most likely to be a strong influence. (Promote yourself through presentations, publications, via the media, i.e., anywhere you can be heard.)

2. Those who become leaders are usually more vocal and dominant. (Volunteer to chair a committee or represent your institution on a panel, and be prepared with a position on the subject. Be decisive, particularly in a crisis situation. Be in charge. Become active in organizations, both in your field and out.)

3. The person who is the usual channel of communication, who has special access to people in power or influence related to the group's goals, or who controls communication in any way is more likely to be a leader. (Write the minutes for a meeting. Publish a newsletter. Author articles for publication. Be active in organizations. Network!)

4. Leaders of effective groups have greater social distance from their followers than the leaders of ineffective groups. (Know when to let go. While members can respect a leader with whom they are friendly and familiar, a leader who is too close to the members may make decisions based on general personal feelings.)

5. Those who can recognize and identify the unique attributes of others gain considerable respect and often leadership status. (Compliment your colleagues. Volunteer to share your experience with them. You'll learn what they are doing and can praise them to others. Send notes of congratulation. In staff meetings, make positive comments about the work of your colleagues.)

As a group leader, you should bear in mind that the leader derives the position of leadership from the followers who see the leader as being able to help them achieve the goal and also to maintain themselves as a group. (Remember the axiom: People look to people who are like them.) Even if you are appointed from outside the group, your status and acceptability will depend on the group's perspective of your ability to meet their needs. Again referring to the "people like us" concept, you will be most effective if you become part of the group (for the task) and model the norms of the group. In this way, you will become a follower as well as the leader.

To gain status, you should also conform to the standards of the group; do not try to make any premature procedural changes in an already established group. Once you have accepted the group's norms, make your contributions to the group's achieving the goals, but in the confines of their norms. Once your input is viewed as a contribution and not as a change imposed from the outside, your place in the group will be assured. It is only after reaching this stage that you can then move toward changing traditional practices and eventually establish new norms. This process is necessary for all new group leaders and is essential if you are the new kid on the block.

The need for good leadership cannot be overemphasized here. Too often teachers do not see any responsibility to an organization as such. They have had no training in organizational systems and see themselves only as being responsible for what occurs directly in their classroom. They have no frame of reference for their role in the school as an organization. Unfortunately, many principals (themselves former teachers) also fail to see the *system* of which they are a part. In addition, most are so burdened with *managing* that they forget to serve as leaders.

STATUS, ESTEEM, AND CHARISMA

Status, esteem, and charisma are by-products, as well as possible precursors, of leadership. Having these three characteristics is not mutually exclusive to being a leader, for a person can be a leader without having status, esteem, and/or charisma; conversely, there are many persons who hold status, esteem, and/or charisma who don't desire or who desire but do not ever attain a position of leadership.

Status is defined as a position in a social system dependent upon the importance of the role and not upon the person. A school superintendency or college presidency is a position of status regardless of the individual who holds the office. A person of status ranks high in the pecking order and other persons defer to the person holding status. If the person of status also is in a position to have direct control over others, she or he is imbued by others with superior personal ability even if the person's actual abilities are more imagined than real.

Status is so powerful that even women administrators in the highest-ranking positions are accorded it despite their gender. This is not to say that the status of men and women in the same position is equal, for the perception of others also enters into the *degree* of status awarded to the position. For example, a male superintendent may hold more status in the community than a female superintendent; among her colleagues, the female administrator is likely to maintain equal status; and among other women administrators of lesser rank, her status will be even higher.

A further example can be shown through an incident using the United States Congress. The position of U.S. Representative is one of status and brings with it certain privileges, yet when the number of women holding congressional seats began to increase, strong status issues arose regarding such privileged amenities as use of the swimming pool and executive washrooms.

Esteem is the value members place upon the person holding a position. Esteem is based on personal ability to lead the group in achieving goals. Esteem is not bestowed upon the holder by virtue of her or his position but by what the person can do with the position. The esteem can be associated with the power of the position and/or personal power, but it must be generated from within the group. Leaders cannot award themselves esteem. Only the group can instill esteem, which usually, but not always, is the result of years of service to a group.

Esteem cannot, like status or position, be mandated or legislated away from the person receiving the esteem, and the holder may retain esteem even after she or he has vacated the position that originally led to the position and its earned status. As might be expected, esteem often leads to status achievement, as promotions depend to some degree on merit ratings of one's worth to the organization.

In interaction with the group, the esteemed member will be listened to by being given as much time as she or he wants to present the information and by being allowed to initiate or terminate activities. Most leaders who are esteemed have a strong motivational commitment to the group and are more valued if they support member independence, identification, and social closeness. They are also looked upon as experts. And, if they live long enough, the esteem may become veneration.

Charisma, like status and esteem, is not limited to holding office or a position of power. Charismatic leaders are said to have extraordinary influence over their followers and "tend to exude confidence, dominance, a sense of purpose, and the ability to articulate the goals and ideas for which followers are already prepared psychologically" (Bass, 1981, p. 152).

Charisma is more than being at the right place at the right time, although very often charismatic leaders emerge in times of crisis. With charismatic leaders, followers often become leaders in seeking more converts for their leader. Charisma is a very personal relationship established between the follower and the leader. Charismatic leadership is rare and places almost impossible responsibility on the participants.

Status, esteem, and charisma are all important factors in leadership, and although none is essential, all are enhancing.

THE LEADER'S ROLE IN SCHOOL REFORM

To be a successful leader in today's educational system you need to consider all persons who are involved in the school community. Everyone needs to understand *what* is worth doing in the school or university and to determine *why* it is important to do it. There will be no meaningful reform in education unless and until all educational institutions at all levels utilize what we have learned through research about organizations as well as about teaching and learning.

Reform is not about change for change's sake, nor is its purpose conformity in all institutions, as many resisters charge. What educational reform is asking is that each institution study itself, determine its real mission, and then gear all processes and resources toward achieving that mission. This will involve questioning fundamental beliefs, as well as daily operations, and it will require rethinking sports programs as well as classroom goals.

Many of these issues are already being debated in the media, such as in criticism of the graduation rate of football players at colleges and universities. Even some major universities that have billed themselves as viewing their athletes as "college students first, football players second" are found to be less than truthful about the percentage of those on athletic scholarships who finish a degree program. Many state-sponsored colleges and universities are also being admonished for lowering standards just to keep the classrooms (and the dormitories) filled. There are complaints that students can't schedule the classes they need in order to complete their undergraduate degrees in the typical four years and that there is pressure on college professors to give good grades. Some say we have created a culture in which students believe they have a right to an A unless the professor can *prove* otherwise. Is this what we want? Do we want coaches to have more authority than college presidents? Do we want all students to be equal in grades "earned"? Do we want a grading system at all? Do we need more or less stringent policies on student harassment or intimidation? What *do* we want from our universities? *Who* should decide? And who will lead in the decision making?

In public education there is an added dimension of legislative control as well as more direct parent involvement than in private institutions. Public schools must answer to both the state government and the local policy makers in the form of school boards. Yet the fundamental question remains "What is it that every student should know and be able to do?" Once that question is answered, we need to develop the process to achieve the ultimate outcome: an educated citizenry. Even that decision is fraught with difficulties, for the school is not a separate entity as it once was. Community and state agencies are much more a part of schools than they were a generation ago.

How, then, do we interact with social agencies? Whose responsibility is it for the welfare of the child? Should the school provide breakfast? Where does your role as the educational leader begin (and end)? It is by asking such questions that we begin to understand the enormity of the task of an educational administrator and the impossibility of single-handedly fulfilling all of the expectations. What should also be very clear, however, is the absolute necessity of good leadership.

As an effective leader you will want to include all of the stakeholders and to marshal the creative resources of every member of the group to search for the best direction for the institution to follow. Based on everything you have read thus far on becoming a good educational administrative leader, you should have a general idea of your own style and realize that if you are to get the job done, you need to take the best of your own natural leadership style and adapt it to a kind of participatory approach to planning.

Systemic reform is the term used to define the impact of change on all aspects of the education system; it also takes into consideration the interrelatedness of all the components that function together in the education system and realizes that as one component changes, so must the others to maintain the integrity, continuity, and consistency of the entire system. (See the section on systems in chapter 3.) Systemic reform is viewed as a shift from a more traditional educational system to one that emphasizes interconnectedness, active learning, shared decision making, and high levels of achievement for all students. Good school reform models show that leadership density can be advanced not through attempts to divide functions but by creating teams that collectively and collaboratively engage leadership assignments (Murphy and Datnow, 2003).

COLLABORATIVE TEAMWORK

Collaborative teamwork is the key to the success of any organization, so the conscientious administrator will use the creative resources and the collective wisdom of the staff and all other stakeholders to build the best possible organization and the best educational institution that will answer the needs of the constituents. Collaborative teamwork holds the following advantages:

1. All stakeholders who become participants will more clearly identify with the goals of the institution and its success.
2. The stakeholders (staff, students, community) will gain a feeling of control and begin to lose the sense of being controlled.
3. The stakeholders, by participating in the process, will learn the complexities of the situation.
4. The stakeholders, by getting to know the leader better, will begin to feel a part of the solution.
5. The resulting decisions will be more acceptable to a wider group of constituents.
6. In addition to becoming key communicators to the community, the stakeholders very often will become the promoters of a program being considered.

7. If we subscribe to the concept of collective wisdom, higher quality decisions should be the result of a collaborative effort.

SUCCESSFUL TEAMWORK

The success of the team effort will depend on the skill of the leader in being open and honest in all communications. Remember, there is nothing wrong in your saying, "I don't know. I'll see what I can find out for our next meeting." You can also use this opportunity to call on the expertise of another member for information you may not have.

Another essential ingredient to building a good team is trust. There must be belief in the leadership, the integrity of all participants, the shared vision, and the goals. Although there will be a modicum of trust given to the leader because of her or his position and status, long-term trust must be developed slowly and consistently:

- First, the team must feel confident that you hold a commitment to the institution and that you bring a clear vision that you are able to communicate to the others.
- Respect is an important element of trust. The members of your team have various talents and must be made to feel that they are safe in venturing to offer their opinions.
- The leader should be willing to relinquish responsibility and to allow others to take charge. (Remember, however, as noted earlier, you ultimately must be accountable for the results, especially if the result is negative. *Never* make such comments as "I tried to tell the committee that it wouldn't work.")
- The leader must be consistent and dependable. When you say you'll do something, do it. Your actions will speak more loudly than your words, so your behavior cannot be erratic or inconsistent. As leader, everything you do becomes symbolic.
- Trust will begin to build when people see that goals are being met, so make sure you set some short-range, achievable goals.
- Trust is mutual, so you also need to show that you trust others by taking time to listen to what they have to say.

To be a successful leader, you must become a part of the group you are leading. You must also encourage the other group members to feel free to speak out and to perform needed functions. Group members need to view you as a member like themselves so that they are free to assess your comments on the merit of their contribution and not because of the person who made the statement.

As leader you must also try to reduce the status differential while serving as a member of the group. This is sometimes difficult because there may be some members of the group who overstep their bounds and think they are now your best buddies. Try to anticipate this possibility and alert, in advance, a member of your staff who can be counted on to help set the tone. For example, if you are uncomfortable being addressed by your first name, then keep formality of everyone's name by addressing them as Mr. _____ or whatever their designation is. You know best your community's culture and need to take that into consideration. To avoid any anticipated awkwardness, you can prepare name cards to be placed on the conference table in front of each person's seat. If you choose to use first names, please always ask the person's preference as to how he or she wishes to be addressed. Not every Robert is Bob.

Don't forget to allow for some levity and some informal time. Providing coffee and/or soft drinks is a way to show your consideration, as is a time scheduled for an occasional stretch break. These breaks, while designed for a bit of relaxation, often result in the participants' talking and exchanging ideas that may be helpful once the group is back on task.

If the meetings are scheduled in the evenings, you are more likely to encounter all kinds of attire. You as the institutional leader need to decide just how casual you yourself want to be. (My advice is not to be too casual. Some of your contemporaries from the business community will be coming directly from their offices and will be dressed accordingly. A neat skirt and a jacket would be in order.) Again, follow community protocol, but be a bit more conservative.

Remember that as the group leader, you do not need to solve the problems; rather, you should serve as the facilitator. Problem solving is a process and, as such, has separate and distinct steps. There are various models in problem solving and decision making. Choose one that will work with your leadership style.

THE IMPORTANCE OF PLANNING

Planning is a process, not a product; however, the planning process should produce a result—the plan itself. Whether you are developing a five-year plan or a plan to implement a new program for the coming year, you need a clear, direct process. This process can be followed whether the plan involves only a leader or has many teams working on the various parts of the plan.

Management guru Peter Drucker (who wrote his first book in 1939 and his most recent in 2004 at age ninety-five) defines planning as "the management function that includes decisions and actions to insure future results" (quoted in Fray, 1987, p. 1). According to Fray himself, planning activities go beyond the determination of strategy and must be integrated into the total management system of the organization. Most businesses have an established formal planning system, which is often termed the "strategic plan." (See appendix D for elements of a strategic plan.) The time covered can range from one to ten years. Five years, however, is the average, for to plan for less than a year isn't worth the time involved, and to plan for more than five years is risky because so many factors change within that period of time.

While businesses have used planning strategies for years, educational institutions have traditionally paid only lip service to whatever written reports and documents were necessary as required by the various state departments of education. Educational institutions relied on employee loyalty and managerial intuition to take care of any changes they might face. Today, educational institutions have become so complex, issues have exploded so dramatically, resources have shrunk by so much, and the public has raised such a cry for accountability that public schools and colleges dependent upon public funds have had to turn to business practices in order to gain credibility.

An educational leader is now expected to know how to run a business every bit as much as, if not more than, how to provide curriculum and instruction. Preparatory programs for educational administrators, already bulging with requirements, are also feeling the pressure to focus more on management courses. To note just how far the superintendency is falling from the role of expert teacher, some districts are hiring persons with a background in business rather than in education for the top job in public schools. Higher education institutions have been looking to businesspersons for their top spot for some time. Good advice, then, to aspiring CEOs in educational institutions is to earn an MBA along with the requisite PhD or EdD.

Knowledge of strategic planning is necessary for any effective leader in business or education. Strategic planning provides a direction for the institution and focuses attention on current accomplishments as well as on future goals. Planning sets priorities and determines the action to meet the goals of those priorities. A good plan can increase motivation and bring credence to the organization. It can also reduce costs by avoiding the expense involved in reacting to events not planned for. A well-run planning process allows for interaction on all levels and should involve all interested constituents. Planning encourages looking at the organization in full bright light and focusing on the question "Where do we want to go and how do we get there in the best way possible?" Best of all, strategic planning provides another opportunity for you to show your own administrative ability.

Whether you are the superintendent or president, a principal or a dean, your understanding of and ability to design a formal plan will be an advantage to you. To be prepared for this endeavor, take as many courses in business as you can schedule and accept any opportunity to participate in any planning process. Familiarize yourself with the terminology and the concepts of management. This will give you leverage regardless of your role in the planning process.

A final note of caution in your strategic planning process: If the members of the group you are working with are not familiar with the terminology, the process of planning, or the system of organizations, use terms with which they will feel comfortable. For example, you can always ease into a planning process with the words "Here's the game plan!"

NOTE

1. The derivation of *chairman* shows that the second syllable comes not from *man* the person, but from *mano*, meaning "hand" or "craft." Therefore, the term is not gender specific.

6

MEN AND WOMEN, MORE DIFFERENT THAN ALIKE

While women have made numerous attempts and have initiated various movements to call attention to the unequal situation of men and women, widespread acknowledgment of that fact is a modern phenomenon. This recent awareness is due in large part to the modern feminist movement, which began in earnest in the 1960s. The women of this movement made their mark by being the generation that led society to finally and openly admit what women have always known but seldom voiced: Women have not been as valued as men.

Mothers have been venerated, daughters have been loved, wives have been respected, women have been admired, and a few female national leaders have been revered, but females—half the population in any human culture—have not been valued. Various services that females have provided have been valued to a lesser or greater degree, but these services have had their value placed on them by males. Women and women's work have been viewed as a convenience for men. And, until the present generation, women were enculturated to feel privileged that they could serve.

This undervaluing of women in our society has not been an easy fact to admit, for most women in today's workplace were reared to believe that they could be anything they wanted to be. They were encouraged to become educated, to be employed or not as they chose, to have children or not as they chose, and to reach the heights of their chosen careers. What someone forgot to tell them, however, was that whatever they decided to do, it might not be valued, and that in many leadership positions there would be barriers and an unspoken, built-in system for failure.

BARRIERS AND BIAS

The barriers to success can be either obvious or subtle; in either case, the barriers are real. Unfortunately, women often don't see particular situations as barriers. We are so accustomed to viewing paths taken by men as being the norm that we view men's paths as being the only way to reach a given goal. For example, women grow up learning that the female characteristic of displaying emotions is not valued and, in fact, is often viewed as proof of women's inferiority, rather than as an authentic way of expression. Therefore, women have tried to suppress their "normal" way of expressing themselves. Fortunately this is changing, with research now showing that emotional expressiveness and interpersonal sensitivity are important in building and maintaining affiliations and relationships. Nonetheless, high-status endeavors still require aggressive behaviors often viewed as appropriate only for men.

In addition to being charged with being "too emotional," women are discounted in many other ways, direct and indirect. There are assumptions and attitudes, both open and hidden, that still prevail and that precede every woman into a room. There also remains a negative connotation when a term is prefixed by *woman*. "Woman's work" implies housekeeping, "women's intuition" suggests guessing rather than knowing, "women's logic" conjures irrationality, and "a woman's place" is still often followed by "is in the home." Comparable negative terms to use with *man* are not to be found.

While some inroads have been made into changing the situation, gender bias is still very much in evidence, in our homes, schools, religious centers, workplaces, and social or service organizations. In fairness to service organizations, however, there have been concerted efforts to include women in the general membership of groups such as Rotary, Lions, and Kiwanis clubs. (Women's auxiliaries of these service clubs—Ki-Wives, Lionettes, and Rotary Anns—are almost a thing of the past.)

While earlier research tended to ignore larger systemic issues of power and ideology as being gender barriers, more recent studies have begun to focus on the organizational structures of schools and their reflection of larger social issues that perpetuate gender, racial, and class inequities both internal and external. Internal barriers include aspects of socialization, personality, values, and attitudes of the individual, and external barriers include environmental circumstances such as sex-role stereotyping, sex discrimination, lack of professional preparation, and family responsibilities (Shakeshaft in Kowalski, 2003; Lewis in Kowalski, 2003). Additional barriers identified by Kowalski (2003) are mobility; negative attitudes toward career opportunities; lack of sponsorships and mentoring; separation of the work of educators by gender (stereotyping); discrimination (both overt and covert); lack of family support; socializing of women not to pursue administrative careers (by hearing things such as "Now, don't be disappointed if you don't get a superintendency"); and experiencing gender bias in professional books and research while in graduate school.

A study by Grogan (1996) found that even though some women had established priorities to accommodate as many of the demands made upon them by their partners as they could, they continued to avoid a possible rupture in the relationship. Thus, their careers were subordinated to their personal relationships. The difference between men and women in this situation is that few of the women who had partners believed they could justify a career move in the same way that their partners had done earlier in their two-career household.

In a survey of women by Gupton and Slick (1996) that was specific to education, the following responses were given as the way men react to women administrators:

Women believed they were

- on the receiving end of a good-ole-boy patronizing attitude
- faced with having difficulty with older males who hated to have a younger, female boss
- not taken seriously
- treated politely, but not as equals
- ignored at meetings

One of the women interviewed summarizes the false hope and naiveté held by many women:

> I never wanted to believe I had less opportunity than the men. I never wanted to believe the cards were stacked against me. I never wanted to believe that when push comes to shove, people can be mean, base, and self-serving. I never wanted to believe people would almost kill to maintain power and control independent of right and wrong. But these were childish and unrealistic principles.

Women also reported factors such as being openly accused of not acting "tough" enough by board members, administrators, and teachers for administrative positions (Tallerico in Gupton and Slick, 1996). Additional perceptions that factor into their not being selected are different interpersonal treatment, less support among the ranks, closer scrutiny of women's dress and behavior, and different, as well as higher, performance standards.

BASIC DIFFERENCES

Research studies confirm that there are many basic differences between men and women and substantiate what has been observed for generations. A highly publicized study by Moir and Jessel (1991)—one that still is considered as important—offers a series of interesting conclusions:

- Men can read maps better. Women do better at locating by landmarks.
- Women have a greater imagination and a keener intuition.
- Men are naturally and innately aggressive.
- Women are better at descriptive language skills.
- Women can recall more seemingly unrelated information than men can, yet men can do so when the information is organized into a coherent form relative to them.
- Girls are better with social, aesthetic, and religious values, and boys with economic, political, and theoretical values.
- Women like "being of service" to society.
- Men like power, profit, and independence.

- Men prefer competition, scientific toys, and principles.
- Women seek personal relationships and security.

In areas of interaction:

- Women pick up better on social cues, and can infer nuances of meaning from a speaker's tone of voice and intensity of expression. This may be attributed to the fact that they also hear better and are more fluent in their own speech.
- Women are also better than men in judging a person's character. This skill may result from their ability to extract social cues from body language and their keen memory for faces and character. All in all, women have a better understanding of what a woman or man means, even when she or he is saying little or nothing.
- Women are also more sensitive in that they are alert to touch, smell, and sound. A woman sees more, remembers more, and attaches more importance to personal and interpersonal aspects of life. She also reacts more quickly and more acutely to pain.
- Men are more single-minded, not noticing distractions. This may be a result of their mild tunnel vision and its accompanying higher sense of perspective. A man is involved in the world of *things*— what they are, how they work, and the space they occupy. He tackles problems in a practical, overall self-interested way. In choosing between any two events, a man will select the one of *most benefit to himself personally.*
- Women are better at social interplay and association. Even when they are not happy, women smile more than men do. Women are nice to people they may not like, and they have closer, longer, and more regular links with friends.
- In dilemma situations, women tend to experience other people's distress as their own, while men respond by searching for a practical solution.

BIOLOGY IS DESTINY

Moir and Jessel spent a great deal of time and effort in studying the differences between men and women in spatial ability and mathematical skills in order to show that (1) there is an experimentally demonstrable difference between the average male and female brain, and (2) the worlds of mathematics, vision, and space are a part of daily life. Their findings demonstrate that testosterone gives men an advantage in focusing a brain already (by its structure) more focused than the female brain. By comparison, it is the high levels of estrogen in women that enhance their coordination skills.

An important contribution of this study is its affirmation that differences in the brains of girls and boys are a determinant of their behavior, emotions, ambition, aggression, skill, and aptitude just as much as social and cultural influences are. School-age boys want dominance and girls want popularity more than success or achievement. With puberty, boys begin to define their life aims in terms of occupations and their prestige, while girls are worried about what others think of them. Social conditioning reinforces this, yet deliberate efforts to reverse this effect do not seem to succeed. Moir and Jessel tell of an instance in which girls were given specific lessons in leadership; their aspirations to lead did not increase, except in cases where the leadership function could be linked to some form of social responsibility and acceptability.

While there still are those who would say that girls are predisposed to choose careers that involve human interaction of some kind and, accordingly, are destined to go into second-class jobs, Moir and Jessel don't accept that kind of view. They believe that because of male dominance (societally influenced as well as biologically determined), aggression, and a sense of hierarchy, women's jobs come to be regarded as second class. In other words, women have been relegated to second-class jobs, not because they are predisposed to seeking jobs involving human action, but rather because men's dominance has prevailed in making everyone think that what men do is first rate and, consequently, what women do is second rate. Thus, it is thought that as any job becomes predominantly female, the position itself loses prestige. It will be interesting to watch as women become predominant in the superintendency just how the prestige of that job changes in the eyes of the community.

Motivation is also different in men and women, say Moir and Jessel. Girls and women are preoccupied with their own identity and their relationships with others, while boys and men are focused on competition and achievement. Moir and Jessel cite studies of college males that show that a majority of them do not choose fields in which conventional success is assured; they choose fields in which there is a *risk* of failure but the *chance* of much greater success. Females in the study usually had different priorities; for them, the nature of the occupation was much more important than formal achievement or financial success.

Along with the male focus on motivation and priority is the issue of money. Success, ambition, and money are all bound together in the thinking of males. Females, on the other hand, see level of salary as not as important as the position (so long as they can make a decent living). This may be part of the reason why women are paid less than men for the same work, especially in careers such as educational administration, in which salary often is negotiated.

When the positions of college president and school superintendent are filled by females and those positions lose their status, the result will be even more women having opportunities to fill the openings vacated by men. What women need to do, therefore, is to negotiate for what the job is worth and not what they think they personally are worth.

BRAIN OR BRAWN?

The findings of Marie-Christine de Lacoste, a noted researcher in the study of the physiology of brains, closely ally with those of Moir and Jessel. De Lacoste's research was the first study of the human corpus callosum to show a possible anatomical basis for sexual differences in intellect, skills, and behavior. Her findings support a prominent theory of Nobel laureate Roger Sperry, whose work is still considered by many to be definitive. Sperry, de Lacoste, and many others believe that male brains are more lateralized than those of females, and, as such, allow for greater right-brain performance, which includes the visuospatial skills. Women, with their theoretically increased bilateralization, excel at verbal skills because, with more cross-communication, they have decreased focus on the right hemisphere (Phillips, 1990).

The actual sex difference in aggression has been found to be characteristic only in certain types of situations. Numerous studies show that males and females are equally likely to engage in aggression when they are provoked, but males are more likely to *initiate* aggression. Men are more likely to be angered most by physical aggression, whereas women are most angered by unfair treatment.

The controversy continues as to the differences between women and men. Most researchers do, however, agree that women and men are different and that there are certain things each sex does better.

FEMALE PSYCHOLOGY

We can say both intuitively and scientifically that *women experience life differently than men do*; consequently, they think differently. As Carol Gilligan, a pivotal researcher and Harvard psychologist, said in her seminal book of the same title (1982), "Women speak *in a different voice*." Soft-spoken herself, she exemplifies the ethic of care she professes in all of her writing.

More than two decades after her original research she remains a strong, but subtle voice. In a recent presentation, Gilligan stepped up to the lectern to speak, only to realize she was being dwarfed by its height and hidden by its microphone. Lifting the large microphone from its mooring, she stepped to the side of the lectern, trying to hold the microphone in one hand and a sheaf of papers in the other without dropping either. She smiled and glanced back at the immense lectern and, speaking as much to herself as her audience, said, "The world is still. . . ." She didn't need to finish the sentence; the audience of both men and women understood, laughed, and applauded.

In much of her work, Gilligan emphasizes the dilemma experienced by girls in early adolescence. They are faced with a choice between remaining responsive to themselves and remaining responsive to others. Unable to choose between selfishness and selflessness, many girls at around age eleven *silence* their voices. It is at this age that girls become less confident and more tentative in offering their opinions, and after a while, the girls speak in a way that is disconnected from how they are really feeling. Girls begin to bury their knowledge. Fearing that speaking up will anger others, adolescent girls still their voices and settle for a view of society in which everyone is "nice."

What various studies have found in the past thirty or so years is that women view human connection as being of paramount importance.

Women use conversation to expand and understand relationships, while men use talk to convey solutions, thereby ending conversation. Women tend to see people as mutually dependent; men view them as self-reliant. Women emphasize caring; men value freedom. Women consider actions within a context, linking one to the next; men tend to regard events as isolated and discrete.

When women are asked to identify themselves, they typically speak of themselves as being a daughter, wife, mother, sister, or friend. They prefer to think of themselves as part of a web of connectedness. They are more likely to bend the rules so that feelings are not hurt, whereas men are more likely to adhere strictly to the rules, disregarding the relationships.

FAMILY INFLUENCES

There are few who would disagree that family influence of whatever variety is very strong on both girls and boys. In most families boys are encouraged to explore areas, space, and things. Their parents admire their daring, even while warning their sons of danger. Boys are always projecting what they are going to be when they grow up, and when they become men, they project what they are going to achieve in the next five years. On the other hand, women rarely think about what is possible for them to become, thinking more of who will be a part of their lives. Thus, boys' self-esteem becomes based on achievement and girls' self-esteem depends on acceptance by others. When society does not place a very high value on feelings between oneself and others, girls have difficulty becoming motivated to succeed.

Former president Clinton frequently boasts that he set his sights on the presidency at an early age and that he confirmed that dream after meeting President Kennedy. We might ask, "What kind of dream did his junior high school female classmates have? Who now influences women in their dreams to become executives?" Generally, not other women.

On the other hand, most of the role models women have are other women, and it is likely that every woman can name her own teachers who inspired her to become a teacher. In the case of women educators, it probably didn't matter so much what subjects their teachers taught; it was the *person* they wanted to emulate.

Most childhood games help shape what and who girls and boys become. In game playing, boys' interest in others is purely functional: "Do you know how to build a tree house?" Girls seek more intimate, personal relationships by forming social clubs. Both boys and men form teams for purposes of winning, while girls and women form groups on the basis of emotional attachments. Males view winning as more important than personal relationships or growth, whereas girls most value cooperation and relationships. Boys insist on boundaries, rules, and procedures often with many intricate rules—rules boys seem to enjoy arguing over. Girls, on the other hand, look disdainfully upon complicated rules and authoritarian structure, preferring shorter and less complex games, and disregarding a quest for victory if it threatens the harmony of the group.

To confuse matters even further, parents unwittingly send mixed messages to girls, particularly in adolescence. They encourage their daughters to do well, yet unthinkingly send signals to not excel by saying, "You want people to like you, don't you?" When the daughters head off to college they are told, "You can do anything you want to do if you apply yourself," yet daughters also hear suggestions such as "Remember your upbringing and make friends" (meaning nice girls like themselves). Boys would never be told, "Make friends," yet they instinctively seem to do so, easily building networks for future business dealings. Girls are more likely to report to parents details such as the hometowns of the girls they have met, while parents of boys will likely hear nothing about their sons' new college friendships.

EXTRAPOLATIONS

By extrapolating this behavior to its logical sequence into the adult workplace, you can better understand similar situations occurring there. If, for example, most of the administrators in an educational institution are male, you can expect the play activities of boyhood to be evident in the working style of the management team. If the management team is close to being divided equally between men and women, a conflict situation could result in which the members of the team are at best uncomfortable and at worst confrontational. This happens because women and men do not know how to play games together. They have learned different game rules and strategies, and neither gender understands the games played by the other. In such conflict situations, you as the leader are going to need to give serious thought to management development, perhaps in the form of a retreat led by an experienced facilitator or trainer (someone with experience and understanding of both men and women).

In the unlikely event that your management team is composed completely, or almost completely, of females, you can expect more decision making by cooperation and consensus. That situation may appear to be positive, but it may not be entirely ideal, for in situations of conflict, females have a tendency to remove themselves from the situation or to cope by unassertive means. In such a case, you may find yourself wishing for some of the assertiveness and risk-taking propensities of males and may even have to take on that role yourself.

Of course, it cannot be assumed that all women and all men work in gender absolutes. Nevertheless, knowing the generalities of the way men and women operate should help you in any administrative position.

It may also be an advantage to have (on your management team) women who grew up (1) with siblings, whether they are male or female, and/or (2) in homes where many discussions around the dinner table occurred. Such family experiences provide more opportunities for girls to learn how to negotiate among their contemporaries and with the older generation. These opportunities for interaction are usually safe ways by which the participants can learn to pick their battles and to take calculated risks, thus sharpening lifetime skills.

SCHOOL INFLUENCE

It should be a lasting embarrassment to educators that they were not the first to call attention to the impact of sexism on the schools, but it is likely that they could not see this unequal treatment because they followed the same assumptions as the general public: that there are insurmountable biological differences between men and women and even deeper differences in temperament and physique. Change happens slowly, and the best we can do as educational leaders is to not perpetuate the sexism and the constraints it supports.

The AAUW Report

It is the work of the American Association of University Women (AAUW) that very likely will be regarded as the most influential report on the crisis in the American schooling of its females. This report has been widely read and frequently cited, and because it is so clear and timely, its impact has been strong. Much of the information on the issue of gender confirms what has already been cited in this chapter. The AAUW report (1992) poses this question: "When girls and boys enter school nearly equal in measured ability, why, at the end of twelve years, have girls fallen behind the boys in the key areas of higher-level mathematics and measurable self-esteem?" (p. 2).

The following listing summarizes the AAUW report in emphasizing the stages at which gender differences are most evident:

1. By age four, children begin to think of girls and girl things as the opposite of boys and boy things.
2. By age six or seven, children have clear ideas of gender, and both sexes strive for conformity to role and prefer sex-segregated play groups.
3. By age eight to ten, children are more flexible regarding occupational roles for women and men, and there is some reduction of sex-segregated behavior.
4. In early adolescence, girls become more unwilling to admit that they ever act like boys. Boys are never very willing to admit acting like girls.

What is of major concern to the AAUW study is the silencing of girls as they move from elementary grades into junior high/middle school and high school. The AAUW report further asks, "If young women of relative privilege, studying in environments designed to foster their education and development, exhibit increasingly conflicted views of themselves and their responsibilities and opportunities in the world, what does this reveal about the cultural norms these schools, and perhaps all schools, are reinforcing for young women?" (AAUW, 1992, p. 12).

Most research, including that reported by the AAUW, shows that early adolescence is a particularly difficult time for girls because they are facing the idealization as well as the exploitation of their sexuality. In addition to wanting the attention of their male classmates, being liked by others of their own sex is especially crucial.

The area of the AAUW report that caused the greatest stir—and has become almost a part of our national identity—is the finding that gender differences in self-confidence are strongly correlated with continuation in math and science classes. Elizabeth Fennema and Julia Sherman, in their classic study in the early 1970s, found a strong correlation between math achievement and confidence. Their research revealed a drop in both confidence and math achievement in the middle school years, and further noted that the drop in confidence occurred first (AAUW, 1992). The implications here are that even though a good grounding in math is a prerequisite for math or science college majors, girls continue to opt out of advanced math (and science) courses. Girls are thereby (although perhaps unwittingly) limiting their career choices.

Girls and Extracurricular Programs

In addition to inequity in academics, the AAUW report also concerns itself with the lack of girls' participation in athletic programs. The report was concerned that no one was telling the girls the very real benefits that playing sports can have in preparing for leadership roles in the workplace. In fact, all extracurricular activities and sports provide important opportunities for leadership, teamwork, and the development of citizenship. Activities provide a chance to explore new areas and to develop skills in an area of particular interest. Of equal importance, and cogent to the premise of this book, is that extracurricular activities provide opportunities for personal contacts with adult role models who can, in turn, provide guidance and support (mentoring). Even more important is the early groundwork training in networking provided by sports and other extracurricular activities.

Anyone who has participated in activities or who has played a role as a coach or advisor has seen this process in action. Friendships formed on a team are lasting ones, and these friendships often become the basis for career networking. Even if teammates follow different career paths, the skills and confidence they have learned on the playing field (or on the stage) are transferable to the world of work. Those girls and boys who have mentors in their specialty, or who are proficient enough to attend district chorus or state track, have the opportunity for even more rudimentary networking. They also have the chance to watch successful female role models if the coach or advisor is female.

Gender and Scholastic Achievement

Well-known researchers David and the late Myra Sadker found that the teachers they studied interacted more often with the boys in their classrooms than they did with the girls. The Sadkers noted that this occurs partly because boys *demand* more attention than girls do, but more often the attention is just another unconscious sex bias on the part of the teachers (AAUW, 1992, p. 69). Other studies support these findings and add their conclusions that boys receive more specific comments and evaluations from their teachers than do girls in the same classes. Because girls are given less attention, some female students do not have the opportunity to learn qualities of perseverance and self-confidence. This lack of confidence in their own abilities is also a reason why girls sometimes abandon academic challenges. Another theory as to why girls avoid striving hard and achieving much is the "fear of success" theory. (See chapter 7.)

Based on the widely held belief that women's colleges are twice as likely as comparable coed colleges to produce achievers and on research studies that indicate that girls often learn and perform better in same-sex work groups than they do in mixed-sex groupings, there is a small but growing trend in high schools to offer single-sex math classes. However, because there is some interpretation that single-sex classes are illegal under Title IX (except under certain circumstances including remediation), there have been some challenges filed against holding single-sex classes. Nonetheless, it is interesting to note that the news media report that girls in these all-girl math classes wholeheartedly agree that they learn more than they did in mixed-gender classes. The girls explain that they do better because they are not distracted by having boys in their classes and because they are more comfortable asking questions and responding to the teacher's questions in single-sex classes. A middle school in Indiana, one of a number of schools exploring single-sex classes, has found that their single-sex classes have cut the failure rate of both girls and boys, but particularly of boys (Kaukas, 2003).

IMPLICATIONS

The extent to which you, as an aspiring woman administrator, identify with the classic scenario of growing up female will vary from individual to individual. Moreover, your own recollections may either enhance or diminish your ability to relate to these typical schooling experiences. You may find yourself surprised at your reaction because perhaps you have not thought about the influence your early schooling experiences have had on your own life choices. If this is the case, now is the time to recall those experiences. The recollection will help you understand yourself better and, while it may not make you any more pleased with the work style of some of those with whom you work, reflecting upon early influences may help you to deal with present experiences in a more enlightened way.

As the leader of an educational institution, you will have a strong voice in determining the direction to be taken by that institution. You will have the opportunity to effect change in both direct and subtle ways. For example, the following changes can be made just in the normal course of operations:

- Establishing committees at every level to spearhead or monitor programs that promote opportunities for girls and women would be a giant stride.
- Placing an equal number of men and women faculty and/or administrators on every committee would be a positive step. (Considering that nationwide about 73 percent of teachers are women, you may have to concentrate on finding enough male teachers willing to serve on the committee in order to have a near-equal representation.)
- Encouraging the library to exercise more discretion in increasing their holdings to include more women authors would also have an impact on the reading and research selections of your student body. (The *best* of both men and women authors should be the goal.)
- Seminars and special speakers, convocations and school assembly programs, field experience and field trips, and/or visiting lecturers on both the college and the high school level could go a long way in raising the awareness of the contributions of women. Make an effort to seek female speakers, particularly graduates of the school.

In addition, try some creative ways to enhance the involvement of the female population in the institution. Once your faculty, board, and students see that you are serious in promoting equality, many more ideas will flow from all quarters. A little publicity wouldn't hurt, either. For example, as your contribution to the spring festival, instead of doing something silly such as participating in the dunking booth, why not offer something fun, yet dignified, such as a debate or a series of male–female contests, both academic and extracurricular? A student–faculty committee could, no doubt, come up with some very interesting and creative ways to highlight the skills and contributions of your female students and faculty. Why not a gender day, in which the historical contributions of each sex are featured—or a special event demonstrating the ways in which each gender approaches particular tasks? This would require research and much planning and coordination, but think of the potential for positive results!

SPEAKING A DIFFERENT LANGUAGE

No one will argue the importance of communication with all constituents—teachers, parents, students, and community. Just as important, however, is the communication of everyday conversation between and among individuals. As most of the day-to-day operations of a business or institution depend on the spoken word, it is necessary to understand that what is being said and how it is being said impacts on the listener.

All of us are all familiar with the cliché "My wife doesn't understand me." We also all have heard such comments as "You're not listening" or "Why don't you hear what I'm saying?" While the first remark is obviously one made by males, it is probably just as apparent to both men and women that the latter two expressions are likely to be made by females. Rather than continuing to blame the men we work with (and/or live with), we should perhaps look at the differences between the ways women and men speak.

Accepting that there *are* differences can be the first step in reconciling those dissimilarities. For example, who among us has not asked our husband to stop at the store to pick up a familiar item—at least one we think everyone in the household recognizes on sight? "Just a box of crackers," you say, "the kind we always get. In the yellow box." Well, be prepared not to be upset when he comes home with Triscuits in a yellow box that says "low fat." You may wonder why he doesn't know you didn't want "low fat," you wanted "original," and he is wondering why you are upset rather than grateful that he took the time to stop. After all, he brought exactly what you asked for. So it is in the workplace.

As the Twig Is Bent . . .

Communication disparities between the sexes begin almost from the time children begin to speak in sentences. A study of conversational patterns of preschoolers and elementary school children found that four-year-old girls volunteered a great deal of information, but four-year-old boys responded with only brief facts:

> When asked by the interviewer to talk about her family, one girl answered, "Well, the first thing we do in the nighttime is we watch some TV, and then we read a book, and then we go to bed, except my mother stays up to read." A boy, when asked the same question, responded, "My dad is on a trip."
>
> When the interviewer asked the girl to talk about day care, she answered: "Well, I have a friend named Sally. Sometimes we play in the tunnels, but sometimes we don't play there because it's muddy and there are worms." With a little prompting, she continued, "And we have snacks. Sometimes we have oranges, and sometimes we have apples, and sometimes we have cheese and crackers."
>
> When the interviewer asked the boy the same question, he answered, "We play with blocks." Hoping to get a bit more information, the interviewer repeated, "You play with blocks?" To which the boy responded, "Yeah." (Wolcott, 1991, p. 22)

These responses are typical and recognizable by anyone who has experience with children, but the differences in the ways boys and girls talk may have an effect on perpetuating unequal status between boys and girls.

In conversation, girls (and women) use elaborations, which are words and phrases adding to the flow of the conversation. Females use these elaborations to add new information, maintain the topic, and form a more definite link with the person to whom they are speaking. Boys (and men), on the other hand, add little or no information in their responses. This allows males (intentionally or unintentionally) to control the interaction, placing females in the awkward position of seeming to flounder and to fill in the conversational gaps (left by the males). For example, in a recent conversation with my son, I was explaining where the outdoor Christmas decorations had been stored last summer, when I had done a major overhaul of the contents of all of the outbuildings on the property. I said to him, "Those items are in the storage room of the guest cottage, on the right hand side in the corner where the cupboard that is now in the third garage used to be, you know, the cupboard that K—— said he wanted but has yet to take." My son's reply was, "So you want the boxes from the storage room taken to the cupboard in the garage." I had given him too much information, information that my daughter readily would have interpreted as I had meant it.

Reflect for a moment on a similar experience you have had in giving directions or how many times you have been in a situation of feeling pressure to ask questions to keep a conversation going. Particularly in social conversations, a woman keeps introducing topics until she finds a topic that interests the man. Women dislike dead conversation and feel the responsibility to fill in. In short, women provide the majority of conversational effort while men maintain conversational control. Think about this—the men are perfectly comfortable saying nothing.

... the Tree's Inclined

Deborah Tannen, a well-known popular commentator on the communication styles of men and women, says that all else being equal, women are not as likely to be listened to as men, regardless of how they speak or what they say. She also cites Eleanor Maccoby, whose research shows that significant sex differences emerge most when children are observed interacting with other children rather than being individually tested. Thus, while males and females have very similar individual abilities, they have somewhat different characteristic styles of interacting, and these style differences often put females at a disadvantage in interaction with males (Tannen, 1994).

In another Maccoby study of children who had not previously known each other, girls playing in pairs at ages approximately two and a half to three were not found to be passive. However, when girls and boys played together in pairs, girls often stood aside while the boys played with the toys (Tannen, 1994, pp. 286–288). The experience of women in meetings where there are both men and women is often similar.

In conversations women are more likely to downplay their certainty and men are more likely to downplay their doubts. This stems from childhood when girls learn to temper what they say so as not to sound too aggressive, that is, too certain. From childhood, little girls learn that sounding too sure of themselves will make them unpopular with their peers, as they discover that groups of girls will penalize and even ostracize a girl who may seem too sure of herself. This kind of learning not to display accomplishments likely plays a part in the reluctance most women have in most speaking situations, be they speaking in meetings or negotiating salary.

Remembering that men and women follow a different conversational pattern can work to your advantage, not only in helping you to understand that even simple conversation is sex biased, but also in aiding you to use this knowledge to your advantage. Make it a practice to reflect on your conversations even while you are engaged in them. In other words, act as an objective observer even while being an active participant. By raising your awareness of gender conversational patterns as they are occurring, you will increase your chances of conversing on an equal footing.

Make your presence and your expertise known. Don't put up automatic roadblocks with phrases that are conditional, such as "This probably won't work, but . . ." Instead speak more directly. Don't wait until you are absolutely positive about an idea you have. If an idea is shot down, you are not going to be remembered as the person who had this dumb idea. It is worth taking the risk that a particular suggestion or solution *is* just what is needed.

Myths and Truths

Contrary to popular myth, studies show that men interrupt women more often than women interrupt men. Boys also interrupt women, where girls rarely do. Studies show that both mothers and fathers interrupt daughters more than they do sons and that women who as children are told, "Don't interrupt!" learn not to interrupt. The unfortunate consequence is that this admonition not to interrupt reinforces a style of docility, humbleness, and powerlessness in the behavior of women. If you ever watched the television program *The Apprentice*, you probably noted—and may have been surprised—to see that Donald Trump seemed to favor those women who interrupted and often shouted down their opponents. While I saw these young women as rude and "unladylike," they were the ones who remained as finalists.

Research further shows that girls and boys learn to use language differently in their peer groups. Girls *talk* and share secrets, becoming best friends in the process. Boys' best friends are the ones with whom they *do* things. Activities become central in their lives. Males' play also is hierarchical. High-status boys give orders and push low-status boys around. On the other hand, girls generally try to include and equalize everyone.

Girls vie for attention in subtle ways, hoping to be noticed, whereas boys grab center stage by showing off their skill or by challenging others. Boys and men also speak out in class more than girls and women because they like the public forum and view it as a mark of status. In addition, many classrooms—particularly those of male teachers—use a debate-like format, with teachers challenging the comments made by students, playing devil's advocate, and generally drawing out comments and counter-challenges. Boys thrive in this atmosphere and have no qualms about speaking out, right or wrong. Girls and women do not like the challenge of debate as a general classroom technique, preferring to work in a small group of people they know well.

As adults in class, men behave as if it is their job to think of contributions, and they try to get the floor to express them. Women, on the other hand, are more likely to pace their participation so as not to appear to be answering too many times. If women speak once or twice in a class, they usually hold back for the rest of the class period because they don't want to dominate. If women have spoken a lot one week, they will remain silent the next. The result is that those who speak freely (the men) assume that those who remain silent (the women) have nothing to say, and those who are pacing themselves so as not to appear pushy (the women) assume that those answering a lot (the men) are showing off.

These behaviors carry over to the professional world and can be observed in administrative meetings. Remember this as you watch the interplay, the challenges, and the debate. Try to make opportunities to speak and to encourage other women to do the same; otherwise, you and the other women may be viewed by the men as having nothing important to add to the discussion.

In situations where information is needed, the person with the information has a higher status. Because of this, most men resist asking women for information because they think it reflects on them that they themselves don't know the answers. When men do ask, women are likely to avoid giving the information directly. Rather, they put the information they wish to convey in the form of a suggestion so as not to appear more knowledgeable than their colleagues. Women conscientiously try not to embarrass those who do not have as much knowledge as they do. Women are likely to say things such as "This may not be the only way to do it," or "There's no guarantee on this," or "What do you think about . . . ?" As a result, women are often perceived as being unsure of themselves.

It is likely you have found yourself more than once in a situation during an administrative meeting in which you make a comment that is ignored. No one says anything. It is as if you haven't spoken. Later, the same comment or suggestion is made by one of the men in the meeting. It is acknowledged, discussed, and often approved, with the credit going to the man for having made the suggestion. Most women experience such situations and most believe that being ignored happens to them because they are women. While there is a great deal of truth to this observation, having a question ignored also may be the result of the way the information is presented. For example, women are more likely to phrase their ideas as questions, rushing through the presentation of information without making strong major points, or they try to be succinct so as not to take up more meeting time than necessary, speaking in a lower volume with a higher pitch. It is little wonder women are ignored by the men who view their style as demonstrating indecisiveness.

Another roadblock for women in presenting information in the way men do—speaking louder, longer, and with more self-assertion—is that they risk being disliked and disparaged as aggressive and unfeminine. Thus, most women find themselves in a dilemma: if they display confidence, they are respected and receive the attention of the meeting attendees, but at the same time, they are disliked for having that confidence.

Another view of male and female conversations shows that male–female group conversations are more like the conversations heard in all-male groups than like the ones heard in all-female groups. In mixed groups, both genders make adjustments, but women make more. In other words, when the two sexes are conversing together, men continue to converse the way they always do and women adjust to the style of men. Thus, women are at a disadvantage in mixed-sex groups because they have had less practice in conducting conversation the way men do.

In addition, women and men are judged differently even if they speak the same way. Women are judged as less intelligent and knowledgeable than men even when both use disclaimers and tag questions, such as "isn't it?" and "don't you think?" Further, when women do not give supporting information with their suggestions, they are viewed as not being intelligent, whereas men who present arguments without supporting statements are not judged as harshly. Thus it appears that when women talk in ways that are associated with women, they are judged negatively, but when men present in that same style, they are not criticized. Unfortunately, no matter how well a woman presents, her information likely will not be as well-received as information presented by a man. We must then conclude that it is not the way women or men talk that affects attitudes so much as it is people's differing attitudes toward women and men.

REVERSING THE TREND

The best tools for an aspiring administrator are awareness, knowledge, and practice. When you schedule a meeting, make it clear in advance what will be expected. Prepare and distribute an agenda at least a day or two before the meeting. If you want information or position statements from your administrative staff, let them know well in advance. This helps to level the playing field, and your staff will appreciate your consideration. At the time of the meeting, make sure you establish ground rules that everyone's ideas are to be given consideration, and that all persons are to be respected. Follow through by allowing time for each person to make her or his presentation. If the men are dominating the meeting, call on the women by name. Bring them into the conversation and the discussion. Do the same for any of the males who are reluctant to volunteer. Set the tone and the expectations by the way you ask questions and engage in discussions. The best approach is to treat everyone as having something worthwhile to contribute. Make it your responsibility to elicit that contribution.

Most administrative preparation programs do not include such basics as "How to Conduct a Meeting" under the false assumption that everyone knows how to run a meeting. If you are inexperienced in facilitating meetings, find a book to help you. There are many such self-help books available in the management or business sections of your nearest bookstore. Don't hesitate to fill your bookshelves with any books addressing management issues; they are well worth your time to read. The successful administrator is one who prepares and turns every situation into a new opportunity to learn.

7

LEADERSHIP STYLES OF WOMEN

The time has finally come in our educational history when opportunities in educational administration are more attainable by women. Women now redesign career paths and establish leadership styles, patterns, and practices that best suit their own gender as well as the culture in which they will work. In some ways it is now an advantage to be a woman, as research is showing that the leadership qualities women bring to an administrative position are those most needed for today's schools and universities.

Sally Helgesen argues that women have an advantage in the role of leadership, particularly in the area of administrative responsibility, because they can easily relate to tasks and transactions. In making her case, Helgesen first cited Mintzberg's findings on the traits of men, which she then followed with a list of traits of women. Table 7.1 is summary of the findings of both Helgesen and Barbara Curry (Curry, 2000; Helgesen in Curry, 2000) in comparing the traits of women to those of men. Successful women, according to Helgesen (1990), have already mastered male skills and have moved beyond them to provide models of what leadership can become when guided by their own "feminine principles." While these feminine principles are not limited to women, they are referred to as *feminine* skills because they are grounded in what research identifies as the general ways in which women do things.

Table 7-1.   Helgeson and Curry's Comparison of Gender Traits

Men	Women
They work at an unrelenting pace, with no breaks in activities during the day.	They work at a steady pace, but with small breaks scheduled in throughout the day.
Their days are characterized by interruptions, discontinuity, and fragmentation	They do not view unscheduled tasks and encounters as interruptions.
They spare little time for activities not directly related to their work.	They make time for activities not directly related to their work.
They exhibit a preference for live-action encounters.	They prefer live-action encounters, but schedule time to attend to details such as mail.
Immersed in the day-to-day need to keep the company going, they lack time for reflection.	They are reflective, but also schedule time for sharing information.
They identify themselves through their jobs.	They see their own identities as complex and multifaceted.

Source: Curry, 2000; Helgeson in Curry, 2000

Business and industry have more recently learned to foster creativity and nurture new ideas (values by which women have been reared), not *because* these are *female* values, but because these values are recognized as being effective. Thus, businesses are patterning their way of doing business—both with their clients and with their employees—on the qualities found in most women leaders: possessing an ease in relationships and a drive for connection; being a whole person—head, heart, and hands; showing an appreciation of complexity and process; having a desire for balance and self-awareness; possessing a sense of artistry, imagination, and playfulness; demonstrating an integrated vision of business and ethics; and displaying courage (Godfrey, 1992).

One of the major changes women bring to the workplace is a *web* style of structuring the organization, a design in which women position themselves in the center of the organization connected to all those around them as if by invisible threads constructed around a center point. Women find this webbing effective, as it is inclusive and allows for flow and movement and connection with any other point.

Women leaders also find webbing comfortable because it is non-threatening and familiar to them and because their whole lives are already integrated much like a web with home and professional tasks overlapping and interweaving. Women learn to integrate tasks because they hold much of the day-to-day home responsibilities, as well as their own professional ones. For example, women have no wives to pick up their dry cleaning or shield them from household problems, so they learn early on to link work and home tasks. Many more women than men plan their itinerary in advance when they have a series of errands to run; they map out the route according to right-hand turns, distances, and the times certain businesses are less busy. They check ahead so as not to waste even a minute on an unnecessary stop, while men just *go*, then become annoyed when a store is closed or their car isn't ready at the garage.

LEADERSHIP STYLES

Leadership styles vary among women every bit as much as among men, and, in many areas of leadership, the differences *among* women are even greater than the differences *between* women and men, even though what is often described as the masculine style uses power based on authority associated with position, title, and the ability to reward and punish, while the feminine style relies on charisma, work record, and contacts (Rosener in Wilson, 1993, p. 27).

The major difference in leadership styles between men and women is that, in general, women are caring and nurturing. Translating this style to a leadership quality, we find that women are more likely to listen to others and to show respect for the views of each individual. Thus, females are viewed to be more democratic and participative than men. As this participatory style is encouraged as a part of management trends that stress quality and excellence, it is important that all who are striving to be educational leaders understand that style and be prepared to use it. In addition, many corporations are seeking the following leadership qualities that are a part of the leadership style of most women: integrative decision making, group problem solving, nonassertiveness, a democratic approach, cooperative planning, and the use of meetings as a forum for discussion.

To further elaborate, women attach importance to personal relationships far more than men do (Moir and Jessel, 1991), in that they tend to manage *people*, not things, and they consider the human dimension in both work and personal lives—both their own and their employees'—as intertwined. Women try very hard to like the people they work with, to understand their needs, and to break down the barriers of status. A woman is likely to introduce or speak of her secretary as "Betty works with me" or "Betty and I work together," whereas a male would objectify the person by her job and say, "Betty is my secretary."

Ironically, however, even with their almost inherent style of personalization, women find it more difficult to form friendships at work. This is partly due to the fact that in administration there are fewer women with whom to form relationships, but the larger reason is that women prefer relationships of *feelings* and not relationships of *functions* that are more typically found in the workplace and favored by men. In other words, women like to make friends based on criteria of emotional connection rather than the fact that they happen to work together.

As you move to a position of authority, you will notice that the first persons to visit you in your office will be the men; they want to make sure you notice them and will tell you they are on your team. Women working for you will be more reserved and will wait to be invited into your group. Generally, their initial overture will be through a memo, a telephone call, a written report, or a copy of an article with a note: "I thought you might find this interesting," or "I think you might enjoy this."

Successful women leaders play by the rules, yet, unlike most men, they retain personal interest in the individual. When there is a conflict between the priorities of the law and of the individual, women are most likely to champion the individual. Again, this is not hard and fast in every case and with every woman, but a woman's leadership style is far more likely than a man's to display the quality of mercy in seasoning justice.

Profiling Feminine Leadership

Interaction, access, flow, conduit, involvement, network, reach—these are the attitudinal words used by women administrators. Note that they are *process* words, all of which emphasize relationships. They also are interactive words that specifically include encouraging participation, sharing power and information, and enhancing other people's self-worth. Women who make it into the top executive spot, according to Rosener (1990), report that they work to make their subordinates' own self-interest work for the good of the entire operation.

Successful women executives are likely to attribute their achievements to personal characteristics rather than to their official positions. Such successful women serve as an affirmation to those who are just beginning to pursue administrative posts since, far too often, women hesitate to leave the safety of a staff position and settle into a lesser position because they fear they won't have the skills for a higher position.

What many women have failed to realize is that the skills and experiences gained in a staff position are very valuable in a line position as well. They have not understood that they can successfully transfer these skills to a "middle-level position" that would at least allow them the flexibility and latitude to work toward the required certification for a line position. What should be emphasized here is that the qualities of female leadership have deep roots and are only enhanced and honed by preparation programs and experiences. Women do not need to remake themselves because the leadership skills and perspectives they bring to the workplace are precisely the ones organizations need. Not so surprising, the ideal management profile, which was originally designed with male managers in mind, has been found to be more closely in line with the qualities actually held by *female* managers.

Breaking the Mold

Beginning in the 1960s with the early "boomers," women moved up the corporate ladder by being aggressive and by trying to think and act like a man. Many of those women prided themselves that they had accepted the terms, and they rarely turned to other women for professional support or advice. Today's female leaders are taking a softer approach—one more natural to women. They are breaking the past corporate mold by talking more openly with their staffs and colleagues, sharing information, and keeping the office door open.

Another way women are breaking the mold is by the way they handle "home-grown" barriers. Recently interviewed female school superintendents were candid about how they overcame these barriers—situations not faced by men—to become principals or superintendents (Archer, 2003):

The barrier for Chris Wright was her daughter's driver's license. As she explained it, "The whole thing was, she had to be able to get where she

needed to be and that had been my responsibility." Once the daughter
passed her driver's test, Wright was ready to move into administration.
She also recalls being turned down by a district that already had hired two
female assistant superintendents. She was told, "We just can't have all
women in the central office."

The heavy demands of the job led to Barbara Moore Pulliam's daughter taking over the dinner duties, making sure the family sat down and had
dinner together.

Libia Gil admits that she didn't even try to keep her life in balance. "I
gave that up long ago; I've accepted that, and so has my family."

"If you look at the 14 percent of women superintendents across the nation, you'll find that 99 percent of us are risk-takers," according to Mary
Summers. "We're the ones who had the guts to take on a superintendency
as a female." (p. 1)

These women also mentioned that meetings of their professional associations often revolve around golf—a sport more popular among men then
women and one that, because it often requires more time than woman can
give, presents a real barrier. Women are breaking this mold, but Gil,
quoted by Archer (p. 14), says it remains a major issue: "Golf is a very serious gatekeeper that people don't fully appreciate." (See chapter 8.)

School Administration

The fundamental tasks of administering schools have no gender identification, and reviewing the list of these tasks clearly shows that they are
not geared specifically to women or to men. They are simply *tasks*.
There is nothing inherent in the tasks themselves that would demand either a strictly feminine or exclusively masculine practice. It is the *doing*
of these tasks that puts a gender perspective to them. This should be
self-evident, but women need to continue to remind themselves and
their peers that there is no administrative task that is beyond their capabilities.

Effects of Hierarchical Structure and Power

It is generally agreed that people well-placed in the hierarchy are already poised for the next position and are constantly playing that position

for promotion and power. It is, therefore, important to understand how women and men become distributed across these structural positions because their placement affects both their behavior and their futures.

Women are more likely to be at the bottom of power hierarchies. As noted above, this lower ranking often leads them to limit their aspirations because they create social peer groups based on interpersonal relationships, reinforcing the patterns of girlhood for the need to be part of a group. Once established in these peer relationships in a low-level placement, many women find themselves comfortable, thus self-limiting their opportunities for advancement.

If you want to move into the higher circles of management, you must not get trapped in comfort of the status quo found on the lower rungs. Rather, find a niche that will give you entry to management. As suggested in chapter 1, this niche should be a specialty, something you know or can do better than others in the same position. Your aim is to be noticed and to have your eye on the next position on the rung of the hierarchy.

DECISION MAKING

Women generally are perceived as being more democratic and participatory than men in their leadership styles. In 1987 Charol Shakeshaft confirmed that perception as fact by summarizing the work of a number of research studies showing that women use more cooperative planning strategies, are less committed to the formal hierarchy, and are more willing to submerge displays of personal power in order to get others to participate in the decision-making process. Shakeshaft concluded that women's participatory style enhances, rather than threatens, their power base, and is more inclusive than exclusive. In addition, women think about and evaluate their decisions more often than do men, are more likely to use strategies that include long-range planning and evaluative data in making decisions, and are rated by both men and women as better planners than are men.

Moir and Jessel (1991) identified differences in men and women's approaches to decision making, saying that decision making is a more thorough, although complex, process for women because they collect more information and take into account more factors than do men. Women also have a capacity to consider the human dimension, with attention given to personal and moral aspects. Men, on the other hand, rely more on calculated, formulaic, deductive processes. In other words, the masculine approach to decision making is blunt and quick, while the feminine is more complex because female decision making utilizes more data, factual as well as emotional.

As a female administrator, you should *not* feel inadequate if you are not comfortable making a snap decision. As a woman, it is natural for you to weigh the facts, consider different dimensions, and seek alternatives if the choice is not what you believe it should be. You may not be as adept in zeroing in on an immediate solution, but you will be better at understanding all of the issues. Give yourself the time you need to make the best decision possible.

Once a decision is reached, you are also more likely than men to second-guess whatever decision you do make because you are clearly aware that very few things are absolute. In addition, as a female, you will be likely to worry about the impact of this decision on others, even though that concern was already a part of your decision-making process. However, once the decision is made, you need to let it stand. Remember, you did the best you could do with the information you had at the time. Do not continue to revisit the decision (unless, of course, there is new information that compels a revisit).

A PROFILE OF PRINCIPALS

While the demand for new principals is growing, the concern is that there will be few applicants to fill the vacancies and fewer yet who will be qualified (Gilman and Lanman-Givens, 2001). If you currently are considering preparing for a principalship, do not delay. The Gilman and Lanman-Givens study anticipated that by 2010, 40 percent of school principals will have retired (and as many as 79 percent in Indiana) and that the door is wide open.

Even so, the principalship positions will continue to be difficult to fill because of the following factors that hinder attracting good candidates (of either gender) to the principalship:

- Too little pay
- Costly and irrelevant requirements
- Too many pressures
- Too many hats to wear
- Not enough time
- Too little authority

In a word, the job, in many cases, is too large, too broad, and too complicated for any one person to be able to do well, regardless of her or his desire, effort, and skill. There are so many demands on a principal's time that many principals find themselves struggling to stay afloat, let alone find time to grow professionally.

You need to clearly understand and accept that principals have huge demands on their time. The typical principal works a sixty-hour week dealing with everything from teacher unions to student behavior and from government regulations to community problems. Because of the wide variety of issues you will deal with, you sometimes will be the target of prejudice, stereotyping, loneliness, and fear. In addition, not everyone will like you, so expect to sometimes feel rejected. Few people will pat you on the back and say you are doing a good job. And finally, remember that sometimes getting a grievance is not because you are doing things wrong but because you are doing them right.

In the eyes of some, for women to even appear at all in the administrative culture is to challenge it, but to appear to do things "different" is especially risky. Women who make changes risk being resented. On the other hand, women principals may have an advantage in implementing school change because typically their administrative style is the style that has been described by many as very effective. The problem may lie in convincing the audience that your style is based on what research has shown to be successful. (You may need to share copies of this chapter with your staff.)

An advantage of being the first woman in your position in your district is that there will be an expectation that things *will* change. View this as an opportunity to meet those expectations. You no doubt already are geared to find better ways to operate a building through ways that are more "people focused," rather than "institutionally" led, and through ways that can meet the needs of clients (students and parents), employees, community, and yourself. Principals learn quickly that change comes through strong relationships built with staff, parents, and students. With some positive strategies, you may have the chance to implement what you believe is best for the students in your charge.

As a female principal new to the position or to a particular school district, you should make it a priority to learn the school's environment. Because studies are incomplete as to how, or even if, different styles enhance effectiveness in different environments, it can only be suggested to aspiring principals that you adapt your own style to the conditions of the organization and/or try to find a school district that is a good match for your style.

Unfortunately, reality dictates that women have less opportunity to be selective in finding a good job match because they are less often considered for interviews and also because they usually are more limited geographically. Therefore, as a female, you are more likely to find it necessary to adapt to prevailing conditions, sometimes at the sacrifice of suppressing your own style. Once you have demonstrated that you can administrate in the *expected* mode (i.e., like a man, or like your predecessor, or *unlike* your predecessor), you can begin gradually to exercise your own leadership style and be even more effective by being yourself. In other words, *first give them what they think they want, and then give them what they need!*

Despite the realities of the position, most principals do survive and many of them thrive in a rich cultural environment they helped to create. Now is the time to find out what the forthcoming trends are in education and prepare for them; this will give you an advantage, both in interviewing and for using as topics of general conversation with your administrative staff and with teachers. Get in the habit, as you read or watch the news, of asking yourself, "How will this impact education in general, my district, and my position (or future position) in particular?"

A PROFILE OF SUPERINTENDENTS

A study by Schuster and Foote (1990) found that the major disparity in the backgrounds of male and female superintendents was not in the classroom or boardroom, but rather in the locker room. More than 57 percent of male respondents to the study's survey replied that they had served as coaches or athletic directors before becoming superintendents, while only 13 percent of the women had had such experience. This suggests that the underrepresentation of women in superintendencies may be even more fundamentally grounded in a sports background or locker room camaraderie than was previously thought. The old joke that the road to the boardroom is through the locker room may not be so far-fetched after all.

Other differences uncovered in this study reveal that women attain their first superintendency much later in life than do men (36 percent of the women were over the age of forty-six, while only 14 percent of the men were of this age). As might be expected from that finding, women in the study remained in the classroom for more years, thus delaying their entry into administration. Also, more women than men reached the superintendency via a central office position and relatively fewer of these women were building principals. The women interviewed were more often firstborn and remained single. They had higher IQs and were more academically successful. More held doctoral degrees, belonged to professional organizations, and read more professional books.

The findings by Schuster and Foote also suggest that, at least for their first superintendencies, women aspirants should seek out smaller, higher-spending districts that have several women on the school board. They should also seek districts that are more affluent with more highly educated constituents. The chances of obtaining a superintendency are increased if aspirants hold a doctoral degree and have demonstrable experience as risk takers and strong decision makers.

Boards most fear hiring a female who is not tough enough. Make sure you have examples, answers, and, if possible, documentation to assure a board that you have what it takes to be a strong leader. In addition, remember to emphasize your collaborative style as being the style currently being shown in journals and the business world as most effective. School boards are increasingly becoming aware that they need a leader with some business perspective and who not only can make hard decisions but who also can work with all constituencies. That can very well be you.

AASA Study

Early findings from the American Association of School Administrators' National Study of Women Superintendents and Central Office Administrators show that women superintendents majored in education twice as often as men did and spent much more time teaching than men did. Strange as it may seem to women, this factor is viewed as a negative. In fact, it can determine whether or not a woman finds a superintendency, as there is an expectation that a superintendent candidate should *not* have taught *too* long because, according to headhunters, those who remain in the classroom "think like a teacher." It actually is believed that this particular perception can create a barrier to the superintendency for women (Brunner, Grogan, and Prince, 2004).

According to C. Cryss Brunner, it is clear that studies and published works over the years have not advanced the innovative and caring models that women often practice. Therefore, Brunner says, women need to know that the way they practice *is* acceptable, especially when they find themselves practicing in ways not mentioned in many books on the superintendency. She continues,

> I found that women who are extraordinarily successful don't act like men. I've also found that men, who practice in the way successful women do, also succeed. Women tend to have an understanding of power that is important for all superintendents. They understand that power is not about how much control you have over others, but rather it's a collective synergy, and they further understand that their roles as superintendents provide them the opportunity to serve and support others working toward a common good. (Brunner, Grogan, and Prince, 2004, p. 36)

Margaret Grogan reminds us that no two districts are alike, and the superintendency looks somewhat different depending on where you are and who you are. The context of the district, the size, the number of students, whether it is rural, urban, suburban, or a mix of all three—all make the superintendency many different positions. Grogan also says that age doesn't need to be a consideration any more than whether a woman is single or married and whether or not she has children. She notes that the AASA research shows that 38.3 percent of the women superintendents in the study had reared two children, 15 percent had reared one child, and only 22.8 percent had no children. As Grogan says,

"That's an important little piece. It demonstrates to women that having a family is not an insurmountable barrier to seeking a superintendency" (Brunner, Grogan, and Prince, 2004, p. 37).

When asked what changes women made in their lives to accommodate the demands of the superintendency, 29–30 percent said they delayed having children, 18 percent said their spouse took a more accommodating job, 20 percent said they had a commuter marriage, and the other 21 percent did not explain. Grogan then tells of a respondent in an earlier study who, when asked if she had had a mentor, answered, "The last thing I want to do is go out there and ask for help. I can do it on my own and I'm very proud that I can do it on my own. I don't want to be thankful or grateful to anyone else." While admittedly taken aback, Grogan agreed that once she thought about her own life, she realized that she, too, just told people what she was going to do and didn't wait for someone to provide the encouragement (Brunner, Grogan, and Prince, 2004, p. 38). Many, however, including this author, believe that a strong mentor can be an invaluable aid.

The AASA study also reflects higher numbers of women obtaining a superintendency in a shorter period of time than is reported in other studies. AASA reports that 50.3 percent of women responding to the survey got the position in less than one year. (It may be that those who responded to the AASA survey were the overall best candidates for the position of superintendent and did not have to search long for a position.) As to the chances of finding a superintendency inside one's own district, the figures are the same for men and women.

A PROFILE OF HIGHER EDUCATION

Although women comprise approximately 58 percent of the nation's 13 million college undergraduates and earn more doctorates than men, breaking through the glass ceiling in higher education can be difficult. According to Leslie Annexstein, director of the legal advocacy fund for the American Association of University Women, "Higher education traditionally has been the playground of male academics. It's their turf. And sharing that turf is difficult for many of them" ("Women a Minority of Tenured Faculty and Administrators," 2004).

The foremost reason for the difficulty faced by most women in academe is the continuing power of the old norms that often are most resistant to change (*change* here meaning *opening doors of administration
to women*) in larger universities. Further, women often are unsure of the
rules of the game in higher education, not foreseeing the full consequences of not recognizing the importance of politics early in the game.
Often in graduate school, women become so involved in their studies
that they forget to build professional networks and political allies. Thus,
when they need political support, it is not readily at hand.

The second reason for the undermining of women's academic efforts
in finding administrative posts is the reluctance of women to convert
their educational accomplishments into *noticeable* professional gains,
such as publications, financial remuneration (grants and awards), and
promotions. This tendency of women not to actively seek attention—or
advancement—is reinforced by the predisposition in many institutions
of higher education to assign women faculty more teaching than research projects. In addition, women who are serving assistantships during their doctoral programs often are assigned assistantships that entail
classroom teaching rather than research that would be to their personal
betterment and professional advancement.

A teaching concentration, once women become faculty members, is
part of the third reason for the weakening of women's efforts to become
professional academics. Because any teaching load takes time away from
research and, therefore, from recognition as well, women (with a heavier teaching load) are not as able to get to know those who can help
them with serious professional advice on how to plan an academic career. Women also find it difficult to campaign (even indirectly) for themselves and to develop a voice of authority as well as an *identity*. Even
when they understand that self-promotion and political gamesmanship
are necessary, the politics of self-promotion remain repugnant to most
women.

In 1980 strategies were developed to widen the pool of eligible and
creditable women candidates for administrative positions in higher education. Among those strategies were the establishment of rosters and
networks and the implementation of training programs to comply with
affirmative action legislation. These efforts resulted in an increase in the
hiring of women, but the hiring occurred almost exclusively at the

lower-level positions of educational administration. In order to be considered for higher-level positions, women had to—and still must—rely on the same tactics as those used in basic education.

There is some evidence, however, that mentoring in higher education is more prevalent than in basic education. The other major difference is that to climb the ladder in higher education administration, there is even more of a need to be willing to relocate, likely at greater distances than for a school superintendency.

To avoid the overall impediments in job progression in higher education administration, many women have found that they can advance faster at smaller schools. This view is supported by Richard Ekman, president of the Council of Independent Colleges ("Women a Minority of Tenured Faculty and Administrators," 2004), who confirmed that women represent nearly 40 percent of the provosts and deans and 30 percent of the chief executives of the 500 schools in the council.

Advice for the individual aspirant to administrative posts in higher education is to begin early with your career path plan. Do not be sidetracked into teaching assistantships without an equal share of research opportunities. Consciously and deliberately seek the friendship of a professional colleague (preferably someone in a position similar to that which you aim for) who can advise you. Play the political game of self-promotion. Do not be deterred from your goal. And do not believe the public relations ploy of some universities that disport "data banks for women" and urge you to apply, implying that this pool of applicants will be given first and every consideration for openings. My own experience in working with aspiring administrators leads me to believe that in many universities such data banks are only window dressing.

Instead, rely on yourself and explore the American Council on Education's (ACE) Office of Women in Higher Education (OWHE) (www.acenet.edu). The council provides the national direction for women's leadership development and career advancement through links such as the following, all accessible through the OWHE website, which itself is most easily found as a menu item on the ACE home page listed above:

- Identifying Women Leaders in Higher Education
- Developing the Leadership Skills of Women in Higher Education

- Encouraging Women Leaders to Make Full Use of Their Abilities
- Advancing Women into Senior-Level Positions
- Linking Women Leaders at All Levels to One Another
- Supporting the Retention of Women in Higher Education

You also may be interested in OWHE's national network of people and activities.

FEAR OF SUCCESS/FEAR OF FAILURE

Whether myth or truth (the studies are inconclusive), there remains a pervasive perception that many women do not pursue "the fast track" of any managerial position because they are (1) afraid they might succeed or (2) afraid they might fail. These two fears are not the same, but rather are opposite sides of the same coin.

Fear of failure is connected to both self-respect and embarrassment. While no one wants to fail at anything, women cannot separate failing at a particular task from failing as a person. As has been established, women connect themselves more to their jobs than men do. Professional women, in particular, identify themselves through their jobs and find it difficult to leave their professional personae when they leave the workplace. Such a characteristic of self-identity is most prevalent in the public professions, particularly if the profession is practiced in the community in which the woman lives and is known.

Educational administration is one of these public professions. Not only is it public in the usual sense, but it also is an area that is not yet typical for women; therefore, many first-time administrators feel particularly self-conscious and vulnerable. They are apprehensive that their performance is going to have far-reaching consequences, not only for themselves and their own career advancement but also for those female administrators yet to follow. They further view themselves as being role models to both the students and their professional staff. They bear the burden of daring not to fail. They worry about the number of people their failure would hurt. And they worry that *everybody* would know if they failed.

Men, on the other hand, see their jobs as only one part of their lives. A man describes his job or position in terms of "what I do" and not, as a professional woman does, in terms of "who I am." Since a woman administrator defines herself in terms of her position, should she fail she believes she would never live it down. In contrast, a man just moves on to the next job or the next place, and he rarely looks back.

The term "fear of success" may have been coined as a result of studies on distinguishing between women's and men's responses to task-oriented situations. Matina Horner created quite a stir in the late 1960s with her suggestions that women have particular anxieties concerning success because success is incompatible with the feminine gender stereotype and thereby may lead to rejection by others. Her study argued that women possess a motive to avoid success. This same motive appears not to manifest itself in men. Women who fear success (which might include all of us, according to Horner), then, either lower their aspirations for success or deny responsibility for their success (Horner, 1969).

This fear-of-success theory became a convenient way to rationalize that women were not competitive because of their fear of success, a success that would prove they were unfeminine. In other words, in business and professions, male goals and male methods were viewed as ideal; thus, if a female followed these goals and methods, she paid a high price by "losing her femininity." Therefore, she made sure—consciously or unawares—that she was not successful.

While later studies refuted Horner, it is her hypothetical case study of "Ann finds herself at the top of her medical school class" that most people remember clearly.[1] In hindsight, fear of success appears a bit ridiculous. However, as an aspiring administrator, you need to know that there are still people who believe that you will trip yourself up because of a deep psychological need to not succeed.

THE ADVANTAGES OF BEING FEMALE

Research evidence strongly suggests that good school administration is more attuned to feminine than masculine modes of leadership behavior. Again and again we hear researchers and practitioners repeat the words of Marilyn Ferguson, "Feminine values and behaviors are exactly what is needed to nurture this new era in human history" (Porat, 1991, p. 413). We need to be guided by our own inner voices, trust our own judgment, and be true to ourselves as women. It is time to recognize and capitalize on the fact that we are female, and that we are not men. There may be some disadvantages to that, but we must acknowledge our own advantages and use them. Women have resources and power, and the time to tap them is long overdue.

Physical Advantages

Throughout the modern world women outlive men, and in the United States, they outlive men by about seven years. Of the top ten or twelve causes of death in this country, every single one kills more men than women. Women also *endure* better. The more a physical competition requires stamina, the better women fare. In diaries kept in wartime are entries noting that in situations of confinement, women had more endurance (and courage) than men did. Women also are more psychologically resilient. A study of areas of London heavily bombed during World War II, for example, found that 70 percent more men than women became psychiatric casualties (Dolnick, 1991, p. 44).

The dire predictions of the 1960s that when women began to go into the fray of offices and boardrooms they would be subjected to the same stress factors and the resulting heart attacks just haven't happened. Not that the stress of managing a home and family along with a job isn't difficult. It is. However, the tension has not brought the predicted ill health. In fact, surveys have shown that "paid work provides women with feelings of self-esteem, responsibility, and camaraderie that outweigh its drawbacks" (Dolnick, 1991, p. 45).

One of the theories for the endurance and longevity of women is the difference in hormones. Rather than being the brunt of jokes, it would now appear that women may have the last laugh. In battles against heart disease, it seems that estrogen is a positive factor and testosterone a negative. In addition to the low-cholesterol, healthy-heart advantage that natural estrogen brings, there have been studies showing the effect of estrogen on scholastic performance. Women compensate for times they don't feel "up to par" by working harder despite physical discomfort. Simply put, we have learned to live with our physical distress and to rise above it.

Even though on a day-to-day basis women feel less well than men, make more visits to the doctor, and take more medicines, it is still thought that the result is positive because women are more in tune to what their bodies are telling them. Even though women are more susceptible to everyday illnesses, they are still overall less vulnerable to life-threatening ones. Women suffer more from depression, but less from schizophrenia. Widows also survive longer than widowers. In addition to general longer life expectancy for women, there is also the fact that, for many men, their wives were their sole confidante, whereas women have a circle of friends in whom to confide, which is a factor in survival.

A common summation is that women *bend* and men *break.* "Women respond to every dip and bump in the road, like cars with springy suspensions. Men, who are trained to keep stiff upper lips, roar over minor divots like cars with rigid shock absorbers. On good roads men do well, but when they come to speed bumps or potholes, watch out" (Dolnick, 1991, p. 48). Thus, greater physical and mental endurance are positive factors contributing to the potential for women's success.

High levels of female estrogen seem to enhance coordination skills in women. From early on, girls are superior in tasks requiring rapid, skillful, fine movements, as well as in everything requiring verbal fluency and articulation.

Social Advantages

Girls excel in social interaction and are attracted to life work that involves some kind of human interaction. Women perceive the world in interpersonal terms, and they tend to personalize the objective world. Women also perform better in noncompetitive situations and are more likely to choose occupations according to what they like rather than what financial rewards or status the position might bring (Moir and Jessel, 1991).

As has been noted throughout this book, women are more attuned to nuances of voice, are more sensitive to the social and personal context, are more adept at reading peripheral information contained in expression and gesture, and process sensory and verbal information faster. They are also less bound by rules. These factors all contribute to the leadership style most appropriate to today's needs and are the characteristics most effective in developing a cooperative, participatory management style.

Advantages of Personal Characteristics

Word choices in describing feminine characteristics have not always been well-chosen. Often in a misguided attempt to be kind or to flatter, researchers and writers have been patronizing in tone. For example, the following terms are often used to describe women: affectionate, sympathetic, sensitive to the needs of others, understanding, compassionate, warm, tender, fond of children, gentle, yielding, cheerful, shy, responsive to flattery, loyal, soft-spoken, gullible, and childlike. In addition, in our society there still lingers a core of imputed feminine attributes; these include, among others, personal warmth and empathy, sensitivity and emotionalism, grace, charm, compliance, dependence, and deference.

At least two-thirds of these terms are words that imply docility and inferiority rather than being strictly descriptive. This is why we must be very careful in using lists of female characteristics. So often they are stereotypical of a perception and not the result of research. Often, too, such lists are used to subtly imply that women do not have the characteristics needed to be leaders.

We need to pay close attention to those researchers who have observed personal characteristics that are enhancements or advantages in the workplace. For example, Helen Regan (1990) speaks of the praxis of administration from a feminine perspective. Her studies show that most women administrators possess the ability to (1) see both the apparent and the hidden; (2) acknowledge both reason and emotions; (3) understand the need for both affect and intellect; (4) legitimize personal experience as an appropriate source of decision making; (5) honor care, concern, and connection; and (6) practice compassion, empathy, gentleness, and collaboration. These are the descriptors of personal characteristics that serve as an advantage to women administrators. They are real, not patronizing.

Skill Advantages

Despite comments made in jest, the prototypical female skill is listening. Women are engaged when they are listening; they are attentive; they hear what is being said; and they synthesize the information in preparation to meet the needs of those speaking. (This may be attributable to a theory that women have an additional imaging function in the brain during the language process; if this is so, it could be said that during this language process a typical woman brings a richer, more expanded, emotional component to this function [Phillips, 1990, p. 46].)

In addition to listening skills, women also have high levels of skill in communication, problem solving, organizational savvy, team building, instruction, and curriculum. Women are said to be especially good at a technique called blending, which refers to doing everything one can to understand the other person's point of view and to match one's motives to the viewpoint of that person.

In a study conducted by Bolman and Deal (1992) on the political, structural, human resource, and symbolic frames in educational leadership and management, women were rated higher than men in every frame. Bolman and Deal say that these findings are consistent with other studies showing that women score slightly higher than men on a variety of measures of leadership and managerial behavior.

A significant study by Neal Gross and Anne Trask (cited in Whitaker and Lane, 1990) identifies the following advantages of women in school administration:

- Women principals had a greater knowledge of concern for instructional supervision.
- Superiors and teachers preferred women over men.
- Students' academic performance and teachers' professional performance rated higher under women principals.
- Women were more effective administrators.
- Supervisors and teachers preferred the decision-making and problem-solving behaviors of women.
- Women principals were more concerned with helping nonstandard pupils.
- Women principals placed more importance on technical skills and organizational responsibility of teachers as a criterion for evaluation.

In the arena of instructional leadership, women also appear to have an advantage over men. In a study by Alan Hein measuring attitudinal perceptions toward the capabilities of women in administration, women scored higher in most categories: practicality, flexibility, forthrightness, ability to give constructive criticism, ability to exercise strong educational leadership, assuming responsibility, tactfulness, and communication (Whitaker and Lane, 1990).

A nationwide study conducted by Executive Development Centers, in association with the American Association of School Administrators and the University of Texas in Austin, rated the skills required of an educational executive. Results show that administrative women tend to possess more expert information than men in the areas of communication, implementation of new instructional systems, curriculum development, and teacher evaluation (McGrath, 1992).

Power Advantages

The classic definition of power includes the use of force and strength, authority, and decisiveness to get things done and to run people's lives. When power is viewed just a bit more broadly, it can be defined as the ability to get things done and to make people's lives better. This is a far cry from the traditional view of the power of women being based on manipulation, helplessness, or personal relationship. Modern corporate or institutional power is derived not from masculine physical strength but from skills that are used to achieve results—skills that women possess. Again it is noted that today's management trends emphasize greater employer participation and less formal structure. Modern management requires, therefore, power sharing, collaboration, and participation—all skills that have been shown to be particular strengths of women.

Newer ways of getting things done don't require power *over*, but rather power *with*, a power mode compatible with women's leadership style. Women generally feel uncomfortable with strong-arm tactics and strive to use techniques that don't require a winner and a loser. Women are socialized to solicit information from others. They use conversation as a way to reach a conclusion, rather than starting with a conclusion before they begin talking, as men more often do.

Women are also more likely to be transformational leaders: (1) able to reconcile a concern for bottom-line results with a concern for people, (2) able to focus on both ends and means, (3) good at planning and communicating, (4) reality based, and (5) able to comprehend all important aspects. Women who demonstrate transformational leadership characteristics focus on getting subordinates to transform their own self-interest into the interest of the group through concern for a broader goal. They typically credit their power to personal characteristics such as charisma, interpersonal skills, hard work, or personal contacts, and they actively work to make their interactions with subordinates positive for everyone involved. They encourage participation, share power and information, enhance other people's self-worth, and get others excited about their work. Transformational leaders, in general, believe that people perform best when they feel good about themselves and their work, and they try to create situations that contribute to that feeling. In addition, women who ascribe to transformational leadership practices give others credit and praise, and they send small signals of recognition, such as notes, public recognition, or praise among their peers. Most importantly, these women refrain from asserting their own superiority.

As it is the usual practice of women to use power to empower others, women are particularly effective in school reform/restructuring movements. School change is predicated on the belief that in order for change to occur, all who will be affected must be empowered, and women are better at sharing power to help empower others. Thus, we are at an ideal time in education for the leadership style of women to be fully appreciated and utilized.

Business Advantages

More and more vendors and service providers are moving from simply making adjustments for their women clients to designing special services to attract their patronage. Travel agencies are eager to help women plan their business trips to include the amenities they expect. Studies (as well as experience of those in the business) show that cleanliness and security are the two most important considerations of women travelers, and hotels listen to the needs of female business travelers. Women clients are also now heavily recruited by investment firms and financial planners, who are offering programs geared especially for women. Banks, insurers, and law firms also are clambering to find new ways to tailor their approaches to women.

While much of this flurry has to do with the rapid growth in women-owned businesses and the realization that women have money and power, the attention being focused on women in positions of importance can't help but enhance the life of a woman educational administrator and increase her chances for advancement by helping to establish a climate beyond mere acceptance. The more attention that is paid to all professional women, the more people will see it as being usual for women to be in top positions in educational institutions as well as in business.

THE POSITIVE DIFFERENCE

Don't ever apologize for your difference, your disadvantages, or your advantages. You are who you are, female and competent. Your style of management is your own and no other style will work as well for you. Your power is built upon both your skill and your sense of caring for others. Be confident in your ability and keep in mind that the evidence is overwhelmingly clear that women's ways of leadership are as effective, if not more effective, than those of men. Trust your own judgment and be true to the lessons you have learned and continue to learn. And remember that you possess knowledge, energy, compassion, and power. Make them work for you!

NOTE

1. The standard test asks participants to complete a story that begins, "Ann finds herself at the top of her medical school class." Most respondents completed the story with having Ann face unpopularity, loneliness, failure, lack of a husband, and loss of femininity. The conclusion reached by the researchers is that both men and women view women who were academically successful as facing unhappiness if they pursued careers.

8

LEADERSHIP STYLES OF MEN

The pursuit of power is overwhelmingly a male trait, according to Moir and Jessel (1991), who also maintain that men and men's styles of leadership will prevail as long as organizations remain structured as power based and hierarchical. Over time organizations may change, but there is no guarantee that organizational structure will evolve into the management style most practiced by and comfortable to women. Furthermore, and at the risk of sounding disloyal to my own sex, I am not sure if this evolution into a female-style management system is preferable.

What concerns me, and what is being overlooked in this whole female management style with its move to "power with" (discussed in chapters 4 and 7), is that we are assuming that eventually everyone will want to move to a style of "power with" rather than "power over." We are banking on a revolution, a way of operating that has not yet proved successful in any major civilization in history, a power style of *empowerment*. We may want to be cautious moving toward something that has not been fully investigated and tested. We have not asked if the concept of empowerment is ill-conceived. What guarantee is there that the new feminine management style really will lead to the best organization? What if this empowered management style is only a Hawthorne effect?[1] What if that which we perceive as improvement is only a result of doing something different for the sake of doing something different, or what if this style is only a means by which to include those who, thus far, have been disenfranchised? Is this reason enough to change? Or should we continue to use what has proved successful, adapting it to accommodate a changing world? Before moving too hastily toward a major organizational overhaul, we should consider the overtones of moving away from traditional styles and toward a feminine—or even androgynous—style of leadership.

LONG-RANGE IMPLICATIONS OF GENDER-NEUTRAL LEADERSHIP

In considering the long-range implications of a "gentler" feminine/androgynous leadership style, there are three questions that should be answered:

1. Should we wholeheartedly adopt a style that may work for a short time, but may be disastrous for the future?
2. Is this the kind of leadership style that will be effective far into this century, or is its success limited?
3. Might this blending of leadership styles be the answer only to problems specific to this time, a time in which women have entered positions of leadership unprecedented in any other time period in history?

Experts in organizational management once thought the factory model of Frederick Taylor was the panacea for work production. No one can deny that this management process was the best way to complete a task in the shortest time, as it was efficient and well engineered. Building upon Taylor's framework, Henri Fayol suggested a method of process management in which administration was based on process through five administrative functions. Luther Gulick expanded Fayol's process management theory to a theory of organization by hierarchy, with each worker reporting to a supervisor and each supervisor being responsible for a certain number of workers. In its own time, Gulick's model worked very well, especially when enhanced by the bureaucratic model of Max Weber. Weber's hierarchy of authority, division of labor, control by rules, supervision by a bureau or department, and orientation toward viewing work as a "career" offered a systematic way for the organization to accomplish its objectives with minimum expenditure of human and fiscal resources.

During the 1930s, traditional management theory lost favor when Mary Follett developed her human relations management theory as a response to the perceived defects of the traditional theory. Follett's hypothesis was based on the increasingly popular movement known as the behavioral sciences, and her proposed management style held as its main concern the motivation and satisfaction of employees. An integral part of Follett's theme of human relations was the interest in group dynamics and interpersonal relations in small groups. Follett's human relations management style served as a transition and laid the groundwork for current management styles of showing consideration for the motivation and satisfaction of employees.

This capsule review of the evolution of twentieth-century management theory serves as a reminder that management styles change to reflect society and are based on what is needed at any particular time. We must be careful not to presume that we now have found the perfect management style in the feminine/androgynous model. We should be wary of giving total and unquestioning credence to the theories that tell us: "Throw out the way men have been operating and institute a (new) feminine leadership style."

I am also concerned that we have paid little attention to the downside of participatory management, collaborative planning, and site-based management. I share the uncertainty of the administrators and classroom teachers in my graduate classes. These students express their fears that under this trend of involving and empowering everyone, no one will be well served. I hear the frustration and impatience in their voices echoing my own trepidation. These teachers who are aspiring administrators are weary of sitting on committees. They are disturbed by their sense that nothing is happening. They are tired of talking and talking, making suggestions, arguing, and trying to come to consensus or agreement. And they are angry because "the system" doesn't seem to allow for either action or closure of the suggestions made. These administrative aspirants are willing to accept the axiom that change is slow, but I see their increasing annoyance with the whole idea of participatory management.

Those who are the next generation of administrators feel ignored and overruled by their immediate supervisors, principals, central office, and board. Many are walking away from voluntary participation, while others are "sitting with their arms folded" where participation is mandatory. Such reactions are troubling.

Of greater concern, however, is the possibility that the participatory leadership style is overrated. The studies that report its effectiveness are not yet definitive, and some reports are barely substantiated. For that reason and because both practitioners and aspirants are weary of participatory involvement, we should not completely turn our backs on what is called men's style of leadership. Let us not malign what has been working just because we are also learning more about effective ways of women's leadership styles. Let us not call for complete change with such oversimplifying statements as "the world would be a better place if it were run by women." To make such generalizations is harmful and self-defeating. Finally, we need to guard against becoming too "soft" in leadership style because if everything is predicated on emotions and "how we all *feel* about this," we may never advance.

These are serious drawbacks to "feminizing" leadership, and we need to heed them and discuss them openly. Rather than taking sides, let us instead look at what has worked well for men and build upon that. Let us learn from both men and women who have been and are successful leaders. Let us ask what it is that men have learned through their centuries of leadership experience while we think about what women can do with that information.

TYPICAL LEADERSHIP STYLES OF MEN

The leadership styles of men are the typical leadership styles. They range from authoritarian (autocratic) to participative (democratic) and touch every point between. While it is obvious that not all men have the same leadership style, there are generalizations that can be made on the typical styles and their effects. The usual characteristics associated with a successful manager have been shown to be more similar to the stereotype of men than of women (Griffin, 1992). In other words, men are expected to act in a certain way and their performance is evaluated according to that expectation. For example, men are rated more positively when they are authoritarian than when they are democratic; this has much to do with expectation and the fact that people are most comfortable with situations that are predictable and that meet their own expectations.

Men's traditional leadership style is hierarchical, action oriented, and, sometimes, quasi-military. The ideal leader, from this traditional viewpoint, is independent, tough, decisive, and individualistic. Men are direct and forthright and are very good at building enthusiasm in employees through short-term crises, according to James Autry, a former Fortune 500 business executive who is a noted lecturer and author (Nelton, 1991). This type of management is thought to be a result of their sports training and their play as children. Men seem to thrive in a "clutch" situation, thrilling to the full-court press with ten seconds to the final buzzer. To most males, the game is all. As they did with games as children, they learn to play with their enemies and compete with their friends.

Male leaders tend to lead from the front, attempting to have all the answers for their subordinates. They have an urgency to be in charge because when they are running the meeting, they become the dispensers of information and the determiners of what will be placed on the table for discussion. This ability to control is important, for it prevents the possibility of being vulnerable to questions raised and topics introduced for which the leader may be unprepared.

Men view and use communication as a tool for acquisition and maintenance of power. They prefer majority rule (possibly because men are usually in the majority at meetings and will generally vote along the same lines). They are goal oriented, rather than process oriented. This is another reason why they prefer the "majority rule" process; it more quickly gets them to the end and takes less time than going through a long discussion. Because they thrive on expediency, men operate on the principle of justice, rather than on the principle of care that is usually followed by women (see chapter 12). Issues are viewed as black and white and either-or.

These characteristics are generalities, of course, just as are the statements made on the leadership styles of women. Not every man's style fits the male stereotype, even though many studies in education, business management, psychology, physiology, and behavioral science point to characteristics that are predominantly male and that we can say are men's leadership styles. The styles of men have also been the measure for general leadership styles. In fact, most of the major studies on leadership have been conducted with only men, or, if women were included in the study, there was no factor established for that variance. The assumption was Leadership = Male Leadership. Therefore, saying "men's leadership style" was redundant. Now that newer studies have concentrated on the differences between men and women in leadership, a clearer profile for each is emerging.

ADVANTAGES OF BEING MALE

Based on the premise that there is much to be learned from the predominant male leadership style, the aspiring administrator needs to review the advantages that male educational administrators possess. Male or female, the aspirant can learn by understanding what it is specifically that continues to give men the advantage in educational institutions.

People Like Us

The first advantage to be acknowledged is that people are attracted to other people who are like themselves. Men are likely to want to work with other men because they are familiar with the way men think and work. Men generally do not want to work with women because they do not understand them. In addition, whatever a person does not understand, that person does not like. Simply put, men don't understand women; therefore, they do not like them very much in the workplace. For example, there still a few people over sixty who will have nothing to do with computers. They do not understand how they work and don't want to know. Thus it is with many men who have not yet worked on an equal footing with women. They don't know how women leaders operate, so they decide they don't like working with them. There is much truth in the words of Jessie Bernard: "Among human beings, there is clear evidence that although individual men may love individual women with great depth and devotion, the male world as a whole does not" (1981, p. 11). There have been countless situations in which women have had better credentials than men vying for the same position. These women make it to the final round of interviews and then the hiring body selects the person most like themselves, a man. This practice of people hiring those like themselves is a distinct advantage for men.

There are two major lessons aspiring women administrators can learn from this primary male advantage: (1) be as qualified as you possibly can be and (2) package or prepare yourself to fit the expectations of the institution. Without compromising your principles, you still can find things you have in common with the institution, the board members, the interviewing committee, and the goals. Is golf important in the community? Then learn to play. Is football the pride of the town? Learn about the game, or at least be conversant in its proud tradition in that town. Is it a working-class community? Make sure you know the key members of the community and find ways to identify yourself with the goals of that community. If community members are accustomed to a male, give them reasons to accept you as one of "them" for reasons other than gender.

Assumptions of Male Success

Men hold a societal expectation advantage in their leadership. They have been conditioned to achieve. They have the male sports attitude that "my team is better than your team." All of this adds to their confidence and sense of superiority. Men have an inherent attitude to win, and, therefore, are not hampered by self-doubts to the extent women are.

Unless they are an ethnic minority, men do not face discrimination the way women do. In any position in which men are placed, it is assumed they will succeed. Every step of the way, from an entry-level position to the presidency of a college, men are accepted for who they are and what they do. Faculties will approve male leadership without demonstrating a "show me" attitude. If their policies and leadership are not particularly liked by those in the educational institution, it is the policies and practices that are criticized and not the person. (In the case of women leaders, the criticism is almost always levied against the person rather than the practice.) If men are not successful in a given position, the blame does not fall on them personally. Some other circumstance is blamed for the failure, and men are left unscathed. Men simply seek, and usually find, another position.

Men are reared expecting to be served. This, too, is a generalization, but is still true for the most part. Their mothers served them their meals, their girlfriends helped them with their papers, and secretaries doted on them, even when they were classroom teachers. Men can always find someone to help them. The expectation of having someone to do the "bothersome" clerical work is used by men as an advantage, for it gives them a power posture. In addition, of course, they have fewer annoying chores to do themselves, and more time to devote to their own careers.

The use of language is also biased in favor of men and is, therefore, an advantage to them. Sexist terminology, whether intentional or unintentional, gives a positive edge to men, as many synonyms reserve the negative connotation for women. For example, a man is called forceful, whereas a woman demonstrating the same characteristics is said to be feisty. Women faint, but men pass out. Men are aggressive, women pushy. Women are "bitchy," but men lodge complaints. The list is endless, the result is the same. The terms and implications in almost every example are more dignified for men.

Physical Advantage

Men usually have a physical advantage in their appearance by their build, their size, and their overall countenance. Height suggests authority, so a tall person is listened to more quickly than a person of shorter stature. Most people have a stereotypical image of a leader: tall, broadshouldered, and wearing a suit or a military uniform; this image most often is of men. The body language of men is also an advantage, as it is more definite, more forceful, more directed. Women are reared to show deference, men to stand their ground. Women are more likely to avert their gaze, while men assume a posture of command, staring down anyone or everyone, if necessary.

Men's clothing is also less of a hindrance than that worn by women. For women there is always the problem of the skirt, the stockings, the high heels, the purse. Men have none of these with which to contend. Men can enter a room with a assertive stride and can sit without worrying about (1) what to do with a handbag, (2) how to sit gracefully, (3) how to avoid snagging stockings, (4) how not to turn an ankle. Just moving around is simpler for men and gives them an advantage and a look of unencumbered confidence.

Setting-the-Rules Advantage

Another advantage men share is that they play the game by rules that ascribe to the belief that the best defense is a good offense. Women have a tendency to respond to an "offensive move" by becoming defensive and to explain, sometimes at great length, why they have taken a particular action. When men are challenged on anything, regardless of the circumstances, they are very skilled at bringing up every other issue upon which there has ever been a disagreement. They will respond to a challenge by attacking on a totally unrelated issue. Women do not like to be put on the defensive in response to men's offensive defense. Such tactics unnerve women, who prefer to stick with the issue at hand and resolve that issue rather that being deflected to a different topic.

The best way for women to deal with this strategy is not to become angry, or at least not to show the anger. If you find yourself in an argument, stick to the point of the discussion and do not be led into arguing about an unrelated matter. Do not respond to challenges and references to other issues. Staying on the subject at hand is the only way to resolve that issue.

The maneuver of keeping people off balance is learned early by boys as they interact in sports and games. Use of this tactic gives men a distinct advantage when there is an issue at stake. Men enjoy the sparring and the constant competition, and the excitement of the contest serves them well. When women are taken off guard, they become resentful, begin procrastinating, and don't feel free to make suggestions. To avoid having this happen to you, you must realize that this method of men is a tactic.

Do not take personally this attempt to throw you off guard. If you are placed in a position of being put off balance, take time to gain your equilibrium. Take a deep breath, think about what has been said, and weigh carefully your response. If you can muster a humorous comeback, that will throw your attacker off guard, so it is well worth anticipating these situations and being prepared with your response.

Men talk more than women. Communication will be discussed more fully in the next chapter, but is mentioned here as another advantage men have over women. Women will allow themselves to be interrupted and will wait their turn to speak. As a result, men gain the floor more frequently and for a longer time. They use this to their advantage and to advance their programs. Men rarely volunteer to take notes for the group or to keep the minutes of a meeting. Thus, they can concentrate on the meeting at hand and not miss an opportunity to speak. In addition, they give the appearance of being more attentive because their heads are not down with their eyes on a pen and notebook.

Job Expectation and Security Advantage

Men are paid higher salaries than women are for the same position. This is not universal, but the higher the level of the position, the more likely that men's administrative salaries will be higher. Their chances for promotion also are much greater, and they have more options from which to choose because many institutions still are not comfortable with women in some of the jobs.

In times of retrenchment or downsizing, women are usually the first to be reassigned. In many instances the women are the ones most recently hired; therefore, they are also the first to be let go from an administrative post. These reassignments are always couched in terms such as "We need you back at the building level," or "The math department has not been the same since you left; we would like you to return to the position of departmental supervisor and get things back into shape," or "The kids really miss you, and the parents would love to have you back as the teacher of the gifted!" You may even be offered the inducement of retaining your present administrative salary. However, you should beware of this incentive, as your salary most likely will be frozen until the salaries of the other staff catch up.

Hearth and Home Advantage

A very helpful advantage most men have is a wife. Wives shield their husbands from problems, not to mention the fact that wives also do most of the cooking and cleaning, take care of the children, and do the shopping (just to mention only a few things). Professional women joke about needing a wife, but, in most cases, they really mean it. The easiest years I lived were the three years following my husband's retirement, before he entered a second career. It was wonderful to come home to a prepared dinner. Of course, the fact that the children were grown also helped, but this experience gave me a great appreciation of the advantage most men hold in that they are rarely bogged down with the minutiae of running a household. As it is unlikely that as a female administrator you will have a wife, your recourse is to (1) accept that your household will not operate as smoothly as it did before you entered administration; or (2) hire as much household help as you can afford, whether it be a live-in housekeeper, a biweekly cleaning service, a window-cleaning service, a laundry service, a child care provider, a shopping service, car detailing and maintenance contracts—whatever will best relieve you. Whatever choices you make, do not feel guilty.

Men are generally more free to relocate than women, as the woman's job is not usually considered that of primary breadwinner. A wife who wishes to advance will, more often than her husband, be the one to take a small apartment in the community where she serves. (This is presuming her children are grown, which they often are, since women do not usually attain the top administrative posts until they are in their late forties or fifties.) In the corporate world, it is more acceptable for either the husband or the wife to have a pied-à-terre, but in educational circles it is expected that families will live together.

Men rarely consider an interruption in their career for the purpose of child rearing. They can remain focused on their careers. They usually are not the ones who stay home from work with a sick child or an elderly parent. They also can devote more uninterrupted time to their educational pursuits. The prevailing attitude is that it is okay for Dad not to attend the children's concerts because he is working on the board report or his dissertation. The same reason is not thought by many to be acceptable for women. And, in interviews, men are never asked such questions as to their plans for a family.

Workplace Design and Expectations Advantage

The environment of the workplace is designed for the comfort of men. Men often understand the rules of business automatically because those rules so closely resemble the rules of boyhood. For example, men play "closer to the vest" and, as a result, are far less vulnerable. They are natural infighters, trained to be competitive, enjoying a dog-eat-dog battle. Men "shoot from the hip" more than women do; their male employers have taught them that they can do this, can miss the mark, and will suffer no penalty. On the other hand, women are not encouraged to react quickly. They are more cautious and reflective before taking action, although this caution is viewed by men as lacking fortitude (Tunick, 1993). Women in businesses and professions also tend to be more honest than men, and that can sometimes blow up in their faces.

In grievance procedures or litigation, men more often win the support of the board or the hearing officer than do women. There is a perception of credibility with men that works in their favor in such cases, and everyone wants to give them the benefit of the doubt. (Just consider sexual harassment cases with major political figures or high-profile media pundits.)

Men have a decided advantage in gaining the interest of experienced administrators to serve as their mentors. Women do not. As has been stated repeatedly throughout this book, the single most important advantage an aspiring administrator can have is a mentor. Also repeated many times is the fact that women have difficulty in finding a mentor, mostly because there are so few women in influential positions. That leaves the men again and again and again promoting the candidacy of even more men.

THE TESTOSTERONE FACTOR

There are surprisingly few studies that attempt to measure aggressive behavior in terms of correlating that behavior with testosterone levels in the blood. Such studies that have been conducted cannot positively show if testosterone causes aggression; in fact, elevated testosterone levels may *result* from aggressive behavior rather than cause the behavior (Bland, 2004). Yet there is an almost universal popular belief that male hormones make men more competitive, better at sports, go-getters in the business world, and ready to fight to prove it. Recent reports confirm this perception and indicate that testosterone levels correlate surprisingly well with behavioral traits such as dominance and being power seeking (Phillips, 1990).

Testosterone has been seen as the villain, as well as the impetus, in male aggression and domination. It may be difficult to separate the myth from the reality, for, with the male ego, it is very likely that life imitates art. In the case of male ambition in the workplace, studies have been conducted that link ambition with aggression. Ambition is considered to be a positive social quality. However, since androgens affect aggression and aggression is related to ambition, then, according to some researchers, it is male hormones that account for the male being more ambitious. To perhaps stretch the point, a study published in 1981 that examined testosterone levels in women in different occupations found that professional or managerial women have somewhat higher concentrations of testosterone than do clerical and service workers and housewives. A too hasty assumption of that study suggested that it was the testosterone level that caused women to pursue professional and managerial positions. Another study, however, showed that stress lowers testosterone levels (Fausto-Sterling, 1985). No definitive conclusions can thus be drawn concerning the advantage of testosterone, and, in fact, a newer study of 933 younger men concluded that "men with clustering of metabolic risk factors . . . had significantly higher scores of total aggression than subjects with the opposite combination of body-mass index and HDL despite similar testosterone levels" (Tomaszewski, 2003). Fausto-Sterling (1992) perhaps said it best: "The claim that clear-cut evidence exists to show that hormones make boys more active, aggressive, or athletic than girls is little more than fancy."

THE IMPACT OF PLAYING GOLF

Golf is an almost requisite skill for those who wish to succeed in the business or professional world. While not quite as important for those who are looking for a position as a school principal, anyone seeking advancement at the superintendency or higher education level had better know the rudiments of the game, even if they don't play. Golf is viewed as the sport of successful business and professional people and affords a great opportunity to network. You do not need to be much more than a duffer, but it is expected that you know the language and the etiquette of the game. Following the advice of Anne Russell (1992) in *Executive Female*, where you stand, when you talk, and where you walk on the green are the *real* essentials of the game.

If you find yourself in a community where most of the leaders are golfers, it might be a good idea to learn to play. Russell suggests that you begin your training by watching some pro events on television. She advises that you learn the language and understand the terminology, particularly *at par, handicap, divot,* and *whiffing.* Don't be the stereotypically slow female player since most men like to complain that women ruin the pace of the game. Be ready at each hole, even if it means carrying two or three clubs with you. You do not want to slow the action by returning to the cart every time you need a club for a particular shot. Don't search for a lost ball for more than one minute, and if you are having trouble with your game, just say so and move to the next hole. That is more acceptable than holding up the game. If you tee up and whiff the ball three or four times, it is advisable to pick up the ball and put it into your pocket. Say that you are a new golfer and are not going to keep score. That is a respectable and acceptable way of avoiding an awkward situation. The main point of the game is for the group to enjoy it. You yourself do not want to be the handicap. Don't spend time a lot of time apologizing. If there is the need for an apology, say it once, and forget it. Do not talk business on the course. Save it for the clubhouse. And find out ahead of time the dress code and the club rules. The suggestion here is no different than any other advice given throughout this book: Prepare ahead of time so that you are ready for the play. The most important thing to remember is that golf is regarded as an indicator of the player's ethics and values, as well as the player's personality. Make sure that yours are ready to shine. There are also those who say that knowing the rules of golf prepares you for the rules of business. The rules of golf do seem to cover the range of "how to's" of business, so get out on that fairway.

Two things you should consider, however: Most of the networking on the golf course occurs among those in businesses. Few superintendents take the time away from work to golf, and even fewer women superintendents are regular golfers. There is also a reactionary approach to golf as the requisite networking venue, as women (again in business) are beginning to network in nontraditional activities based on pastimes many women enjoy more than golf. (See chapter 11.)

THE MALE DILEMMA

We can say all we want about the advantages of being male in a male-dominated society, but we also need to at least mention some of the dilemmas now faced by the male gender members beginning to feel their very world crumbling under them:

1. From a strictly objective point of view, men now have more peo-ple against whom to compete. The professional population has vastly increased with the influx of women into professional fields. In a given field of 501 school districts, as in Pennsylvania, there may be eighty to one hundred openings or turnovers in superin-tendents in a given year. There are probably 400–500 people who hold the certification for a superintendency and who conceivably could be vying for these relatively few positions. Before the tenfold increase in the number of women completing doctoral programs in educational administration, these premium positions would be expected to attract 90 percent male applicants, and a total of per-haps 200 men. Today, however, each man is now competing with twice as many people as he once did. Regardless of how fair-minded he is, he can't help thinking that his chances for obtaining a superintendency have decreased because of the enlarged num-ber of female applicants.

2. There are many men who believe that, even disregarding num-bers, their chances for any position of choice are threatened by the push to give equal opportunity to women. They believe that, in some cases, women are being given an "edge" just because they are women. The statistics do not bear this out, but the perception on the part of the men who have been interviewed and have lost the position to a woman is that they were not selected because the board must have been pressured to select a female. Rarely do men who are not chosen believe that the woman was chosen because of her capability and not because of her sex. (According to findings of the National Association for Female Executives, one of the reasons the "old boys' club" is still strong is that men do not want to have to compete with women as well as with other men [Dee, 1993, p. 27]. By maintaining this informal, yet very powerful, network, the men can continue to play politics, making selections and promot-ing their own kind both in their own institutions and in other in-stitutions in which they have male colleagues.)

3. Younger men who already hold the post of superintendent are concerned that the position of superintendent will be diminished

if it becomes a job in which the majority are women. History has shown that once any profession becomes primarily female, it loses prestige, not only in the eyes of the men who hold the position, but in the eyes of the public as well.

4. Most men are not comfortable with women colleagues who are in the same level position. They would rather attend meetings and conduct business the way they always did. Having women in the group changes the dynamics. Men and women do not communicate in the same way, do not view things from the same perspective, and do not approach problems in the same manner. Their style of leadership is not the same, and even if leadership styles begin to blend, men still may not be comfortable with women sharing their status.

5. When men lead other men, they lead as equals. Men now face the dilemma of how they are to react when women have the position of leadership, whether in a committee or as a presiding officer of an organization. Women do not lead in the way men are accustomed to. The men now must worry about how to respond since they can't always read the signals women send. If men try to respond in a favorable, friendly way, they wonder if their male peers will find this acceptable. Can they return a question with a retort, or will an off-the-cuff or off-color remark be frowned upon?

6. Men are uneasy as to the expectations of their women colleagues: Should the men continue to open doors, let the women enter first, help them with their coats, offer to do the driving? What are the new rules? Will a female in an equal professional position resent the man who is following the good manners he has been taught? Should he compliment a female colleague on her appearance or must his compliments be confined only to an aspect of her job performance? Will this be viewed as only flattery? Or will it be mistaken for an uninvited, personal overture?

7. Men wonder if they are being ingratiating to a fault or not respectful enough of the position if it is held by a woman. Many have a difficult time treating a woman in any way other than the stereotypical attitude of daughter, wife, or mother. Even if they are making a very conscientious effort to speak in a neutral tone, how do they know whether or not they sound condescending, paternalistic, or deferential without meaning to?

LEADERSHIP STYLES OF MEN

While these examples have focused on school superintendents, similar plights are faced by male administrators on all levels of educational administration. The passage of time and the increase in numbers of women in educational administration should see a lessening of many of these predicaments. The new rules of conduct have not yet been written and vary from woman to woman, thereby making a consistent response to any given situation almost impossible for any man.

MEN WHO ENCOURAGE WOMEN

Perhaps this topic belongs with the section on dilemmas faced by men, as certainly a supportive male can find himself in a dilemma if his own colleagues do not share his enlightened views on women in educational administration. It is only fitting that we acknowledge the countless men who have encouraged women to enter the field of educational administration, who have supported them in their endeavors, who have promoted their candidacy for administrative positions, and who have stood beside them, shoulder to shoulder, as colleagues. There are a growing number of these men and that is very positive for women in management.

No one makes her or his way alone in this world. Each of us has had help from many sources, not all of which we realize at the time. At the risk of sounding patronizing, yet in the name of fairness, we salute these men who are not afraid of equality of the sexes, who are secure in themselves, and who are willing to reward merit, regardless of the sex of the recipient.

It is generally agreed that men who are perceived to be most helpful are the following:

1. Those who have made a conscious attempt to change their attitudes toward competent women
2. Those who earnestly work to change their perceptions about women's management abilities
3. Those who recommend capable and credentialed women for promotions
4. Those who offer words of encouragement or good advice

5. Those who actively teach female aspirants about the everyday details of school administration
6. Those who share inside tips
7. Those who request that women be included in the pool of candidates
8. Those who are willing to take a risk not just of hiring women, but of bearing the comments of their male colleagues because of it
9. Those who openly compliment the work of *all* administrators, including women
10. Those who overtly demonstrate respect for the dignity and worth of all persons

The importance of the support and encouragement of men in educational administrative positions cannot be overemphasized. Women are not asking for special favors. All that is wanted and needed is for women in educational administration and those who are aspiring to positions in that field to be taken seriously and to be accorded the same consideration that would be given to a man in the same position.

A MEETING OF THE TWAIN

Men and women can work comfortably together at the top and their differing styles of leadership can be complementary, producing a synergism that gives the organization benefits it would not receive if only women or only men held the top posts. The fortunate institutions are those in which differing styles are viewed as complementary rather than confrontational and those that encourage women to learn from men and men to learn from women. As many studies are showing, women are well suited to leadership, especially in leadership practices that are based on greater openness and interaction with people. As Edward Moldt, director of the John Pappajohn Entrepreneurial Center at the University of Iowa from 1994 to 1995 and 1998 to 2000, once said,

"[Women's approach is] one that is right for the times." Today's companies require leaders who not only are risk takers and visionaries but also are "strong enough people that they're capable of hearing the ideas of others and really empowering them to use some of those ideas in changing business and in making themselves successful." (Nelton, 1991, p. 17)

In institutions in which there are both women and men in the top management positions, it is not necessary for the women to handle the soft areas and men to deal with the more difficult. Such a division of labor only perpetuates stereotypes. Rather, all issues should be considered the concern of everyone. Not all duties have to be assigned to everyone, but matters that require problem solving or strategic planning will benefit from the various skills and perspectives of both genders. All men and women educational administrators have much they can teach one another—as well as the members of their own sex—about leadership. As they learn from one another, they can bring heightened leadership abilities to their educational institutions. The following suggestions are offered as ways in which both women and men can learn to work together for the benefit of all:

1. If you are a woman, consider being more decisive. Women often lack a sense of timing about when to stop building consensus and gathering information and to make a decision.
2. Be a good listener. Women are usually better listeners than men. Men need to work on their listening skills, and to realize that listening doesn't impose on the listener the obligation to make the decision based on what the speaker says.
3. Women need to develop the ability to focus on short-term goals, and men need to develop the patience and the skill to take the time to weigh the ramifications of all possible consequences of a long-range goal.
4. Be willing to express your emotions, even to cry. This goes for both sexes. Men need to learn to be comfortable in expressing their own emotions and to learn that when women cry, they are not showing weakness, looking for sympathy, or trying to manipulate. If you are going to be on the leading edge of management, you sometimes must be on the emotional edge as well.
5. Don't let your ego get in the way. No one person makes an institution successful; it's a team effort and a team attitude.

6. Be yourself. Keep to your natural style, but learn from the style of others.

Both men and women bring strengths to positions of leadership. The woman who can learn from men to be more decisive and to exude an appearance of being in control and the man who can learn from women compassion and the absolute necessity of listening to what others are saying and acknowledging their worth will both gain greatly. The best leadership style may, indeed, be a combination of the best that both women and men have to offer, and persons who learn to be both caring and commanding will discover the key to a leadership style to which both genders can relate. It is they who will make the best leaders for the complex times in which we live.

NOTE

1. A result of experimentation that shows that productivity increases when there is a change in environment or in attention paid to those being treated.

9

COMMUNICATION

Communication is the ingredient that makes it possible for an organization to function and is vital to an organization's success. It is the major activity engaged in by school administrators. Communication styles and skills influence how people treat each other, how they solve conflicts, and how they exchange information. From saying "Good morning" and answering the telephone to writing the strategic plan, you are being evaluated by everyone with whom you are communicating. No matter how well you think you are speaking, listening, or writing, unless the respondent understands, you have not communicated effectively.

To be fully effective, communication must be conducted (1) accurately, (2) properly, and (3) with the understanding of the other's perspective.

- *Accurately* means that your communications are as error-free as possible. You use standard English, correct choice of words, and careful syntax, and you follow all of the rules of good speaking and writing learned throughout your education and experience. If you are not absolutely sure of your skill in these areas, take a brush-up course and/or purchase style books (Strunk and White's *Elements of Style* is still considered the best), a basic grammar reference book, books on public speaking, books on business writing, any of Deborah Tannen's books on communicating, and a style manual, such as *The Chicago Manual of Style* or the *Publication Manual of the American Psychological Association*.

- *Properly* implies that you understand form and protocol, such as when is it best to write, phone, send a memo, or use electronic methods such as voice mail, e-mail, and faxes. Also included in "properly" is appropriateness of the message. Remember, once something is said, it cannot be taken back, and once it is written, it becomes a permanent record.

- *Understanding the other's perspective* is also very important and will place you in the realm of caring individuals. Your regard for the listener or the reader's perspective not only will save you time in clearing up possible misunderstandings, but also will indicate your sensitivity to and regard for others. It shows that you are open to the views of others, and that you have given forethought to what you are communicating.

It is said that language is a great motivating force. Used positively, it can inspire people to do their best; used negatively, it can lead to uncertainty and self-consciousness in both the sender and the receiver. Worse, negative communication can lead to alienation without the sender of the communiqué realizing the consequence. It is imperative, therefore, that you become very aware of the kinds of messages you are sending.

Your "voice" and the language you use will help to set the course for your role in the educational institution in which you lead or serve. Your voice is distinctive, expressing your own personality, as well as that of the institution, and your management style will reflect itself in your voice, whether it be written, oral, or through body language. Every word and all actions bespeak who you are and what you value.

UNDERLYING COMMUNICATION: GOOD MANNERS

I can still hear the reminders: "Say thank you to Mr. Bressler if he offers you green beans from his garden." "Stand up when Aunt Jessie comes in." "Remember not to answer Linnie's questions if she asks anything personal about the family. Just tell her you don't know." And, even as a toddler, I heard, "Say 'Please.'" In our family, having good manners was as important as having a straight part in our hair. That was the expectation, and to not demonstrate good manners was not permitted.

As children we learned good manners by rote, without knowing why. I remember wondering why certain rules were enforced, and while answers were supplied, they had to be taken solely on faith. I recall very clearly some of the explanations my older sister gave me, and I, in turn, dutifully relayed that wisdom to my next younger sister. For instance, we thought that the reason the older sibling walked on the curb side of the sidewalk was "because if a car comes up on the sidewalk, the older person, who has lived longer, will be the one killed." It wasn't until years later that I learned that this particular courtesy was based on the civility that a gentleman would walk curbside to protect the lady from the splashes of passing carriages (or from runaway horses, which seems to be closer in explanation to the reason given us). Not slamming doors also was an ironclad rule, and, even today, if I inadvertently close a door too abruptly, I find myself reopening it and closing it again very quietly, just as Mrs. Houser, our sixth grade teacher, insisted that we do. I'll admit that I must look slightly ludicrous reopening a door only to re-close it, yet my automatic reflex to do so is staunchly engrained.

I recall in detail the gaffe made in such innocence by my ingenuous baby sister, a sin of commission the family never forgot. This ten-year-old made a telephone call to our pastor and guilelessly requested to speak to "Ezra." At the time, I thought we would never recover, but in today's more casual society, perhaps this form of address would not even be noticed.

Specific manners *do* change, but you should always err on the side of more formal rather than less. Good manners are always fashionable, but an even better reason to learn and practice good manners is that knowing how to behave in both social and business situations is essential to anyone who wants to be taken seriously. It makes business sense to have good manners, and those who expect to advance in their positions must reflect in their everyday actions that they are courteous and respectful of others.

Manners are based on using common sense and kindness in interactions with fellow human beings. They may appear to be artificially and superficially imposed without any thought, but almost all mannerly behavior has evolved from a need to show regard for and consideration of others. While some courtesies are designed to show respect and deference to one's position, most simply establish protocol that leads to a smoother operation of both business and social communication.

Social graces and executive manners are not that different from each other, and demonstrating your understanding of both marks you as a considerate person and one who "belongs." Comporting yourself well is one of those sometimes indiscernible, unspoken ways by which you will be judged. Letitia Baldrige, social secretary to two U.S. ambassadors, chief of staff for Jacqueline Kennedy during the Kennedy administration, and an expert on corporate and governmental protocol, relays a telling story:

> I once watched an aggressive young manager take the comfortable front seat next to the company president, who was driving his own car, while the chairman and two other executives were wedged into the small back seat. When I saw the CEO the next day at a North Carolina furniture plant and asked him how the three-hour drive had been, he said, "Fine, but I learned something about young _____ that I had never known before." Before I could ask what, he continued, "Anyone who is insensitive enough to hog the best seat in the car during a very hot, long ride either has to be the chairman of the company or someone on his way out of the company. I'll let you guess which one *he* is!" (Baldrige, 1993, p. 29)

Baldrige is probably best known as the author of a revised edition of *The Amy Vanderbilt Complete Book of Etiquette*. Her newest book, *New Manners for New Times: A Complete Guide to Etiquette* (2003), is well worth your consideration. This guide, along with her earlier *New Complete Guide to Executive Manners*, addresses areas in which the rules have been clear and workable for years as well as those that are changing, such as "opening a door for a lady—or a gentleman." There are very helpful chapters on appropriate stationery, traveling with a colleague of the opposite sex, entertaining for business, dressing for success, correct forms of address, and other areas of human interaction.

MANNERS AND WOMEN ADMINISTRATORS

As an administrator, you will set the tone for your area of responsibility, so you must subscribe to an affirmative and exemplary code of behavior. Where others might be allowed some latitude, you are not. Not only must you follow the general rules of good corporate manners, but also you must be pleasant and gracious to *everyone*. You will be expected to have a good sense of humor, and to laugh at yourself in an appropriate way (not as the brunt of jokes).

A woman executive should be compassionate and not apologize for being so. You should particularly be a sympathetic mentor and good role model for aspirants, female and male. Never forget those who have helped you, mentioning them in your conversation, speeches, or reports. Crediting others enhances your own image as well. Remember also to keep your private life separate from your professional one, and do not chat about your family or your relationships.

You should always be on time, both for appointments and in meeting deadlines. It behooves you to be well organized and thorough in preparation. If an emergency situation causes you to be late for an appointment, always contact the person whose appointment may need to be rescheduled. If possible, make this contact yourself. If not, get back to the person as soon as possible. When you are meeting with someone, do not look at your watch; it is insulting to your guest.

If you have the authority to set protocol, carefully consider the forms of address to be used in the office and throughout the institution. The trends of society are becoming more informal; however, you may want to set a more professional tone by not using first names among the professional staff. Using first names in an office atmosphere suggests to parents and other visitors that they may do the same. A good procedure is to use first names in speaking to one another, but to use the title (Mr., Mrs., Ms., Dr.) when *referring to* persons, as in "JoAnn, please take this packet to Mr. Riley." Arrange for such protocols to be reviewed periodically, and for persons new to the organization to be informed of them. Make sure you understand the hierarchy of the organization and always follow protocols and procedures, not skipping over someone to speak to the person at the top.

Never blame others for your mistakes. Accept the responsibility for your errors, and do what you can to correct them. If your mistakes have caused a hardship or an embarrassment for a colleague, set things right immediately.

A woman should totally refrain from the use of foul language. Regardless of gender equality, bad language still sounds far more offensive coming from a woman.

Helping someone on with a coat, holding a door open, or offering to carry a package is not a gender issue. If you find someone offering any of these amenities, accept gracefully. If, on the other hand, you really don't want or need the help, simply say, "Thank you. I can manage." Add a smile to assure the other person he was not wrong in offering. The purpose of good manners is to put others at ease, so don't make an issue of something innocuous. And, yes, you should stand up to shake hands if you are sitting and someone new comes into the room, regardless of the person's age or gender.

It is not expected that you will never lose your temper; however, you should be prepared to deal with situations that might trigger your anger, so you don't react in a way that could damage your career. Rather than getting defensive and angry, remain in control.

Do not embarrass anyone in front of others. If you need to take issue with a person's misstep, do it behind closed doors. If in a meeting it is obvious that errors have been made, address those mistakes in a kind way to avoid placing the offender on the defensive.

Whatever courtesies you extend in the name of business must be carried out with grace. You are a representative of your institution and you may need to set aside personal values in dealing with people whom you might not choose as your friends. You do not have the opportunity to select your constituents, but you must develop the ability to connect with them without being condescending. Good manners are not reserved only for those who share the same values. In an educational setting, as in any business or professional setting, courtesies need to be extended to everyone.

LISTENING

Before you speak, you should listen. Many people are uncomfortable with silence, especially if silence to them means only that they are not talking. Fortunately for women, they are more comfortable with silence, as they have learned to listen and to be reflective. These listening skills, which women have honed throughout their lives, serve them well in their administrative roles. We have seen that women interrupt far less often than men do. As a result, they hear more, absorb more, and can, therefore, respond in a more informed manner. Women usually do not have to try to guess what the speaker is going to say next because they are paying attention and can intuit the progression of the conversation.

Women are also very good at paying attention to or appearing to be interested in the person speaking. In a business situation this can be turned to a very real advantage. By concentrating on the speaker, you can pick up on visual cues. In turn, the speaker will be responsive to you and more likely to draw you into the discussion following delivery of the message.

Another good tactic you can use as a listener is to ask open-ended questions of the person with whom you are having a conversation. A question such as "What do you think of _____?" is very flattering and forces the other person to speak. "Tell me a bit more" or "How did you feel then?" are other such leading questions that can increase the flow of the conversation or the meeting.

If you expect to be in a situation or a meeting in which the discussion may be so diffuse that even the best listeners cannot grasp all the nuances, let alone the key points, take with you a designated "listener." This person's responsibility is to take notes while you concentrate on listening intently as each point is made. Such a technique allows for you to maintain eye contact, as well as to respond to the speaker, rather than being distracted with note taking.

There is much to be said about silence. Silence gives you a chance to collect your thoughts and keeps you from saying more than you need to, particularly in difficult situations. For example, if you are dealing with a staff member who is unhappy about a situation, not only can you learn more about his or her perspective by listening, but also you give the aggrieved person the feeling that you *care* enough to listen. Sometimes, by simply asking each party in a dispute to "start at the beginning," you are able to get a more complete, coherent, and connected story.

Another situation in which you should only listen is when an answer by the other party is unsatisfactory. By not responding immediately, you are likely to get additional facts or a different kind of information. As most people do not like the voids caused by silence, you can use these voids to your advantage by being patient.

Keeping silent after giving a major presentation can also be effective. Finish the presentation, ask for comments, and do not speak again until there are questions or a reply. Do not reiterate while you are waiting for a response and do not use fillers such as "I know this is a difficult decision." Do not feel compelled to fill in the silence. By rushing to fill the void, you may say something that will break the concentration of your listeners, resulting in their responding to your *comment* rather than to the points of your presentation.

SPEAKING

Verbal skills shape and support every interpersonal relationship. These skills are a vital resource for developing your competence as a professional and your credibility as a communicator. Whether you are making a speech or speaking with a colleague, it is important to be aware of what you are saying and how you are saying it. Always strengthen your facts with good judgment, making sure that your words serve your best interests. You may have the most forceful evidence on your side, but if you cannot make your recommendation acceptable to the people who will be affected by it, it is useless.

If you find yourself as the reactor to open-ended questions and long pauses, have your responses ready. In reply to an open-ended question, ask, "Can you be more specific?" Force the questioner to ask a direct question so that you have time to formulate an answer and not say more than what you intended to say.

Your speaking skills are not, of course, limited to formal occasions. Much of your day is spent in speaking to others. Although each person you interact with is different, there are general techniques, such as the listening and speaking suggestions above, that can be applied to most situations.

The first thing you, as an administrator in a new position, should do is to meet and talk with all of the staff members. Ask their concerns and make your own expectations clear. Tell the staff, too, what they can expect from you. Do not make any promises you cannot keep. Be honest and open without being too blunt.

Public Speaking

On occasions for which you make a speech or presentation, do not hesitate to seek professional assistance if you are not comfortable with your own speech-writing and delivery skills. Not everyone feels at ease speaking in public, and there is no reason why you should not obtain help. If you have no idea where to find assistance, contact your state professional organization or ask a trusted colleague in business to recommend someone. I am not necessarily suggesting a speechwriter, but if you know you need help, don't hesitate in getting it.

A good way to practice delivering your speech is in front of a mirror or by using a video camera. You also can practice standing behind a lectern in an empty auditorium, or by visiting the room in which you will be speaking. In preparing speeches, there are two major points to remember: (1) select a topic of interest to the listeners, not the speaker, and (2) speak with your own voice. The thoughts and vocabulary must be yours. Additional tips might include the following:

- Have something interesting to say. Otherwise, don't make a speech.
- It is usually more helpful to have the entire speech in front of you, rather than notes. Use larger size type and double-space the text. It is a comfort to have it in front of you—just in case. However, don't read your speech. Deliver it.
- Use eye contact. Looking directly at various people in the audience for three to four seconds each. You might even pause for emphasis after an important or well-worded point.
- Don't slouch. Stand upright in a natural posture.
- Use humor sparingly, if at all, and don't use gimmicks. Also keep in mind that PowerPoint presentations are becoming clichéd.

ONGOING INTERACTION

Communication must be constant. Talk to your staff—individually—and find out what is on their minds and what motivates them. What makes them want to come to work in the morning? What is important to them, personally and professionally? What do they believe is successful for them now and what do they need to have increased success?

Because educational institutions by their very design make it difficult to talk with every staff member every day or even every week, try scheduling regular meeting times throughout the year to engage individuals in dialogue. Try "brown bag" meetings of small groups to discuss issues in education or in your own institution. Through this informal method, you can resolve many issues before they become problems. Encourage your staff to visit your office. Prepare a comfortable seating area, so that visitors do not have to sit across the desk from you. Offer coffee, soda, or bottled water (along with cups or glasses).

The more you can interact as professional colleagues, the more the staff will see that the mission of the institution is a shared one, and that you view all staff as important elements to the success of the venture. They need to understand the overall mission and to think beyond their own situations. In turn, you need their input and trust. Provide your staff with the most recent and accurate information possible but do not discuss what others on staff have shared with you, except to mention that you are hearing the same concern from several other staff members.

IN A MANNER OF SPEAKING

Since its invention the telephone has been the primary tool of communication. It is, perhaps, the most convenient and most direct way to reach someone. The following suggestions are offered to make telephone calls more pleasant and effective for those trying to contact you:

- Answer your own phone, when possible, identifying yourself with your full name. Callers will appreciate not having to go through a switchboard or a secretary.
- Place your own calls when possible.
- The purpose of a business call is to conduct business. Certain initial pleasantries ("How have you been? Did you get to the state conference?") are expected, but do not prolong personal conversational topics.

- Call your own number when you are out of the office to see how your calls are answered.
- Use voice mail; that way you can guarantee you are getting the message as intended.
- Do not have music playing while the caller is placed on hold. Many people find recorded music distracting, particularly if they want to use the wait time to read their mail or review a document to be used in the conversation.
- Don't be multitasking by using your computer while on the telephone; likely the person can hear the keyboard clicking.
- For important calls, make an appointment so that both you and the person you are speaking with can fully concentrate on the conversation.
- If you find yourself in an unpleasant situation, such as speaking with an irate parent, be polite, but do not subject yourself to unreasonable demands, threats, or abusive language. To extricate yourself, suggest the caller make an appointment so that everyone involved can be a part of the discussion. If the caller's language is offensive, calmly tell the person that you do not wish to hear such language and, if it does not cease, you will terminate the conversation until such time that he/she can speak in a more acceptable manner. Then, if necessary, do it. Say, "I am closing this conversation now. Good-bye." Then document the call, recording the abuser's exact words.

FIRST PERSONS, FIRST IMPRESSIONS

The initial impression anyone has of your institution is made by the first person the visitor encounters, either by telephone or written communication. You want that initial contact to be a positive one. To check the impression your institution makes, look for the following:

- How does your central switchboard operator answer calls? Or, if you must use an automated service, how easy is it to use? Does the automated response allow for "Stay on the line and someone will be with you shortly"?

- Does each secretary receive written instruction as well as personal training in the protocol of answering the telephone so that there is consistency in every answer?
- Is there a designated greeter at each building, someone who can help the visitor through the locked doors? Has everyone in the building been given guidelines as to how to report a suspicious person?
- What kind of message is being sent through your newsletter? Have you conducted a survey to find out what kind of information would be most helpful to your public? Are administrators and teachers/professors identified by name and proper title? Are telephone numbers or e-mail addresses listed? If articles are reprinted, do you give proper credit to the original source?

UNSPOKEN LANGUAGE

A pat on the back, a reassuring hand on the arm, a friendly arm around the shoulder—all send messages. For example, standing when someone with an appointment enters your office sends a different message than standing when someone uninvited enters your office, interrupting your work.

Women particularly need to be cognizant of their body language because women unwittingly give off signals that convey insecurity and weakness. Women tend to shrink when they feel vulnerable, by pulling their arms in, hunching their shoulders, and putting their heads down. Showing this type of posture indicates powerlessness. Men display authority by spreading out with their legs apart, their arms flung over the back of a chair, and their heads up. Women cannot sprawl in this manner because of their clothing styles, but they can convey an image of confidence by opening their stance a bit. When standing, keep your head up and your feet slightly apart. When seated, sit back in the chair with your arms resting on the chair arms. Ask a man to sit down when you are speaking to him, especially if he is taller.

Typically in conversation, women face each other when they speak, while men stand shoulder to shoulder, talking into the air. Men "face off" only as an act of aggression, so when a woman faces a man while speaking to him, the man may instinctively read this as a move of aggression. On the other hand, when a woman is speaking to a man and he stands next to her instead of looking at her, she thinks the man doesn't care about what she is saying. When men nod, it is in agreement with what is being said, while women nod to mean "I hear you." (As full interpretation of body language is beyond the scope of this book, you may want to purchase a book on the subject.)

WRITTEN COMMUNICATION

Any correspondence you receive that requires an answer should be responded to within three days. It is also important that you personally respond to most of these communiqués. A personal response is courteous, it keeps you in touch and makes connections, and it provides an opportunity for you to make positive comments.

Use notes for quick, personal messages to individuals. Unless a formal notice is absolutely necessary, do not use preprinted memos. These are viewed as highly impersonal. It takes no longer to place your message on a card or even a standard sheet of paper, and it will be more positively received. A good technique, more often used by women, is to add by hand a personal commentary on a message that may be formal in tone. A personal addition adds a softness and takes away any suggestion of abruptness.

Establish a routine of informal written weekly reports from all of your managers. Ask them to list concerns, unusual occurrences, anticipated roadblocks on projects, or anything else they want to let you know about. If you are out of town, have these reports sent to you as e-mail attachments, thereby signaling the importance you place on them. These reports make good openers for the individual meetings you have scheduled with each administrator. If you can make the time, occasionally stop by and chat with the writer or arrange to go to lunch. If the report sends a serious or urgent message, go see the sender immediately. Another technique is to send open-ended questions, asking for responses, either in the weekly reports or as the basis for discussion at group meetings. Just make sure the questions do not appear threatening.

All who deal with the public should be trained in how to communicate with constituents. Many of your staff may be sending negative messages without even realizing it. A little time taken to review suggestions such as the following will return major dividends:

1. Use simple, direct sentences. Fifteen to eighteen words is a good length for messages.
2. Write short paragraphs. Readers are more likely to read what is written.
3. Be factual and specific. Highlight the specifics by placing them at the beginning or end of sentences and paragraphs.
4. Be positive. Use words that convey an upbeat attitude, but keep the tone neutral.
5. Set off important material. Use headings, numbers, dashes, or bullets.
6. Do not lead with the bad news. Emphasize what *can* be done, not what cannot.
7. Proofread. Ask others to read anything that is going to the public over your name. If you need to send something quickly, try reading the message aloud. Obvious errors will be more evident.
8. Set the tone for quality.
9. Tailor your letters to the readers. Your choice of words may vary according to the intended audience.
10. If you possibly can, set the letter or message aside and come back to it later to make sure it is saying what you want it to say.

If writing is not your strength, there are many books and manuals available on business writing. Use these until you become more comfortable with the writing process. There are also computer software programs that may be useful. Adapt the examples to your own needs.

ELECTRONIC COMMUNICATION

The power of technology has put a new face on communication, and can enhance every area of interaction. A computer, however, will not think for you, software will not make you an expert writer, and voice mail will not automatically give you proper syntax. What technology can do for you, however, is to make many things easier, faster, and, yes, even *more* personal. Technology makes it possible to work smarter.

Voice mail is today's answering machine. It is an efficient way to transmit valuable information. If you use a voice mail system, however, do not forget the human element. If at all possible, have a person answer the phone and offer to direct the incoming call to the voice mail of a particular individual. Nothing is more maddening to callers than to reach a system that requires them to spend time listening to recordings and punching buttons, without ever speaking to a person. Worst is a system that instructs the caller to "Press zero now to speak to an operator," only to direct the call to yet another round of messages. When leaving a voice mail response, remember the tone of your voice as well, as the message itself can be played over and over again by the receiver. Don't leave messages that are confidential, harsh, or negative.

Fax machines are wonderfully convenient, but a cautionary word is in order. A fax is a letter without an envelope and can be read by anyone who happens to walk by the fax machine. Remember that employees don't always check the in-boxes, so it is wise to call to verify the fax number and to alert the intended recipient that sensitive documents are on the way. Make sure your document has a professional-looking cover letter or header with all contact information.

People in business find it acceptable to send personal messages of congratulations and other compliments by fax or e-mail, but never use electronic mail to send thank-you notes or condolences.

Cell phones are time-savers in that you can be taking care of business en route without having to be interrupted with a phone call the minute you reach your destination. In the event of an emergency, you can immediately change your destination. However, be selective in who has your cell phone number.

E-mail is best for conveying key information, confirming appointments, documenting decisions, or contacting a decision maker directly. Remember, conventional grammar, spelling, and punctuation will always help your message be more easily understood. Don't ignore greetings, closings, and subject lines; they help the recipient file or act on the information contained within.

COMMUNICATING THROUGH GENDER

As has been stated throughout this book, men and women communicate in different ways in terms of content, style, and structure. Men and women also listen for and hear different information. For example, when a male administrator discusses an instructional issue with teachers, a woman may be listening more for the underlying tone or belief, the man for the facts. Women administrators have to work harder to get male teachers to "hear" them at all because male teachers tend to exhibit more hostility against women administrators (even though many admit they prefer women administrators) and, consciously or unconsciously, tune them out.

One approach to this dilemma is to imitate some of the speaking techniques of the opposite sex. The follow suggestions may be helpful for women:

- **Get to the point.** The first thing you need to concentrate on is speaking clearly, quickly, and concisely. Men don't want to hear explanations for the way you arrived at the information you are giving or the decision you are making.
- **Use humor.** Most women tend to take themselves too seriously.
- **Talk about sports.** Many advice givers in the area of communication between genders suggest that you initiate a conversation about sports as a way to build rapport with male colleagues and employees. However, do this only if you can be sincere.

On the distaff side, women would appreciate men who try the following suggestions:

- **Learn active listening skills.** Try paraphrasing or repeating what the woman says to show you are listening to her.
- **Talk about feelings.** This is not easy for many men; however, it is essential for good communication with women. Try emphasizing people and relationships.
- **Use equivalent gender forms.** This advice should be aimed at both men and women, for women are as remiss as men in this area.

If men are referred to as Mr. or Dr. Someone, the formal equivalent for women should also be used: Ms., Miss, Mrs., or Dr.

COMMUNICATING THROUGH MEETINGS

The success of the institution depends upon the ability of each staff member to learn from the best ideas of every other member. To assure this, the leader needs to establish a trusting atmosphere, one in which each member of the team feels valued and is led to believe that what is contributed is important. You, as the administrator, can set the tone and comfort level, but it will take the efforts of everyone to be successful.

First, make sure to provide an agenda and a time frame and follow both (but if discussion seems to flow from item A to item C, go with the flow). One good technique is to send out a question prior to the meeting so that people will come in with thoughts to share.

During the meeting, give equal speaking time to everyone, inviting those who haven't yet spoken to do so. Be aware of the participants' body language: leaning forward, an open mouth, raised eyebrows, or looking at the speaker are good indicators of a person's desire to speak. Ask questions that require responses. Then accept the answers that are given, acknowledging the responses with a positive comment. Address persons by name as a way of including and valuing them.

You can create a positive atmosphere by taking a genuine interest in what others are saying. Ask for their reaction to the issues. Comment on points you find particularly helpful; for instance, you might say, "That clarifies what we have been struggling with." Thank people for their contributions to the discussion and to the solutions, if appropriate. Give genuine praise frequently, but do not be overly effusive.

Make connections to what others are saying. Pay attention to what they say, and repeat their words and terminology in further elaboration or comments. Point out similarities to or differences from ideas on the table. If what has been offered is not quite clear to everyone, try summarizing what has been said. This not only will give credibility to the person making the comment, but also it will underscore the suggestions already made and will allow for correction and modification. Use an introductory phrase such as "If I am understanding you correctly . . ."

If you sense a problem of either operation or content, do not neglect to resolve it. For example, if people are talking too softly and cannot be heard, tell them. If there is conflict, resolve it before ending the meeting. If someone becomes hostile, say something placating, but acknowledge the anger, as in "I sense that you are upset. Would you like to elaborate at this time?" Do not make sarcastic or demeaning comments about anyone's actions, words, temperament, or appearance, and never embarrass anyone. Finally, as the meeting chairman, you are expected to keep the meeting on an even keel. Maintain your dignity at all times and move the meeting forward.

Save five minutes at the conclusion of the meeting to recap what has been discussed and decided. Clarify the potential outcomes, the next steps, and who is responsible for each step.

COMMUNICATING THROUGH PRAISE

Praise is a very effective method of communication. It is clear, direct, and positive. There are various ways to praise, all of which must be sincere in order to have value.

First, praise should be specific to an action. General comments such as "Good job!" are not explicit enough. Specify what it is that is being praised, for example, "You handled the parent disagreement problem very well. I appreciate that you took care of it at the building level." Focus on the action, not the person. This technique sets the tone in case you need to comment negatively on some ill-advised action. It also behooves you to show praise in a public meeting. Say something like, "Thanks to the work of Dr. DeLiberty, we can move forward in our state plan."

Another method of praise is to award the person increased responsibility and added autonomy. Reward outstanding performance by allowing the person the freedom to formulate plans in a new area, one that can serve as a career builder for the person. Make clear that this is serving as an accolade and not an addition to the person's workload.

Praise will pay off for the institution as well as the individual. A staff that receives deserved praise and awards will be more creative and more motivated. In addition, as praise continues, lines of communication will increase, and people will see you as someone who is secure in her own position and appreciative of the efforts of others.

RECORD KEEPING AND DOCUMENTATION

Keep a record of everything you do. Document, document, document. Keep notes on what any incident or conversation was about, who was involved, and what you said you would do. Keep a file folder on every area of your job responsibilities, keep a log of telephone calls and conversations you have with everyone, and, if you deal with students, keep a card file (or electronic file, if you have a foolproof backup system).

For efficiency and to control extra clutter, use a daily or monthly calendar as a schedule reminder. The two most popular methods of keeping track of your life—your appointments, projects, expenses, birthdays, telephone calls, and the like—are the leather-bound planner (such as Day-Timer or Day Runner) and the electronic planner, which can be either a software program for your personal computer or a handheld device. Whatever the method, you need to keep records and document what you are doing and have accomplished. Keep these appointment books and planners from year to year. They are helpful when you are trying to reconstruct the progress of a project or the number of times you met with an individual. If you need to keep track of your mileage, your appointment book also can be a good record of your travel.

Save everything that concerns you. Make a copy of everything you do or produce and keep extra copies in a file at home. This will be helpful in building a portfolio, either for your job review (evaluation) or for future job searches. Keep the original or a copy of all letters, memos, or complimentary notes that reflect favorably on your performance or ability. Write acknowledgments or thank-you letters recapitulating verbal compliments or conversations so you have a record for your personal file.

Don't ever assume that your job position is secure. Most positions in educational administration are not tenured. You serve at the pleasure of the board and/or your superintendent. You never know when someone may decide that your position is expendable. You may need to present a case as to the importance of your contributions. In a worst-case scenario, you may need documentation for your attorney's use. If you sense that you are being targeted, keep a daily journal, as detailed as possible. You must make daily entries, as you will not remember all the details of what happened and who said what to whom.

Keep every note and every report you make on an incident or interaction with those you supervise. Even if you keep copies of these reports in other files, make sure that everything having to do with every individual is in that person's file. (These are your files, not to be confused with the personnel files kept elsewhere and accessible to others.) Date all material. You may not use all of this documentation, but keep everything because you never know in advance whose file will be crucial to a case you find yourself involved in.

The same advice holds for student files. If you handle discipline, it is essential to keep thorough records. No matter how good your memory is, you cannot rely on it for every detail of every student you meet with. Even though I can vividly recall nearly every detail surrounding my first two discipline cases, most of the infractions of all the other students now run together in my memory. It was the bright red card file that ruled the students' lives and documented their deeds and their misdeeds, and it was those file cards that convinced parents that I had talked with their children on such and such a date, and that we had decided thus and so. Computer records can also be effective, so long as there is a reliable backup system. I would still advise that you print out the notes from each encounter and keep these in file folders, as parents find the printed word more credible, and you don't want to be printing from your computer during a parent meeting. If a recalcitrant student finds herself or himself facing suspension or a hearing before the school board or even the district justice, your records are essential.

Keep minutes of every meeting. These minutes are your official records of the meeting itself, those in attendance, agenda items, action taken, and who is responsible for what. If you are chairing the meeting, ask someone else to take notes. If it is your meeting, however, you should write any official report or review it before it is released. Keeping records and minutes of meetings also helps to keep everyone informed and current. Keeping good records is the mark of an organized professional. It may take extra time at the beginning to set up a system, but it is crucial to your success and, perhaps, your future.

COMMUNICATING WITH THE PUBLIC

It is important to keep your public informed about their educational institution, even if 75 percent of that public does not know much about the daily operation of the school district. The public of a college or university usually is even further removed both geographically and fiscally from the institution it supports. Nevertheless, the need for and the process of communication are very much the same on both levels. All educational institutions have students, parents, public or private financial supporters, governmental regulations, and local citizens among their "publics." Because of dependence upon these publics, all institutions must communicate information about their organization to promote understanding of the programs, demonstrate accountability, help clarify and build commitment to goals, and promote cooperation among other institutions.

Throughout the history of public education in the United States, educators have gone through periods of interactive cooperation with citizens followed by isolationist withdrawal from the public. Associated with these cyclical trends is growth in the public confidence followed by damaging loss in credibility of educational leaders. Within the past twenty years educators have been faced with publics who question their trustworthiness. The credibility gap for college administrators also has greatly widened. One has only to follow the reports in the *Chronicle of Higher Education* to see the rapid, and sometimes unpleasant, turnover in the presidencies at many universities. The trend in basic education seems to be following the same pattern as the term of a superintendent in any given school district continues to decrease. There have been decimating reductions in legislative appropriations to all educational institutions, both basic education and higher education. In many cases, private donations to universities have also drastically decreased.

Some observers place the blame on societal conditions in general, while others believe that young people themselves have created a loss of credibility with the public. It is, however, the children of the 1970s youth generation who are among the loudest complainers that the schools and colleges are not doing their job. And it is often this same "protest generation" that screams the most that their own children deserve every opportunity, yet they are not willing to be taxed or to pay

the tuition costs of a private school education. They demand to know
what is "wrong" with our educational system and in the same breath
they ask why students aren't learning and why education costs so much.
They are angry when their own children are disciplined, yet want better
control in the schools. They are upset when their child is not accepted
by the college of her or his choice, yet they complain that there are no
academic standards.

Better communication may not resolve these issues, but promoting
better relations with the public through a planned process may help.
How the organization is achieving its mission should hold top priority in
your public relations plan. Recurring issues of interest to parents of elementary and secondary children include grading, promotion or retention practices, homework, methods and materials of instruction, special
services, state assessments, behavior, accountability, and school safety
and security. Of greatest concern to parents of college students is the
safety of their sons and daughters, increasing costs, and the job market
for their offspring once they are graduated.

One of the keys to a good public relations program is to recognize the
importance of personal interaction. While you as an administrator can do
much for the organization by your presence and willingness to serve as
the district's advocate to the public, it will take more than the effort of
just one person to make any impact. The day-to-day contact that parents,
students, and citizens have with teachers, administrators, support staff,
and other educational personnel, such as the board members or service
contractors, is of primary importance. Therefore, you should begin with
preparing your own staff. Remind them of the mission of the institution
and provide direction or training to raise the awareness of the importance of positive responses to public questions and challenges. Also educate your staff to the realization that every time they make a comment
about education in general or their place of employment in particular,
they are serving as spokespersons for their school or university.

NEWSLETTERS AND OTHER PUBLIC COMMUNICATION

Nearly all institutions publish a newsletter or other periodical. These
can be very effective in communicating to the public. Use these publi-

cations to present issues of concern and current topics in education as they affect your institution and your students.

Most of the information contained in a department or building newsletter should be specific to department or building concerns. If the publication will have wide dissemination, be selective in the articles, so that they will be of broader interest. The tone of the newsletter should be professional, yet personal to the institution. It should speak to the reader respectfully, offering information about programs, activities, and current issues, such as the yearly budget, strategic planning, or state guidelines, as well as any other areas of concern. If there is a hot topic in the news, you should address how that issue affects your institution. Make sure, if you are addressing a controversial issue, that your style is reportorial; do not take sides until and unless your board has taken an open stand on the issue.

Another good administrative practice is to write a column in the newsletter, making sure that it is your voice speaking. Do not plagiarize. If you are using the findings of a research article or educational journal, give credit to the publication and its author. It is very obvious when you use a "canned" article you have read, even if you reword it. Also, be careful that what you are stating reflects what you are doing. Do not be placed in a position of advocating or advising parents to do something when your district is not practicing it.

Much as we may disdain slick public relations campaigns, there are lessons to be learned from the techniques of experts. Because we live in a world of sound bites and "the news in brief," there often is not the luxury of time to explain everything in a beautifully written or eloquently delivered declamation. We live in a world so full of fast messages that we must adapt media methods to our own repertoire of communication skills.

We are in competition for the ears and the minds of our public. If most of the world believes that education is deteriorating, even if we know it is not, the public perception will not change unless we take our own case to the public. As an educational leader, you need to take some pointers from the spin doctors in the political arena, so that you can at least have better control over what message your institution sends:

- **Keep the message simple.** Focus your attention on the issue. Do not cloud the issue with other information, even though that information is just as important. Simplify the issues and your responses. Present the facts, and repeat them every time you are questioned on a critical matter of concern.

- **Use controlled emotion.** People respond to emotion and you must respond in kind. Play on whatever emotion it takes. Tailor your messages to assuage the fear, guilt, shame, or any other emotion the fearmongers have raised in their attacks on education. Even we as educators find ourselves alarmed at the fears these critics try to instill in the public. Compose a brief response to each emotional charge, and be ready to use it in response to the next person who questions you.
- **Reinforce your message.** Repeat the answers, restate the phrases, and design or coin new terms for educational trends. Use positive words and repeat them in everything you write or say.
- **Use the "fatal flaw" technique.** Turn any weakness into a strength. In response to such criticisms as "Why are not all students achieving?" you can respond by extolling the virtues of American democracy in providing an education for every child and explaining that schools do all they can to help each child achieve.
- **Frame questions and answers in priority order.** If you ask a question, always know the answer you want to receive. In addition, if you want agreement on a series of questions, ask the easy ones first. If you want a negative response, ask the difficult questions first. If you are answering a question, reframe it by rephrasing it to ask the question you want to answer. You also can postpone your answer, or divert attention by asking another question.
- **Get to the source.** If the message is blatantly in error or is directly aimed to discredit you, invalidate the message. Raise such questions as to the credibility of the facts and the reasons for the attack.
- **Delivery counts.** You are performing and your voice must sound alive and positive. Use visuals, either actual ones or descriptive verbal images. Use a format with which you are comfortable. Use students as your references, or as "props," if appropriate.
- **Leave them with something to remember.** A big finish is a good technique, and using a clear example of your point makes a good ending: Use a metaphor, a mission statement, an emotional appeal, or a well-crafted quotation (preferably your own, but that

of another will do). Tie yourself to your final remarks, either visually or figuratively.

DEALING WITH BAD NEWS

When you or someone in the organization receives "bad press," there are two inviolate rules to follow, according to Mike Wallace (1993). The first rule is to recognize that the bad news is news and that is what you must deal with, not bemoaning the fact that you are not getting coverage for all of the positive things you do. The second rule is to never hide and never lie. You need to make yourself available, if only to say, "No comment." If possible, explain that you cannot address the issue at the moment, but do not avoid or mislead the media.

If you need to discuss the matter with the press, prepare your remarks. Consider the key points, and deliver them briefly in a prepared statement of about fifty words. If there is a potentially volatile situation, speak to the press in a neutral location.

Most importantly, follow the golden rule of bad news: *Tell the truth. Tell it all. Tell it now.* Full and prompt disclosure is best. You may look bad, but at least you come across as an honorable person who is not lying to cover the facts (which will come out eventually). If this is a building situation or in your area of responsibility as the principal, you should do the responding. If the bad news is very serious, impacting others, the top person in the institution should make the response. Make clear what action will be taken. If the issue is delicate, follow the advice of an attorney. If the bad news personally involves you, the attorney may advise you to say nothing. Weigh this advice carefully because according to Wallace, "It's important to get at least some of your side of the story out immediately rather than waiting months or years for the legal system to clear your good name" (Wallace, 1993, p. 17).

Whatever the area of communication, you must be as proactive as possible. Get in the first word, send the first information flyer, make the initial telephone call, and be on top of the situation. Keep a step ahead of what people need to know and you'll assure your credibility and leadership.

BUILDING YOUR OWN CULTURE

An organizational culture is elusive to explain or demonstrate, but can best be defined as "those phenomena which account for patterns of behaving that cannot be *fully* explained by psychobiological concepts" (Kaplan and Manners in Sergiovanni et al., 1992, p. 295). An organization's culture also has been called the "personality" of an institution. A culture is the unwritten "way we do things around here," as well as the reflection of beliefs and a demonstration of the environment. In some ways, culture can be compared to the ambiance of a restaurant; it is the "tone" of the place, the atmosphere, the environment. A culture is, in part, tradition and, in part, the reflection of its current leadership. It mirrors all who are a part of the institution, from the board to the staff and students, and is seen by the community as everything the school or university stands for and everything it does.

AN ENTRY PLAN

With every new leader there will be some effect on the culture of the institution, and, likewise, that culture will affect the leadership style and capability for success of any new administrator. Few administrators are able to start with a completely new slate because even if a new educational institution is being established, there will be the nucleus of the present culture in those who are initiating the founding. The responsibility of the administrator is to become part of the existing culture before attempting to effect any change or to build a new vision for the future.

In beginning any administrative position, always have an entry plan, a plan for what you want to achieve and how you want to achieve it. The entry plan and direction must be your own, and you should plan in advance of beginning your tenure. Whether or not you are new to the institution, you are new to the position, and, therefore, you want to present a clear direction for that position. Even before applying, you should already have asked yourself, "What would I do if I held that position?" The answer to this question is the basis for your entry plan.

If you are to be the chief administrator of a school district or university, it is essential that you have a written blueprint to share with the board of directors. The need for a written plan is one of the main reasons why it is so important to learn in advance as much as possible about the institution, its people, its culture, and its community. During your screening interview, make sure to mention that you will prepare an entry plan for your second-round interview. If you are applying for an internal position, have a complete plan prepared for the first interview.

I have used folders with pockets, folders with plastic sleeves, and, for a major position, a bound booklet titled *Pride in Yesterday, Excellence for Today, Planning toward Tomorrow: A Blueprint for Success*. This twenty-page document included an introduction, an action plan, eight target areas (that most needed attention in that particular district), a "profile of a superintendent" (outlining in two sections the leadership qualities I would bring to the district and the pledge I would make), and a summation that began, "In closing, I thank you for your consideration of my candidacy. . . . I would like to leave you with the following list of reasons why I have applied for the position and why those who have urged me to apply believe that I am the person to take the reins as the educational leader and superintendent." That document served as both a review of my qualifications and, more importantly, as a proposed entry plan.

In preparation for a different position, I prepared a booklet with sixteen pages of text, plus appendixes, which included reprinted photographs of various areas of the building that represented proposed solutions to the concerns I addressed in the text. The title of that document was *Academe High School: A Time for Tradition, A Prospective for Pride*. The cover was in the school's colors and imprinted with the high school shield. The focus of the document was my plan to restore pride to the high school, an overriding concern of that district at the time.

If the selection and appointment process happens very quickly and you do not have time to prepare a complete plan, at least prepare an outline of how you will proceed the first six months. Not everyone may agree with your views; nonetheless, most will be willing to give you the benefit of the doubt because you are showing that you have given thought and foresight to the development of an action plan.

It should be assumed that you need time to get to know the institution. In case there is not that assumption, make learning the ways of the organization a part of the entry plan. In delivering the plan to the staff (and board, if you are the CEO), begin with honoring the past, stating that your long-range goal is to perpetuate what is best while preparing for the future. Do not make promises for things that may not be possible to deliver. In fact, do not propose solutions to specific problems if you are not fully knowledgeable about the institution, as there may be circumstances and politics to which you may not yet be privy. Your best tactic is to let everyone know what you plan to do first, which should be to learn as much about the institution and its personnel as possible.

The actions you take during your first three months will largely determine whether you succeed or fail. This period of time is a period of opportunity, a chance to start fresh, and to make whatever changes may be necessary. Failure can precipitate the end of a career. The following five propositions from Harvard Business School (Watkins, 2003) are worth considering:

1. Failure of successful people happens not because they are flawed but when new leaders either misunderstand the essential demands of the situation or lack the skill and flexibility to adapt to them.
2. There are systematic methods that leaders can employ to both lessen the likelihood of failure and reach the break-even point faster.
3. The overriding goal in a transition is to build momentum by creating cycles that build credibility and by avoiding getting caught in cycles that damage credibility.

4. Transitions are a crucible for leadership development and should be managed accordingly.
5. Adoption of a standard framework for accelerating transitions can yield big returns for organizations.

In addition to the advice in the above list, consider the following as a guideline for your first day (or week) on the job, using the items that best apply to your situation as the new leader. This list was developed for superintendents, so adapt it according to your position:

1. Call board members individually and let them know you are on the job.
2. Walk through the central office and introduce yourself to everyone.
3. Sit down with your secretary and see what's pressing. Determine how you'll take calls and whether they will be screened. Determine who will keep your schedule.
4. Get an update on how planning for the first day of school is going.
5. Read whatever has been left on your desk.
6. Find out the status of any litigation in which the district is involved.
7. Have your secretary set up meetings with athletic boosters; special education interests; community and business leaders; former board members, if appropriate; all elected officials; and other community stakeholders. Make plans for visiting schools, meeting teachers, and talking with all the principals.
8. Schedule briefings by people handling each division to learn what's going on.
9. If summer school is still in session, visit a school.
10. Be prepared for calls from the press; if there is one major newspaper, meet with the education reporter. Schedule a meeting with the editorial board.
11. Spend time with your predecessor, if appropriate.
12. Meet with heads of various employee organizations.
13. Call neighboring superintendents and introduce yourself.
14. Avoid offering too many solutions at the start.

15. Establish how people should address you and others in your charge.
16. Put your personal stamp on the day (Demmon-Berger, 2003).

Note the importance of meeting with everyone under your supervision or jurisdiction. As you prepare to meet with these various constituencies, be ready to ask each person or each group, "What do you see as the top three strengths in the organization and what are three areas to which I should pay immediate attention?"

If your organization is small or the area of responsibility is limited, first meet with your staff in groups and then meet with each person individually. For example, if you are the building principal, meet with the entire faculty first, followed by scheduled meetings with each department or grade chairman, and then meet with each teacher individually. (Schedule these individual meetings at a time convenient to them.) The purpose of these meetings is for you and each staff member to get to know one another on a more personal basis. Do not take notes, unless you ask the person if you may jot down something that requires your attention.

Next meet with other stakeholders, such as student leaders, support personnel, parent organizations, student activities coordinators, and/or community leaders—depending upon your position. The point is that you must meet with all who have a vested interest in the well-being of the organization. Spend time getting to know the campus, the district, the community, and the area. If you are in a school district, visit classrooms, even if you stay in each one for only a few minutes. If you are a new principal, you might even go to each classroom and introduce yourself to students. Begin immediately to attend student events. You need to "see and be seen" as soon as possible. Be accessible to anyone who wants to meet you.

Your next step should be a needs assessment. You can begin with the teachers, conduct the assessment as an administrative collaborative, or engage the services of an outside agency. Regardless of the extent, this assessment must be part of any entry plan. Then you are ready for the real work that includes the strategic plan, beginning with your vision for the building or institution.

A VISION

Vision is what guides actions. Vision provides the "magnetic north" that aligns all stakeholders with the higher purpose of the institution. When everyone in the organization shares the common vision, each person should be not only inspired and motivated, but also clearer about how to contribute to the success of the institution.

A vision should incorporate universal themes to which most people respond, such as improvement in the quality of life, provision of the best possible service, or being part of a winning team. Most people will mobilize around a vision that urges them to be the best at what they do and to truly make a difference in the world, in the workplace, or in their own lives. Your vision should be that which strikes you with the greatest passion, that which you fervently believe, and that for which you dedicate your professional life. Your vision should become your mission statement, which, in the best of circumstances, will be refined as you communicate it to, and activate it with, your team of stakeholders.

It is those with vision who are the most successful leaders. They are ardent in their beliefs, and are willing to do whatever is necessary to achieve the object of that vision. Some may have a vision of a new building that will allow for a better configuration to deliver instructional services. Some see an expansion of parent involvement. Some envision the community as a working partner with the school, using the facilities equally with the students. Others have a dream of an academy, or of a cooperative management system, or of collegiality among everyone in the institution, or of a vibrant plan for transactional leadership.

Most of you first entered the classroom because of a vision and a belief in the power of education; the vision was usually to make a difference in the lives of students. Further, you pursued or are pursuing an administrative position because you believe you can achieve that vision on a larger scale. You have a vision of the ideal curriculum or of helping students with disabilities. You have a vision of how a high school, an elementary school, or a school district should operate to best deliver the services to the students, or you have a vision of what a university should look like by the mid-twenty-first century. Whatever the scope, you are passionate about what can be and must develop a clear plan of what you want to achieve. Your vision should energize you, motivate others, and then create that same vision in the minds of those others.

THE STRATEGIC PLAN

Planning is essential, and those who take the time to plan will reap the benefits. Even if strategic planning (for public schools) were not mandated by most state departments of education, planning is necessary to achieve desired and consistent results. Planning ensures more efficiency and effectiveness, provided the plans are followed, and even if they are not, the planning at least forces the planners to take stock of themselves and to ask compelling questions. Strategic planning implies the involvement of all stakeholders, is based upon a broad consensus among various interests within the system of the institution, and should be integrated into the total management system of the organization. As such, it suggests the following priorities:

- A concern for planning implementation, rather than just the exercise of a planning process and the production of planning documents
- A concern for the integration of plans and strategic action programs with all of the other operating and control systems employed by a company
- A concern for instilling in management at all levels a continuing awareness and a balanced orientation to the future in carrying out all of their responsibilities (Fray, 1987, p. 2)

Other benefits of strategic planning include the following:

- Planning establishes direction. An institution that has clearly defined itself can better discern its strengths and weaknesses.
- Planning focuses action. It sets priorities, then integrates them at all levels. The focus, then, is on a shared goal.
- Planning increases motivation by focusing perspectives on shared goals. It instills in the minds of all stakeholders a high sense of legitimacy and of knowing where they are going.

- Planning reduces costs by reducing risk. It encourages risk-taking, but on good risks that have been studied and approved.
- Planning heightens communication by lowering barriers at all organizational levels, thereby reducing perceived differences.
- Planning fosters creativity by encouraging planners to see things in a new context. Planning establishes new relationships and associations. It may uncover new work assignments and organizational relationships. Most of all, planning shows alternate routes and options, thus creating proactive rather than reactive choices (adapted from Fray, 1987, p. 4).

As an administrator, you should be very much involved in strategic planning, and should approach the task with enthusiasm and view it as an opportunity to use your leadership skills. Too often a staff will show great reluctance to participate in strategic planning, not realizing the importance of their input. You can make this process more palatable by providing the tools and information your staff may need. Do not assume that everyone is familiar with the process or the terminology, yet do not be patronizing as if you are the great dispenser of knowledge. Treat everyone as a colleague, as a task force working together toward a common goal.

If at all possible, meet during the normal working hours, particularly in the morning when everyone is fresh. With an increasing number of businesses and industries allowing for flexible work schedules, morning meetings may not be a problem for parents and board members. Provide refreshments and periodic breaks. Be task oriented, but allow for some humor. Set the tone of the importance of the strategic plan, for it is the single most important document you will generate. It should be the driving force behind every other decision yet to be made. Many strong disagreements can be avoided if every decision is held to the golden test: Does this further our mission and is it part of our strategic plan?

Lay out the entire process, complete with a time line. Then concentrate on sections of the process, one section at a time. Establish reasonable expectations. The way you conduct this process will be viewed by the participants as the way you do business.

The Mission Statement

The first task of the strategic planning committee is the creation of a mission statement. To begin this discussion, ask the following question: "What kind of school district (or university or institution) do we wish to become?" This question should drive the discussion. The mission statement should not be a series of platitudes, nor should it be too idealistic. As you wrestle with the phrasing, keep foremost in your mind the *implication* of every word. Even a simple phrase can have serious implications and set you up for failure. For example, "to educate every child" is dangerously simplistic. What is meant by "educate"? by "child"? Since all states are mandated to educate the children, this kind of mission statement is not at all reflective of the thoughts and the specific needs of your own school community. The committee must wrestle with such decisions as: Do the citizens want basic or comprehensive education? How far are they willing to go with course offerings? What commitment are they willing to make to extracurricular activities? What additional services may be necessary to serve the students? Not all of these questions need to be addressed individually in a mission statement, but the mission statement will determine what goals are established. Keep the mission statement succinct, but make sure it reflects what is important to the institution.

The Organizational Goals

The educational (organizational) goals should be written in practical terms and should focus on the students. Your planning committee should be led by questions such as these:

- What do the students need?
- What are we now supplying that meets those needs?
- What are we now supplying that the students do *not* need?
- What are we not supplying that they do need?
- What are our resources?
- How can we best use these resources?

The reaction and answers of your planning committee will become the basis for your organizational goals. Developing these goals will take time before consensus is reached. Completion of this task may not be accomplished in one session, unless the members of the committee have already held discussions with those they represent (such as other teachers, parents, and community members). Keep in mind that whatever part an individual plays in the process, that person is important to the whole.

Whatever you do, do not request the input of various stakeholders only to rewrite what they have submitted. Do not waste people's time if they are not to be regarded as valuable. This holds true for any committee. Even if the board of directors rejects what is submitted, return the strategic plan to the original planning committee. They should be given the first opportunity for revisions. To do otherwise is insulting. You must always be considerate of the time, the work, and the feelings of all whose services were used.

The Action Plan

Once you have established the organizational goals, formulate an action plan. Devise an outline of that action plan so that the goals can be placed on a matrix of specific short-range and long-range goals with specified target dates. Indicate in the action plan who is to do what and by when. While it is not the intent of this book to provide all of the steps of a strategic plan, it should be noted that the strategic plan is very important in developing your organization's culture, for the decisions and direction of the strategic plan will determine, to a great extent, what will be the priorities of your administration. In addition, and just as important to the culture, the strategic plan should produce a commitment to the plan from all involved. The strategic plan provides a mind-set for the operation of the organization and is the basis for its organizational culture. Your action plan needs to reflect that it is carrying out the plan. (See the sample action planning worksheet in appendix E.)

COPING WITH CHANGE

Change has always happened. It is fluid and it cannot be stopped. You are not the same person you were yesterday nor the same as you will be tomorrow. You do not teach each class the same way even though you have taught the lesson many times before. Circumstances change, personalities of students change, new interpretations of the content change. Nothing is constant. Things will always change; the choice you have is to decide if you will lead the changes or be led by them.

Volumes have been written about the change process; in fact, *change* as an entity was a phenomenon of the last quarter of the twentieth century. There have been such tremendous changes and upheavals in all areas of our daily lives that dealing with the change process has evolved into a specialty in management studies. In educational circles, however, "change" is most often seen as synonymous with school reform.

Resistance to Change

Even though educators do not admit that their thinking is parallel to the beliefs of the early eighteenth-century writer Alexander Pope, who stated, "Whatever is, is best," members of each generation confidently believe that what they are doing is "best." To believe otherwise is tantamount to invalidating their life's work. Rather than reacting like physicians who embraced magnetic resonance imaging (MRI) because it allows a diagnosis to be more accurate or like surgeons who are enthralled with laser surgery for the same reason, educators become defensive when faced with change. They say, "This is right because it is the way we have always taught math." While willing to look upon medical breakthroughs as miracles, educators view educational innovations as heresy. Educators like familiarity and the security it provides. They defend their position by claiming they have learned how to do a task and do it well, so why is it necessary to change? Resistance becomes resolute.

Cultures are difficult to change as well, particularly because change is a process, ongoing, never static. There is no definite beginning and ending point. Change is an event that does not occur for everyone at the same time. When any single individual reaches the point of wanting things to change, others are not at the same point. While some are changing, others are standing still while things around them change. They resist change, not realizing that, even in that resistance, they are changing.

Change does not necessarily set teachers against other teachers, or teachers against administrators, or even administrators disagreeing with other administrators. It is educators at all levels who are unsure of what the changes will bring. That is why it is so important to build trust before change is even considered as a planned course of action. Therefore, it may be best to begin with the resistance to the proposed changes. Acknowledge the resistance and perhaps even honor it as the first step to accepting change.

To complicate things even further, you may also find yourself in a situation in which you find it prudent and necessary to follow the party line on a matter of change. For example, if there is an issue of school reform that your board does not favor, you must support the decision of the board. If there is an issue that you do not favor and the board does, you must support the decision of the board. If your faculty strongly objects to a particular change that the board wants, work with your faculty to address their concerns; relay their concerns to the board, but do not publicly take issue with the board. If your faculty is committed to a project they are presenting before the board, support your faculty in their presentation, but accept the board's decision, whatever it is.

The Pain of Change

Understand clearly your own responsibilities in the change process. If you have a line position, do not assume that because you have communicated with your superordinate, she or he has shared that information with the board. Do not be caught in the middle, assuming that the board knows what change is occurring, just because you prepared reports for the members. You might expect that the information is being shared, but there is always a possibility that it is not.

I recall vividly a major restructuring initiative that I was charged to implement. Those on the committee were given the resources to do the work, and the faculty, administration, students, and parents were kept informed through frequent reports and meetings. The superintendent was supportive, both in his words and in providing release time and other resources. He and I met often to discuss progress and concerns. He relayed to me conversations he had had with various board members about the initiative. The committee prepared reports for the board, and several times the superintendent told me that we were scheduled to meet directly with the board members. That meeting continued to be

postponed, each time with the superintendent's reassurance that everything was fine; it just was not yet "the right time" to do a full presentation. After many delays, we finally made the presentation to the board.
Each member of the faculty committee had a part, and students also
were presenting an account of their experiences and positive reactions
to the new program.

It was only as we felt the verbal stings of the board aimed at both the
students and the faculty that we realized our superintendent had not
shared with the board his charge to us, our mission, or our efforts and
results, let alone the fact of his ongoing financial and verbal support of
the project. I suppose I should have guessed what was happening because I was in the habit of attending every board meeting and had seen
that there was no formal discussion of our work. However, I had no
choice but to believe the superintendent, who had been insisting the
entire time that he was keeping the board informed both orally and by
including our reports in the board packets mailed to the members prior
to every board meeting. In actuality, he had done neither. To no one's
surprise, the reform initiative was totally rejected by the board. To
everyone's surprise, the faculty committee and students were openly
chastised by the board. Unfortunately, what was learned from this incident was distrust. A year or so later, the superintendent left the district,
but the damage to our team (and to my administrative leadership) had
been done.

What can be learned from this is just how painful an attempt at
change can be. You must be very careful in initiating change in your institution. First, accept that it is highly unlikely that any significant, long-
lasting change will occur without the involvement of the entire school or
university community. Though the specific content of each change will
depend on each institution's particular situation, virtually all effective
change models call for some version of the following basic steps:

1. Agree that a problem needs a solution. (You may be surprised to
   discover that you might be alone in your belief that a problem exists.)
2. Set clear goals that get beyond surface issues. (When change is
   warranted, there are usually underlying reasons for the need.
   These must be addressed.)

3. Understand what in the institution's current structure and culture works for and against these goals. (Again, get to know the institution first.)

4. Establish a participatory structure that allows those affected to organize how and when changes will happen. This structure should accommodate new ideas and conflict when they arise. (You cannot effect change all by yourself.)

5. Start making the changes in an orderly way according to that structure, which must include steps for ongoing evaluation and reflection. (Involve others in actually making the changes as well as in organizing for the change process.)

These steps, of course, are simplified, but are reminders that change does not just happen. Those of us who have struggled through school reform and have the scars to prove it are the first to admit that, while change is slow, it must have a process and it cannot happen until and unless the commitment to change is present.

ADVISORIES

Establishing advisory boards can be a very positive way to engage all who have an interest in what happens in the institution. The most important factor in forming and in operating these groups is to have leaders who believe in the purpose for having them and who have had some training in how to chair such groups. Without a skilled and committed chairman, advisories will wither.

Community Advisories

The importance of community advisory boards in building good school-community relations and a positive organizational culture cannot be overemphasized (see chapter 3). Because of their status, community advisory members feel some ownership in the decisions made by the managing board and they, in turn, speak well to the rest of the community about the openness of the board and administration. Through their service to the school board, community advisory boards contribute to formulating policy (through their legwork, not through any voting privilege) and then carry the message of the institution to the public. As liaisons between the public and the school, they should be encouraged to inform the public of facts in order to keep speculation and hearsay to a minimum.

Parent Advisories

Parent advisories are another positive way to include those who have a vested interest in the educational institution. Parent advisories can be beneficial in both basic education and higher education institutions.

In most public schools at the elementary school level, interested parents are limited to parent-teacher organizations. The major activities of these elementary school parent organizations include raising funds and sponsoring extracurricular activities for the children, as well as serving as room parents or as chaperones on field trips. On the secondary school level, parent-teacher organizations usually dwindle in number of active members and the amount of support. Parents are more reluctant to actively participate in the day-to-day operation of the school because traditionally (1) parent involvement decreases as children mature, (2) parents feel less "ownership" of a consolidated school attended by children from more than one elementary school, and (3) students discourage their parents' involvement as they themselves seek more independence. Advisories can—and should—address these limitations.

Colleges and universities that sponsor parent advisories have found them to be successful, but as might be expected, state universities and smaller colleges and junior colleges have had the most success with involving parents on a personal basis because of relatively shorter traveling distances for the parents. These college parents assist with homecoming activities, plan special events, and serve as a sounding board for new policies and other pending decisions such as tuition rates, campus security, and housing. The extent of their involvement, of course, depends on the need as perceived by the individual colleges. College and university parent advisories rarely become politically active, except on matters of state legislation, in which case they may be asked by the administration to lobby legislators, either personally or by making a group statement.

Elementary School Advisories

Even with an active parent-teacher organization (PTO) or parent-teacher association (PTA) in the district, well-planned parent advisories can be of great benefit to both the parents and the school because they are an important element in building the institutional culture. Elementary parent advisories can be organized at the building level or the district level. They are, however, most effective as a district-wide organization, to include all buildings in one endeavor. A district focus also distinguishes the advisory from the PTO or PTA, both in structure and purpose. An elementary parent advisory board meeting that includes the superintendent provides a forum for parents to discuss issues ranging from general educational issues to specific school board policies affecting them and their children. Contrary to the fears of some administrators, parent advisory boards are not "out to get something" (or someone). They are parents with a genuine interest and willingness to assist the school district in its mission. What they seek is direction and a person willing to listen to them.

A general information article in the school district newsletter or each elementary school newsletter about the inauguration of a parent advisory board should pique enough interest to establish a board. Membership must be open to any interested parent. Unless your district is very large and there is a history of high numbers of involvement, you will not need a system of representation. If a district serves a large suburban or metropolitan area, the deputy superintendent is the most likely person to establish a parent advisory in her or his area.

During the initial meeting of the group, make clear the purpose of the organization. Depending upon your district's procedures, you may want to have prepared a statement of purpose and guidelines for the operating policy and procedure. A typical purpose reads something like the following:

> The Parent Advisory Board is a district-wide forum of interested parents whose purpose is to focus on improving academic achievement in the elementary grades. The Parent Advisory Board is chartered to identify issues and to make recommendations to enhance the effectiveness and value of the learning experience.

The operating policy might include such information as time and place, membership, how a chairman is selected, the role of the advisory board, the procedures for recommendations to be presented to the administration and a system by which the administration will respond, and the method of information distribution to all parents. You may also choose to have an agenda review committee that would decide the merit of items submitted for discussion. The agenda should be prepared by the co-chairmen (the administrator of record and an elected or appointed parent). Topics of discussion might include any of the following: building conditions, classroom aides, class size, curriculum, foreign languages, transitional kindergarten, protocol in working with the school board, review of district management goals, testing procedures, or any other issue important to the parents.

Secondary Schools

Parent advisories are especially appreciated by the parents of secondary students, as these parents often feel helpless and isolated from the schools, especially the high school. As high school–age students are not known for their eagerness to provide information to their parents about anything occurring in the high school, a parent advisory could fill an identified need. By providing a forum for these parents, you will be offering a valuable service, as well as building a supportive culture for the school.

Send an open invitation through the district newsletter or add a letter to a general notice of any event that uses a mass mailing; also, make personal contact with parents you think may be interested. Many who read the newsletter may not take the information seriously or may think there is an ulterior motive. Some may be hesitant to attend because they have never heard of such a forum before, their children say it is "stupid," or they aren't quite motivated enough to take the initiative. If you do not receive a large response, start the advisory with parents you know will have an interest and ask them to bring another parent with them. Explain that this advisory is of mutual benefit and that the desired result is a better educational experience for their children. The number of attendees will probably not be as large as the number who attend the elementary meetings, so do not be discouraged. The dedicated parents will be a positive force in the school.

An effective way to heighten interest is to begin as a focus group on a particular issue, such as academic improvement. Send a questionnaire to the parent(s) of each student, asking for their response, either by mail (or electronically if your school is set up to do surveys) or by attending a special meeting. Clarify that you are looking for parent input on this and other issues and ask if the parents would be interested in helping. Pose the question: What can the following groups do to identify weaknesses and make recommendations for improvement in academic achievement?

- Students
- Parents
- Teachers
- Administration
- Community at large

Suggest specific concerns:

1. What do you see as problems?
2. What improvements would you like to see?
3. What do you particularly like about our academic program of studies?
4. What do you not like about it?

Regardless of the number of parents who respond, conduct the meeting with a professional attitude. The key is to treat your committee, council, board, or whatever you decide to name it with the utmost respect for the opinions and suggestions of all. Make it a rule to *not* mention names or discuss personalities or individual classroom situations. Keep in mind that the purpose of the advisory board is not to attack, but to make recommendations for solutions. The list of topics for general discussion is endless, and the more established your advisory becomes, the longer the list of concerns will be.

A special service an advisory board can provide to other parents is to host an evening of information about the procedures of applying to and selecting colleges. There are always a number of parents in a school district who have not attended college themselves or who are preparing to send their first child. To some of them the whole process is a mystery. A presentation by parents who have gone through the college visitation, application, and selection process is very beneficial, readily appreciated, and accepted as being practical and personal advice. These parent college meetings should not, however, supplant the meetings held by the guidance counselors or college representatives, as each serves a separate, but related, purpose.

Student Advisories

Student advisories can be very effective in helping build a positive school culture. They differ from the typical student councils in both structure and purpose, as the members serve as a direct line of communication to the administration.

One way to launch a student advisory is to start with a small group of students and one issue. I found this to be an effective way to ease into the concept without making it a major production or a status attraction. I began by forming a special committee of volunteers who wanted to address a series of minor problems we were having in the cafeteria. There were no qualifications for membership, only a willingness to participate. We met only as a "cafeteria committee" for the first half of the school year. By spring, the committee members began to raise other school concerns, and the duties of the committee expanded. The following year the membership was increased from nine to seventeen members to include (1) two student school board representatives, (2) the presidents of the four classes, (3) the president of the student council, (4) two at-large members of the senior class and two members of the freshman class, and (5) three at-large members from the sophomore and junior classes. This gave the following ratio of representation: five seniors, five juniors, four sophomores, and three freshmen. (This method is viewed as "equitable," but is only as good as the students holding office and/or being selected by the study body. Personally, I preferred the initial self-selected and principal-invited group, as they were motivated only by a desire to help.) Some of the issues addressed included hall traffic control, school assemblies (and how to educate the student body in regard to the purpose and expected behavior), formation of a spirit club, review and revision of the student handbook, lines of communication (informal and formal), educational issues (especially such topics as school reform), and school facilities. The possible topics in any school setting are endless and will vary according to the culture of the institution.

A student advisory board works best if it meets with the high school principal, with semiannual meetings with the superintendent if she or he is willing. Most of the concerns can be resolved with the principal, thus providing a direct line of discussion at the nearest level. If you are the adult in charge, you need to be open and nonjudgmental. You cannot become defensive when the students confront you with issues important to them. In every school there are pet projects that you think are working well, but that the students may view otherwise. Listen attentively to what they say before you reply. List their concerns and try to answer them without sounding defensive or telling them, "You don't understand." After all, the purpose of the advisory board is to learn from the students what it is they do not understand and try to solve what they see as problems.

Keep minutes of the meetings and send them to the members, as well as to each homeroom for posting, prior to the following meeting, along with the new agenda. If you treat this group with respect and let them know that you value their input, you will learn much more about the hidden agenda of your students.

A variation on a student advisory board is a yearly principal's forum or superintendent's symposium, held off site. In this format, a larger number of students can participate. Assign discussion groups and topics in advance, one issue to each discussion group because the discussion is more productive if all participants know in advance their assigned topics. Invite selected faculty facilitators, perhaps on a rotating basis—although the facilitators should be those who are interested and who have the skill to facilitate and not to direct the discussion. Include guiding or leading questions for each topic with the suggestion that the forum participants discuss the assigned issues with their peers in advance and also do some background research or conduct informal polls. Student forums are much livelier and the information more accurate with everyone's advance preparation.

The forum itself should follow a schedule and include breakfast or lunch. Following the discussion, one student from each group should present an oral report of her or his group's discussion, including recommendations to address the issue. (Each group must be given the same amount of time, no more than five minutes.) It is the further responsibility of one student and the faculty facilitator from each discussion group to prepare a written report of the discussion and their recommendations. To be most effective and credible, you must follow with a response to all participants—in fact, to the entire school—as to the actions to be taken on the recommendations. Then make sure you take those actions! Such a process can do much to develop a culture in which students feel that their input is valued.

Faculty Advisories

A faculty advisory board is important to the well-being of the staff. This should be separate from both the regularly scheduled faculty meetings and the meetings for team leaders or department chairmen. The purpose of a faculty advisory is the same as that of the community, parent, and student advisories. A faculty advisory board can address educational issues, building operations, and any other topic that affects the faculty in their roles in the school. This group provides an excellent forum in which to discuss the issues addressed by the other advisory boards as well as issues of concern to the faculty themselves, things they don't bring up at a faculty meeting. Many of the issues are the same, but there is no better way to seek solutions than for all to work from these same issues. Such a group should meet informally during the day, preferably in the morning. If that is impossible, then schedule it in the evening rather than at the end of the school day when everyone is most tired. Membership should be open to any faculty member, not by faculty vote or administrative selection. You can certainly informally invite some of those who will be most productive, but the open invitation needs to be extended to all.

Those who serve on a faculty advisory board say that they gain a great deal of understanding of how the educational system works. They find themselves more positive in helping to find solutions to problems and less ready to criticize. I am reminded of a teacher who told me about a memo placed in each faculty member's mailbox during the time of the Gulf War. The message offered assistance to anyone who felt stress and/or who had a loved one involved in the conflict. The teacher revealed that her first reaction was overwhelmingly positive because she felt that the administration was showing a great deal of caring and concern for the needs of the staff. Then she read the note at the bottom of the page: "Please read this to your homeroom and post." She felt such a letdown, she told me. As she said, "Schools show such little regard for the adults." There is no forum for concerns, no safe haven for moments when one needs to compose oneself, no place to be alone for even a brief minute or two.

Often professional staff members feel very alone, lonely, and left out. A faculty advisory board might be a place where these kinds of concerns could be discussed in a nonthreatening way. More attention needs to be paid to the staff because it is their attitude that can promote or harm the culture of the school. If the faculty feel positive, and believe that they *matter*, that attitude will be reflected in the students as well.

ALUMNI—YOUR BEST HIDDEN ASSET

Alumni are the best hidden and least utilized resource school districts and universities have, yet few school districts have established a formal working relationship with the people who have the potential to be the school's best, most productive, most supportive, and most rewarding asset. High schools have thousands of graduates, most of whom do not maintain any contact with their alma mater, and most of whom have not set foot in the school since graduation. Yet alumni can be the best source of service a school could imagine. Not even the band boosters can match the potential power of alumni. While the boosters have a single focus, the interest of alumni spans every activity the school offers. Alumni are draftsmen, artists, attorneys, physicians, and teachers. They can write well, speak with confidence, build, design, sell, craft, and raise funds. They can plan an event or tutor a student, help build floats for homecoming, or serve as graduation speakers. There is no end to the talent they can contribute to their school. They represent every walk of life, and they and their attendant skills are just waiting to serve their alma mater.

If you, as an administrator, are willing to invest just a little time to help your alumni become an organization, you will reap the rewards many times over. Alumni are among the most loyal support groups you can cultivate. Their interest does not wane, like that of parents once their children have been graduated, for alumni remain alumni forever. The time you spend in assisting them to formally organize is minimal, for alumni are independent adults and their interest in the school is their own. That ownership means something to every graduate, for high school is an event in all our lives. It is an experience that matters, that determines who we are and what we will become. The high school years, the associations formed, the experiences shared all make an indelible impression on every one of us. This is what you, as an administrator, can build upon: love and loyalty. All you need to do is provide the catalyst for an association to begin. Once it is operational, your role can, and should, diminish. The rewards, however, continue. By supporting the formation of an alumni association, you are creating a very positive piece of the school culture, one that can support the programs you are proposing for the institution.

If you are the superintendent, suggest to your high school principal that such an association could be of direct and indirect benefit. Extend your support to any effort she or he is willing to expend in forming an alumni association. Offer your own time to meet with a steering committee and offer the resources of the district for an initial mailing, the services of the district to print a newsletter, and any other help that may be needed. If you are the high school principal, your first step is to approach your superintendent as a matter of protocol as well as courtesy. Most superintendents will approve and applaud your efforts. If yours does not, ask if you can return with further information. Once the sanction of the superintendent is obtained, you should outline a plan of action based on the following ten steps:

1. Form a steering committee.
2. Hold an organizational steering committee meeting.
3. Determine purpose and basic goals by the conclusion of the second meeting.
4. Establish a process of contacting graduates.
5. Hold an organizational meeting for all interested persons.
6. Establish a budget, file for nonprofit status, and begin a membership drive.
7. Plan a high-profile project.

8. Publish a newsletter.
9. Offer services to alumni (such as providing lists of names and addresses and allowing their initial mailing through your bulk rate stamp, or promoting an alumni night at a sports event).
10. Plan a variety of projects to meet various interests of the alumni and needs of the school (Witmer, 1993, 1994).

Alumni are a very important part of your organizational culture; they represent the best efforts of the past and are living proof of the school's success. Use the vested interest of these graduates to enhance your plans for the educational institution. They are its past and will help you to build its future.

A POSITIVE ATTITUDE

Your own skill, determination, vision, and positive attitude are the main thrust behind developing a school culture. What you do and say will guide the building of that culture. You set the pace and are the role model for the institution. You are always "on," and all others involved in the working of the school or university take their cue from you. It is your responsibility to convey a positive attitude. When speaking about your educational institution itself or about any of the people involved in it, never make negative comments. A single negative comment can undo all of the positive steps you make.

You are also expected to be proactive rather than reactive, and to stay on top of what is happening in the organization. Make sure everyone keeps you informed. To ensure a communication flow, always thank people for relaying information to you, even if it is bad news. If you fall into the habit of reacting negatively, your staff will begin to keep things from you, waiting for a better time to tell you something. Encourage those who have to tell you about problems to (1) report promptly; (2) give the necessary facts, neither understating nor overstating; and (3) offer a solution, if they have one, particularly if the problem is in their area of responsibility.

Always answer questions as completely as possible. Be direct and give as much information as confidentiality permits. Do not ever tell a subordinate, "I shouldn't tell you this, but . . . ." If you should not tell, then do not. In no way be misleading. Truthfulness and accuracy are crucial ingredients in establishing credibility and in setting the basis for a positive culture.

Keep everyone informed. It is the only way to avoid misinformation and rumor. People who do not have the facts are more likely to speculate, voice their speculations, and have those speculations repeated as facts. Never forget what it was like as a subordinate, not knowing what was going on in the organization. When people aren't sure of what is happening, they are more likely to reflect negative attitudes.

Always acknowledge your own mistakes. Make it clear to everyone that you accept responsibility when things go wrong. This does not mean that you should overlook errors made by others, but never use these others as scapegoats. As the administrator, you are the responsible party.

Treat your staff as valued clients. This shows your respect for those who work for you. Do not make thoughtless comments about others and never humiliate anyone. Think about any casual comment before you state it; what appears innocuous to you may be hurtful to someone else. I recall a luncheon I attended with a group of a dozen administrators, two of whom were female. We were honoring a retiree and the conversation turned to vacations. The highest-ranking administrator made a careless comment about preferring vacations without his wife, and the other nine men joined in with similar comments, laughing and punching one another. Not only were they being disrespectful of their own wives (even though they were not present), they were disregarding two of us who fit the category of the persons being made fun of.

Never allow anyone to be the brunt of a joke. I recall one superintendent who always made fun of a building principal who had a weight problem, and another one who relished making his business manager blush, particularly at board meetings. Such action is totally uncalled for and is remembered long after the comments are made. Don't ever express an attitude of superiority. If you were blessed with more ability (or luck) in certain areas, your staff will know it without your calling attention to it. Be generous in your praise of whatever skills and talents each person in the organization has.

Be visible! This allows for people to get to know you and for you to know them. Make a demonstrated effort to learn the names of all of the staff as soon as possible. This is especially important in an educational institution where there is not a high turnover in personnel. Using people's names when you see them is an indication that you are a sincere and positive person who is interested in your staff.

Make liberal use of praise. This is easily done in an educational setting because there is always something good to say about instruction and students. Make absolutely sure that your secretary keeps you informed of any honors earned by anyone on the staff. Ask people to tell you of their achievements. Send congratulatory notes. Stop by to offer congratulations. This is important at all levels.

Do not overreact to problems. Do not treat problems as if they are crises, unless they really are. Handle situations calmly and with good humor. Adopt a "let's get to this" attitude, and begin immediately to gather facts and to find a solution to any problem. Do not cry unless it is unavoidable. If you have a tendency to tears, make an opportunity to tell those who work most closely with you that your crying should not be taken as a sign that you are upset. Your candor on this matter should help the situation and at least avoid some awkward moments. Better than that, of course, is to *not* cry in the presence of anyone. If you must weep, go behind closed doors or get in your car and take a drive. Return with a smile and with a resolve to "get to it" and attack the problem. That's a positive attitude!

One final note on establishing a positive culture: Even with collegiality and team management, be careful not to allow lines of established authority and responsibility to be bypassed. For example, if a faculty member comes to you with a request that is the responsibility of her or his department chairman, without first having spoken to that person, you should not grant the request. To do so, you create an environment of resentment and special favors. It also begins to erode the authority of the manager. A request for a favor may seem trivial at the time, and you may be tempted to be kind, but, before responding to any request, think of the ramifications your decision might have on the attitudes and responsibilities of others.

A positive corporate culture is dependent upon many factors, but, most of all, it depends upon the person who is taking the lead. Your vision sets the direction and your leadership gets you there. In summation, you can achieve that vision and establish that culture by (1) building relationships based on integrity and respect, both of your own worth and that of others; (2) verifying every statement for accuracy of information; (3) being trustworthy; (4) being a team player and involving all stakeholders in decision making; (5) providing a clear direction; (6) following through; (7) being dependable; (8) accepting responsibility; (9) getting the job done; and (10) being able to answer "Yes" to the following question: "Does this decision or action make a positive contribution to the institution?"

11

NETWORKING AND MENTORING

NETWORKING

The term *networking* has many definitions, but dictionaries do not list the origin of the word. Until the 1980s, networking was strictly a biological term; today, its use as a computer term and as a way of describing relationships is universal. From relative obscurity in biology textbooks to a position with cachet in the business world, *networking* has taken a strong hold on our organizational vocabulary and way of thinking. Prior to the coining of *network* as a term to define a support system and a means of connection to others, there was the phrase "old boys' club" (OBC). While the meaning of both networking and old boys' club is similar, networking encompasses a broader concept than OBC, as a network is not limited in definition to a male support system.

Both network and OBC imply a set of fundamentally instrumental relationships in which the goal is the use of one another's resources or connections. The drive for those connections suggests a fuller experience of mutuality—not just taking and using, but giving and being present in ways that enable all parties involved to come to know, trust, and support one another.

Networking as a support allows those within a system to move from one-on-one relationships to multiple relationships and to access information not otherwise readily available. Networking signifies actively working on problems and issues with others; it also implies moving up through the offices in a service organization and hints at gladhanding influential clients or members of the board of directors. Most of all, however, networking is *knowing and connecting with those who can help you*.

Networking is important to you as an aspiring administrator because, regardless of who is doing the networking, the process of that interaction will affect you. If you are not a part of it, you risk being isolated from informal channels of what is happening, who's doing what, and where the job openings are going to be—information not generally known by those not in the loop. You cannot disregard the network in any system; it is there and, whether or not you choose to be a part of it, the network will affect you. While you might have prided your independence in the classroom or in an entry-level administrative position, disregarding the network is too high a price to pay for standing alone. The world does not operate in seclusion, and you will be left behind if you remain too independent.

Formal and Informal Networking

The formal network in an educational institution is its organizational chart. Everyone knows the hierarchy, with its line and staff charts, circles and squares, solid lines and dotted lines, all depicting who is who in relationship to everyone else. (While webbing is a different way of structuring an organization, it is still a formal network system, in that there is a definite, prescribed relationship among and between positions.) Everyone in the organization is expected to go through the chain of command in reporting or in giving orders. There is a procedure, and it is followed.

In contrast, the informal network is composed of various characters and informal roles played by those characters. The informal network provides the links between and among those characters and is the organization's primary means of communication. This informal information network provides the *real* reasons behind the official ones for decisions made or actions taken by the organization. The informal organization may be obvious or it may be underground; however, it is always there, and is a very active system in the institution.

Deal and Kennedy (Conran, 1989) identify underground networkers as spies, storytellers, priests, whisperers, and cabals, and they believe that every organization has them to a greater or lesser degree:

1. Storytellers change reality to suit their own perceptions. The best of them are in the center of activity and always know enough of the real story to make their version believable to any eager listeners. Storytellers love to indoctrinate new employees.

2. Priests are the guardians of the institution's values. They have time to listen and they willingly give advice and offer solutions to dilemmas. They use stories, but always in relation to past events. They often see it as their duty to provide historical perspective because they are usually also the school's self-appointed historians.

3. Whisperers may be found anywhere on the hierarchical ladder. Their source of power is that they provide information directly to the chief administrative officer. They are astute in reading the mind of the CEO and tap their sources throughout the organization to find information for her or him. Whisperers are intensely loyal to *whoever* is in charge, and their loyalty changes accordingly.

4. Gossips are the "know-it-alls" of the present. They make it their business to befriend all new staff and learn enough from them to appear to others as if they are the confidantes and mentors of the newcomers. Gossips reinforce the culture, and can be instrumental in increasing or decreasing others' reputations. Gossips like larger audiences than either storytellers or priests.

5. Spies are usually loyal buddies who keep administrators informed about what is going on. The best of them are well-liked and have access to many different people and sources. Their positions are usually secure because they are unthreatening in that they have no career ambitions other than being the boss's eyes and ears.

6. Cabals are groups of two or more people who secretly join together to plot a common purpose, usually that of promoting themselves or one of them at a time. Cabals are not highly regarded by the administrator in charge (Conran, 1989).

As the administrator, you should acknowledge that this informal, sometimes underground, network exists and find trustworthy individuals who themselves may have access to their motives and actions and who can forestall any potential harm to you. While you need to acknowledge all of these characters and their subcultures, you do not need to be placed in an uncompromising position by them. Proceed with caution.

Networking Lessons Learned

Many people have a skewed view of networking in that they think it is false and self-serving. Such may have been true at one time, but in today's world, networking is the acceptable way people do business. There is, no doubt, insincerity to the networking system in some instances, but taken all in all, networking is both necessary and mutually beneficial. I like to think of it as an extended circle of friends.

As one who did not enter administration until her forties, I was secure in my own success as a classroom teacher who believed strongly in merit, integrity, and responsibility. "Who needs a support system, let alone a network?" I used to scoff. It would annoy me to see my husband, a career high school principal, "working the crowd," as I called it. He insisted it was a sincere effort to meet and greet people, but it wasn't until years later that I saw he was absolutely right! Because he was an extrovert and I am an introvert, I assumed we simply had a difference in style. He enjoyed talking to people and could shake hands and be very cordial, even to the point of sharing a laugh with someone with whom he had had a dispute earlier in the day. It didn't matter whether the person he was chatting with was a superior who may have taken issue with him on some matter or a teacher or student whom he had had to reprove. His manner, after the issue was over, was one of more than just civility; it was downright friendliness. I would say to him, "Why were you so nice to that person?"

It took a lot of practice for me to learn to be comfortable in similar situations. I remember feeling very awkward the first few times I shook hands with people I met during my administrative preparation program and in the early stages of my administrative career. Now shaking hands comes as second nature.

Other lessons I have learned about networking is that it really does make life easier for everyone if you know the people you are dealing with in a setting other than the business at hand. As an educational consultant I meet many people in upper administrative positions and have found almost all of them to be wonderfully open and caring individuals. All it took on my part was to be friendly and to express an interest in what they were trying to accomplish. I learned a lot, not only about their work, but also about them as people. I now realize that the aloofness that I used to attribute to them was really my own shyness. I am not presuming to say that networking is simple, but for women, sometimes that initial getting over the nervousness is the most difficult part of connecting.

There are many other ways in which networking occurs; it is not all handshakes and smiles, even though that is often the beginning of personal networking. Linking (networking) can also be carried out through conferences, telephone calls, air travel, books, professional organizations, workshops, social gatherings, mutual friends, professional development, graduate courses, committees, and advisory boards on a county, regional, state, or national level. Serving on state committees or as an officer in your professional organization, or as a presenter at conferences, provides many opportunities to network.

Again, drawing on my own experience and that of other administrators of my acquaintance, I have found that making a concentrated effort to become visible and to be involved is one of the best ways to be in the mainstream of things. Whenever my superintendent asked me to represent the school or to attend events in his stead, I eagerly agreed. Even though I was not always authorized to speak for him or to cast his vote on an issue, I always learned something of value, and, better yet, I learned to know other superintendents in a way not otherwise possible. These kinds of occasions are to be embraced; they will broaden your perspective and, possibly, your opportunities.

Classmates in your administrative preparatory or degree program will become a special kind of network. They are already people on whom you can rely for advice and, sometimes, comfort. Those with whom you share the struggles of an administrative program are likely to be the only ones with whom you can discuss some issues, both because you are likely to be in similar professional positions and because you trust one another. In addition, they are very often the people who will be hiring, or who will know of openings. Value these relationships and the opportunities made through them, and cherish the friendships above the favors you may or may not be able to do for one other. Best of all, it is from friends that you learn the truth.

If you are fearful that you cannot network once you enter administration, set those fears to rest. The problems shared by administrators are more similar than the problems faced in the classroom, and you will find discussing these problems among colleagues much easier than discussing classroom management or teaching strategies with teaching peers. Part of the reason is that your self-confidence level is raised as you enter administration. Be assured that you will find support from fellow administrators, both in your own institution and in outside meetings you attend. Administrators are a friendly lot, and welcoming to those new to the ranks. It won't take long before you are a part of the network.

The Male Network

As with all other administrative and organizational strategies, men and women do not network in the same way. The male network is described by Carol Kleiman in her book *Women's Networks*, as cited by Schmuck (1986):

> It is secret and it is informal, but it is such an inbred, automatic response that men don't think twice about it. Good Old Boys don't say, "Well, today is the day to pick out one of our own as the new vice-president in charge of transportation." They just do it. Men grow up knowing all about how to network. They play team sports. They are taught to collaborate and work with each other. They learn not to hold grudges. They learn to share. Along with reading, writing, and arithmetic, they absorb the fact that they *need each other* [to advance]. (p. 61)

Men's OBC networking system has three primary characteristics: it is unconscious, informal, and private. Men don't make conscious decisions about whether or not to join the network. They are a part of it just by virtue of *being men*. They do not have to explain, justify, or even comment on being with "the old boys." The buddy system, the old boys' network, or the old boys' club—whatever it is called—is the informal establishment and an understood construct that does not require clarification. There are no guides to networking for men. Networking just *is*.

Women's Networking

Women's networking is a different story. While women recognize that the ladder to success is supported by networking, they also realize that the usual OBC and its methods will not work for them. As a result, a number of popular trade books have been written for women. Although we cannot imagine a book titled *Networking Secrets for Men*, we acknowledge the need for this kind of guidebook for women.

Women have had to duplicate a process that had no definition. They were faced with delineating something intangible, something that is, as stated above, unconscious, informal, and private. Women, even though they play together as girls, do not internalize the lesson learned by men that they *do* need one another. According to Schmuck (1986), "For women to network, they must consciously acknowledge that (a) 'I am a woman,' and (b) 'I am a woman who must connect myself to other women'" (p. 61).

Quietly, women have been developing an alternative to the traditional old boys' club because they realized that men's ways are not suited to women's schedules or preferences. Rather than cocktail hour gatherings, business card exchanges, or sports events, women prefer more individual and personal ways of connecting. Following are several nontraditional ways women have originated to network with one another:

- **Online groups.** WomenWIT (Women, Insights, Technology) (www.worldwit.org) is a global online and offline network. Typical online messages include job postings or questions ranging from how to fire a friend to how to find lodging for a college student in another city. Offline, groups have been formed in specific cities, regions, and countries, including MassWIT in the Boston area.
- **Book clubs.** While seemingly unrelated to networking, book clubs can be the beginning of great personal and business relationships. One such club began as a discussion group about women's career issues and has become a professional resource for its members. "It turned out to be good for business although it wasn't created for that," says its founder, who has secured clients for her company through contacts she made at the book club. "The women get to know each other as people first, and people like to do business with people they like."

- **Dinner groups.** Professional women who work for Sun Microsystems in the Boston area meet for dinner the first Wednesday of each month to discuss their jobs and career issues. Because about half of Sun's 35,000 employees work out of their homes or satellite offices, the night out helps the women feel less isolated from each other, says one of the members. Breakfast or lunch groups can also be effective.
- **Hobby groups.** Such groups can be started with a few people who share an interest or through a source called Meetup (www.meetup .com). Those involved in these groups say they share information on a topic or hobby, but end up forming relationships that go in all different directions. A member of a group that meets for parlor games (in contrast to men's poker nights) notes, "You talk about your thoughts and feelings and break down barriers."
- Other possibilities include manicure salons or spa sessions for groups who schedule a common time. According to one participant, "We know business opportunities exist or we wouldn't be meeting, but this gives us a chance to learn about each other as women" (Capell, 2004).

Women can also become involved in the Women's Caucus of their state association of school administrators, where they have opportunities to attend seminars such as "Women Preparing for the Principalship," "How to Negotiate a Superintendent's Contract," and "Networking Women in Academe."[1] Such seminars are very supportive for aspiring administrators and also demonstrate that women cannot and should not replicate the networking system of men.

Boys and Girls Together

William Goldman, in his seminal novel of the 1960s, struck a chord in those who were growing up in early 1960s with his realistic and sensitive insight into the relationships formed between and among boys and girls (*Boys and Girls Together*, 1967). Goldman, with a refrain haunting yet today, revealed—without ever using the term (not yet coined)—how networking operated. In tracing the lives of his fictional boys and girls, he staged a masterpiece of understanding of how relationships evolve and, in doing so, showed why men succeed in making the right connections and why women do not.

As a rule, women's strongest relationships are with other women; however, such relationships do not usually provide entry to professional networking. In the educational workplace, women do not congregate, leaning against the windows and chatting prior to the first morning class. They have not made the social contacts that sports provided to the men on their own high school or college teams, in their current coaching, or even in their Monday morning quarterbacking of the games attended or viewed the previous weekend. These social contacts and skills, which are second nature to men, are not usable skills when men and women network in the same stream. Nor can we assume that women who play sports—even as stars—can interact with men that way men interact among themselves. I recently observed a young woman, who had been a star basketball player on a collegiate team that had placed in the national championships, with a mixed group at the opening convocation of a new academic year. Presently employed in the development office of the same university, she displays an air of quiet confidence. Even so, from my vantage point of participant-observer, I noted that the conversations men held with her during that morning mixer were strained, more from their part than hers, but still strained. I could easily understand why other women, with perhaps less assurance and fewer conversational topics in common with men, would find such a situation even more difficult. That scenario was also a reminder to me how men generally look past most women in such settings, as I began to feel like the invisible woman, but then I don't play basketball.

To not allow ourselves to be left standing alone, whether physically or metaphorically, women need to build on their own strengths of affiliation, caring, and nurturing. Our networking needs to stand on the strengths of women. We need to view the areas women see as needing improvement as opportunities to establish professional relationships and bonding, which encourage confidence and affirm female identity. Women need to weave their own webs of connection, where talent is nurtured and encouraged, where there are a variety of interconnections, where lines of authority are less defined, and where there is a reliance on a moral center.

However, the fact still remains that women must network with men, and not just with other women, because men still hold the power positions in most organizations, particularly in educational institutions, even those with women as board presidents. Men have the experience and status, and they can provide sound advice. The trick is to learn from them and use what is learned to your advantage. As has been said before in this book, do not be afraid to go to both men and women and ask for advice, either specific to a desired position or advice in general as to how to "throw your hat in the ring." Most people will be pleased to be asked for their advice and will assist you, if only to tell you how difficult the path to an administrative position will be. However, what is important is that you will have established a contact.

You may be pleasantly surprised as you make these contacts just how attuned some men will be. They don't always interact ideally (according to women), but at least many more men are making the effort. One successful executive in a major telecommunications company immediately comes to mind. After working with Philip for more than a year, I shared a concern I had. We had just concluded a committee meeting of a volunteer group in which every man at the table had been asked if he would be interested in serving in a particular capacity, while the women had been ignored. I recounted for Philip my observations and he listened intently, without interruption. When he responded, he admitted that maybe he wasn't as gender aware as he needed to be. That conversation was the beginning of a far more relaxed and collegial relationship between the two of us. Sometimes, as in this case, all that is needed to initiate a relationship that can result in networking is to take the time to talk informally after a business meeting.

The more you make connections, return telephone calls, and go forward to introduce yourself, the more people you can later call for advice on anything of a professional nature. Accept that men's ways of networking are different, but work within that difference by persevering. The more natural you can be, the less different you appear. Don't try to be one of the boys or even one of the girls; just work toward being a member of the network.

Women Networking with Men

Since the networking that aspiring administrators are most concerned with involves both men and women (even though predominantly men), it is women who will have to adapt. They must put the potential male contacts at ease and smooth the way to workable networking experiences.

In mixed-gender settings, women and men should open with neutral conversations, picking topics everyone feels comfortable with: current events, movies, even the weather. Both genders need to be conversant in educational issues as well as finances and governmental agencies. In addition, a sense of humor is helpful. It is often difficult for women to understand that in many situations, pecking order, status, and ultimate acceptance is based on humor.

An easy way for women to gain experience in this style of conversation is through membership in service organizations such as Rotary, Lions, or Kiwanis clubs. This club setting is a bit more comfortable than a professional arena where your job may be at stake. In most service organizations, there is no professional competition, so you can practice your ripostes without jeopardizing your career.

Special Interest Networks

Special interest groups, such as superintendents' councils or state university associations of provosts, are established for the purpose of networking and discussion of topics related to the interests of the professional position. These networks can be invaluable, but you must understand the cardinal rule that privacy of the group and the individuals in it must be respected, and there must be an understanding that what is said there, stays there.

Close attention is required to maintain these relationships. The environment must be safe, with no competition. In such networking groups, problems can be discussed without fear of information leaking. For example, if you are a member of a special interest group, you may request reaction and input from those who may have faced situations similar to those you face at your institution, yet who do not necessarily have a vested interest in your institution.

In an atmosphere of such security, you are free to look at alternatives to solving problems and to have the benefit of brainstorming with an audience that is not biased concerning the decision you must make. While this group should not be compared to support groups that meet for therapy or counseling, there is a similarity in that the confidentiality, the effort to curb defensiveness, and the ability to see solutions for others more easily than for oneself are common to both kinds of groups. The difference is that the special interest network sessions are not dealing with emotions. Their purpose is not social, but is for tending to common issues or problems faced by individual members in their administrative responsibilities.

If you are in an area with a large enough number of female administrators, you may want to form a special interest networking group for women. You should have at least twelve members with similar positions in order for the group to be effective. If this is not feasible, form a small support group in the original sense of the word. This will at least give you a safe haven in which to discuss mutual concerns.

Body Language (Again)

Body language is a part of verbal networking. If you are seen as approachable, you will find it easier to meet new people and have conversations. Because in discussions of feelings or attitudes only 7 percent of the message is conveyed through choice of words, while a full 55 percent is conveyed by facial expression and 38 percent by tone of voice, it is important to present your message with positive body language. Make sure that the message your body is conveying is consistent with what you say. People may not consciously interpret nonverbal signals, but they do react to them. If your body language and your words are not saying the same thing, you create an enormous credibility problem.

The "safe" distance between persons talking in a social situation is one to three feet. Most people are disconcerted by those who encroach on their space, so watch your approach. Greet associates with a firm handshake, reserving a kiss or double-handed handshake for very close friends. Do not make the mistake of assuming that the two-handed shake is more friendly; it also can be interpreted as being patronizing.

Your height can also be a factor in networking interaction. Since you cannot change your size, you may have to make adaptations. If you are short, you need to concentrate on appearing confident and in charge. If you have a choice on where you stand, avoid juxtaposition with tall people. Upon joining a group, try to stand by someone near your own size. Tall women must try to avoid seeming to intimidate those who are shorter. Stand a few inches further away than you would from someone your own height. Take your time in entering the room, pause occasionally, and try to relax, but maintain excellent posture and walk energetically. Be aware that space is related to status; the more space we use, the higher our status.

Networking Referrals

As you develop your networking relationships, find a way to be of service to others. Before you ask someone to do something for you, look for ways to be friends—to do some service for that person and be willing to give more than you receive. When asking for a referral, or any help that may, in turn, reflect on the person whose assistance you are requesting, make sure the reference knows your job responsibilities and how well you fulfill them. Be gracious if a network contact declines to help, and show gratitude through personal notes when receiving help.

Networking as a Sales Technique

By its very nature, networking presumes that you have a business reason for wanting to talk to someone. The skill of the conversation lies in introducing people to what you have to offer without offending them by seeming to be too forceful. Keep in mind that in networking, you are supposed to give first. If you first make a contribution, people are more likely to trust you and want to work with you. The following tips may be useful:

1. Don't be too aggressive. On the first meeting—or any other time—don't overload someone with too much information.
2. Attend structured professional meetings, where promoting your services is an expected part of the agenda.
3. Take an active role. Be visible, sign up for a leadership position, chair a meeting, edit the newsletter, volunteer for committees.

How to Get the Most for Your Investment

Networking will not happen naturally. You must structure it. You must make the contacts. If you are new at this, begin by making specific appointments to meet with people and by attending professional activities. Look for seminars and conferences with set agendas, so that there is a forum in which you can begin discussions with others. This will eliminate the awkwardness you may feel with initial introductions. You might even want to prepare in advance, so that you can ask informed questions and make appropriate comments during the sessions.

Another way to structure introductions and to define your purpose is to volunteer to work at the registration table for the conferences you attend. This gives you the chance to see who is there and to better match names with faces.

Other ways to see and be seen were addressed in chapter 1. These suggestions include writing for publication, offering to help with newsletters, corresponding with others in your field (or in positions to which you are aspiring), making presentations, and serving as an officer in organizations. (Program chairman is a good position, as it can serve as a way to contact people to serve as speakers for your meetings.)

Barriers: Our Own and Others

Every list enumerating the barriers that hinder the advancement of women in administration includes lack of networking skills. As most of the factors associated with advancement are in some way connected to networking, the lack of networking skills is further compounded. Mentors, sponsors, and role models; lack of encouragement from both men and women; cultural, social, emotional, mobility, and attitudinal barriers; training that is often male oriented; limited interviewing skills; general lack of confidence; and a later entry into the field all are tied closely to networking.

There is some evidence that our greatest strengths as women—our caring and sensitivity—also define our greatest weaknesses: overpersonalizing, lack of self-confidence, and ambivalence about competition. According to Helene Lerner-Robbins, a management consultant who worked with Fortune 500 companies to address women's issues (Harnischfeger, 1994),

In relationships women naturally reach out, to nurture and to be nurtured. It's when we enter the workplace with its hierarchical structure that we're in conflict: We want to reach out, but the workplace fosters competitiveness. But our strength and success lie in our ability to bond in the workplace. We really need to learn a new vocabulary to come together. (p. 56)

None of these barriers, however, is as discouraging as the impediments placed by women themselves. Women may expect too much from those of their own gender, and assume that because all are women, they will stand up for one another. Such is not always the case. Women are people and people are not always supportive of others. Some women who see others of their kind get ahead are not as gracious as they might be. Some women are jealous that others have moved ahead in their career paths, for reasons as far reaching as a belief that women should be home in the evenings tending to their families or the career women's serving as reminders that they themselves have not made any plans to further their own careers. Some who are particularly jealous defy or will even try to undermine their peers who are aspiring to administrative positions (Woo in Gupton and Slick, 1996).

Beware the Queen Bee

This conflict is particularly graphic in the phenomenon of the Queen Bee Syndrome, the situation in which a woman who makes it into management neglects to support the advancement of other women. A Queen Bee resists efforts to include women among her ranks for a number of reasons, including the fun of being the only woman, wanting the rewards of her hard work to be hers alone, and believing that she has succeeded and those who do not succeed should blame themselves.

In defense of these women, we must keep this phenomenon in perspective; most of the Queen Bees fought hard—mostly without support from either women or men. Their style is not collegial or participatory, as they patterned themselves on the male management style. They did what they had to do at the time in which they entered management or administrative positions. They also may believe that the newer women coming into administrative posts neither appreciate nor understand that the "pioneers" had to achieve their positions against all odds and often at great personal sacrifice and much loneliness.

When you find Queen Bees, give them the deference they have earned, much as you honor any historical vanguard, but do not seek them for your network or as mentors. Let them know you appreciate their achievements in cracking a few glass ceilings, for they did not have the equal opportunities now beginning to open to you. Be gentle and generous, for they are not of this new world and their ilk is a waning breed.

Arrogant Women Administrators

This also may be the place to warn aspiring and new women administrators to *not* be arrogant or condescending once you reach a position of authority. You are going to need your former network of teachers, particularly if you ascend in your home district, and you must include them in your networking system. Don't separate yourself too far from your roots.

Bear in mind that your new position does not automatically entitle you to a greater personal status. An attitude of superiority is particularly irritating to the rank and file who view new "star-struck" administrators as forgetting whence they came. A wise friend—and astute observer—remarked that some administrators were not even competent, let alone outstanding, teachers, yet once they reached management positions they believed the position anointed them as experts in everything, making them even better than those who remained in the classroom.

Never forget that some great educators remain teachers all their lives and are not to be viewed as lesser because they chose not to go into management. Remember, it usually is *not* administrators who have lasting positive effects on individual students.

MENTORING

Mentoring is defined as guidance, training, support, and one-on-one counseling that can be both formal and informal. The term *mentor* has its origins in Homer's epic poem, *The Odyssey*, in which Odysseus entrusted the education of his son Telemachus to his trusted friend and counselor, Mentor. The term has continued to mean an older, more experienced guide who trains a younger, less experienced newcomer in the ways of a profession or business. Until recently, most mentors and those they mentored were men.

The system of mentoring simply evolved and there was little written about the relationship or the process. Since the entry of ever increasing numbers of women into the ranks of aspiring managers and administrators, mentoring has become more of an issue and, in some organizations, more formalized.

Traditional Mentoring

Traditionally and historically, a mentoring relationship was an informal process. It was a chance relationship based on common goals and interests. Mentors were not, and still are not usually, assigned, although that is changing in some corporations. A mentor typically enters a person's life at a time when changes are about to occur, helps the person, and either departs as a mentor or remains as a friend.

Mentors do a lot of different things. They counsel and advise, possibly open doors to new opportunities, and provide connections and introductions. They instruct those they are mentoring in the ways of the profession, its formal processes, and informal networking. They smooth the way, introducing their protégées to others who can help them; they advise as to career moves; and they offer personal advice, if needed, on such things as appearance, speech, and any other characteristic that may be used to evaluate the protégées' qualifications. Mentors can save time and provide shortcuts for those they are mentoring, advantages that might otherwise come only after a more circuitous path. Mentoring is considered a very powerful training tool and the one that is most likely to guarantee mobility within an organization.

Mentoring has become an important focus in a person's career path, and more aspirants are seeking mentors. Administrative positions have become much more competitive, and more aspirants are seeking an edge in the job market. Mentoring provides this edge. Further, mentors are found to be *critical* to the advancement of women. That finding has had a major impact on the concept and practice of mentoring. Any time there are more people than positions available, there will be a problem, and applicants are finding that one solution to finding positions is through mentoring.

The practice of mentoring has been compounded by the fact that more men are mentors than women; it therefore follows that more men than women are being mentored because men are more likely to mentor men than they are to mentor women. In addition, even the few women, proportionately, who are in positions of power do not mentor as much or as often as men in comparable positions. Aspiring female administrators are thus faced with a series of mentoring dilemmas:

1. There are more men in administrative positions. As a result, there are more men available to serve as mentors.
2. Of this available number of potential male mentors, a high percentage are willing to serve as mentors.
3. There are fewer women in administrative positions. As a result, the pool of potential female mentors is small.
4. Of this pool of potential female mentors, only a small percentage are willing to serve as mentors.
5. Men prefer to mentor other men because (a) they are more comfortable working with people like themselves, (b) people tend to promote people like themselves, and (c) for obvious reasons there is an added risk in mentoring someone of the opposite sex.
6. Women are more reluctant than men to ask someone to serve as their mentor.
7. Men are scrambling for mentors because they see their chances for advancement decreasing as more women enter the job pool.

Legislation and affirmative action programs have helped women in their pursuit of administrative opportunities, but mentoring relationships cannot be legislated. The mentoring process must be voluntary and intentional in order to work because both parties must want to be involved in the relationship.

Of great help to women has been the trend toward formal mentoring programs established by companies and professional organizations. The major advantage of these formalized programs is that they provide readily accessible opportunities for capable people to be mentored and for more experienced people to become mentors. These programs do not rely on luck or chance in finding a mentor. Furthermore, they ensure that women and minorities will have mentors. Formal, structured mentoring programs lead to a faster mentoring process because they eliminate the need for sending signals, responding to signals, and the bonding that is necessary for successful programs to begin.

Formal mentoring programs have been helpful in meeting the needs of women and minorities and also have given organizations the opportunity to provide services to their members. However, to be more effective, organizations need to go a step further in requiring that mentors be trained, perhaps with an added incentive of earning professional in-service credits. With more attention being paid to these mentoring needs, opportunities for women to find mentors should increase. Until that time, however, mentoring opportunities for women continue not to meet the need.

An often unspoken roadblock in men mentoring women is the belief by some that because mentoring is such an intense relationship, a man and a woman can't engage in this working affiliation without a love or sexual relationship forming. Because of this potential risk, many from both genders shy away from what could be excellent mentoring relationships.

Another drawback for mentoring women is that the task is different than it is for mentoring men with similar career potential and aspirations. In a study conducted by Ann Schneider (1991), the findings indicate these differences:

- Women require more feedback and frequent monitoring to develop assurance.
- Mentors need to model and reinforce strategies more frequently with women.
- Women need more mentor-initiated contact.
- Relationships with women are longer in term.
- Women remain in a readiness phase longer than do men. (The women felt they needed more time to prepare for the role to which they aspired.)
- Women spend more time in each mentoring stage.
- Men who mentor women must expect that personal crises and individual needs will surface in the mentoring relationship.

Despite all that has been written of the need for women to help
women and the fact that women administrators should realize how
important mentoring is, current research continues to indicate that
women administrators are not carrying their weight as mentors to other
women.

Gardiner, Enomoto, and Grogan (2000) report that most of the
women in their study desired a female mentor yet had not connected
with anyone. Of a conversation with five women currently in educational
leadership positions, Sobehart and Giron (2002) report that the women
spoke openly about the reality of threat and competition among women
who may vie for a single top spot. They agreed that with as few as 10 to
15 percent of the top positions currently occupied by women, there are
plenty of top spots to go around, and that the excuse of "helping the
competition" was no reason to not mentor.

Alternatives to Mentoring

Ruth Owades, founder and CEO of Gardeners Eden and Calyx &
Corolla, says,

> I never had the female mentor I would like to have had. But I did have a
> wonderful collection of professors and teachers who encouraged me. My
> brother was very smart and preceded me everywhere. But one of my
> grade school teachers took me aside and said, "You are Ruth, and you are
> very smart and capable," implying that I did not have to live in my
> brother's shadow. I think that had an enormous impact on me, though
> then I had no idea what she was talking about. (Godfrey, 1992, p. 155)

Mentors may not be where you expect to find them, and may not even
want to think of themselves as mentors, but rather as advisors or "sounding boards." Take them where you find them and if you need to be the
one to make the contacts, do so. People you meet and contacts you make
while networking can serve as individual advisors when you cannot find
a permanent mentor.

Women can write their own rules for their mentoring style. There are
many alternative ways to connect without needing to be in the same organization or even in the same state. You can devise a formal program

or a basic "keep in touch" approach. Whatever works for your particular situation is the style you should pursue, whether you are the mentor or the one being mentored. Consider any of the following—some typical and others not—as possibilities to meet your needs:

1. Go out to breakfast, lunch, or dinner with other women.
2. Try to interest someone you have met at a nonprofit organization.
3. Keep your eyes open to any opportunity, such as a meeting or seminar.
4. Try a long weekend retreat with several other aspiring and practicing women administrators.
5. Consider an electronic mentoring relationship through one of the computer bulletin boards.
6. Establish a long-distance mentoring relationship via letter.
7. Keep in touch by telephone.

If you can find no attentive mentor, no guide, and no support group, turn to the women peers of your acquaintance. A study group can be an excellent source of support and provide honest feedback in a secure environment. Another possibility is the Women's Caucus of the American Association of School Administrators. This organization provides leadership opportunities for its female members.

The Committee of 200 is another possibility. Founded in 1982, the Committee of 200 (www.c200.org) is a national organization of women in the executive ranks of business and industry whose contacts with each other allow useful exchanges of information and support. The National Association for Female Executives (www.nafe.com) is another good place to start. This group has regional or local groups in most states. That information can be found on their website; begin there because the local groups do not all use the same name.

Also consider the American Association of University Women. This group, founded in 1881, is the strongest advocacy organization for the education of women and equality in the workplace. Membership is not limited to those in higher education. Their resources are many, so visit their website at www.aauw.org. There are also other professional organizations that should be able to offer assistance. Seek them out and join the ones in the specialty to which you are aspiring.

Another pathway to consider is private leadership coaching. This is common practice among corporate CEOs and middle and upper management in business.[2] Leadership Coaching for School Change is one such program of executive coaching that provides confidential, ongoing support for school leaders, identifying strengths and weakness, and helping the leaders make the changes they need to reach their goals.

At the beginning of each relationship between coach and school leaders, a baseline assessment is conducted of each leader's strengths and areas for development. This becomes the basis for improvement and provides more self-awareness for the leader. The assessment also helps the leaders see why certain problems may arise. Following a half-day kick-off session, four months of weekly, 45-minute follow-up sessions are held by telephone. These coaching sessions are always private, enabling coach and leader to brainstorm solutions to challenges they are facing. Each session ends with specific actions to implement during the week. According to Karla Reiss, a coach for Leadership Coaching for School Change, the process is effective, in part, due to the accountability built into the coaching relationship (Reiss, 2003).

The affiliation is always confidential, enabling an open and honest conversation about growth areas, leadership crises, and the obstacles that prevent leaders from implementing new practices and policies in their districts. It differs from mentoring in many ways, although both roles focus on helping the client succeed. A mentor is one who has been in the role (job position) of the other person and shares experiences, while a coach has specialized training in the process of change and hundreds of hours of practice developing coaching skills (Reiss, 2004).

In addition, there are numerous published articles available for you to educate yourself. Some are in current professional journals, and others are available through ERIC (Education Resources Information Center) and other electronic retrieval services. Further, there are a number of books written in the past few years that offer advice on mentoring. There are even professional associations on mentoring, including the Mentoring Institute. And, finally, there are other guidebooks in the field written especially for women who are aspiring educational administrators. You may have to be your own mentor. Many of us were!

NOTES

1. These are sample sessions from the Women's Caucus, 2004, of the Pennsylvania Association of School Administrators.

2. In November 2001, MetrixGlobal LLC reported an almost 529 percent return on investment for an executive coaching program for a Fortune 500 company. The company using executive coaching placed its value at more than five times the cost and increased the value to 788 percent when including financial benefits from employee retention and improved culture (Reiss, 2003).

(12)

POLITICS AND ETHICS

Had this book been written a generation ago, there would be no need for a full chapter on politics and ethics. Whether it is only in retrospect that we view the past with naiveté or whether there really was not the strong political influence on education does not matter. What is important is that schools were not political in the sense they are today, and the typical practicing administrator did not think in terms of ethics. This is not to say that people were not ethical, just that *ethics* was not deliberated the way it is today.

With the increased awareness of the political system in education, there also has been a growing interest in the study of ethics, as problems pertaining to ethics are viewed as political when they are collective. No longer relegated to the religious community, ethics and ethical decision making have become a popular topic in education, as well as in other areas such as business, medicine, and law. One cannot help but speculate that the need for understanding ethics is a direct result of the growing politicization occurring in education.

POLITICS

When I first entered teaching, I recall a visit to my classroom by the county superintendent. A tall, pleasant gentleman, he reminded me of the school visitor in "Among School Children" by William Butler Yeats (1926). The only difference is that he was not there to see the schoolchildren but rather to ask me about myself and the process of my being hired. I thought it rather odd at the time, but I told him of reading in the newspaper the preceding spring that a new school district had been formed, the junior-senior high school was to open in the fall, and the administration was seeking teachers. I told the gentleman that being part of a new school appealed to me. I explained how I first had had difficulty finding the small town, that the interview had taken place in a basement office on the square, how kind the secretary had been, and that I had been offered a position a few days after the interview. I did not see this as anything but very routine.

It was not until some weeks after the county superintendent's visit that someone explained that this gentleman had been checking for political appointments. It had not occurred to me that such things happened; in fact, it was not until many years later that the ramifications of "political appointment" became clear as I began to interview for administrative positions. In the 1960s I thought "politics" meant whether or not I was of the prevailing political party in the county. In the 1980s I came to see that "politics" meant a lot more, as I began to encounter my share of politically *wired* job interviews.

Beyond the politics of hiring, however, today's educational institutions have become political in nearly every aspect of the organization. Numerous interest groups, a dramatic surge of educational legislation at both the state and federal levels, controversial court cases, contested school board elections, contracts for supplies, ousted college presidents, short-tenured superintendents, citizen tax groups, powerful coaches' cliques, and lobbying efforts by teacher professional organizations are just a few of the ways the political nature of educational institutions is brought straight to our attention today.

Harry Broudy (1981) succinctly states the dilemma faced by public schools in the political arena: "The school operates on the principle that it must reinforce the ideals the community professes and not the behavior it tolerates" (p. 23). And therein lies the problem as well as the ethical dilemma. The educational institution is charged with upholding standards, while at the same time it is expected to make adjustments and exceptions for nearly every situation. In addition, educational institutions are constantly faced with and must respond to essentially political questions, such as what objectives should be emphasized and how resources will be allocated, along with who will determine who gets what, when they will get it, and how it will be accomplished.

As an administrator, you will have to answer these questions. The dilemma is that the process of answering is far more complicated than the questions. While you may be the educational leader, you will not unilaterally be making the decisions. Throughout this book we have referred to the overriding question of education: What should students know and be able to do by the time they are graduated from high school, college or university, or professional school? Even if you have the answer, consider all that is required in providing the curriculum necessary to fulfill that outcome. Who, what, when, and how all must be decided, planned for, and implemented. Who decides what is an appropriate education or what kind of system will bring it about? The answers to all of these questions are determined by politics.

At the core of politics is the notion that some individuals or factions will prevail over others by obtaining policies closer to their own preferences. Every stakeholder in the educational process and in the educational institution has a view as to how the educational system should operate. No two stakeholders will agree on every point, and there will be some issues on which it will be difficult to find two people who can agree at all. If you are a member of any organization, you no doubt have seen examples of this in action. Resolution of differences, and, consequently, political supremacy, is determined by influence, power, and authority. (See chapter 4.)

In education, the power question has shifted from "Who exercises power?" to the equally important question "Who benefits?" In any given community there has always been the question of who exercises the power in matters of the public school. Is it the political party to which the majority of the board members belong? A community's "power elite"? Is the education profession itself a kind of power broker? Are the teachers' unions, or are the students and their parents? With the question now being "Who benefits?" the question must be rephrased in terms of the recipient of what that power brings about. Does the political party benefit? The community power elite? The profession? Teachers' unions? Students or parents?

Who decides and who benefits? Should businesses have input since they (collectively) will be the utilizers of the educated students? If the schools are asking business and industry to help them, should not these benefactors have a say in the education of the students? What about major foundations? The Ford Foundation, the Carnegie Corporation, and the Kellogg Foundation are but three of the many charitable corporate foundations generous to education. Should they determine what policies are established? For example, the Getty Foundation sponsors many arts education programs, research, and policy. Should their advocacy of a particular process of arts instruction be the standard in the schools they fund?

In the case of public schools and state universities, the educational institutions are ultimately responsible to the citizens they serve. As such, should the citizens determine school policy? There is a tendency to say yes because we are a democracy and the schools are a reflection of the community. There is also an inclination to say no because most citizens have neither detailed knowledge of educational issues nor more than casual interest in how these issues are resolved. The astute (political) administrator will involve the citizens by keeping them informed and by asking them to serve on committees so that public opinion remains favorable. Yet how much influence should these groups have? While there is the tendency to believe that there is everything to gain and nothing to lose by having an informed citizenry, we should not lose sight of the fact that the public as a body politic is fickle. How, then, do we balance by including the public without being overrun by it?

Through the Murky Waters

How do you negotiate through the murky waters of school politics and survive? The single most important technique is to be honest and forthright. If you keep your word, do not hide the truth, and always get back to people, you will have a solid base on which to build your reputation. Notice that no one is saying to have an open-door policy—that is a matter of leadership style, not honesty. The honesty comes in having respect for others by showing them courtesy and regard for them as worthy persons. You won't like everyone and not everyone will like you, but giving and gaining respect is better than liking and being liked, so put your energies into what you can control. Try to remain above the fray and the cliques. Be friendly by standing "among them, but not of them."[1]

Always follow protocol. Even if you are told that everyone is equal and all doors are open, make sure *you* knock. Build a base of supporters not through favors, but through merit. Earn respect, not paybacks. Stand up for what you believe, but be ready to compromise (not your integrity, but some of your pet points) when it is time to reach consensus. Remember that as the leader, you will be followed. Make sure others follow because they believe in you, and not because they fear the authority with which you are imbued. Demonstrate that you care about the people in the organization through your taking time to listen to what they are saying. Be accepting of what is important to others and be tolerant if they do not share your values.

Be keenly aware of the political systems in your school. (This is a polite way of saying, "Watch your back.") Remember that because you are the leader, most people will be nice to your face, telling you things you want to hear. Make sure you stay grounded as to the agendas of your constituents. This is one reason why it is so important to establish advisory boards. (See chapter 10.) These groups will help you keep a pulse on the organization as well as build a *political* base of support.

Finally, do not make promises you cannot deliver. There are ways of reassuring others that you will consider their needs or requests without promising results they want. Make it very clear that you will give full attention to their needs, but that you require time to think about their requests. Never, ever, accept favors that may have strings attached. Make sure your recommendations are educationally sound, and not just pet projects. And certainly, never make recommendations that are primarily for your own benefit.

The Strategies of Politics

The strategies of politics for an educational administrator should be like the strategies used by power strategists who understand the significance of events without being influenced by current opinion or their own biases. Power strategists can make quick decisions. They also can follow through by taking necessary action without letting fear hold them back.

Following is a summation of characteristics and practices, found throughout this book, that are useful in planning power strategies. Even if your area of responsibility is limited at this time, by establishing these practices and developing your characteristics and/or style to match, you can become a political strategist to be reckoned with.

- **A vision.** Every great leader has a vision of what she or he would like the institution to look like. The vision serves as an orientation point to all who are a part of the institution. Your vision should so galvanize your constituents that it becomes the rallying point for all endeavors.
- **A mission statement.** Your institution's mission statement should reflect the vision and should appear in every office and in every classroom. The mission statement should also be published in every newsletter. If it is not too lengthy, a portion of it could be incorporated as part of the letterhead of the organization's stationery. I know at least one school district that has engraved the school's mission statement on the reverse side of the nameplates used by the school board during their public meetings. These placards serve as a constant reminder to the board members of their purpose.
- **A school philosophy.** A philosophy is the set of principles by which the institution operates. These principles should be stated in concrete terms and be in evidence at every board meeting.
- **A competitive edge.** You need to be aggressive in your pursuit of the goals and objectives of the organization. Your public needs to know that you offer the very best for the students.
- **Site-based management.** Your institution should act as a confederation of educational leaders, with each manager (e.g., building principal, dean, department chairman) vested with both authority and responsibility. These leaders should focus on the school's mission, but each leader must be given the latitude to carry out the mission with her or his own initiative and creativity.
- **Cooperative strategic planning.** All stakeholders should have input into the design of the strategic plan, and those charged with implementing the plan must support it.
- **A clear organizational culture.** The culture should reflect the strategic plan. It will, if you empower your staff and students to

take the initiative in implementing the goals and objectives of the institution. The culture also will be enhanced by an atmosphere of trust in and respect for all persons.

- **Openness to new approaches.** Listen to what others have to say and incorporate their good ideas into your own goals. Be humble and realistic enough to know that you personally do not have all the best answers.
- **Awareness.** The two little words "Be aware" can be very powerful in their full application, for true awareness opens vistas not previously considered.

Most of all, power political strategists are not deterred from their vision. They intuitively see the big picture, and remain above mundane matters, deliberately avoiding identification with them. They ask themselves, again and again, "What have I done to make this organization a better place?"

Being Politically Correct

The movement to be "politically correct" began its sweep in the 1980s and has come to mean many things, ranging from inclusionary language (nonsexist and nondiscriminatory) to a very politically active move toward multiculturalism and diversity. As an educator, you cannot ignore these political attitudes, as you are likely to be confronted by one or another interest group claiming that the institution you represent is either (a) not politically correct or (b) overreacting to political correctness.

The most immediate impact of political correctness (PC) appears to be on institutions of higher education with the central thrust involving the replacement of the traditional core curriculum—consisting of the great works of Western culture—with a curriculum flavored with minority, female, and Third World authors.

Opponents fear that in flavoring the traditional curriculum with minority, female, and Third World authors, we as a culture will lose too many of the traditional and historical studies known as the liberal arts. Those whose lives and thoughts were shaped by traditional studies are grieved by what some call the attempted brainwashing that deprecates Western learning.

The origin of the PC movement, or enlightenment, depending upon your point of view, lies in the belief that young Americans should be taught to live in and govern a multiracial and multicultural society. Immigration from Asia and Latin America, combined with relatively high minority birthrates among our own citizens, is changing the complexion of America, and many universities—as well as public schools—are creating samples of how a more diverse and pluralistic community might work for our society.

Opponents say they do not object to goals such as pluralism or diversity, but voice their concern about how these goals are being pursued. Criticism is particularly levied at universities that are accused of not carefully monitoring the special interest groups influencing the curriculum. Adversaries of PC fear that much of the traditional material is being replaced by authors of diverse ethnic backgrounds whose works have not been evaluated by any standard.

The battle over political correctness (or political balance) is far from over, as more minorities become majority voices, and as minority voices continue loudly to demand the establishment—or expansion—of women's studies, African American studies, and studies of other ethnicities, and to lobby strongly for the hiring of minority faculty. Proponents cry that minority faculty are needed to offer distinctive black, Hispanic, and Asian perspectives to scholarship and to students, while critics claim these voices are not always academically objective. Critics also fear that the colleges are being transformed from a place of learning to a laboratory of indoctrination for social change.

While not as prevalent in basic education as it is in higher education, political correctness has encroached into public schools. As schools wrestle with decisions of "what every student should know and be able to do," teachers and administrators alike are struggling with what should be included in the school's curriculum. If a school has a diverse population, should more ethnic history be included? Should alternative lifestyles be presented as acceptable or desirable? Should English be taught as a second language, with the courses being taught in the first language (native tongue) of the majority of the students in a given neighborhood elementary school? Should Milton be omitted because he was a Eurocentric white male sexist who arranged for his daughters to be taught to read Greek so that they could read to him in his blindness?

Should Wordsworth, whose wife and sister devoted their lives to his comfort (with sister Dorothy, in particular, serving as his personal secretary and note taker), be eliminated from the poetry collections for the same reason? Is George Eliot's work any better or worse because for twenty-four years she lived with George Henry Lewes, who was married to someone else? Or do these facts only add to our understanding of the authors' creative contributions to our literary heritage? Should a less well-written history text be used because it was written by an ethnic minority? Should you permit Bible clubs? Neo-Nazi student organizations? Gay boys' and girls' advisory councils?

Should you carefully monitor every article in the student newspaper so that inclusionary language is used, or is it enough to use inclusionary language only in the organization's newsletter? Do you need to form a review committee for all publications to make sure you are not offending any group represented in your student population or in your community? Can you schedule a Cultural Awareness Fair without offending the cultures being honored or without appearing to be patronizing? Should your hiring practices be revised in order to attract a population that will reflect your student body?

The answers to such questions will not be easy, for the controversy surrounding political correctness is likely to continue. You as an educational administrator must confront these issues as they apply to your institution. You must try to be objective in your approach to this prevalent trend. You must be sensitive to the views of all of your populations, but also be wary that in meeting the needs of the few, it is not at the sacrifice of the needs of the many.

Dealing with Difficult People

Politics doesn't stop at the classroom or office door. Politics has to do with not only the affairs or governance of the institution, but also the relationship of persons in the institution. While both administrators and teachers face their share of difficult people, teachers usually have most of their problem situations with their students, while administrators have more possibilities of encountering difficult people among their staff, and their skill in dealing with such persons can very much affect their success as a leader.

While it is not within the realm of this book to describe all of the difficult people you will encounter, you do need to know that there are techniques that can help you to effectively deal with most personalities. You may want to add to your library a book or two in which specific approaches are suggested for dealing with various difficult people. The major types, however, include the following.

Liars

There is no polite way to label liars except by that term. They do not deserve the dignity of a euphemism. Liars are the very worst people to have in any organization. They are sneaky, internal troublemakers, invisible and disrespectful, garnering attention from those gullible enough to believe them or foolish enough to be entertained by their lies.

The major problem in dealing with a liar is that you never know what else a liar might do in addition to lying. A liar is hard to catch, and when and if you do catch one, it will be extremely difficult to pin the person down. However, you cannot let liars get away with lying. Find them and stop them, not only for the sake of stopping them, but also so that no one on your staff sees you letting a liar get by.

There are two defenses against liars. One is fear, the other respect. The latter is the better choice. You need to project honesty and integrity by always being truthful yourself. If your staff members know that you are always truthful (except, perhaps, to tell a white lie, out of caring for someone's feelings), they will also be very reluctant to lie to you. Leading by example is the best way to deal with liars.

Naysayers and Faultfinders

Every organization has its share of naysayers and faultfinders, who also fall into the category of whiners and complainers. If you ask most educational leaders what part of their job is most difficult, it is likely they will answer, "Working with negative people." Negative people can ruin, or try to ruin, your best day, your best year, or your best attempts at school change. Naysayers erode your efforts to develop a pleasant atmosphere where most people are positive about their work and confident in themselves. They are hazards to your institution and everything good you are trying to build. Naysayers are constant irritants because you can't dismiss people for having a negative attitude. These persons are smug in that knowledge, and if they know they are annoying you, they may spread even more of their toxicity.

How can you neutralize the poison of the approximately 15 percent of the people in any organization who are negative? You'll have 10 percent who are positive, and 75 percent who are somewhere in the vast middle—the undecided majority who reflect on a situation before they decide to react negatively or positively. Your best tactic is to keep the undecided 75 percent informed with accurate, positive information. If you do not, the naysayers will provide only their viewpoint, while the positive 10 percent are unlikely to say anything, as they always look on the bright side.

You may be able to curb the activities of the faultfinders by counteracting their influence in the following ways:

- Be a good role model. Be positive in your own actions, and maintain an upbeat attitude. Consider the verbal and nonverbal messages you send. Show that you disapprove of negative people.
- Identify the negative people on your staff. These may not always be the obvious gripers; however, most negative people display a sour outlook on life. Use positive people to counter comments made by negative people, especially if the negative comments are made in an open meeting.
- Limit the leadership opportunities available to negative people. Place the positive people in positions of leadership, and if you are in a situation where the negative people are always the ones encouraged by their peers to volunteer for committees, don't ask for volunteers.
- Seek committee members in advance and appoint them. Or if you must open the membership to volunteers, make sure that in advance of the meeting, you have asked positive people to volunteer, and call on them first.
- Practice polite nonrecognition. Let the negative people have their say, but refuse to acknowledge their negative comments unless members of the majority express the same ideas, in which case you might want to attend to the comments.

- Avoid contact with negative people. Do not engage them in conversation, and when you see one approaching, greet the person and move on. Don't ask a naysayer how things are going. If you encounter negative people in the presence of others, respond to their negative comments with silence (Chalker and Hurley, 1993, pp. 25–26).

Another tactic with naysayers may sound contradictory to the above, but advice from business says that a good technique to use when people say negative things is to respond by asking for their advice (Wolter, 2004). Repeat their statement back to them and say, "You're right. Achieving the success rate we want can be difficult. What would you suggest to make it possible?" The thought behind asking naysayers for their suggestions is that they are used to people dismissing them rather than listening to their ideas. So, make them feel appreciated by being listened to. You may just gain an ally. As you listen to their suggestions, their defenses should fall. On the other hand, if they don't have an answer, case closed.

Time-Grabbers and Interrupters

Time-grabbers and interrupters do not realize that they are problem people. They usually think of themselves as friendly or helpful. They are not nearly as harmful as liars and naysayers, but they can be deterrents in your getting your own work taken care of. You need to develop strategies to deflect their good intentions. Following are typical time-grabbers and strategies you can use to deter them:

- "I Need Your Help with This." Make sure the person understands what is expected. Set up a time schedule for a progress report, but make it clear you do not expect a litany of events. Let the person know that you are counting on her or his ability to complete the job independently.
- "Can You Spare a Minute?" This is my personal pet peeve. I have found, however, that even when I reply, "Not right now," the requester still intrudes. The suggested method of defense is to reply that you can spare a minute, and then, when a minute has passed, right at that moment pick up your appointment book and schedule another time to meet with the interloper. (Saying, "Not right now.

Can we schedule another time for this call?" to an interruptive telephone caller may work in that situation as well.)

- "I Have an Urgent Problem." Everything for this person is an
  emergency, and you need to determine if you really want to be
  drawn in. Stress your own urgent business and suggest someone
  else who might be able to help this person who is always distressed.
- "Let Me Finish Telling You." If you can't stop this person with
  words because you are made to feel that you are interrupting, then
  take action. Pick up a paper, your pen, the phone, your coat—
  anything to signify that the conversation is over.
- "Drop What You're Doing and Do This Instead." If your superior
  makes a habit of wasting your time, you have two choices: (a) discuss it with her or him, or (b) say, "I'm working on the board report
  and will have it on your desk by the end of the day if I have no interruptions." This must, of course, be done with a smile.
- The Good Friend Who Just Wants to Talk. Chances are that if you
  do not do "drop-in" visits, neither will others. To discourage this
  further, suggest that the two of you have lunch together.
- "Don't Let Me Interrupt You." This is the person who walks in
  while you are on the phone or otherwise engaged. She or he may
  thrust a note under your nose, trying to get you to attend to her or
  his concern. Give this person the cold shoulder by ignoring such
  notes thrust upon you (adapted from "Foil the Time Grabbers,"
  1992, pp. 9–10).

These are but a few of the most obvious kinds of difficult people.
There are no doubt others as well, all of whom are vying for your precious time. Deal with them in a friendly but firm manner, basing your
approach on one of the techniques suggested.

Dealing with People Who Do Not Like You

While none of us likes to think that there are people who simply do
not like us, it is particularly difficult to be at odds with one who is your
immediate superordinate or subordinate. If your boss is new to the position you thought would be yours, there can be a tense situation. As
soon as it is possible, meet with this person and offer your support.

Chances are that someone has told this new person that you were in line for the position, so there is no need to feel secretive about the situation. Acknowledge that the choice has been made, and that your position is now to support the new agenda. If the person is gracious, she or he will accept this offer on your part, and will avail herself or himself of the skills you can use in furthering her or his vision. If, however, the new person sees you as a constant reminder of the competition she or he faced, any overtures on your part will be futile. In this situation, you should try to find another niche in the institution until you can remove yourself permanently.

When the person who is your subordinate does not like you, keep the relationship strictly business. If your initial extension of friendship is rebuffed, then meet with the person, lay out your objectives, explain the expectations, and make sure the person understands the reporting order. If things do not improve, you may need to hold a second meeting in which you verbalize your concerns and ask why the person is being resistant. If necessary, meet daily to review tasks and performance. At the same time, work hard at establishing and maintaining relationships with others. Do not allow one negative relationship to override the other positive ones.

If you run into a situation in which your secretary (or another support person) is hostile because she or he still feels loyalty to your predecessor, you need to have a straight talk with her or him. An elementary principal tells of her own situation in which her secretary had always prepared coffee for the former principal, and the new principal preferred to get her own. The secretary's feelings were hurt, as she wanted to bring the coffee. Ms. L _____ 's sensibilities were offended, as she saw herself as a very capable woman who did not want her secretary to play such a servile role. Neither is really to blame, although the secretary should be the one to comply with the personal preferences of the new principal.

ETHICS

Ethics, like politics, is also enjoying a renaissance of interest. Neither concept is new; both have their roots in antiquity, with public interest in each waxing and waning throughout history. In recent years we have seen a dramatic increase in journal articles on the subject of ethics. It was not too many years ago that the subject of ethics was mentioned only in passing in the typical textbook used in introductory courses in educational administration. Until recently, ethics was thought to be only in the purview of philosophy departments, and to mention ethics in the world of public education branded the speaker as self-righteous. The renewed interest in ethics likely is a realization that in a complex society, with many dilemmas facing decision makers, we need more than opinion to guide our actions.

Ethics, most philosophers agree, is a subset of morality. It is a systematic, rational reflection and/or judgment of morals. While ethics apply to morality, the term is not a synonym for morality. Morality refers to standards of human behavior, such as right and wrong, while ethics is based upon a set of principles that attempt to apply moral rules to specific situations. Ethics as a practice is typically applicable in environments in which professionals are expected to make moral choices among arguably correct alternatives. It has, however, lately been used when news writers don't want to say an action is *illegal*.

When viewed in the context of professional practice, sound professional judgment requires grounding in an understanding of ethics, its history, and philosophy. A profession, by its very nature, emphasizes responsibility for making ethical choices that go beyond informed judgment by not only accepting the rules, but accepting them because of understanding how they were derived and why they are currently accepted.

The Ethic of Justice

Most civilizations are governed by observing justice in which persons treat one another according to some standard that is (a) approved by most citizens in the society and (b) applied uniformly to all relationships between and among the citizens. Beginning with Socrates' exploration of the basis for justice in Plato's *Republic* and continuing through the work of Lawrence Kohlberg and his followers, a theory on the ethic of justice has evolved. It is, however, the work of Immanuel Kant and John Rawls that most closely relates to this ethic of justice.

Kant maintains that moral law dictates the following conclusion: An act has moral worth if it is done from the conviction that the principle of the action is capable of being universalized—that is, made applicable to all persons. Kant termed this a categorical imperative. It implies that no matter what may be desired, *the moral necessity to act is unconditional* (Witmer, 1989). "Act," said Kant, "as if the maxim of your own conduct were to become, by your will, the maxim of all the world's activity" (quoted in Witmer, diss., 1989, p. 97). One therefore must have the will to follow the moral law, regardless of profit or loss for herself or himself. She or he must, in short, perform the expected duty.

John Rawls' theory of justice expands upon the Kantian principle and aims to find principles to govern social and political life rather than individual behavior. It also begins from a moral basis. Rawls' theory of justice is an elaboration of a simple idea: A fair system of arrangements is one that persons can agree to without knowing how it will benefit them personally. In other words, *persons would make a decision based on not knowing how that decision would affect them personally* as individuals. Both Rawls and Kant call upon a person's reason and both agree that it is innate, be it termed duty, justice, fairness, or principles.

Kohlberg carried on this tradition, adding his own belief of moral stages. His studies show that as humans move from one moral stage to another, they move toward the highest moral stage, that of principles and universality (Kohlberg, 1981). Kohlberg further believed that moral reasoning and choices, while decidedly individual, were best made in a community setting. He was very active in the promotion of "just community" schools, in which all members of the school determine its governance, much like a New England town meeting.

An educational administrator who follows an ethic of justice will choose to encourage specific ethical learning activities structured within curricular and extracurricular programs to discuss individual choices as well as school community choices. In a school that takes site-based management seriously, decisions on the day-to-day governance of life in the school are mandatory. The ethic of justice demands that the institution serve both the common good and the rights of the individuals in the school. To cite just one example, in a just community or site-based management school, issues of grading and testing could be examined from the perspective of justice, with such discussions leading to the development of alternatives to present practices that benefit some to the disadvantage of others (Starratt, 1991).

The Ethic of Caring

One of the limitations of the ethic of justice is the contention that what is "just" for one person might not be considered just by another person given the same situation. Carol Gilligan and Nel Noddings, in particular, have taken issue with the ethic of justice as being too narrow and not inclusive of all persons. Gilligan claims that there is sex bias in Kohlberg's stages. Her seminal study (1982) of adolescent girls makes a strong claim that females do not show the expected pattern of movement through Kohlberg's moral stages. According to Gilligan, because the values of compassion, responsibility, and obligation are more likely to be stressed in the socialization of females than in that of males, females who base their reasoning on these values are classified at a lower level of (Kohlberg's) moral development theory. Noddings (1984) concurs, saying that it cannot be presumed that women make choices for the same reasons as men do. Women may choose an alternative form of moral conduct, a conduct and moral decision based more on caring than justice.

The ethic of caring focuses on the needs and demands of relationships, not from a standpoint of justice or the law, but from a standpoint of personal or professional regard. According to Starratt,

> An ethics of caring requires fidelity to persons, a willingness to acknowledge their right to be who they are, an openness to encountering them in their authentic individuality, a loyalty to the relationship. . . .
> Such an ethic . . . postulates a level of caring that honors the dignity of each person and desires to see that person enjoy a full human life. (p. 195)

Educational administrators who follow the practice of an ethic of caring will demonstrate that the integrity of human relationships is sacred and that the institution should hold the good of human beings within it as sacred. There must be a relationship of regard, mutual respect, and honesty between and among all individuals in the organization.

The leadership style of women more often lends itself to the ethic of caring for all of the reasons thus far discussed in this book. However, women should be cautioned to not overemphasize the ethic of caring to the harm of the ethic of justice. As a society we are far from ready to embrace caring as *the* way of governing. Change is slow for a reason. Concepts, ideas, and theories all should be tested against what is already in place and (apparently) working.

There is much good in the ethic of caring, just as there is much good in the ethic of justice. The successful transactional leader can learn from both, as there are elements of each theory in the other. Moreover, each ethic *needs* the strong convictions embedded in the other. The ethic of justice needs the humanistic point of view and regard for the dignity of the individual found in the ethic of caring, just as the ethic of caring needs the fairness of the ethic of justice as well as its larger attention to social order. School restructuring can be enhanced by attention to both the ethic of care and the ethic of justice, especially if they are integrated to provide a comprehensive and multidimensional foundation for an ethical school governance.

Integrity

There is nothing so important to your personal and professional character as integrity, and there is nothing more personally and professionally important than protecting the quality of that integrity. Integrity is in the essence of a person; it is your very character. While ethics deals with what you do and how you conform to accepted professional standards of conduct, integrity implies incorruptibility and holding firm to a personal moral code. Integrity begins with honorableness based on a sense of doing your duty and having an unwavering regard for what is morally right. It is a conscious choice and requires carefully weighing every decision as to its being right and equitable. Persons of integrity live their lives by the fundamental universal principles (Kolhberg's universal moral principles, in Reimer, Paolitto, and Hersh, 1979, p. 84) upon which most civilized persons agree:

1. Law and rules
2. Conscience

3. Personal roles of affection
4. Authority
5. Civil rights
6. Contract, trust, and justice in exchange
7. Punishment
8. The value of life
9. Property rights and values
10. Truth

Even though it is possible to disagree with particular values Kohlberg has chosen as being universal, it is difficult to deny that there are some values or moral institutions that are universally common, even though their practices may vary with each society.

Questions can arise when a person of integrity steps into a public area, such as educational administration: Should you remove the mantle of personal integrity when you don the robe of public authority? Is it possible to set aside personal beliefs when you become a (public) administrator? How do you make value choices in a position of power in which your decisions will affect other people? How do you resolve the moral conflicts between such values as truthfulness and loyalty, candor and kindness, freedom and equality, or justice and compassion? Such decision making is not easy, and that is probably why the concept of decisions based upon ethical principles has, until recently, been left out of typical educational discourse.

Educational leaders, in particular, must demonstrate integrity. Every function of the administrator's role and position involves making decisions based not only upon the standards of the school and community, but also according to sound ethical judgment. In addition, school administrators are expected to make the right choices for all of the students under their charge.

This brings us then to the argument for courses of study to be offered for the training of educational administrators in making ethical decisions. Training is important, for even though educators with integrity face each decision with truthfulness, candor, and fairness, they still will find themselves in the middle of ethical dilemmas. Through training in ethical decision making, they will learn to base their decisions in ethical principles.

Training Educational Administrators in Making Ethical Decisions

It certainly is acceptable to admit that as educational leaders, we do not have all the answers. We can be reasonably secure in our abilities to solve problems, but we are not always just quite sure how to deal with questions of ethics. Advice on ethics can be found in both popular magazines and scholarly journals, with the most popular format being case studies with a closing paragraph such as "What would you do if . . . ?" While this is appealing to readers, the scenarios of the case studies usually have no more lasting value than a crossword puzzle.

Life, however, is not a game. Real life holds consequences for erroneous decisions. The problems that educational administrators face are all too real, and the results of their decisions can have a lasting impact. They need a specific program that will build upon their innate sense of doing right, a course of study especially designed to train them in making ethical choices.

Every day educators are faced with ethical situations such as the following:

- As a student, you see another student cheat on a test. As a teacher, you observe a student cheat on a test.
  Is this the same dilemma?
  Is your obligation the same?
- You overhear a fellow administrator say she is going to call in sick tomorrow because she needs "R 'n' R." You hear a teacher make the same comment. You hear the same statement from a student.
  Do you deal with all of them in the same way?
- The students complain to you about a teacher you also believe is substandard.
  What do you do?
- A student needs a particular course to win a full athletic scholarship to a major university. He is on the verge of failing.
  What, if anything, do you say to his teacher?
- A student asks your secretary to copy 300 pages of a book for him. She turns to you for your approval.
  What do you say to her?

- The student senate wishes to invite a very controversial speaker to campus.

  How do you handle this?

None of these situations have easy answers. Even if your first reaction is made quickly, these are the kinds of situations that require more than snap decisions. Because a strong case can be made for any of several correct answers, these situations are termed *dilemmas*. A dilemma has no obviously correct answer. Rather, it presents a valid argument that concludes with a choice between two equal alternatives. A dilemma (a) assumes there is no way to avoid choosing one of the alternatives, (b) assumes there is no way to know the truth of the premises, and (c) demands resolution in the course of daily life. A dilemma becomes *moral* when it concerns the duties and obligations one person has to another.

A moral dilemma must contain these three properties:

1. It asks, "What is the right thing to do, fair and just?"
2. It cannot be settled simply by facts.
3. There is a conflict of moral principles present.

Unfortunately, there has been more rhetoric than research in the area of ethical training for educational administrators. While most other professions have begun to review their ethical practices, education is sadly lacking in such a self-study. A few writers have addressed the subject, but have not specified the need for the training of educational administrators in making ethical decisions. Textbooks in the field barely touch upon the general subject of professional ethics; professional journal articles are usually very general in their approach to the subject; and, while the number of books that deal with ethics is abundant, very few address the issue of *how* to be an ethical educational administrator.

Educational administrators must learn to develop skills for making choices based on sound judgment. They must become, to borrow a term from Maslow (1959), "good choosers." Maslow tells of an experiment with chickens choosing their own diet. The results show that good choosers can choose better than bad choosers what is better not only for themselves, but also what is better for the bad choosers. The purpose, then, of training educational administrators to be good choosers is that very often they must do the choosing for all within their charge. It is this charge to do the choosing for others that necessitates that educational administrators be trained in making ethical decisions.

Standards of Ethical Practice

While learning about moral standards and ethical conduct may raise awareness of right and wrong, and of good and not-so-good decisions, such knowledge does not necessarily make one an ethical person. However, a person who has had training in ethical decision making will be more prepared to make ethical choices at every level of administration.

The higher a person rises in the corporate structure or professional ladder, the greater will be her or his power to act and the more she or he will be called upon to make choices affecting increasing numbers of people. Also, the more public the responsibility and power are, the more the person with the power will be looked upon to make decisions that are ethical. In a public position these ethical decisions require explicitness of reasoning. The person in charge should be able to give an account of the reasons for the choices, both as a defense of the choices that are followed and as an explanation or justification of following them. This public person needs to be understood as to how she or he understands the basic moral issues. As the organization's leader, she or he establishes the ethical tone by applying standards to the organizational behavior. Chances are that if the person (1) is beyond reproach, (2) rewards right behavior in others, and (3) is intolerant of wrongdoing, most others in the organization will also behave ethically.

In addition, the educational administrator must be all things to all people. She or he must, first of all, be a scholar and know about education; she or he must have a humanistic philosophy of education; she or he must stand for something—that is, the person must have a values framework. Most of all, the educational administrator must be a responsible person of integrity who is intelligent enough to make decisions based on values as well as caring enough to consider others because educational administrators must make not only satisfactory decisions in terms of the school's goals, but also decisions that are morally appropriate. In short, all value conflicts must be addressed from both an institutional basis as well as a humanistic one. It is impossible to separate morality and responsibility, assuming these characteristics and criteria.

Educational administrators must have a commitment to a value system that sets an ethical standard. The call among educators is to discover a consensus of these value systems that can serve as standards of good practice for the ethical administrator and become the basis for a code of ethics.

A Code of Ethics

A method used by all professions that choose to bring external controls to bear and to establish boundaries for conduct is the development and adoption of a professional code of ethics. The purpose of a code of ethics is to provide some general guidance, some regimen of life, and a pattern of values (Berkson, 1968). A code of ethics (a) is a means of social control, (b) defines professional conduct, (c) represents the judgment of leaders, (d) prevents control or interference by government or social agencies, and (e) develops higher standards of conduct (Titus and Keeton, 1973). There are those who say that to some extent ethical codes have become substitutes for higher moral standards once expected by society, but it is more likely that codes were developed to give shape to standards as our civilization became more complicated.

Professional codes of ethics are directed at particular occupational groups, and while occasionally they are used as banners, their basic intent is sound. Certainly no code can claim to solve ethical problems, as no two ethical problems are exactly alike, and no code can delineate every consideration a person needs to address in making an ethical choice. Studies indicate that there is a notable difference between what some professions profess as a code of ethics and how the members of those professions behave in actual situations (Witmer, 1989). These studies conclude that a significant discrepancy exists between acceptance of a professional code of ethics and adherence to that code in actual practice. However, codes do provide guidelines, and give credence to their intent.

Building an Ethical School

A much larger issue than making ethical choices in separate incidents is the task of establishing a school environment in which education itself can take place ethically. As an educational administrator, you are charged with an educational program that is supposed to serve moral purposes (the nurturing of the human, social, and intellectual growth of the students) (Starratt, 1991). Thus, you have a moral responsibility to be proactive about creating an ethical environment for the conduct of education. This should be of primary consideration as you draw up your entry plan, your strategic plan, and your action plan.

With school restructuring a major force in education today, the time to infuse ethical practices is now. True and effective restructuring is based on systemic change, change in every system of the institution. This requires a new way of viewing educational policies and practices. The ethical challenge in restructuring is to benefit all segments of the organization—most of all, those who are served by it.

An ethical perspective provides a framework in which educational administrators can move from the way things always have been done to an awareness of moral issues involved in making decisions about every aspect of the way a school is governed. As an administrator, you need to think about how to construct an environment in which an education can take place in an ethical manner.

Taking the Lead

To build an ethical environment, it is most important to be principled and to demonstrate the virtues of honesty, probity, respectability, fidelity, honor, and justice. Educators must demonstrate a deep and passionate concern for integrity—in the classroom, in personal relationships, in the use of language, in community life, and, most of all, in themselves. As models through which children see the truth, educators should also talk about—and demonstrate—honesty.

Stephen Covey, author of the best-selling *The 7 Habits of Highly Effective People* and *Principle-Centered Leadership*, says that the secret to success and leadership is rooted in unshakable principles and character traits, such as integrity, justice, patience, humility, and fidelity (Huffman, "Taking the Lead," 1993). Covey explains principle-centered leadership as "integrating your life around a fixed set of principles, applying those principles interpersonally and organizationally in your management responsibilities so people come to trust you" (quoted in Huffman,

p. 97). The seven habits he espouses parallel the suggestions made throughout this book:

1. Be proactive and take responsibility.
2. Begin with the end (vision) in mind.
3. Live by that vision; have integrity.
4. Respect others and seek to benefit them as well as yourself.
5. Seek to understand first, instead of being impatient to be understood.
6. Value differences. In an organization, conflict and tension should be respected because disparate points of view often can lead to better, more creative results.
7. Renew yourself. You must constantly recharge your own batteries (Covey, 1989).

In the last analysis, you may want to consider the wisdom of Emerson, who offers these words: "Nothing is at last sacred but the integrity of your own mind. Absolve you to yourself, and you shall have the suffrage of the world" (*Self-Reliance*). Act honorably, more rationally, more prudently, and more sympathetically than those around you, and remain whole when all else is losing its center.

NOTE

1. Lord Byron, *Childe Harold*, canto 3, stanza 113.

13

PROFESSIONALISM

The issue of professionalism in educational administration has not been resolved completely. In fact, the question of whether or not education is a profession continues to be argued. Most educational administrators maintain that educational administration is a profession, but there are contentions being made on both sides of the issue of professionalism, even by those in the field. The criteria for what makes an occupation a profession are not completely clear, although there are many substantiated reasons given by those who continue to debate the issue.

It is, however, generally agreed that

1. a profession requires special knowledge and skills in a widely recognized body of learning that is derived from research, education, and training at a high level;
2. it is expected that practitioners exercise their knowledge and skills in the interest of others;
3. professionals are self-supervised and make their own procedural decisions;
4. standards of competence and conduct are established and monitored by an association that represents the profession as a whole and operates under a charter or articles of association;
5. practitioners adhere to a code of conduct.

Ministers, lawyers, doctors, and university professors, all of whom are considered to be members of the original professions, "derive their status from the education they receive and the individual and collective autonomy they claim and enjoy in the exercise of their professional duties" (Herbst, 1989, p. 6). Sergiovanni (1992), a well-known education professor at Trinity University, however, is not entirely sold on the idea that those in basic education are truly professionals. He says that while teaching (and administration) may be designated as a profession, this designation does not render it a "recognized profession" (p. 97). Sergiovanni has noted, "If there is nothing specialized about the knowledge base of educational administration, then it cannot be considered a profession in the strictest sense" (1991, p. 523). He will concede, however, that educational administration may be able to claim a professional status higher than that of teaching, but does so at some peril to a democratic unity of administrators and teachers.

On the other hand, Peter Clamp (1990) writes that professionalism is a state of mind and has little to do with occupation, position, rank, years of service, clientele, hours worked, seniority, personal ambition, remuneration, holidays, office size, degrees granted, or codes of conduct. Clamp defines professionalism as "an ideal which guides individuals in dealings with others in their chosen vocation" (p. 53). He goes on to affirm that professionalism is grounded in a set of characteristics and that an individual earns these characteristics:

1. Competency, derived through training that is thorough, comprehensive, and well-earned
2. Integrity, based on one's good name and reputation for fine quality workmanship and fairness, honesty, and trust
3. Reliability, including punctuality, stability, and commitment
4. Empathic humanism, displayed through consistently genuine feelings and behaviors for others (Clamp, 1990, pp. 54–55).

Clamp concludes that the mark of a true profession is that it is self-standardizing, self-disciplining, and self-governing (p. 56).

MOVEMENTS TO LEGITIMIZE PROFESSIONALISM

Self-named professional associations, by their very existence, have made the hallmark of membership that of being a "professional." The National Education Association (NEA), the largest and best-known education association as well as the leading lobbying force in matters concerning their members, lacks the name "professional" in its title only because of the longevity of the organization. NEA professes professionalism because it serves a purpose: professionals can command more respect, increased benefits, and higher salary. NEA's support of movements to elevate the status of teachers is legend, yet there are some educators who worry that NEA is not fully supporting other initiatives that are thought by some to be requisites to be termed professional.

The National Board for Professional Teaching Standards (NBPTS) has developed policies, processes, and standards for a professional certification for all subject-area specialists as well as for an area called "generalist." While the process is voluntary (with a fee), certification by the NBPTS signifies to school districts that teachers are "board certified" and that they have met the NBPTS knowledge-based standards of theory, pedagogy, content, and performance. NBPTS is not, however, an association (or union) in the way NEA is. Rather, it exists solely as a certification board.

Administrators belong to organizations that include their occupation specialty, such as the American Association of School Administrators (AASA) and the National Association of Elementary and Secondary Principals (NAESP), to name the two best known in public education. The University Council for Educational Administration (UCEA) is a comparable example in higher education.

The main difference, however, between NEA (to which most teachers belong) and AASA (administrators), NAESP (administrators), or UCEA (professors of educational administration) is influence. NEA is a union that represents its members in contract negotiations. The associations to which administrators belong do not involve themselves in contract negotiations, although they do offer workshops in this area for their membership. The main purpose of teachers' unions is salary and benefits, while the overriding purposes of administrator associations are networking, professional development, and setting standards.

Educational administrators usually claim a professional status higher than that of teachers based on these reasons: (1) teaching is a prerequisite for administration, (2) there are fewer administrative positions, and (3) administrative posts are less easily obtained than teaching positions. As one example, administrators do not have to set their schedules around the ringing of bells and they do not have to plan their work around a particular group of students. This flexibility of time thus gives status, as the arranging of one's own day is a privilege of professions.

FEMALE ADMINISTRATOR: PROFILE AND PERSONA

Most researchers and practitioners would agree that the professional profile is based on the male experience and on values generally associated with masculinity because the three parties who exercise instrumental control over the professions—practitioners, professors, and the state (councils, legislatures, civil servants, and courts)—are predominantly male. While this dynamic is changing with the increased number of women in administrative positions, women may still have to play by old rules for a time, creating opportunities to change the rules. In the meantime, they must be aware of the view others have of any administrators and realize that they are *constantly* on display and are being evaluated on everything they say and do.

Because a professional person identifies with and is identified by the profession, you will be carrying this persona with you at all times. When you go to the grocery store, you are not just a shopper. You are the Principal, the Superintendent, or the President. Especially as a woman, you must maintain the decorum of the position no matter where you are. A male administrator can go to the community pool without too much notice. A female, however, is subject to scrutiny not only of her swimming style, but also of her swimsuit. Attending a social function, a male administrator can more easily accept an alcoholic beverage; a female had best stick with one glass of light wine, if anything. A woman finds herself in a double standard wherever she turns. She cannot be loud and boisterous, for while a man will be viewed as "letting his hair down and having fun," a woman will be accused of "being out of control."

The female administrator must present a professional appearance in every situation. She cannot ever "escape" from the duties or the expectations of the position. The public is not yet completely comfortable with a "woman in charge," so more eyes, both literally and figuratively, will be upon her. You will find that you are always "on." You need to be careful not to speak about any employee, even in the most casual conversations, for someone is sure to repeat your comments and give them more weight than you ever intended them to have. Do not discuss business for the same reasons. Men are viewed as being "regular guys" when they say more about a situation than may be wise, but women who discuss issues or events relevant to the institution are looked upon as "talking out of turn" or gossiping. And remember to play by the same rules expected of everyone else. Don't be delayed for an appointment or meeting because of something at home, unless it is a real emergency. Make sure contingency plans are in place for such situations as a sick child or a change in the child's schedule; if you are late or miss work frequently because of these situations, you put yourself in a vulnerable position on many fronts.

PROFESSIONAL RELATIONSHIPS WITH OTHERS

Professional relationships should not be anything special. This means that you should not be playing a role when interacting professionally with others. If uncomfortable situations occur, as in anger displayed by an employee or a constituent or parent, it is then easier for you to sustain a businesslike relationship, maintaining your dignity and not losing your patience. Rather than argue with someone, suggest that the discussion continue at another time and place. If that is not possible, just sit quietly until the other person regains composure.

Do not take opposition personally. Very often, differences of opinion do not have anything to do with personalities. Keep any discussion to the issues and respond only to the process, not to the person. Following the discussion (or confrontation), do not relate any unpleasantness to others; rather, keep the matter between the other person and yourself. You may want to discuss this with a third party outside the organization, but be wary about doing so, and avoid it if possible.

PROFESSIONALISM WITHIN THE RANKS

Administrators are often accused of "closing ranks" against opposition. This is not necessarily a negative. You need the kind of support that only those in the same or a similar position can provide. Trust within the ranks is crucial to a good professional working relationship, and is worth the time it takes to build.

If you are the lone female administrator, you may have to work to earn the trust that men naturally give to one another. One way to do that is to maintain confidentiality among your colleagues. Support the decisions of any member of the group and do not repeat anything that is stated among the group.

When you are the new kid on the block, you must wait to be included. Don't push your friendship on the others. Don't walk into conversations that seem to be private, but do join in group conversations. Be friendly, contribute to the dialogue, but do not overdo it. Most importantly, do not gossip or make jokes at the expense of anyone. Leave that to the men.

Be loyal to the administrative team and support its decisions. Do not go out of administrative sessions and share the information with those who are not a part of your group, unless it is information intended for that audience (such as your staff). Do not comment to others about the decision once it has been reached. To be a team player (a professional, if you would), you need to do whatever it takes to win for the team. Use female strategies such as persuasion and interpersonal relationships, as well as cooperative approaches, to make the team decisions work for you!

PROFESSIONAL PREPARATION PROGRAMS

Educational administration is basically a self-selecting profession in which prospective members are academically prepared in part-time programs on university campuses, far from the school sites. The main criticism of most educational programs is that they are too theory oriented, removed from reality, and taught by those who do not have experience in the field. These criticisms, however, are not valid for all institutions. The better educational administration programs strive to keep current and they constantly self-monitor and make changes in the program.

Universities that offer specialized doctoral programs in educational administration are successful because they understand the importance of "theory into practice" and instill in their graduates the desire to be academicians as well as administrators. The very best programs align themselves with organizations, such as the Danforth Foundation, that aid universities in developing top-notch practitioners who leave the program not only with a solid foundation in theory but also with the skills to handle the practical application.

The Danforth Foundation is a nonprofit organization that helps universities to improve their instructional programs for educational administration. As a direct result of their efforts, universities identify the need for new courses, including public relations, curriculum assessment, and problem solving. The foundation has provided both financial and advisory assistance to universities grappling with reform of their administrator preparation programs.

THE ROLE OF THE DANFORTH FOUNDATION

In response to the rampant criticism that hit educational administration preparation programs during the 1980s, the University Council for Educational Administration reviewed preparation programs in "Leaders for America's Schools." This review found that there was a need to (1) define educational leadership, (2) recruit promising candidates for educational leadership, (3) develop collaborative relationships with school district leaders, (4) make programs more current and clinical, and (5) encourage minorities and women to enter the field (Milstein, 1992).

In 1987 the Danforth Program for the Preparation of School Principals began a study of five university administration preparation programs. It found that if improvement was to occur, a readiness for change, leadership, and partnerships between and among key participants would be essential. Internships, field experiences, and the use of cohorts were also identified as important to successful preparation programs. The Danforth Foundation offered to use its resources to challenge universities to change the way they prepare educational leaders. Four universities joined in the founding of this program, and, by 1992, membership had expanded to include twenty-two universities (of the

500 higher education institutions that prepare educational administrators). As a direct result of the intervention and resources of the Danforth Foundation, great strides have been made in the preparation of educational administrators, not only in the twenty-two member universities, but in most of the 500 university preparatory programs. Since its inception, the efforts of the Danforth program have had a positive effect on the way educational administrators are prepared.

In the early nineties, Philip Hallinger and Joseph Murphy (1991) advocated that what was needed in the preparation of educational leaders was the establishment of a professional knowledge base, driven by practice and based on real problems. Their model stresses the codification of knowledge into a sequential body of understanding and skills, guiding the educational administration students in a thoughtful, sequential program with cohorts. Many of their recommendations provided the basis for the reforms.

Jerome T. Murphy (1991), shortly before he became dean of the Harvard Graduate School of Education, recommended that educational administration programs focus on a curriculum designed to balance reflection, action, and commitment. He specified that issues should be studied from various points of view, such as political, social, economic, and organizational, so that administrators realize the implications of any decisions. He said that graduates should leave preparatory programs with the capacity to act with integrity, judgment, and skill—in a manner consistent with their personal conceptions of leadership. This requires a focus on "'thinking (and acting) like an administrative leader,' a nebulous notion akin to the law school notion of 'thinking like a lawyer.' . . . [This] means thinking [and acting] like an administrative leader, . . . approaching problems in an action-oriented way: scanning the environment, thinking strategically, asking the right questions, collecting and synthesizing useful data, anticipating problems, thinking about process, working cooperatively with individuals and groups, and worrying about the future—constantly taking action to move the organization ahead in an ethical way, consistent with its values and its mission" (J. T. Murphy, 1991, pp. 508–509).

As part of this reform movement, Carnegie Mellon University established what at the time was considered an unusual program for its school administrators (Gursky, 1992). There, educational leadership students undergo the same academic training as leaders from business, industry, and the public sector. All graduates of the program are certified administrators, earning a master's degree in public administration. Courses include financial analysis, organizational management, data analysis, and economic principles of policy analysis. The program is based on the theory that schools are like businesses, and administrators need business acumen, interpersonal skills, and leadership talent to run their institutions. The education students are required to take only two education courses—supervision of instruction and educational leadership—in addition to their core courses on finance, management, and other business areas.

Another trend in educational administration preparation programs is the use of reflection, a process for developing administrators' thinking and decision-making skills. The rationale for the process is based on research in cognitive psychology. Hart (1993) reports on the work of a design studio in which students are required to apply content knowledge acquired in their traditional course of study to school problems. They are expected to defend their proposed actions.

While the results of Hart's research are mixed, many preparation programs encourage the use of reflection in journal writing or case records (Short and Rinehart, 1993). The use of reflection may be most helpful in problem-solving courses that use dilemma situations such as the supervision of teachers, student performance problems, conflicts with parents, disagreements about curriculum or instruction between teachers, and accusations of racial discrimination.

THE NEEDED SKILLS

Many studies have been undertaken to try to define just what skills are necessary for beginning administrators. Previously, we looked at the skills and functions of an educational administrator. (See chapter 3.) Anyone planning to enter an educational administration preparation program should look carefully at these as well as the results of studies of various programs in educational administration. Familiarizing yourself with these programs should help you in choosing an institution that can deliver instruction in the areas identified as being most useful and/or choosing electives that will be of most benefit to you.

A study in the early 1990s, sponsored by the National Association of Secondary School Principals, surveyed principals and assistant principals regarding their previous preparation programs and recommendations on how to improve future programs (Ashe, Haubner, and Troisi, 1991). The National Leadership Network's "Strengthening Support and Recruitment of Women and Minorities" (1992) then reviewed the many recommendations that various groups proposed and reviewed the following frameworks built on skills needed to be a good administrator in the entry year:

1. **Knowledge-based skills**, including district policy manuals; special education and special needs programs; legal processes related to students and personnel issues; staff evaluation procedures; relationships with students, parents, and staff; professional growth opportunities for staff; and organizational skills.
2. **Survival skills**, including leadership, planning, instruction, personnel, law, finance, facilities, and community relations.
3. **Performance skills**, including demonstration of an understanding of system expectations, procedures, and resources; demonstration of increased competence and comfort in addressing building or unit outcomes or concerns; enhancement of professional and personal growth; development of a personal support system; acceptance of personalized assistance in coping with building or unit problems; and acceptance of formative feedback and assistance toward strengthening administrative performance.
4. **Climate, orientation, and individual assessment skills**, including (1) assessing the climate (human relations skills, communication skills, leadership style appreciation, and understanding political structures); (2) orientation (basic administrative skills, problem-solving skills, and local procedures and expectations); and (3) individual assessment (continuous assessment of the individual on the job and specialized skills development).
5. **General administrative skills**, including interpersonal relations, instructional supervision, staff development, goal setting, problem analysis, decision making, communication, coordination, conflict management, and stress management.

6. **Principalship skills**, including problem analysis, judgment, organizational ability, decisiveness, leadership, sensitivity, stress tolerance, oral communication, written communication, a range of interests, personal motivation, and educational values.

7. **Domain area skills**, including (1) functional (organizational processes and techniques by which the mission of the school is achieved, including leadership, information collection, problem analysis, judgment, organizational oversight, implementation, and delegation), (2) programmatic (scope and framework of the educational program, including instructional program, curriculum design, student guidance and development, staff development, measurement and evaluation, and resource allocation), (3) interpersonal (connections to the school, including motivating others, sensitivity, oral expression, and written expression), and (4) contextual (the world of ideas and forces within which the school operates, including philosophical and cultural values, legal and regulatory applications, policy and political influences, and public and media relationships).

The studies that generated the above lists are indicators of what those who finished preparation programs believe most helped them. In addition, in my own experience with the students in the educational courses I have taught, the topic of politics always arises. These aspiring administrators want to know how to handle the politics of administration and are concerned that their sheltered lives in the classroom will be a deterrent in dealing with the political system. They also voice concern over vulnerability, the importance of a career path, dealing with the "spin doctoring" of the media, and relationships with boards. Some cite a fear of losing touch with the classroom and the students, and many are concerned with how one person can handle all of the demands placed upon an individual school administrator today. Most, however, are almost desperate to talk about day-to-day issues and how to solve problems. They are hungry to exchange ideas and to work out solutions to common problems.

Jerome Murphy (1991) supports this practical practitioner's approach. He avers that students of educational administration need experience in dealing with demanding groups: unions, interest groups, the media, and—most important—school boards. They also need experience in "responding to unpredictable, high-stakes crises" (p. 509). Murphy says that the capacity to act can best be learned through simulations, the case method, and internships, and through working with practitioners who reflect on their practice.

CERTIFICATION AND NATIONAL STANDARDS

One of the most important initiatives to develop out of the concerns of the 1980s for some kind of standard for educational administration was the formation of the National Commission on Excellence in Educational Administration, under the leadership of then UCEA executive director Patrick Forsyth and the leading academic figure in the field of school administration at the time, Daniel Griffiths. The commission was formed "to galvanize collective action on the challenges, opportunities, and problems confronting the field of school leadership" (Murphy, 2003, p. 2). One of the most important outcomes of their efforts is the existence of the National Policy Board for Educational Administration, a coalition of ten major education organizations with a large stake in school administration, including, from the academic section of the profession, American Association of Colleges for Teacher Education (AACTE), the National Council for Accreditation of Teacher Education (NCATE), the National Council of Professors of Educational Administration (NCPEA), and UCEA.

In 1994 the National Policy Board for Educational Administration (NPBEA), under the leadership of its then corporate secretary, Scott Thomson, created the Interstate School Leaders Licensure Consortium (ISLLC) to develop standards to anchor the profession as it headed into the twenty-first century. At its inception, ISLLC was composed of twenty-four states, most of the members of the NPBEA, and other key stakeholder groups, such as the National Alliance of Business, with an interest in the health of leadership in America's schools and school districts. In order to better link the standards work to the policy machinery of licensure and accreditation, ISLLC was housed with the Council of Chief State School Officers (CCSSO). This move made additional sense because the Interstate New Teacher Assessment and Support Consortium (INTASC) to develop standards for teachers was already located with CCSSO.

The Interstate School Leaders Licensure Consortium standards state that a school administrator is an educational leader who promotes the success of all students by:

1. facilitating the development, articulation, implementation, and stewardship of a vision of learning that is shared and supported by the school community
2. advocating, nurturing, and sustaining a school culture and instructional program conducive to student learning and staff professional growth
3. ensuring management of the organization, operations, and resources for a safe, efficient, and effective learning environment
4. collaborating with families and community members, responding to diverse community interests and needs, and mobilizing community resources
5. acting with integrity, with fairness, and in an ethical manner
6. understanding, responding to, and influencing the larger political, social, economic, legal, and cultural context

Despite some criticism, such as not being comprehensive enough, the ISLLC standards were approved in their final form at the end of 1996. Even though the project is no longer active, the standards exerted influence on the profession of school administration.

With the advent of national certification, it is even more important for those entering the field to choose their programs from (a) accredited universities, (b) universities that support the National Policy Board for Educational Administration, and (c) universities whose professors of educational administration are members of their own professional organization—the University Council for Educational Administration, one of the ten member organizations of the National Policy Board for Educational Administration.

Another important initiative is the Forum for the American School Superintendent, a decade-long effort funded by the Danforth Foundation. The Forum was designed to strengthen the ability of school superintendents to provide effective education for all children, particularly students at risk of school failure. The effort involved sixty superintendents (new and experienced; from urban, suburban, and rural districts; women and minorities) with at least 50 percent of the student population in their districts classified as high need and high risk. Through two Forum meetings each year, superintendents engage in thoughtful, structured discussions around significant problems identified by the superintendents and the Forum Advisory Board.

To widen the impact of the Forum, five in-depth initiatives (early childhood, leadership, public engagement, principal, race and class) involve selected Forum lead superintendents in the development and implementation of local plans to enhance learning opportunities for all children in the community. As lead superintendents, these sixty members share their plans, progress, and "lessons learned" from each Forum meeting.

Specifically, the leadership initiative is designed to engage superintendents in the difficult task of inventing, constructing, and sustaining learning communities where all participants—children, teachers, parents, support staff, administrators, and board members—learn at high levels. The focus is on reconceptualizing structures, relationships, and expectations that support this vision.

Another initiative created to assist school administrators is the Leaders for Learning project. Its purpose is to create technology-based instructional materials aligned with the standards of the Interstate School Leaders Licensure Consortium. With funding from the Missouri Department of Elementary and Secondary Education, faculty from fourteen institutions that prepare school leaders formed annual cohorts to collaborate on the development of vignettes, case studies, and problem-based learning modules to prepare aspiring principals (Dalton, 2004). Since the program's inception in 1999, it has expanded to include the development of a module to train adjunct faculty; portfolio frameworks and scoring guides; and instructional materials focused on the superintendency. These can be found at www.umsl.edu/~mpea.

THE EMERGING ROLE OF THE WALLACE FOUNDATION ON PREPARATION PROGRAMS

The Wallace Foundation, one of the largest private nonprofit supporters of public education, is leading a major new initiative to advance student achievement by improving school leadership. The foundation has committed to a multiyear program to support districts and states in developing comprehensive approaches to attracting, preparing, and placing a more effective, able, and diverse corps of superintendents, principals, and other education leaders, and to improving the conditions that enable leaders to foster the academic performance of all children.

In January 2004, the Wallace Foundation convened a Leadership Effectiveness Knowledge Exploration Committee to review how collected data has guided leader development in leadership preparation programs and in the ongoing professional growth of practicing leaders. Their work resulted in a set of recommendations. These recommendations were still in the review stage at the time this book was written.

Among several other research studies being funded by the Wallace Foundation is one by the Stanford Educational Leadership Institute (in conjunction with The Finance Project, a Washington, DC–based nonprofit research organization) that, among other studies, explores the state policy and finance structures that foster effective programs. The School Leadership Study is taking place in several phases, the first report of which was released August 10, 2005. *School Leadership Study: Developing Successful Principals* is a review of research—an examination of existing knowledge in the field. Investigators identified the ways that school leadership and school performance are closely linked, and examined the essential skills of good leadership, key features of effective principal education programs, structures of effective programs, and successful financing and policy reform strategies. The lead authors of the report are associate professor of education Stephen Davis, professor of education Linda Darling-Hammond, research director Michelle LaPointe, and associate professor of education and professor of organizational behavior Debra Meyerson, all of Stanford University.

In an introduction to the report, M. Christine DeVita, president of the Wallace Foundation, writes,

> Researchers . . . will be conducting an in-depth investigation of . . . unanswered questions about improving the preparation of school leaders so that the field can move from criticism to knowledge and effective solutions. Better training alone won't solve America's mounting school leadership challenges. Well-trained leaders placed in near-impossible job conditions aren't likely to succeed in improving learning. But if better training

isn't the whole answer, it is surely a big part of it. That's why this first report on what is and isn't known about improving the preparation of school
leaders, and the reports in the months ahead that will deepen our knowledge about what works, are so timely. (Davis, Darling-Hammond, La-
Pointe, and Meyerson, 2005, p. 1)

With the review of research completed, Wallace Foundation–funded
researchers are now compiling a series of in-depth case studies of eight
highly developed pre- and in-service programs in five states. These studies will examine the programs and the perceptions of participants, and
will track graduates into the schools they lead. This phase of the School
Leadership Study is being conducted by a team of more than a dozen
researchers from around the country.

It is likely that the impact of the efforts of this undertaking by the
Wallace Foundation will equal—if not exceed—that of the Danforth
Foundation two decades ago. Readers are encouraged to follow this
work, as it surely will guide changes to education administration preparation programs. Information on the Wallace Foundation's initiatives in
this area can be found at www.wallacefoundation.org/WF. Information
on the School Leadership Study, as well as other related research being
conducted by the Stanford Educational Leadership Institute, can be
found at seli.stanford.edu/research/sls.htm. Another good source for
keeping current on the reports funded by the Wallace Foundation, as
well as many other useful related documents, can be found at the Education Policy Information Clearinghouse of the Education Policy Leadership Center, www.eplc.org/clearinghouse_leadership.html.

INDUCTION AND IN-SERVICE
FOR ENTRY-LEVEL ADMINISTRATORS

In general, there has not been much research conducted on the problems of first-year administrators. What is known, however, is that begin-
ners need assistance and support if they are to be successful. Some of
the most frequently mentioned concerns are the following:

- New administrators need to be oriented to the characteristics and
  culture of particular school systems.

- Mentor systems should be designed specifically for the needs of administrators, and not consist of adaptations of teacher mentor programs.
- Reflective activities should be facilitated through peer support and observation that provide time for reflective analysis, either through a mentor on site or by arranging for the new administrators to be a part of an area organization.
- Professional growth and development activities need to be developed and provided for all administrative personnel.
- Workloads should be adjusted so that beginning administrators have sufficient time to develop productive working relationships with staff, students, and parents.
- Frequent, specific, and accurate feedback should be given concerning job performance.

It is incumbent upon an institution to offer the kinds of support needed by administrators, for if it does not, the institution risks losing on its investment. Not every institution will, however, have the leadership or the means by which to provide such support or professional development. In such instances where the institution is remiss, entry-level administrators will need to seek their own continuing professional development opportunities.

If you find yourself in an institution that does not provide formal support for professional development, then plan your own continuing education. Request to attend seminars, workshops, and conferences. Suggest hosting workshops, perhaps through your county or regional associations or support institutions. Offer to make your own arrangements, if you must, but do not neglect your own professional enrichment.

SPECIAL CONCERNS OF WOMEN REGARDING PROFESSIONAL DEVELOPMENT

Again and again we read of the imminent shortage of qualified school administrators, as various organizations and government agencies make employment projections. Further, we hear that there are even greater shortages of minority administrators and of women administrators. In other words, we are told (1) that there are not enough qualified people to fill administrative vacancies and also (2) that of the total number of administrators in place, few are either minorities or women. Reality indicates that there are many women and minorities who are very qualified but who are not in administrative positions. Mathematically, this problem should be self-solving. Realistically, however, this is not happening even though there are very well-qualified women available for the vacancies. Campuses have been successful in their recruitment of women and of minorities to enter educational administration programs, yet the women and minorities are not being hired after having earned university certification and, in fact, have made few significant inroads into the male world of administration.

In 2003, 14 percent of the superintendents in this country were female. Across the first five years of the twenty-first century, 12 to 15 percent of superintendents were women, double the numbers of the previous decade but about the same as a century ago. Currently, approximately one-third of assistant superintendents are women (indicating that only about half of these women attain a superintendency). In higher education, according to the American Council on Education, women represent nearly 40 percent of the provosts and deans and 30 percent of the chief executives of the 500 schools in the council.

In addition, women constitute more than 50 percent of the graduate students enrolled in educational administration programs and are being awarded more than half of the doctorates in the field. However, about only 10 percent of women in doctoral programs are opting to earn the superintendency credential along with their educational specialist or doctoral degrees.

The percentage of women enrolled in and graduating from administrative degree programs continues to increase, yet males continue to dominate the field. Women are encouraged to apply for job vacancies, but when hired, they often are placed in positions beneath their education, skills, and experience. As recently as 1999 the U.S. Department of Labor described the superintendency as the most gender-stratified executive position in the country (Bjork, 1999, in Skrla, 2003).

More recently, women researchers have been adding to the knowledge base of female superintendents, showing that women generally do not follow the traditional paths of male-centered paradigms. Unfortunately, much of this information has been marginalized—just as women themselves in the field have been—and the research findings have had little noticeable effect on educational administration practices. Conferences (with the exception of women's caucuses) pay scant attention to gender issues, and research publications often ignore these issues; for example, in the second edition of the *Handbook of Research on Educational Administration* (Murphy and Louis, 1999), only one chapter out of twenty-four discusses gender.

With the majority of doctoral degrees in educational administration now being earned by women, to continue to blame women's lack of aspiration as a reason for low numbers of female superintendents makes little sense, and while some would like to think that women don't seek the superintendency, such is not borne out by the research. Linda Skrla ("Normalized Femininity," 2003) believes that, in large measure, nothing has changed for women in the superintendency because at deeper levels nothing has changed. Skrla notes, for example, that in a statewide Iowa study on the crisis of filling school administrative positions, there was no acknowledgment that gender was an issue. Regardless of paying token regard to "gender issues" in the text, no strategies were ever put up for discussion on addressing them. Women in the state were qualified but, as must be surmised, not wanted.

What may be an important unspoken reason for women's not attaining the top positions, when it is clearly shown that they are well qualified, is a phenomenon recently noticed by researchers who have interviewed women superintendents for various studies. These researchers have noted women's reluctance to mention, let alone acknowledge or blame, sexism and discriminatory treatment as a cause of not being selected for the jobs. The researchers all wondered why women didn't discuss this or mentioned it only in later interviews, and some researchers suggested that maybe this reluctance occurs because the women being interviewed accepted sexism and discrimination as part of the job or because they were so accustomed to it that they didn't find it unusual. Some researchers speculate that perhaps women candidates consciously or unconsciously ignore this situation as a way to manage working in such an environment.

SELF-SILENCING

Skrla ("Mourning Silence," 2003) explains what she calls self-silencing as women's downplaying isolation and sexism, failing to comprehend how gender serves to segregate and how social constructs make certain discriminatory phenomena unobservable. She further explains that this cultural self-silencing is a strategy used by a dominant culture to stifle the lesser and, in this case in particular, to erase women's voices and prevent the possibility of their speaking out against the sexism and discrimination. It is almost as if the women the researchers interviewed had become inured to its presence.

Such silencing is prevalent throughout U.S. society, but the overwhelmingly male-dominated culture of educational administration has created a situation in which the silencing of women's views is particularly acute, according to Skrla. Worse, she says, the silencing has been so effective that it is invisible to the vast majority of those who work in educational settings—teachers, administrators, principals, superintendents, board members, professors, and students in school administration. "The silence on women's issues in educational administration, thus, is a feature, a product, an effect of the normal situation—what Daly (1998) labeled 'numbing, dumbing normality' (p. 19) and what Foucault (1980) termed 'the procedure of normalization'" (Skrla, "Mourning Silence," 2003, p. 107).

Thus, somewhere in the subconsciousness of these women is the "sense" that to be feminine is to suffer in silence and to do otherwise is to risk censure or being labeled as a complainer, someone who expects special treatment, or who is a feminist. To be appropriately female is to be silent (Skrla, "Normalized Femininity," 2003). Simply put, the women were unable to talk about the discrimination they faced.

RECOURSE AND ACTIVIST ORGANIZATIONS

Affirmative action *may* get you an initial interview, but it is not reliable as a career path. Litigation is accompanied by a high price, both monetarily and in career consequences. Those who have used the legal system find it slow and difficult. They may receive personal satisfaction, as well as recompense, but there are many who find doors closed following a discrimination suit. Proactive organizations, such as those described below, may be of interest to those wishing additional information on activist opportunities.

The National Coalition for Women and Girls in Education (NCWGE), founded in 1975, is a nonprofit organization sponsored by the U.S. Department of Education's Office for Civil Rights. It comprises more than fifty organizations dedicated to improving educational opportunities for girls and women and to providing leadership in and advocacy for the development of national education policies that benefit all women and girls. Their website provides information on current activities, updates on relevant federal education legislation, and other resources (www.ncwge.org). NCWGE also holds an annual gender equity and educational achievement conference. One of the conference sponsors is the National Education Association.

The Feminist Majority Foundation (FMF), founded in 1987, is an organization dedicated to women's equality, reproductive health, and nonviolence (www.feminist.org). In all spheres, FMF utilizes research and action to empower women economically, socially, and politically. Their research and action programs focus on advancing the legal, social, and political equality of women with men, as well as other feminist issues.

The Association for Gender Equity Leadership in Education (www.agele.org) identifies its mission as providing leadership in the identification and infusion of gender equity in all educational programs and processes. Their focus is on (1) leadership and advocacy, (2) professional development, and (3) collaboration, networking, and outreach. They also sponsor an annual conference.

The National Women's Law Center (www.nwlc.org), established in 1972, is a leader in the move to ensure that women and girls have equal educational opportunities. The center's education program fights for strong enforcement of Title IX and promotes programs that remove barriers to girls' educational opportunities. The center's employment program addresses these barriers by fighting for equal treatment of women in all aspects of their employment. Current priorities include fighting for equal pay and benefits for women, protecting the right to take family leave when necessary, gaining strong enforcement of laws prohibiting sexual harassment and other job discrimination, and promoting the creation and preservation of affirmative action programs in the workplace.

RETENTION OF WOMEN

Because the U.S. Department of Education and most states do not keep historical data on gender in the superindendency (Blount, 1998), some conclusions must be extrapolated from available research. A study conducted on women who exited the superintendency reveals that the substantive areas these women felt were most lacking in their own sense of security include the following:

- Understanding current school board dynamics
- Vulnerability in the superintendency
- The importance of one's career path
- Analyzing external and political influences
- Understanding the media's influence on shaping, expanding, or constraining conflict
- Awareness of board turnover and knowledge of how to prevent, cope with, or capitalize on it
- Ways of dealing with the relentless scrutiny on the job
- The predictable mobilization of teacher or administrative union forces (Tallerico, Burstyn, and Poole, 1993)

Beekley (in Brunner, 1999) also did a study of women superintendents who voluntarily had left their positions. She found the following:

- All were marginalized by their gender.
- Their school boards were predominantly male.
- The women knew no other women superintendents.
- They lacked role models and a support system.

Beekley's conclusion in this study is that capable women are exiting the school superintendency prematurely for reasons that primarily have to do with their gender. They are disadvantaged by cultural and social discrimination, professional and organizational isolation, and a diminished quality in their personal and family lives. In short, the women simply weary of all the effort.

STRATEGIES FOR RETENTION

Once women finally find administrative positions, they are faced with planning strategies to assure their retention or promotion. All administrators—but particularly women because their positions are more tenuous—must continually improve their skills. Thus, any improvement you make, from budgeting to strategic planning, will enhance your present position, but, more importantly, will provide new skills for a post you may not have yet considered.

One particularly good choice for continuous in-servicing is reflection and self-assessment. Often, in a formal preparation program there is little time to reflect, take stock, and plan the next step. Further, because most preparation programs are planned from a male perspective, there is less likelihood that studying reflection will be included because it is considered "too feminine." Therefore, pursuing reflection processes as professional development, in conjunction with self-assessment, could be very beneficial.

Examination and understanding of individual ethical or moral choices is another area that most educational administration programs do not include. Unless you have had a personal interest in ethics or philosophy, your understanding of the framework for making ethical decisions may need some guidance. You may have to search for specific programs in learning how to make ethical decisions. However, if none are found, you may have to learn this skill on your own. (See chapter 12.)

Another extremely important skill in building retention strategies is constructing a personal support system. Family, friends, clergy, mentors outside your immediate position, your cohorts in your administration courses—all of these can be helpful when you need someone to lean on. Do not take these persons for granted. Rather, take the time to cultivate relationships, beginning with sharing your initial positive excitement in your first administrative position. Continue to touch base, discussing just enough of your job responsibilities so that those in your support system are kept current. Do not neglect to listen to their comments and concerns about their own situations. This support system runs both ways.

Make building a support system a priority goal in your first year as an administrator and the system will likely remain in place. Administrators are isolated, and a strong personal support system is needed to compensate for what may be missing at the organizational level, especially for women.

Another retention strategy that most administrators overlook is to be prepared with legal options. As such information is not always readily available in times of crisis, you need to be prepared in advance. Find out what your professional association offers in the way of legal counsel. Most professional associations do not provide actual legal services (unless your case has state or national implications), and many novice administrators are not aware that the attorney of record for an association is not retained for the personal use of its membership. Your association should, however, be able to provide you with a list of attorneys who specialize in school law or labor law. If you do not have your own attorney, now would be a good time to establish a professional relationship with one. Take the time to find someone you like who has a good track record.

You also may want to have on file the names of personal counselors or therapists. Do not, however, expect that your professional association will have such a listing. In fact, you probably do not even want to ask, as you do not want anyone in that office mentioning to the association director (or anyone else) that you called requesting the name of personal counselors or psychologists in private practice. Even if you do not anticipate needing the services, you will feel more secure in knowing the names of reliable professional therapists, just in case any turmoil becomes overwhelming in your professional or personal life or you need to provide a referral for a colleague.

In the position of chief executive officer you should initiate an inservice program for the edification of your board members. Such workshops can enhance your professional relationship with them. Bear in mind that most board members are men, so you may want to consider training related to gender stereotyping and gender expectations. (Do not, however, make this the topic of your initial sessions.) Another topic to consider in educating your board is the different leadership styles of educational leaders. Such a workshop can help them to better understand your style, and will help make them aware of some of the advantages women bring to the position.

As board membership changes and new members arrive with personal agendas, training in conflict resolution is worth considering for the board (and as a hedge against their misunderstanding of your agenda). Another possible training session might be a presentation by consultants who do job recruiting. Consultants can best raise the awareness of the board and can be a key to shaping board members' perceptions of what to look for in hiring and, in particular, the qualifications of women.

Most students in a preparation program worry that they do not have an opportunity to build political skills. Development of these skills, then, is appropriate in your professional development plan. Politics can be a very positive force and you need to develop political skills to make that force work for you. (See chapter 12.)

Sometime during the first or second year in your administrative position, you should begin to polish your interviewing skills. This training will aid you in conducting interviews of prospective employees, and, even more so, it will help you learn the fine points of being interviewed. The training may also assist you in interviewing those who will be conducting the interviews for positions in which you may be interested. Skills perfected in this training can be especially helpful in your ongoing interaction with your board.

Some universities sponsor regional programs to provide continuing support to their educational administration alumni. Check with your university for such programs. If they are not available, you may be able to initiate such a program by contacting colleagues and approaching the university to sponsor regional programs with the guarantee of delivering the number of participants they require. By contracting with the university, you and your cohorts can request the kinds of programs you need.

University study councils are another possible source for professional development. Particularly if you can obtain a grant to sponsor such a program, you should find very willing university partners. There are federal and some private funding sources that sponsor grants to serve women and other underrepresented groups in educational administration.

As we are painfully aware, both personally and through research findings, because there are so few women administrators, those in the positions often suffer feelings of isolation. Forming women cohort groups
can help combat that "lonely-at-the-top" sense of isolation. Even if there
are not enough women in your administrative specialty, it is helpful to
form a support group of women in similar positions. Your professional
association may be able to assist you in this endeavor. A few organizations have special ad hoc associations for their women members; for example, the American Association of School Administrators (AASA)
sponsors a Women's Caucus with its own agenda and meeting times.
Women members of AASA are automatically also members of the
Women's Caucus. Other professional organizations, such as the National
Association of Women Deans, were specifically formed for women.
Seek out associations that offer support to women. (Also see the section
on networking in chapter 11.)

Keep informed of your association's own professional development
activities, and encourage the association to establish referral systems or
"hotlines" for problem solving, information sharing, and reflective listening (Tallerico, Burstyn, and Poole, 1993, p. 19). Perhaps you could be
instrumental in persuading women who have retired or exited administrative posts to serve as resource persons.

Do not overlook the importance of your own research. In higher education, research is an expectation, if not a requirement. On the other
hand, in basic education, research is almost never a prerequisite for an
administrative—or, for that matter, a teaching—position. This is unfortunate because research is important in professional development. The
research process keeps your skills sharpened, and both the process and
the content provide you with additional knowledge. Even if you are in
an institution that does not require research, your publications, or even
evidence of the research in the form of reports, can provide substantia-
tion for retention of your position and can give you an edge in your application package when you are ready for professional advancement.

Informal women-to-women connections are also very important in
your professional development. These connections can be very powerful, but you must initiate them. One natural way is to keep in contact
with the women professors in your preparatory program as well as your
women university colleagues. This kind of informal contact can form the

basis of a women's networking or webbing infrastructure. (See the section on networking in chapter 11.)

State departments of education can also provide information and assistance to the enterprising female administrator. If your state has not already established records, you may be able to interest them in forming a state or national resource database or registry for women in educational administration. In fact, you (in collaboration with your state department of education) may find this to be an opportunity to apply for a federal grant. Affirmative action regulatory agencies are another possibility for stirring interest in a national database or registry for women in educational administration positions. The following site has an extensive list of job registries that may give you some ideas for such an initiative: www.niu.edu/crc/major/HigherEducationJobListings.htm.

Finally, you should become proactive in support of the work of such key coalitions as the National Policy Board for Educational Administration (discussed above). Call (202-293-2450) or e-mail for information (www.npbea.org). Ask to attend their meetings, and offer your help. It is to your advantage for national standards and certification to become a reality for everyone in the field.

The list of possibilities for professional development is limited only by your own inventiveness. The one positive thing about being in a profession in which there are not many women is that you can have a larger hand in shaping the future of the field and your own professional career.

A WORD TO WOMEN

Each one of us can help further the cause for all women aspirants by offering to mentor both men and women and to educate all audiences at every opportunity. It is by being active in outside organizations, as well as in our own professional organizations, that we can demonstrate the competency of women in positions of leadership. We need to be heard through our own voices and in our own words. That is why throughout this book the reader has been encouraged to write, to speak, to volunteer for committees, to be seen, and to be heard. We must continue to do this again and again and again, for we will not always be heard the first time.

We must make a conscious and deliberate effort to encourage other women to consider opportunities that will give them experiences in leadership. Let us also encourage all teachers—women and men—to take courses in administration so that they can be better prepared decision makers, curriculum developers, supervisors, and public relations agents, and so that they can become more politically aware and more socially conscious. All faculty should be provided training in budgeting and scheduling as well because these are additional skills that make for better understanding of the entire school system. The more that everyone knows and understands about the complete educational process, teaching and learning notwithstanding, the better our educational institutions will be.

To those readers who are not sure they want to be educational administrators, I advise you to take the educational administration courses, meet the people, and find a forum for discussion. You have nothing to lose and everything to gain. Even if you decide that administration is not for you, I guarantee you that your eyes will be opened, your horizons expanded, and your outlook changed.

14

DIFFICULTIES AND DILEMMAS

Those who follow the calling of educational administration can count on being faced with many difficulties and dilemmas; as a result, problem solving has become the single most important function of an administrator in today's educational arena. Every professional career has seen its challenges increase in complexity in the past thirty years, but educational administration has traveled the furthest from being a quiet, safe, well-respected, low-stress, almost routine job to being one of the most stressful, controversial, and complicated positions in our society. Problems almost unheard of a generation ago now dominate the life of an educational administrator. Problem areas have multiplied almost before our eyes during the course of our careers: Bible reading, racial slurs, prayers at graduation, the Pledge of Allegiance, access for people with disabilities, desegregation and resegregation, freedom of speech and assembly, contract negotiations, Individualized Education Programs (IEPs), home schooling, school choice, charter schools, distribution of religious material, censorship, inclusion, academic freedom, campus crime, discipline and students' rights, freedom of the (school) press, gangs, sex education, Title IX, lawsuits for disqualification from participation in activities, drugs, textbook and library book choice, copyright laws, libel, search and seizure, school safety, and ever-tightening school budgets. Almost more

than one person can fathom, these issues have become our modern-day
behemoths, yet are not as easy to slay as the dragons of yore.

While it is beyond the scope of this book to address all the myriad
problems you may face as an educational administrator, it is the intent
of this chapter to look at the six general areas most likely to cause you
concern, either personally or in your daily dealings: (1) discrimination,
(2) pressure groups, (3) sexual harassment, (4) interpersonal relations,
(5) employment, and (6) personal considerations. We will look at these
areas from the point of view of how you can handle some of the "tough
stuff." We live in very litigious times and you are urged to use caution
and to seek advice of an attorney to review any decision that will affect
you or others in your charge. Because administrators find themselves in
hot water more often over being hasty and arbitrary than for any other
reason, be advised to keep a level head, gather the facts, and *do your
homework* before taking any action.

DISCRIMINATION

Discrimination takes on many guises. The term as it is being used here
refers to the practice, whether intentional or unintentional, of showing
favoritism toward one individual or group at the expense of others or of
excluding any individual or group for reasons arbitrarily decided by another individual or group. The three most prevalent areas of discrimination in the educational setting are gender, age, and race. You very
likely have been the victim of at least one of these discriminatory practices, and some of you may have faced all three.

Gender Bias

Gender bias is not restricted to educational administration, even
though the premise of this book assumes that gender bias is a contributing factor reflected in the low percentage of women administrators. In the corporate and professional world, many women are coming
to the painful realization that even when they reach the upper ranks,
they still lag behind their male counterparts in pay, perks, and power. As
this realization increases, so do the lawsuits charging sex discrimination.

Such complaints have taken on more seriousness since 1991 when Congress passed a civil rights bill that, for the first time, allowed women to sue in federal court for damages for discrimination. This, of course, places more importance and focus on sex discrimination cases and has led to even more challenging decisions on the part of women who have been discriminated against.

According to lawyer Jerry Liddle, "People who are discriminated against on the basis of age or race are angry that they've been treated shabbily, but the women who come into my office with a case of sex discrimination are often embarrassed. They feel they should have been able to handle it on their own" (Gordon, 1992, p. 68). As they see men being promoted, women are often told, "Titles aren't important," or they are given token titles that never appear in the official records. And, of course, flattered as you are, you accept the "promotion" at face value and feel rewarded. The same person who says to you, "You belong here," is often also the one who forgets to make your title clear to everyone else and who tells you, when you ask for a raise commensurate to the position, "Maybe we can do better for you next year." Do not trust spoken words. Get everything in *writing*.

Filing Suit

When you realize that you have been discriminated against, either by lack of promotion or reassignment to another position, you have a choice to make. In considering whether or not to file a discrimination suit you must, of course, remember that there will be a high price to pay. The risk is your professional career. Not only does word get around that you have filed a suit (and you may find it hard to be hired elsewhere), but also, while the suit is in litigation, you most likely will become an outcast in your present position, often ignored and relegated to duties a clerk could do as well. It also does not help your reputation when the employer's defense is based on trying to prove that you are professionally incompetent, despite years of excellent performance evaluations.

In other instances, however, filing a suit is the only way you can regain your professional stature and, in some cases, compensation for lost wages and the expense of bringing suit. It is certainly not comfortable being in litigation, but then neither is being a doormat.

Justice

You may find yourself asking, "What price justice?" Are you willing to face your peers and your board? Will those who came to you privately to voice their support and to profess their dismay at your mistreatment be willing to speak openly on your behalf, thus placing themselves in potential jeopardy with the institution against which you are bringing suit? Most of your colleagues will not be willing to do this.

Before you make your decision, write everything out, either in a narrative or as an outline. You might request your professional association to ask its legal staff to review your material, but don't count on their running to your defense. They select the cases they will support based on the wider-reaching impact of the potential outcome. If what happened to you could happen to other members, and might make case law, your chances are better that the association will handle your case. Be very, very careful, however. Professional association or not, there is no guarantee that those who read your documentation will keep your information confidential. The attorney will keep the professional confidence, but do not be too sure of the other persons on staff.

Another area you should consider is the politics of the situation. Career administrators have suggested to me that some state associations tend to protect the CEOs of institutions and will not help any subordinate administrator who may be taking legal action against the superintendent or the president of the institution in question.

You may want to find a good labor attorney or one who is experienced in labor and school law. Make discreet inquiries and get a referral from someone who has been in a situation similar to yours or from your own personal attorney (*not* the attorney for the institution where you are working). She or he should willingly offer you a list of names and should be able to give you a brief background on all those on the list. If you live in a rural area, your choices may be somewhat limited. If so, select the attorney with experience in discrimination suits, wrongful termination, or a specialty as close to your problem as possible. Interview any prospective attorney to determine whether she or he is familiar with gender discrimination, and ask for information about other gender discrimination cases she or he has handled.

Age Bias

Older employees are the fastest-growing segment of the workforce and usually are also the most productive. Unfortunately, they frequently face age discrimination. Despite research showing that older employees, administrators included, are very often superior performers and that their performance output increases with age, there is still an assumption that contributions decline in proportion to the years worked. This should be a concern of an aspiring female administrator because, if you fit the statistical profile, you are already older than your male counterpart when you begin your administrative career path.

Often, however, the real culprit in age discrimination situations is a younger CEO or a younger board of directors who regards anyone older as a threat. Many younger new CEOs do not want any of the old guard around to remind them of the way things were. Even if the old guard is in the vanguard of school reform and on the cutting edge of new programs, they can be viewed by new bosses as reminders of the past. You are especially vulnerable if you were a major part of the history of your institution. Even if this younger head of the institution thinks she or he might learn from you, her or his youth (and maybe insecurity) may not allow her or him to ask. She or he will feel much more comfortable if you are not around and will be pleased to show you the door.

Do not, however, be pushed out unless you are ready to go. The law is on your side. The federal Age Discrimination in Employment Act (ADEA), enacted in 1967, is based on an important policy and fact: that ability, not age, should determine an individual's qualifications for getting and keeping a job. Most states have also passed laws against age discrimination that provide even greater protection than the federal ADEA. In instances where the state system is more favorable than the federal ADEA, you may wish to pursue a claim with the state agency.

Age discrimination is not an easy thing to prove, especially if you are not blatantly dismissed, but rather suffer subtle, not easily substantiated, slights, such as being passed over for promotion, not being sent to professional development seminars, not being placed on important committees, or other situations that could affect compensation or benefits. If you suspect that you are being discriminated against because of age, first obtain a copy and interpretation of the ADEA. You need to know your rights as age discrimination becomes an increasingly significant issue in our society.

Be alert to any comments about your age or unsolicited comments about retirement or being tired of working. Make sure that you yourself do not make any kinds of comments along these lines either about yourself or about others. It is not appropriate to discuss anyone's ability based on her or his age. Not only is it not good manners, it also could lead to a lawsuit. What might at first appear to be genuine concern for your years of service may be a way of laying the groundwork for discriminating against you. Unless you really do prefer a less demanding position, do not take an easier job without thoroughly investigating all of the ramifications. A lateral move is particularly suspect. Make sure that lateral move is not a dead end or a position that may be slated for phasing out. A reduction in responsibilities is a sign of being eased out, as is a sudden drop in performance evaluations. Be alert to these actions and document them.

If any action sends a signal that you are being discriminated against because of age, start keeping records of conversations and actions. Talk with your superordinate and share your concerns. Do not allow yourself to be brushed off, and don't become confrontational.

If you have been discriminated against, you should file a charge of discrimination with the Equal Employment Opportunity Commission (EEOC) and the state agency for two reasons: (1) it makes the EEOC aware of discriminatory practices and allows them to investigate and attempt to informally resolve the charge, and (2) it preserves your right to file a lawsuit. Should you decide to file a lawsuit, find an attorney who specializes in employment law. In addition to checking the sources suggested above, you can also request names of attorneys with a specialty in labor relations from the National Employment Lawyers Association (www.nela.org), the local bar association, AARP, and the EEOC itself.

Tell your attorney all the facts of the case and what you consider to be an adequate resolution. Listen to the advice of the attorney about the merits of the case, the likelihood of success, and the practical considerations about bringing a lawsuit. Weigh the pros and cons carefully. You stand to gain back pay, lost wages, benefits and reinstatement, and possibly damages, as well as attorney's fees. However, if you win and are reinstated, you may find a very uncomfortable situation awaiting you.

Racial Bias

So much has already been written on racial bias that it has become almost a cliché, except to those who are affected. Title VII of the Civil Rights Act of 1964 made clear that discrimination in employment based upon race, color, sex, religion, or national origin is prohibited. The EEOC is empowered to enforce Title VII through investigation and/or federal lawsuits. In fact, a private individual alleging discrimination must pursue administrative remedies within the EEOC before that individual will be allowed to file suit against an employer under Title VII. This legislation, along with affirmative action, has been instrumental in alleviating some of the overt racial discrimination in the hiring of minorities. It has not, however, been able to affect the still prevalent covert racial discrimination in minority hiring.

One of the major difficulties minorities have faced in any affirmative action or civil rights cases is that courts will not find a violation of a minority plaintiff's civil rights unless the plaintiff proves by a preponderance of the evidence that the school board allowed race to affect its employment or promotion practices. Courts will not intervene where the school board can prove that its decision not to hire or promote a minority was based on legitimate criteria, for example, academic qualifications, work experience, licensing, attitude, or job performance.

On the other hand, it is illegal for employers or managers to avoid charges of racial bias by simply not criticizing the work of minority subordinates. The Fifth Circuit U.S. Court of Appeals declared such nonaction to be unlawful discrimination. Further, the court found, it is a violation of the 1964 Civil Rights Act to use race to deny workers the opportunity to improve, as having faults pointed out is viewed as an effective way to get better at the job. Thus, employers cannot simply "hire and ignore" because that may prevent persons from learning from mistakes and, in turn, possibly being promoted.

Nevertheless, for most minorities, the larger problem lies in being hired in the first place. While there are scattered statistics on the small number of minorities in educational administrative positions, there have not been major studies of the problem of racial discrimination in the hiring of minority educational administrators. In addition, there have been even fewer studies of minority female educational administrators, mostly because there has not been a definite population from which to draw a sample.

Most minority women have found that being female and a racial minority makes it twice as complicated to break into the hierarchy of administration. They have little problem gaining entry-level elementary principalships or staff positions, but find it nearly impossible to move out of middle management. In addition, many minority women suffer from the same problems women in general have experienced in the field. As has been stated throughout this book, people tend to hire people like themselves, and minority women, even more than women in general, do not fit the typical administrative model, regardless of their competence.

The recourse for racial discrimination is the same as that for gender and age bias. If you are discriminated against because of race or color, you should seek the assistance of an attorney. Contrary to what the advice in this section appears to be, I am not necessarily advocating that legal steps be taken in all presumed cases of bias or discrimination. Rather, the reader is cautioned to learn her legal rights and the recourses she has. Do not simply rely on the advice of well-meaning friends. Seek counsel, review the facts, project the consequences, weigh the issues, and then decide what is best for *you*.

PRESSURE GROUPS

While pressure groups come in all forms, what they have in common is zeal and loyalty to a cause. Pressure groups can be formally organized with officers and a treasury, or they can be informally organized with a wide spectrum of individuals who come together only because they feel strongly on a particular issue. An example of an informal group is parents of students attending an arts magnet school who are reacting to the school board's vote to no longer pay the tuition to the school. Chances are that prior to the board action, the parents of students attending the arts magnet school did not know one another. More than likely, individual parents decide to attend a board meeting, and it is there that they discover they are not alone in their reaction to the decision of the board. Depending upon the outcome of the board meeting, this informal group of parents who share a similar concern may be drawn into organizing formally. More than likely, once the issue is resolved, the group will disband and the parents will not meet together again.

On the other hand, a formal group, on the local level, is usually organized around an issue and will present a united front or a single position statement on behalf of the group. Many such single-issue groups form to lobby for a particular program. If the educational institution has a policy and guidelines for presenting requests, there is usually very little problem. In most cases, there will be a process of presentations, discussion, and review by the administration and the board, which then results in a decision. Case closed.

It is when "request" or "issue" groups become pressure groups that problems can arise for the administrator in charge. Pressure groups usually have an agenda or issue that is, if not downright controversial, then at least very emotional. The difference between pressure groups and other groups is that the pressure groups are usually very well organized, and will not take no for an answer. They will use everything in their power to get what they want, even to the point of campaigning to elect "their" candidate(s).

Everywhere we turn today we see self-appointed groups who view themselves as the conscience of American education. Groups that once were dismissed with a shrug and perhaps a scoff have become more sophisticated and have learned how to use the system to their advantage. Regardless what they call themselves—their names often include the words "Right" or "Citizens"—they have become a force. Even the use of *Right* in their titles is studied, with its suggestion not only of political leaning but also of being correct, and *Citizens* implies they are speaking for the majority. These groups have taken a battle position against social issues with which they do not agree. They have placed a smoke screen in front of these issues by publicly proclaiming that their agenda is "clean living, solid academics, and family values," making it difficult for others to take issue with them.

Unless you have personally witnessed the debates or presentations the members display (rallies might be a better word), you cannot imagine how well they work the crowd. They dominate a debate because they do not allow fair practice and equal time the way most of us understand the formal process of debate to be. They are masters at misrepresenting the views of the opposition and experts at speaking in generalities. They know all the right emotional buttons to push, and those who try to present logical responses to their challenges find it impossible to be heard, either because of being interrupted or because of having to answer defensively—not a good position from which to make points.

What Is Your Recourse?

As an administrator, you are expected to show consideration to all constituents, so when such groups attend your meetings, you must be polite. Never be confrontational, but gear yourself in advance not to be vulnerable. You cannot win by debate with these groups, so your best strategy is to have a procedure in place for *all* persons who wish to address the board or to meet with you personally. (Personal meetings are less likely to occur, as pressure groups like large audiences.) Hire a consultant to train your board, or do the in-servicing yourself, but make sure you do it. Your procedure should include a time limit for all presenters and/or all topics (in case a group brings many speakers, all on the same topic), and stick with that format for everyone at every board meeting. Your board members should not respond to the presentations, except to thank the presenters for attending the meeting. Neither you nor the board members should be baited into answering.

If the pressure group attends an open forum, rather than a board meeting, again you must have ground rules and adhere to them. There should be equal time given to all sides, but not in a debate forum. You will feel an urge to respond to untrue allegations or implications; however, you should think carefully before answering and may choose not to respond at all. Do not be placed on the defensive. Should you choose to respond, remain calm and state only the facts. Do not feel that you must answer point for point, and never, ever get in an argument with a pressure group.

SEXUAL HARASSMENT

As volumes have been written on this subject and most readers are presumed to be familiar with the points of law, the most helpful information for aspiring women administrators on dealing with sexual harassment is to (1) look at sexual harassment as just another form of a power play and (2) empower yourself against those who are abusing that power.

Sexual Harassment as Power

In the animal kingdom, the old prey upon the young and the powerful upon the less powerful. One would think that in a civilized society, we would have more befitting ways to interact with one another. In an age that preaches fairness and equality and in a nation that legislates against those who do not practice parity, we should expect to find tolerance and good will. Such is not always the case.

It becomes more and more clear that cases of sexual harassment have less to do with sex than with gender. Sexual harassment is not new to our culture, but ever since 1991 when professor Anita Hill accused Supreme Court nominee (now justice) Clarence Thomas of lewd and overbearing conduct toward her, the country has been trying to determine the difference between innocent fun and genuine pain.

The pain felt by most women who suffer indignities in the workplace is not the pain inflicted by men's overtures of sexual desires. Women feel pain because they are made to feel inferior intellectually, emotionally, and professionally in situations where they have every right to feel equal. What women are feeling is not harassment, but bigotry being played out through power of position, physical size, or just plain "macho" ego used to lord over women.

Recall situations when a man has said to a woman, "Now, honey, you may be right, but . . ." This is certainly not a sexual "pass," but it has an edge of condescension and belittlement. Such terms as *honey* or *young lady* (when the person being addressed is well past debutante age) are used to lessen the value of what a woman is saying, even if the person using these engaging terms does not believe he is doing so deliberately. These patronizing tactics send the message that it's still a man's world and what the woman says is of little consequence. Most women resent being addressed in terms of endearment, but rationalize that men are teasing or just being good natured. I would go so far as to say that in many instances the men themselves aren't consciously aware of just how these comments are put-downs. That is what makes the situation so maddening. I would go further to say that in even more instances, the women ignore the comments at the moment they occur, but internally harbor the consequences. These subtle messages, repeated over and over and over again, year after year, from childhood through adulthood, all add to the reminder that some are still trying to keep women "in their place."

The most unfortunate results of sexual harassment, bigotry, and power plays are loss of a job, loss of opportunity for advancement, and loss of self-worth. Loss of self-worth is worse than lost employment because it is more insidious and longer lasting. Being devalued is insulting and hurtful to the very core of one's being. That is the point. Once you feel devalued, the harasser has won, and bigotry prevails.

Empowering Yourself

The best way to combat sexual harassment is to empower yourself and to strive to eradicate this harassment from your life and your educational institution. As an administrator, you will be in a position to combat harassment of all kinds in any area under your jurisdiction. Don't be swayed by those who try to dismiss this very real issue as not being a problem. To ignore it, you condone it.

Empowerment in the institution. Men identify fewer behaviors as harassment than do women. When men do identify a behavior as harassment, they still often maintain the belief that women will be flattered. That is why "harassment behaviors" may need to be specifically listed in a policy. Make sure your institution develops and adopts a strong policy on sexual harassment.

A good policy should address harassment of both employees and students, explaining what sexual harassment is and providing examples of unacceptable conduct. The policy should clearly describe the grounds for taking disciplinary action against alleged offenders and explain grievance procedures and other processes of recourse. Individuals should be encouraged to report any unwelcome sexual conduct. It is a good idea to designate several persons in the institution to be "first contacts," as often the supervisor is either the accused harasser or a friend of the accused and, therefore, should not be the only contact person available. Both men and women should be involved in designing the policy, and at least one of the available first contact persons should be female.

Organizational climate plays a significant role in legitimizing or discouraging sexual harassment. The entire institutional atmosphere must be made free from gender (and other) inequities. Professional development and/or training programs should be made mandatory for everyone. Awareness needs to be raised among students, staff, and administrators.

The program should be divided into separate sessions for administrators, supervisors, classroom teachers, and support staff (as well as students, of course). Make sure the emphasis is on changes in *behavior*. It would be a bonus if, in the process, attitudes also change, but you will find more success in attempts to initiate behavioral changes. Sessions on preventing sexual harassment should be conducted annually.

The use of inclusionary language is another way to address the issue of sexual harassment in a supportive, subtle way. A committee on equality in the workplace is another positive step you can take. You can also, by your own example, set a tone of equality and respect for the dignity and worth of all persons. Simply by your treatment of others, you can lead your institution to a heightened awareness and improved relations among all members. To maintain a sense of moral integrity within your institution, you must take the lead to ensure that students and employees have a safe, equitable environment in which to learn and work.

Empowerment in your personal situation. You have been sexually harassed if you feel violated, intruded upon, or exploited. You have been harassed when you are uncomfortable around the alleged harasser and you find yourself avoiding him because of what he might say or do. (The masculine pronoun is used here for convenience and because it is mostly women who are here being addressed and mostly men who are their harassers.) And you have been harassed when your heart knows you have been assaulted as being something less, something not worthy, or someone not quite human. Health problems associated with harassment are also a good indicator that you may be suffering from harassment. These health problems are similar to those that result from other stressful situations and include headaches, chronic fatigue, nausea, sleep and appetite disturbances, more frequent colds, and urinary tract infections.

The first step to your own empowerment in these situations is to face the harasser. Tell him that you do not appreciate his words (or actions) and that you want him to stop. Don't get into an argument; simply state your purpose and then leave. Go to your desk and document what happened. Record the incident itself as well as your follow-up words to the harasser. You may never need these records, but if you document everything, you will have accurate information if you ever do need it. Another option is to write to your alleged harasser, but I would recommend speaking with him first; then, if he does not take you seriously, send him a memo.

Second, talk about this to someone you trust implicitly. The emotional support can be helpful, but do make sure that your confidante is someone on a similar professional level, but preferably not in your institution. This first-line support may be all that you need, but don't impose on a friendship if you feel the need for a professional counselor.

Next, make sure to not take the harassment personally. That statement may sound contradictory because harassment is quite personal, but if you understand that sexual harassment is a weapon used to gain power over you, you can then direct your anger at the weapon, not at yourself. The harasser wants you to feel cheap, devalued, and powerless. Do not let him get to you. You do not need your personal or professional validation from someone who uses intimidation.

Take time to reflect on what is happening to you, and to gather your inner forces. In addition to keeping a record of events, try writing a daily journal. Think about how you would write your story as an article for publication, focusing on the facts. Writing can be both cathartic in externalizing what has happened and helpful in gaining a more objective perspective on your situation.

This also might be a good time to concentrate on updating your resume. Reviewing your accomplishments can help you regain your confidence, and rewriting your resume will help you put things into a more positive framework. In addition, you will be ready if you decide to pursue another position.

If the harassment is seriously affecting you and your work performance, take some time with your family or a close friend to learn a new skill, travel, or just retreat. If you can afford the time and the harassment situation is tense, get away for at least a week. This will help you clear your head and plan your strategy (either while you are away or, better yet, upon your return).

In a major harassment situation in which speaking and writing to the perpetrator is not helping, talk to an attorney. Even if you are not planning to file a lawsuit, consulting an attorney can help you regain control. She or he can serve as an informed advisor, clarifying your rights and how they may have been violated. An attorney can also evaluate the documentation you have made and can advise you as to whether or not you have a case. (Bear in mind, though, that while most attorneys will not advise you to file a lawsuit if they do not believe you have a strong case, attorneys are trained to be contentious.)

Most important is your own attitude toward what is happening to you. Approach this problem step-by-step, by gathering information, documenting, reviewing the evidence, looking at options and long-range implications, and making informed choices. Keep away from anyone who tries to tell you that what happened is your own fault. It is not.

INTERPERSONAL RELATIONSHIPS

The subject of interpersonal relationships could fill several volumes. Here, we are briefly touching on the basics of coping with conflict, anger, criticism, and familiarity, as these issues can cause problems without ever coming to the surface. If you can learn to recognize the signs, you can deal with the underlying issues before major problems develop.

Conflict Resolution

Most people think of fighting when they see the word *conflict*. They also think of someone with physical size and strength as the logical choice to resolve the conflict. Such stereotypical responses die hard, despite evidence to the contrary that it is women who have more real-life experience than men in conflict resolution. Regardless of the extent of their formal administrative experience, women know more about conflict resolution because of the way they were reared. Most girls are brought up to please, and are, by nature and/or nurture, conciliators because they want everyone to be happy. That nature is a distinct advantage in dealing with conflict resolution.

According to Shakeshaft (1987), studies of women and men find that women approach conflict resolution somewhat differently than men do. Women, says Shakeshaft, are more likely to withdraw from conflict or to use collaborative strategies, while men rely more heavily on authoritarian responses. Further, women are said to be more effective at resolving conflict among staff members and in using conflict-reduction techniques more often than men. Women also have been found to be more respectful of the players, especially of teachers, than are men, and it may well be that this regard for the dignity of individuals is the key attribute in resolving conflict.

Women see conflict as a negative state and prefer to eliminate it, whereas men are more combative and are more likely to enjoy the contention. Women, prepared as they are in the traditional roles as wife, mother, and daughter, are more likely to try to promote and maintain harmony to retain the group interaction. This promotion and maintenance of harmony begins in the way girls play games in childhood. Girls typically quit a game rather than fight among themselves (believing, it can be assumed, that the quarreling is not worth the price of friendship).

As a woman administrator, you can use these natural strategies to your advantage. Rather than taking the typical (male) entrenched stance of a firm position, you can ask the parties in conflict to look at and list their various points of priority. By knowing what is of priority to each party, you can help mediate by having each side review its own concerns, as well as the concerns of the opposing side. By reviewing each other's concerns and talking about those rather than the overall position, you can help resolve things, piece by piece.

In the case of a stalemate, where neither side wants to lose face by backing down, you can help each side save face by maintaining the integrity of each side's position and the dignity of each one's personal self. This is more important than winning all the points. Follow your natural inclination in serving as peacemaker and you'll see that your own calm, respectful approach can do wonders in dealing with conflict as a people issue, rather than as a position issue.

Anger

Despite the fact that most women can hide their anger better than men can, all executives have occasional temper flare-ups. Anger is perfectly normal. What is important is how you deal with it. Taking the wrong approach can have serious repercussions. For instance, if, as a female, you ever shout, you will be labeled forever after as a shrew or as having a short fuse. If you lash out at your staff, either professional or support personnel, for mistakes they have made, it could destroy their motivation (and perhaps loyalty). It is expected that as an administrator you will be in control of yourself at all times. You cannot afford to ever lose your temper in front of anyone. Wait until you get in your car or are in your own home—alone.

Learning how to manage anger is the key to avoiding negative consequences. View this as another process. First, *frame* the anger by taking a step away from the situation and collecting yourself. Take a walk, read something unrelated to what angered you, or visit a place where there are children. Next, *claim* the anger, by admitting that you are upset. To deny the anger can trigger migraine headaches, stomach ulcers, or even heart attacks. Instead of focusing on being mad, identify the true issue causing the anger. Once you have determined the cause, then you need to *deal* with it. Ask yourself, "Is the problem something that isn't really important or is it upsetting to the point where my self-worth is being eroded?" If you decide that it is of great importance, then decide to take action, but take the action on the issue, not the anger.

The dialogue process for dealing with anger goes something like this:

"When you talked to the faculty about things we discussed in private, I felt . . . (betrayed, angry, surprised)."

"The effect of this behavior on me was . . . (embarrassment, upset, anger)."

"In the future, I would like you to first discuss with me before you relay to others what we have discussed in private."

After making this or a similar statement to the person with whom you are annoyed, you should stop and wait for a response. Deal only with the current issue and not with any other unrelated issues or the personality of the individual. Don't make comments such as "You *always* . . ." or "You *never* . . ."

Criticism

When you are on the receiving end of criticism from your superior or the board, do not take it personally. The criticism is aimed at an action, not at you as an individual. Most women (unless they were active in organized sports) have not had the childhood experiences of criticism of an action, and, as a result, tend to personalize all such comments. Because mothers, aunts, or sisters generally criticize only appearance or personal behavior, women in general are not used to constructive or directed criticism, and often view it as something to be avoided at all costs, or as a sign that they are total failures at everything.

When faced with criticism, set your emotions aside and calmly ask, "What specifically did I do to upset (or anger) you?" Hold the criticism away from your personality. Accept the criticism as a comment on an aspect of your performance, not as a universal statement of your worth. Even if the criticism is directed to one of your personality traits, ask the critic to pinpoint the behavior that is upsetting her or him. Try then to lead the criticism into a positive direction so that you can learn from it. Apologize, but do not overdo it. If you believe that the criticism is unwarranted, you can tactfully say, "I'm sorry you feel that way about it." With those words you are not admitting to something that does not deserve criticism, yet you are acknowledging the critic's anger.

Familiarity

Beware of overtures to a too-friendly relationship. Collegiality is wonderful, but can be overdone. I am reminded of one superintendent's attempts to institute collegiality by announcing to all staff, both professional and support, that the school district would thenceforth operate by collegiality, as if saying the word would make it happen. As he neglected to define the term, except to say that everyone would be on a first-name basis, one of the building secretaries, with great glee, explained the concept to several faculty members, "It will be just like all of us being in college together!"

Certainly there should be a certain amount of camaraderie, and a united spirit is good for morale, but cohesion can go too far if you are not selective in the activities you sponsor. For special events, such as birthdays, marriages, births of babies, and graduations, the staff should be encouraged to supplement the coffee break or lunch with a cake or cheese and fruit tray. Do not, however, condone a "one big, happy family" atmosphere, or you are asking for problems. It is too complex to be both a buddy and a boss.

When a team—collegial or otherwise—is too close, one of two things usually happens: (1) resentment builds up against the one "not pulling weight" or (2) teams that are too intimate tend to cover up for the weaker members. You, as the supervisor, face an awkward situation in such instances where a team member is slated for firing, reassignment, or retrenchment. How do you fire or reassign a buddy?

It is far better to set boundaries at the beginning. By doing so, you help define the culture of the institution and the limits it puts on all employee social interactions. As you demonstrate where and how to keep your distance, your staff will pick up on the message you are sending: Some fraternization is fine, but a lot is not.

After-hours socializing is particularly risky. You need to respect your staff's private time as they need to respect yours. If they schedule evening events and do not invite you, so much the better. If, on the other hand, they do extend an invitation to you, you could attend occasionally for a *brief* time, but miss enough of the events to send a clear message. It is always polite to express appreciation for the invitation, but you should beg off attending most.

Seek and maintain friendships away from work. Good friendships require a sharing of yourself, which is unwise in a professional relationship, especially in a mix of supervisors and the supervised. Find friends outside your institution who share a similar background and with whom you can be yourself in a social situation, as well as in situations of sharing professional concerns. By doing so, you can separate business from socializing and will be able to maintain a more professional atmosphere in your educational institution.

EMPLOYMENT CONFLICTS

The higher you rise in the organization, the more potential there will be for employment conflicts. In administration the stakes increase, the responsibilities multiply, and the likelihood of problems expands. If you accept that employment conflicts are a natural part of being an administrator and prepare yourself to expect them and to cope with them, you will learn to take these problems in stride.

Passed Over for Promotion

Suppose you were expected to be selected for a particular administrative position. Everyone told you so. You were assured by the CEO (or the board of directors) that the job would be yours. Now you find out that the position—*your* position—has gone to someone else. What happened? What do you do? What do you say?

First, find a way to vent your disappointment or anger, but do it away from the job. Then plan your next two moves, which will be to congratulate the person who was chosen for the position and to speak to the person who had assured you that the position would be yours.

Go to the person who was selected, extend your congratulations on her or his promotion, and offer your support. You need not linger, as no doubt this meeting will be awkward for both of you. Your remarks should be genuine, and you should not express your own disappointment to the person appointed to the position. If she or he should mention your candidacy, be prepared to say something kind and tactful, such as "I'm sure you'll do a great job and I'll be here to help in any way I can." Don't act like you have something else wonderful lined up. For many reasons, this is not the time to talk about your own possible future plans.

Next, speak to the person who made the promotion decision to find out why you were passed over. Express no recriminations or accusations. Say something like, "I understand Terry has been selected as the new provost, and that's a good choice. However, as you know, I was very interested in that position and had received encouragement from a number of people in the organization. It would be helpful to me if you could tell me why I was passed over and what I could change to be the best candidate if another position opens up." Never remind her or him that the position had been promised to you, as you do not want the discussion to start off defensively.

You may not be told the real reason for the choice because decisions on promotions can be very subjective. Often the real reason is either your personality or that you were not the best match for the position. As has been mentioned numerous times, people are drawn to people like themselves. The reason you have been passed over may simply be that people think you don't fit. If that is the case, and you are astute enough to recognize it, you may have to face the fact that, very possibly, you will not get where you want to be in your present institution. The best thing to do may be to cut your losses and start looking for another position in another institution.

If you decide to look elsewhere, wait until at least a month after being passed over for promotion and then return to speak to the chief executive. Tell her or him of your decision to seek a position elsewhere

and ask for her or his support in your efforts. Chances are you will receive help. You may not only be making the best choice for yourself in
this, but you also may be alleviating an awkward situation for all concerned, and may receive even more assistance in relocating than you
would have under usual circumstances. The initial disappointment can
result in your favor through the CEO's feeling more of an obligation to
aid you in finding other employment.

Women, in particular, need to take a good look at the opportunities
they are (not) given at work. If you find you are not getting the assignments that will help you advance in your career, then move to a job in
another institution where you can get the right experience. Women tend
to be too loyal to institutions and employers, assuming those employers
have their best interests in mind. You should not place the charting of
your career into someone else's hands. That someone, more than likely,
has his or her hands full looking out for his or her own career, not yours.

When Your Contract Is Not Renewed

Even worse than being passed over for promotion is being let go. Not
fired. Just not retained. If you are in a nontenured position, you are always in danger of not having your contract renewed. That is one of the
risks of being in top management.

Most times, you should have some warning signs, but, occasionally, a
board of control will simply decide among its own members that they
want a change for apparently no particular reason. I have seen this happen, leaving superintendents totally bewildered. Unexpected nonre-
newal of contracts occurs more frequently in public schools than in
higher education, although the operative word here is *unexpected*. Either college presidents are more astute than school superintendents or
they can read their boards better. In addition, in public education where
school boards are elected by the public, the politics and agenda can
change overnight.

Your best hedge against unexpectedly being left out in the cold is to
negotiate a good, clear contract when you first accept a position. Consult an attorney if you are inexperienced in negotiating a contract. Regardless of how good your relationship with your board appears to be,
especially if you have come up through the ranks, keep foremost in your

mind that you are entering into a business relationship. You must protect your own interests. (See appendix C for a sample contract.)

If you maintain regularly scheduled performance evaluations with your board, you should have a good idea of their attitude toward you. You should always ask for a periodic written evaluation, with objectives, as well as assessment and evaluation. If you have a record of positive evaluations, you have a better chance of negotiating a settlement to your benefit.

Should your board vote not to renew your contract, you are entitled to know the reasons, as even a nontenured position has some protection against arbitrary and capricious dismissal. Obviously, you do not want to stay in a position where you are not wanted, but you need to leave with a good recommendation and with your reputation unsullied. Once it is definite that your contract is not being renewed, begin to negotiate the terms of your severance. Depending on the terms of your contract, as well as the circumstances under which your services are being terminated, you need legal assistance. There may be an opportunity for a buyout, a sabbatical, or other options. Get busy, so that you can come out a winner, with your dignity undamaged.

Between Positions

When you have worked all of your life and/or must work to maintain yourself, it is very difficult to be between positions. Educational administration at any level is not as secure as it once was, so don't feel singled out, even if you are the only one *you* know to whom this has ever happened. No one wants to be perceived as being out of work, so you should be prepared with responses to new acquaintances and with a strategy to get back into the workforce.

Your best approach is to be positive. When you meet someone new, talk about the challenges you anticipate from a new job or from starting your own business. Practice a one-sentence self-introduction that highlights the content of your previous job. "I'm a public school administrator" or "I work with college alumni" keeps the description of your professional self in the present tense, yet does not mention the educational institution. If you are committed to looking in a new direction or field, you might say, "Most recently I was the chief financial officer for Academe University, but now I'm looking for a similar position in the private sector."

Be realistic enough to know that the market will not come to you. You need to let it be known through professional friends or your professional association that you are seeking a new position. Make sure you sound upbeat and positive and that your energy level and commitment to finding a new position are high. You will find people far more willing to help you if it is evident that you are first helping yourself. Keep your networking alive. This means all the time, not just when you need help. Whether you are looking for a position in the same field or have decided to go into business for yourself, you should set a goal to attend at least two functions each month related to your field. Keep up your contacts at all costs.

Prepare letters to send to those with whom you dealt in the position you have left, informing them that you no longer are with Academe University, and that you can be reached at the following number (preferably your cell phone number). If you use your home phone number, use voice mail or make sure your answering machine has a professional-sounding greeting and that you and everyone in your household are prepared to respond to callers.

Before you leave your position, it may be worth discussing the benefits it would bring to the institution if you would include in this announcement letter an introduction to your successor. Perhaps an arrangement can be made for the institution to bear the costs of mailing. Such an arrangement, of course, depends on your own purposes and the conditions under which you are leaving the institution.

Keep current in the reading material in your specialty, and work on your general conversational skills. When you meet new acquaintances (who could become clients or provide leads to a new position), be ready to make small talk about current news events, general educational trends, or other common issues. Decide in advance what you can offer the people you meet, and think about ways to be in touch with them afterward. Sending a clipping relative to your conversational topic is a reasonable follow-up. Never ask new acquaintances if they know of any job openings. That is too presumptuous and not fair. If someone asks for your business card, give one, but do not offer it unless asked. You can have a small number of new cards—with your home address and cell (or home) phone number—printed quickly and inexpensively so that you have them for such occasions.

In the meantime, start a self-improvement program. Conduct a self-assessment and decide what your strengths are, what you need to do to prepare yourself for the next position, and even if you want to stay in the same kind of work. Do not continue to define yourself by who you were, but rather by who you are and who you want to become. Remind yourself of when you were in the classroom and could not imagine having the skills to transfer to any other line of work. With additional course work, you soon found yourself to be a skillful administrator. You certainly can now turn those skills into something new. Don't limit your possibilities.

I remember well when I left public education by mutual agreement when I had reached the point of the next-to-the-top position and had had reasonable assurances that I had the support for the top position. When the scenario was played out, I was passed over for the superintendency and, within nine months, was gone from an institution in which I had spent my entire professional career to that date. After leaving, I used the first three months planning to go into business for myself, and the next three getting the business started. In addition, I sorted through thirty boxes of files, a lifetime of work, keeping what I thought could be helpful and discarding what would not. That process was cleansing and gave me time to grieve and reminisce privately, yet also to close a chapter by putting things in order. I floundered for a short time, but was determined not to quit. Since that time I have discovered that the skills I spent a lifetime developing were ready to serve me well in completely different capacities.

If you live in a large enough population center, you may consider locating or forming a support group of women who are between jobs. Make these meetings (probably over breakfast or lunch) productive by preparing an agenda or a specific topic for discussion. Don't let the meetings turn into "bemoaning sessions."

Recognize that a part of you feels relieved not to have to arise and dress very early every morning, but also accept that this feeling should be only temporary (unless you really are relishing retirement). It is a good idea to organize your day. Create routines that are productive, whether they are formal or informal. It's reasonable to take more time for yourself in reading and/or writing letters, but don't become inactive professionally.

The length of time it takes to find a new path is not predictable. Sometimes things will happen more quickly than you are prepared for, and sometimes waiting for other doors to open will take longer than you can imagine. There are, however, new beginnings for all of us. You need to concentrate on being prepared for your new beginning by learning additional skills, staying active, and remaining positive in outlook.

PERSONAL RELATIONSHIPS

Your relationship with yourself and your personal well-being can present some difficulties. Certainly, you are capable and well qualified to be in your administrative position. Not only that, you have worked—and maybe even fought hard—to attain a position in administration. Why then should there be any doubt in your own mind? Why do you occasionally have a nagging doubt of being able to cope with everything?

Can You Have It All?

Every person's life is different and every woman's life is her own. If you can begin from that premise, you have a good foundation for determining how much you can have in your life. Everything has a price of time and/or money, and only you can choose how much of each you want to invest in different areas of your life. Can you have a successful career and a successful marriage? I think so. Can you be a professional star and still be a good mother? I believe so. Can you also pursue graduate school and keep up with both professional and leisure reading? Probably. Can you also be active in your neighborhood association and your children's schools? Perhaps. Can you excel at all of these? Maybe not.

You will second-guess yourself many times, but if you follow your own path and choose what is important to you, the rest will follow. Some things will not get your full attention, but those that require it will. You need to trust in your own judgment, for only you really know yourself.

Life on the Fast Track

For those determined to have it all, it can be done. There will be trade-offs and personal sacrifice. There will be inner conflict and maybe an outward struggle. You will encounter bias and some setbacks solely because of gender. Know that, and you won't waste your energy on unexpected roadblocks. You'll know the glass ceiling and the maternal wall are there, and you can expend your energy on real impediments and not ghosts.

Those who want to combine a family life with a career can succeed. The desire to find time for family life is certainly not unnatural; in fact, a successful career combined with a happy home life seems to be the hallmark of women in the twenty-first century. Despite many obstacles and not a few nightmares, women are making it.

Many of the women who are succeeding are women who work more than fifty hours a week. Their secret, if there is such advice, is their ability to manage their lives and their time, and the support they have from others, either family or paid assistants. Most must rely on an equal partnership at home, and, at the same time, refuse to let themselves be consumed by their professions. Those whose own mothers worked outside the home find that they themselves make far less of an issue of combining working and a family than those whose mothers worked only in the home.

What you need is an organizational plan and established family rituals, particularly if there are children. Most people like predictable and reliable routines in their private family time, and a routine is particularly necessary for children. If at all possible, one parent should be home in the morning when the children are beginning their day, and one parent should be there at the end of the day. There should always be a system by which contact is made by both marriage partners sometime during the day, even if it is only by telephone.

A good rule to follow if you are in an administrative position—or any professional position, for that matter—is *not* to talk about family issues at work unless it is critical. If you must take your child (or parent or even spouse) to a doctor appointment, that appointment should be referred to as yours. If it is necessary to attend a conference with your child's teacher (even if it is in your own district), call in to say you will be an hour late or leave during the day as you would for any other appointment that must be scheduled during working hours. Your personal life is really no one's business. It is expected (without mentioning) that you will make up the time or the work missed. Do not make an issue of it. This cannot be stressed enough: *Keep your personal business to your-*

self. I even advise that you not let it be known when your birthday is. You do not need to have a birthday party, nor do you need to call attention to speculation about your age. If birthday celebrations are part of the company culture, make sure your secretary knows your personal wishes, as she or he is the one the others will ask. If it is expected that the birthday celebrant treats the others to a cake or morning donuts, then provide the treat several times throughout the year, just in celebration of teamwork or for no special reason at all. Discourage any undignified calling of attention to particular birthdays such as reaching age forty or fifty. Silliness is in poor taste in a business or professional office.

Most fast-trackers begin their families at a later age, but that is a personal decision. Beginning your family early in your career can work, and may even be a good choice in the field of education, as studies show that women enter administrative positions at a later age. You also may have to make some difficult career choices if they involve relocating. Sometimes an advancement is not worth the price of moving if, for instance, it is your child's senior year in high school.

While we know that "superwoman" and "supermom" are myths, there is still some truth in the concept and the jokes made (again, at the expense of working women). A woman who works in a high-profile, highly responsible administrative position that makes great demands on her time and talent must find superhuman energy to manage her life. You will have to make adjustments. You may have to start your workday earlier, and you certainly will have to develop a clearly defined plan as to who does what on the home front.

You must make every second count. There is little, if any, downtime and you will be thinking and planning every minute. You will devise ways to save time, such as shopping by phone or online, and planning your wardrobe for the week. Learn to concentrate on the major things and the minor ones will take care of themselves. Most of all, tune out negative judgments from others as well as advice as to how you should lead your life.

The Cheerleader Syndrome

Lynn Snowden (1992) once summarized the "have's and the have not's" by observing that cheerleader tryouts are "the moment when you learn nearly everything you'll ever need to know about the business world" (p. 72). The three most elementary maxims—"Life isn't fair," "Ability doesn't guarantee success," and "Yes, of course, looks count"— are the first harsh realities of life faced by young women. Snowden compared failing to make the cheerleading squad with being passed over for promotion, and noted that "no company policy, no matter how heartless and inhumane, will ever match the level of public humiliation and institutionalized cruelty of cheerleader tryouts" (p. 74). It is the cheerleaders, she said, who go through life with a quiet confidence, as if they never have to prove anything again. In contrast, failed cheerleaders (the rest of us) tend to be intense, as if they (we) have to prove everything over and over again.

It doesn't help the noncheerleaders much to know that those who were not cheerleaders are usually more successful professionally than the girls who made the squad. All we ever see is that we have been compensating ever since high school for our failure to make the squad.

All kidding aside, the point is that many of our experiences in our formative years determine our fortitude to be successful in our adult years. You will find, however, that success is far easier to attain if you stop viewing every job as a cheerleading tryout!

SSStressss

According to the Department of Health and Human Services, 40 percent of adults say they find high stress in their jobs. Princeton Survey Research Associates found that three-fourths of employees believe the worker has more on-the-job stress than a generation ago. St. Paul Fire and Marine Insurance Company says that problems at work are more strongly associated with health complaints than are any other life stressors ("American Workers under Pressure," 1992), and a study by Northwestern National Life indicates that one-fourth of employees view their jobs as the number one stressor in their lives ("Employee Burnout," 1992). If you are one of these workers, you may want to find ways to better deal with the pressures causing the stress. Make sure your doctor is aware of any stress symptoms you may have so that medical reasons for the stress can be ruled out or attended to.

There are three basic strategies you can use to deal with stress: (1) alter your environment, (2) avoid the situation, or (3) accept it. To alter your environment is to first understand that you cannot change other people. Too often we say, "If only she/he would . . ." You cannot *force* anyone do anything, so to alter the environment, you need to change your *own* behavior. You can express to others how you feel, but do not keep saying that someone else "should . . ." Instead, try saying, "I need," "I want to," or "I'm going to."

Although you may be viewed as weak if you make a habit of avoiding uncomfortable situations, there are times when it is better just to walk away. Come back to the problem when you have the time and patience to deal with it. One instance in which it is preferable to avoid a situation is when you are angry or upset and you know your coping skills are at an ebb. Go for a walk and come back later.

When you can do nothing about a situation to alter or avoid it, you may just have to accept it. Being stuck in traffic is an example of something about which you can do nothing, as is bad weather. Working yourself up over your tardiness will only increase your stress. Accept the unavoidable delay, and if you really need to let someone know the immediate problem, use the telephone.

This capsule review of stress is by no means the answer to the myriad problems that can cause feelings of uncertainty, powerlessness, burnout, or isolation, or the reality of a really bad job or home situation. If you have a sense of helplessness and mounting frustration, please seek professional help. You owe it to yourself.

Personal Crises

It is extremely stressful to concentrate on your job responsibilities when a crisis is occurring in your personal life. You cannot possibly be working at your best, but you do need to maintain effectiveness. You owe it to your staff to let them know that you are going through a trying time, but you do not owe them an explanation of all the details. You need to share just a bit more information with the person closest in rank to you, both your subordinate and your superordinate. If you are the CEO, speak with the president of the board and your immediate assistant.

Tell them that you may need some time off and ask them to support you in the delegation of some of your responsibilities or in the delay of others. Choose carefully how much detail you want to supply, however, even to those closest to you. Again, your personal business should remain so. You do not want to become the center of office or institution gossip, even if it is in sympathy. To do so may cause you to lose status (need I add, especially if you are female).

Find support away from work, either with a good friend or with someone who has been through a similar crisis. Even if you are a stoic, you probably need someone to talk to about your feelings and/or ways to cope with the personal crisis.

Some people prefer to continue working even as they are coping. This is acceptable, but make sure you are not playing martyr. You may do more to lessen people's regard for you if you try to "tough it out," as you may be seen as being uncaring and insensitive to your own problems.

If you have suffered the loss of a family member or a similar tragedy, you need to thank all those who were/are supportive. Upon your return to work, stop at each person's desk and simply say, "Thank you for your support/caring/sympathy card. It meant a lot to me." If you do this, with just brief words to each individual, you will take care of the awkwardness that usually accompanies a return to work after such an absence.

More Successful Than Your Mate?

Let me begin this by quoting a sentence from a newspaper article published when a new superintendent was appointed in a school district in central Pennsylvania: "Mrs. S_____ has been elected as the new superintendent of _____ Area School District. She is the wife of Paul S_____, a teacher in the district." What is more disturbing than the actual wording of the article is the fact that of the half dozen people I asked to read it, not one saw anything wrong in how the announcement was written.

It is not easy to be married to a husband whose career path does not reach the height yours has. While your husband may be very proud of your accomplishments and genuinely pleased for you, beware the possible backlash. Most male egos are very fragile, and, while I wholeheartedly maintain that that is *their* problem and not the problem of their wives, reality dictates that you may need to handle this delicately. If your husband balks at attending institution functions with you, do not insist that he attend. You're a big girl, and you can go alone. It would be a bonus if your husband is wonderfully supportive and enjoys the limelight with you; however, if he does not, do not make an issue of this.

Remember that men live in a male culture in which the following epigram is only too true, and you need to let your own partner deal with this in his own way: "If a woman marries a man more successful than she is, the world congratulates her. But if a man is married to a woman more successful than he is, the world asks him how he is coping with it."

15

IT'S YOUR TURN

"If you have forgotten how to have fun, how to play, how to love, then no matter what you set out to do, you will not do it well."

(Ray Bradbury in Godfrey, 1992, p. 29)

At this juncture you should see that where women walk is not the same as where men walk, that women speak in a different voice, see the world through a different lens, and experience a world different from the world men experience. Women have traditionally had to follow the precepts of administration established by men, and while these precepts are not bad, they may not be as suitable to women as ones designed specifically for the path that women walk. Women need their own validated leadership style, based on what best works for them as female administrators. They need to follow the beat of their own drummer, in concert with the bugler who may be playing the Pied Piper of the male administrators. This is not an either-or situation. There is room in educational administration for both men and women. In fact, there is a need for both in order to achieve a balance of viewpoints as well as styles. In order to flourish, education must have leaders of both genders and build a community to embrace all ages, races, and genders. I don't ever want to hear again that "what we need is a man in this position" or "what we need is a woman in this position." Let's strive to reach the point at which we can say, "We need the best person for this position." And I don't ever want to hear another friend say, "I know I've earned my doctorate, but I'll be remembered for whom I married, and not for what I have achieved."

TIME FOR ONE'S SELF

Through all of your work and your achievements, remember to take time for yourself. It is too easy to fall into the habit of working constantly. If you are a workaholic, there is probably nothing that anyone can tell you about taking time to relax. I have heard that admonition for years, and while I believe it, I have yet to follow the advice I am urging on you who are aspiring administrators. I ask you to at least make time to laugh and to love, to play, and to be involved with other people.

You must take time for yourself, even if you need to schedule it. It doesn't matter what you find relaxing or invigorating, as long as it is something different and more creative than what you normally spend your time doing. Take a walk at lunchtime, go to a museum, listen to jazz, read a book, paint, write poetry. Join friends for dinner, play golf, join a tour to Egypt, or collect antique porcelain. Your mind and your body both need diversion from work. If you prefer to spend this precious time alone, by all means do so; however, you should also find something that you enjoy doing in the company of others, if only for the social interaction. It is better if these activities are shared by those with whom you do not work on a daily basis, as in such company you are further removed from the problems of the workplace. It is healthful to spend time with people who are not in education. It assists you in keeping a perspective on the world and in reminding you that your institution is not the center of the universe. Too many of us become so engrained in the life of the organization that we forget that there are larger issues, as well as lighter ones. Lest we forget, let us not take ourselves too seriously. A good reality check is to ask yourself, "Will this still matter five years from now?"

TIME FOR FUN

You also need to take time for some basic, down-to-earth fun. In addition to extracurricular adventures of your own, you should schedule some activities in the workplace that are geared strictly to fun. Such activities help to relieve the tension that builds in any institution and will indirectly lead to more creative ideas for solving problems.

Breaking Bread

Office lunches, brown-bag lunches, picnic lunches, breakfast meetings, evening sessions, weekend brunches, and midmorning breaks are all ways to establish a fun atmosphere. If you are considering a special project and want some brainstorming activity that is not a formal meeting, try throwing a get-together in which the food is provided. Even late-night pizza or popcorn can be an inducement for creativity and good fellowship. With a focus, these gatherings not only will build camaraderie, but also can be very productive sessions. If you want to create more attraction to these meetings, try making them "by invitation only" to people who have volunteered for other projects and have shown their interest in the institution. You can continue to add members at any time.

Sandboxes and Skunkworks

For the purpose of creative problem solving, try the sandbox or skunkworks method. These are brain sessions with a purpose: to create an idea, a project, a solution, a process, or a mission that has not heretofore been a part of the institution. Certainly it takes more than just fun to guide a creative process, but try the sandbox idea as an approach. Establishing a sandbox provides an opportunity for collective brainpower to be creative in the way that children are—spontaneous, free, and uninhibited. A classic skunkworks is a group of eight to ten people, housed in an out-of-the-way spot away from the main headquarters, who come up with innovative solutions to problems. Major companies, such as IBM, 3M, United Airlines, GE, BP, and Bristol-Myers Squibb, to name a few, have supported skunkworks. Two of the best-known examples are those that laid the groundwork for Apple computers and invented Post-it Notes.

Educational institutions, of course, cannot justify hiring persons full-time to produce innovative solutions, but we can adapt this method by holding retreats away from central headquarters and by providing a supportive, informal atmosphere. Some of the educational organizations working on school reform have been very successful with this method. It can be particularly effective with a nurturing, yet risk-taking, style of leadership.

Joline Godfrey (1992) tells of using a fun learning culture with in-service training through a storyteller. She has also used movies, game nights, and imagination sessions. I have seen films and film clips used very effectively as a source of inspiration and as a basis for creative discussion. I once attended a workshop in which a well-known and powerful clip from *The Miracle Worker* was shown. The clip showed the breakthrough of teacher Anne Sullivan to the illiterate young Helen Keller. Just asking a leading question, "How does this relate to service learning?" opened the discussion to areas that the moderators, including me, had not anticipated, but that gave a totally new view of some of the difficulties in establishing a service-learning program.

Using films or stories that appear to not be related to the topic at hand can also be used in creative thinking. Questions such as "How does this relate to the problem we are trying to solve?" can be productive by focusing on something seemingly unrelated to the central issue in order to gain a fresh perspective. Reading a short story, an article, or a novel; going to a play; or attending a football game—all of these leisure activities can be the catalyst for creative problem solving.

TIME MANAGEMENT

Utilizing time-management techniques can be helpful in balancing your workload and your attitude toward the countless tasks facing you every day. The major administrative functions can be organized into the following six: (1) planning, (2) organizing, (3) directing, (4) controlling, (5) communicating, and (6) decision making. Each function has built-in potential for stress and time wasting, but each also can be made more effective through the use of time management skills:

- *Planning.* Do not try to accomplish more in a single day than is reasonable, and do not try to do tomorrow's tasks at the expense of those scheduled for today. Build in time for daily crises, as they are bound to occur, and make sure your plans are flexible enough to accommodate interruptions that are beyond your control.

- *Organizing.* Arrange your workspace so that your secretary can screen visitors and keep unplanned interruptions to a minimum. Do not use your desk to stack letters, reports, and other reading material that you will be looking at only once before you file it. It is suggested that you do not handle a piece of paper more than once.

- *Directing.* Do not resist delegating tasks to others. Assigning responsibilities to others helps them to capitalize on their strengths.

- *Controlling.* If you do not control your own environment, others will. Stand when greeting those uninvited to your office so that they do not sit down (if you are busy). If meeting with a subordinate, schedule it in her or his office so that you can terminate the conference when you are ready to leave. Assign your secretary to screen your calls, and, to effectively manage returning telephone messages, set aside a block of time each day.

- *Communicating.* Invest time in giving clear instructions the first time. Express things as you view them, not in terms of what you think others want to hear. Communicate in meetings by concentrating on sharing information, generating ideas, and gaining consensus. Do not continue a meeting one minute longer than necessary. Provide an agenda, and keep accurate records, sending copies of the minutes to participants within forty-eight hours.

- *Decision making.* Delegate routine decisions, and spend time in making decisions immediately so that similar ones need not be revisited. Do not allow fear of failure to make a good decision deter you from coming to closure.

These, of course, are only proposals on how to make your life simpler and perhaps a bit more organized. Beyond these suggestions you need to follow a management style that works for you. Do not let others dictate *how* you should operate in your area of responsibility. Maintain confidence in your own ability. After all, *you* are the one in the administrative position.

FAST-FORWARD TIME

Women preparing to enter the field of educational administration have learned that a fast track can mean many things, including your home life as well as the work world. However, to remain on the fast track both at home and in the office, you may need to rearrange your personal time schedule. For example, you should constantly maintain contact with your family, in the morning, in the evening, and when you are out of town. Establish rituals that are inviolate, such as phoning at breakfast time when you are away, making sure one parent is always home in the morning and one is home by 6:30 each evening, and limiting weekend work hours to when the children are asleep.

Remind yourself that you cannot do everything alone. You need support people in your personal as well as your professional life. Whether that person is a hired aide or a supportive partner, you need someone.

You should establish a practice not to encourage business calls in the evening unless there is a real emergency. Some educational institutions are notorious for expecting people to be "on call" at all hours of the day and night; this is an unrealistic expectation and you should discourage it once you are in a position to do so. You need to make the decision whether or not to discuss work at home. A lot depends on the kind of work your partner is involved in and how interested that partner is. However, even if your partner encourages you to discuss your work, you are the one who needs to choose how much you want to talk about your job. On the other hand, as advised earlier in this guidebook, do not discuss family issues at work unless it is absolutely critical.

Swiss and Walker (1993) surveyed successful women, who offered this advice:

- Establish a support system.
- Become a master at management in the office and in the home.
- Take care of yourself. Exercise and find time for friendships that are your own.
- Establish a career before beginning a family. (This, of course, is a matter of personal choice, but the women in the survey who waited to start a family felt that their senior positions gave them the confidence that motherhood would not affect their professional ability.)

- Don't let trivialities get to you. Concentrate on what is important. *Tune out negative judgments from others about how you lead your life.*

TIME TO BE YOURSELF

Do not lose sight of who you are. You are you and nobody else. There is no "typical female administrator" and no "average working woman." Don't compare yourself with others, and don't rate yourself by the standards, opinions, and abilities of others. Keep in touch with your own beliefs and values, living by your own standards (based on acceptable universal principles, of course). Do not do anything that you personally believe to be wrong, as that is the source of guilt. Stay in line with your conscience and moral standards.

When you make mistakes, acknowledge that you were wrong, correct the mistake, and learn from it. Forgive yourself, and then put it completely out of your mind. Remember that you are yourself, and not your job title. Your ultimate value comes from what you are and what you do as a human being.

Learn to accept compliments and do not live by false modesty. When someone compliments you, reply simply by saying, "Thank you very much." Do not embarrass the person by rejecting the compliment with an expression such as "It was nothing." You got to where you are on merit as a result of planning, hard work, and sacrifice, so accept the compliments on your success.

TIME TO READ

In an information age, you must know how to find information. Keep up to date on accessing information through books, articles in journals, newspapers, computer information-accessing services, the electronic card catalog at your community or college library, and the Internet. The well-read person has always had an advantage, and the person who knows how to find information can jump-start any project.

Newspapers and News Magazines

You should read one newspaper daily, preferably the *Wall Street Journal*; second choices include the *New York Times*, the *Washington Post*, and the *Los Angeles Times*. The *Wall Street Journal* is the leader in news, so if you want to be the first person to know what is new, make this your newspaper of choice. Its syntax is elegant and its style impeccable. Assign your secretary to review the city daily newspaper and the weekly local that serves your area, and to clip articles relevant to your institution. One news magazine a week is enough. Choose from *Newsweek*, *Time*, or *U.S. News and World Report*, as the basic contents of each do not vary significantly.

General Culture

For general culture and ideas, try the Sunday *New York Times*, *The Atlantic Monthly*, or *The New Yorker*. For lighter, yet sophisticated fare, try *Town and Country*, and for fashion, *Harper's Bazaar* or *Vogue*.

Science

For science and technology, I recommend *Wired*, *Science*, *Scientific American*, or *New Scientist*. The latter is staffed by some of the most able science writers around, and the writing is intelligent and timely.

Education Journals

In addition to the journals that are targeted to your specialized professional positions, the following are recommended. There are two methods you can use to choose which of these best serve your needs: (1) you can subscribe to all of them for a year, and at the end of the year eliminate the one(s) whose issues remain in the "yet to read" stack; or (2) you can subscribe to one or two of them each year until you decide which are most helpful.

- The *Chronicle of Higher Education* tabloid, published weekly, is probably the most widely read publication in higher education, in departments of education, and among those who just want a review of the week's events in higher education. In addition to a comprehensive, multipage classified section containing job postings, it provides its readership with basic information on what is happening on campuses and in the world of academe and elaborates on the snippets daily newspapers tend to print.

- *Educational Administration Quarterly* is published quarterly with the sponsorship of the University Council for Educational Administration. It is the journal of choice among faculty of educational administration programs. Its purpose, which it fulfills in an exemplary manner, is to stimulate critical thought and disseminate the latest knowledge about research and practice in educational administration. It serves as a rich source of information for many doctoral students as well.

- *Educational Studies* seeks to help fulfill the stated mission of the American Educational Studies Association to enhance scholarship in and among the educational foundations disciplines by providing a vehicle for articles and essays that feature analysis of the foundations, methodology, applications of such methodology to key issues of the day, and significant research that evolves from and unifies the foundations disciplines, all focusing on the interdisciplinary nature of the educational foundations fields. Most contributors are university faculty.

- *Educational Leadership*, the monthly, flagship publication of the Association for Supervision and Curriculum Development, is the most widely read and most often quoted of all the publications in basic education. While intended primarily for leaders in elementary, middle, and secondary education, it also appeals to anyone interested in curriculum, instruction, supervision, and leadership in schools. It is well informed on whatever is happening in education today.

- *Educational Policy Analysis Archives* is published by the Education Policy Studies Laboratory of Arizona State University. It publishes research on educational policy and practice at the local, national, and international level. An interdisciplinary perspective illuminates important debates in education with a focus on schooling and higher education, as well as nonschool settings.

- *Education Review* publishes reviews of recent books in education, covering the entire range of education scholarship and practice. It is made available (online) to the public without cost as a service of the College of Education at Arizona State University and the Michigan State University Libraries.
- *Educational Review* is published by the University of Birmingham (UK) through Carfax Publishing Company and publishes general articles and accounts of research of interest to teachers, lecturers, researchers, and university students. Special consideration is given to articles dealing with research, with descriptions of experimental work in schools, and with critical reviews of teaching methods of curricular content in schools. Occasionally, there are articles on administrative problems, tests and measurement, child growth and development, and the relation of schools to the community.
- *Educational Theory*. The general purpose of *Educational Theory*, published quarterly by the University of Illinois, is to foster the continuing development of educational theory and to encourage wide and effective discussion of theoretical problems within the educational profession. This journal is devoted to publishing scholarly articles and studies in the foundations of education, and in related disciplines outside the field of education, that contribute to the advancement of educational theory.
- *Theory into Practice*, published four times a year as a journal of the College of Education of the Ohio State University, is organized around a single theme and features multiple perspectives and scholarly, yet accessible, discussions of current and future concerns of interest to today's educators. It has been nationally recognized for excellence in the field of educational journalism. Its goal is to stage a forum for the creation of an educational literature that represents the highest quality in a field of inquiry.
- *Thought and Action* is the higher education journal of the National Education Association (NEA) and is a vehicle for its policies. Membership on the editorial board of review represents a broad spectrum of backgrounds. Contributors to the journal are, for the most part, university faculty.
- *Women in Higher Education*, originated in 1992, is a monthly practitioner's news journal. Each of the 240-page issues is designed to

help smart women on campus become more savvy about how gender affects their being successful in the world of higher education. The goals of the publication are to enlighten, encourage, empower, and, sometimes, enrage women on campus.

Management and Business

As education becomes more and more a business and follows the practices of good management, it is wise to include at least one business journal in your "must-reads." *Fortune, Barron's, Forbes*, and *Business Week* are usually found among the top choices. *Business Week*, in particular, is timely and tends to items of one page. Its longer items are given an enthusiastic "thumbs-up." Another fine publication you may want to consider is *Inc*. Also recommended is a journal exclusively for members of the National Association for Female Executives, *NAFE Magazine* (formerly known as *Executive Female*), which offers in-depth articles, savvy tips, and member news and resources.

Reference Books[1]

There are many dictionaries on the market, and among those most recommended are *Webster's New World College Dictionary*, fourth edition; *Webster's Third New International Dictionary*; and *Merriam Webster's Collegiate Dictionary*, eleventh edition. Additional reference books that should be near your desk include the following:

The Elements of Style, fourth edition (William Strunk, Jr., and E. B. White)

Roget's International Thesaurus, sixth edition (A word of caution: do not rely on the ersatz thesaurus in your word processing program. An actual thesaurus provides explanations about the differences in seemingly synonymous words.)

The Chicago Manual of Style, fifteenth edition

Publication Manual of the American Psychological Association, fifth edition

Zip Code Finder (Having this at your desk is sometimes easier than going online.)

Merriam-Webster's Dictionary of English Usage

Barron's Profiles of American Colleges
The National Directory of Addresses and Telephone Numbers

These lists are by no means exhaustive, but should get you started, particularly if you are a novice. You will want to add your own choices as you become more experienced and begin to plan your own professional development. If you are still in your preparation program, these are the resources that would be very helpful in your course work.

IT'S YOUR TIME AND YOUR TURN

Despite obstacles, this is still a good time to prepare yourself to enter educational administration. There are doors to be opened by those who are ready. My parting advice to you is to periodically revisit the information contained in this book and always to be open to learning and to change. Competition in the field becomes stronger every year, so you must keep current. Do not be discouraged with disappointments; even the best have occasional setbacks. If you are well prepared and have the desire and enthusiasm to succeed, the opportunities are out there.

Success is like a spiral: it circles, yet constantly moves forward, building on what has been experienced; therefore, in conclusion, we return to where we began:

So, here you are. You've come to the crossroads. You've reached the point where you need to make some hard decisions. You know how to become a successful educational administrator and you are excited at the prospect. You are willing to take the steps necessary to become certificated and you accept the kinds of work required to reach your goal. You are on the cusp of a new adventure. You are prepared to take the plunge. You have done what you needed to do to get where you want to be. Nothing can stop you. *Absolutely nothing.*

NOTE

1. Most of the time you will want to purchase the most recent edition of a reference book. The newest available at the date of the publication of this book are included here.

APPENDIX A:
APPLICATION FOR SUPERINTENDENT
OF SCHOOLS (SAMPLE)

Personal Information

Name: _____

Address: _____

Home Phone: _____ Work Phone: _____

Social Security Number (optional): _____

Application Information

1. Complete and sign this application form.
2. Enclose three letters of reference including at least one from your last employer. (Explain if this is not possible.)
3. Include a current resume.
4. Submit college/university transcripts.
5. Include a copy of your current certification.
6. Complete personal statements requested on page 3 of this application.
7. Send all information to:

> Office of the Superintendent
> P.O. Box 000
> Anytown, Your State 00000

I. CURRENT INFORMATION
   A. Are you presently under contract in a school system?

      Yes _____ No _____

   B. If so, when does your contract expire? _____

   C. Name of system or district: _____

   D. Position: _____ Present Salary: _____

II. CERTIFICATION INFORMATION
   A. Are you currently certified as a superintendent of schools in this state?

      Yes _____ No _____

   B. Are you eligible to be certified as a superintendent of schools in this state?

      Yes _____ No _____

   C. Are you presently certified as a superintendent of schools in another state?

      Yes _____ No _____

   If yes, what state(s)? _____

NOTE: Candidates who do not hold certification in this state should contact the (state) Department of Education, Division of Certification.

III. ACADEMIC/PROFESSIONAL TRAINING
College/University Attended   Location   Degree   No. Years Completed

_____   _____   _____   _____

_____   _____   _____   _____

_____   _____   _____   _____

_____   _____   _____   _____

_____   _____   _____   _____

Please have copies of your college/university transcripts sent to the Office of the Superintendent if not enclosed in your application packet.

IV. MEMBERSHIPS IN PROFESSIONAL ORGANIZATIONS
_____

_____

_____

_____
_____
_____
_____

V. PROFESSIONAL EXPERIENCE

Position/Responsibilities	School System	No. Years	From/To

VI. OTHER RELEVANT WORK EXPERIENCES/ ACHIEVEMENTS

Position/Responsibilities	Employer	No. Years	From/To

VII. PERSONAL STATEMENTS: In giving your answers to the following questions, please limit your responses to one typewritten page each and attach these to this application.

1. Why would you like to become Superintendent of Schools in this system/district?
2. What do you feel are the most pressing challenges we face today in public education?

The board of directors of (district) is committed to conducting a thorough screening of applicants for all positions and requires the completion of the following questions of all candidates:

Have you ever been disciplined, discharged, or asked to resign from a prior position?

Yes _____ No _____

Have you ever resigned from a prior position after a complaint had been received against you or your conduct was under investigation or review?

Yes _____ No _____

Has your contract in a prior position ever been nonrenewed?

Yes _____ No _____

Have you ever not been nominated for re-employment in a prior position or ever had your nomination for re-employment not be approved?

Yes _____ No _____

Have you ever been charged with or investigated for sexual abuse or harassment of another person?

Yes _____ No _____

Have you ever been convicted of a crime (other than a minor traffic offense)?

Yes _____ No _____

Have you ever entered a plea of guilty or "no contest" (nolo contendere) to any crime (other than a minor traffic offense)?

Yes _____ No _____

Have you ever had a professional license or certification suspended or revoked in any state, or have you ever voluntarily surrendered, temporarily or permanently, a professional license or certificate in any state?

Yes _____ No _____

Has any court ever deferred, filed, or dismissed proceedings without a finding of guilty and required that you pay a fine, penalty, or court costs and/or imposed a requirement as to your behavior or conduct for a period of time in connection with any crime (other than a minor traffic offense)?

Yes _____ No _____

If you have answered YES to any of the previous questions, provide full details on an additional sheet including, with respect to court actions, the date, offense in question, and the address of the court involved. Conviction or other disposition of a crime is not necessarily an automatic bar to employment.

My signature below constitutes authorization to check my employment history, including, without limitations, criminal arrest and conviction record checks, reference checks, and release of investigatory information possessed by any state, local, or federal agency. I further authorize those persons, agencies, or entities that are contacted in connection with my employment application to fully provide any information on the matters set forth above. I expressly waive, in connection with any request for or provision of such information, any claims, including, without limitation, defamation, emotional distress, invasion of privacy, or interference with contractual relations that I might otherwise have against the system/district, its agents and officials, or against any provider of such information.

I understand that information submitted in and with this application may be disclosed to a screening and/or interview committee, which may include board members, administrators, other staff, and members of the community. I give my consent to this disclosure.

Confidentiality of application information will be maintained in accordance with (state) statutes. No information will be released to the public without prior notice being made to the candidate.

_____   _____
APPLICANT SIGNATURE   DATE

APPENDIX B: SEARCH FIRMS

The following is a sample listing of search firms that conduct searches for executives, higher education positions, superintendents, central office, and/or building-level administrators and that could be confirmed as of press time.

The Bickert Group
1340 Wilmot Drive
Deerfield, IL 60015
Phone: 708-361-4997
E-mail: robarnes@indiana.edu
Website: www.thebickertgroup.com

Bracewell & Patterson, LLP
711 Louisiana, Suite 2900
Houston, TX 77002
Phone: 713-221-1415
E-mail: jthompson@bracepatt.com
Website: www.bracepatt.com

Castallo & Silky Education Consultants
P.O. Box 100
Syracuse, NY 13215
Phone: 315-492-4474
E-mail: wdsilky@aol.com

Floyd Consulting
P.O. Box 34523
Bethesda, MD 20827
Phone: 301-229-4480
E-mail: jfloyd3208@aol.com

Focus Consulting Associates LLC
P.O. Box 516
Carmel, NY 10512
Phone: 845-225-1031
E-mail: brucekb@rcn.com

Goens/Esparo LLC
P.O. Box 271740
West Hartford, CT 06127-1740
Phone: 860-567-1945 or 860-284-9888
E-mail: gagoens@snet.net or esparoloumae@aol.com
Website: www.goensesparo.com

G. Tryon and Associates
P.O. Box 265
Johnston, IA 50131
Phone: 515-727-5807
E-mail: gtryon@mchsi.com

Harold Webb Associates
6532 Lost Horizon, Suite 201
Austin, TX 78759
Phone: 512-342-9777
E-mail: info@haroldwebb.com
Website: www.haroldwebb.com

Hazard, Young, Attea & Associates Ltd.
1151 Waukegan Road
Glenview, IL 60025
Phone: 847-724-8465
E-mail: hya@enteract.com
Website: www.hyasupersearches.com

Heidrick & Struggles International
Sears Tower
233 Wacker Drive, Suite 4200
Chicago, IL 60606-6303
Phone: 312-496-1200
Website: www.heidrick.com

Herbert William Consulting
P.O. Box 404
Avon, CT 06001
Phone: 860-673-9616
E-mail: SuperSearch@herbertwilliam.com
Website: www.herbertwilliam.com

Isaacson, Miller
334 Boyleston Street, Suite 500
Boston, MA 02116
Phone: 617-262-6500
E-mail: info@imsearch.com
Website: www.imsearch.com

J. A. Roy Associates
P.O. Box 582
Dennisport, MA 02639
Phone: 508-398-7257
E-mail: jaroyassoc@aol.com

Korn/Ferry International
1800 Century Park East, Suite 900
Los Angeles, CA 90067
Phone: 310-552-1834
Website: www.kornferry.com

Leadership Associates
23052-H Alicia Parkway
Mission Viejo, CA 92692
Phone: 949-461-9119
E-mail: CatherineWheeler@msn.com

McPherson & Jacobson LLC
P.O. Box 7346
Omaha, NE 68107
Phone: 888-375-4814
E-mail: mail@macnjake.com
Website: www.macnjake.com

N&P Educational Associates
5020 Neely Ave.
Guntersville, AL 35976
Phone: 256-582-8428
E-mail: hdpat54@aol.com

New England School Development Council
28 Lord Road
Marlborough, MA 01752
Phone: 508-481-9444
E-mail: nesdec@nesdec.org
Website: www.nesdec.org

Northwest Leadership Associates
724 Lancashire Lane
Liberty Lake, WA 99019
Phone: 509-255-6170
E-mail: dennisray@superintendentsearch.com
Website: www.superintendentsearch.com

PNR Associates
P.O. Box 765
Springfield, OR 97477
Phone: 541-747-3967
E-mail: pnrassoc@aol.com

PROACT Search
200 N. Jefferson St., Suite 100
Milwaukee, WI 53202
Phone: 414-347-0200
E-mail: info@proactsearchinc.com
Website: www.proactsearchinc.com

RBL Enterprises
1300 Clay St., Suite 600
Oakland, CA 94612
Phone: 510-622-7707
E-mail: rblenterprises@aol.com
Website: www.ruthlove.com

Ray and Associates
Executive Plaza Building
4403 First Avenue SE, Suite 407
Cedar Rapids, IA 52402-3221
Phone: 319-393-3115
E-mail: rayassoc@netins.net
Website: www.rayandassociatesonline.com

Richard Lerer Educational Consulting Services
57 Clarewood Drive
Hastings-on-Hudson, NY 10706
Phone: 914-478-7700
E-mail: lererecs@aol.com

Sockwell & Associates
227 W. Trade St., Suite 1930
Charlotte, NC 28202
Phone: 704-372-1865
E-mail: sjernigan@sockwell.com
Website: www.sockwell.com

Superior Search Systems
716 Beryl Drive
Kent, OH 44240
Phone: 330-677-0408
E-mail: mkonnert@kent.edu

TD and Associates
6818 Old 28th St. SE
Grand Rapids, MI 49546
Phone: 616-977-9980
E-mail: terredavis@aol.com

Western New York Educational Search Consultants
222 Baldy Hall
State University of New York at Buffalo
Buffalo, NY 14260-1000
Phone: 716-645-2932
E-mail: vcoppola@buffalo.edu

Wilson Riles and Associates
1140 Chargene Way
Sacramento, CA 95822
Phone: 916-448-0600
E-mail: priles@wredu.com
Website: www.wredu.com

APPENDIX C: SAMPLE SUPERINTENDENT'S CONTRACT

THIS CONTRACT, entered into this _____ day of _____, between the Board of Education, hereinafter called the "Board" and _____ hereinafter called "Superintendent." WITNESSETH:

1. DUTIES

The Superintendent agrees, during the period of this contract, to faithfully perform his/her duties and obligations in such capacity for the school district including, but not limited to, those duties required by the School Code. He/she will act as an advisor to the Board on matters pertaining to the school administration or the School District, and he/she will inform the Board as to administrative action taken on its behalf. The Superintendent shall recommend, effect, or cause to be effected, the policies and programs of the Board of Education as may be adopted. He/she will faithfully and diligently fulfill all the duties and obligations incumbent upon him/her as the executive head of the administrative section of the school system and the School District.

2. TERM

The Board agrees to employ _____ as Superintendent of its schools for the term of _____ years from _____ to and including _____.

The Board shall review this contract with the Superintendent annually, and shall, on or before March 31 of each ensuing year, take official action determining whether or not it is extended for an additional year and notify the Superintendent of its action in writing. If no action is taken by the Board, the contract shall be deemed to have been renewed for an additional year.

(OR SUBSTITUTE FOR PARAGRAPH 2)

The Board of Education shall, not later than March 31 of each year during the term of this contract, consider the extension of this contract for an additional one-year period.

3. EVALUATION
The Board shall evaluate the Superintendent, at least annually, using the criteria and an evaluation process mutually agreed to by the Board and the Superintendent.

4. TENURE
The Superintendent shall not be deemed to be granted continuing tenure in such capacity but shall be deemed to have been granted continuing tenure as an active classroom teacher in accordance with the provisions of the (state) Teacher Tenure Act.

5. PROFESSIONAL LIABILITY
The District agrees that it shall defend, hold harmless and indemnify Superintendent from any and all demands, claims, suits, actions and legal proceedings brought against Superintendent in his/her individual capacity, or in his/her official capacity as agent and employee of the District, provided the incident arose while Superintendent was acting within the scope of his/her employment and excluding criminal litigations. The Board shall provide public liability insurance for the Superintendent to cover legal expenses in defense of claims and payment of judgments resulting from his/her functioning as Superintendent and will reimburse him/her for any portion of such expense and judgments not covered by insurance. In no case will individual Board members be considered personally liable for indemnifying the Superintendent against such demands, claims, suits, actions and legal proceedings.

6. PROFESSIONAL GROWTH

The Superintendent may attend professional meetings at the local, state and national levels, the expenses of said attendance to be paid by the District.

The District shall reimburse the Superintendent for all reasonable expenses resulting from the performance of his/her duties as Superintendent.

7. PROFESSIONAL DUES

The District shall pay the Association dues of the Superintendent for the American Association of School Administrators, the (state) Association of School Administrators and the Region in which the School District is located, as well as other appropriate affiliations as approved.

8. MEDICAL EXAMINATION

The Superintendent agrees to have a comprehensive medical examination once every year. A statement certifying to the physical competency of the Superintendent shall be submitted to the President of the Board of Education and shall be treated as confidential information. The cost of said physical examination and reports shall be paid by the District.

9. COMPENSATION

The Board agrees to pay the Superintendent for his/her services during each year of said contract in equal installments unless otherwise agreed to by the parties. Compensation shall be $_____ annually. Said salary shall be reviewed annually and is subject to upward revision by agreement of the parties. In no case will the salary be lowered.

10. MOVING EXPENSES

The Board will pay expenses reasonably incurred for the moving of the furniture and furnishings from the Superintendent's present home to his/her new residence in _____, (state).

11. FRINGE BENEFITS

The Board of Education shall provide the Superintendent with the following benefits:

- Health, dental, vision and long-term disability insurance provided other administrative employees.

- Life insurance in the amount of _____ times his/her annual salary.

(OR)

- Life insurance in the amount of $_____.

- ____ sick days per year to be accumulated without limit. The Superintendent shall be awarded ___ days of accumulated sick leave upon
  approval of this agreement. (The second sentence applies if this is the
  Superintendent's initial contract.)

- ____ vacation days per year to be accumulated without limit. These
  shall be in addition to the holidays recognized by the District.

- ____ personal days per year.

- ____ days of bereavement leave not to be deducted from sick leave.

12. TRANSPORTATION

The Board shall provide the Superintendent with an automobile. The
School District will incur the cost of insurance and gasoline and all
maintenance costs of said vehicle.

(OR)

The Board shall provide the Superintendent with a monthly automobile
allowance of $_____.

(OR)

The Board shall reimburse the Superintendent ____ cents per mile for
use of his/her automobile in conducting business in accordance with the
position of Superintendent of Schools.

13. ANNUITY AND/OR DEFERRED COMPENSATION

The Superintendent shall annually receive a tax-deferred annuity in an
amount equal to _____ percent of salary.

(OR)

The Superintendent shall annually receive a tax-deferred annuity in the amount of $_____.

(OR)

The Superintendent shall annually receive deferred compensation in the amount of $_____.

14. TERMINATION PROVISIONS

The Superintendent shall be subject to discharge for good and just cause, but the Board shall not arbitrarily and capriciously dismiss him/her. No discharge shall be effective until written charges have been served upon him/her and he/she shall have an opportunity for a fair hearing before the Board after ten (10) days' notice in writing. Said hearing shall be public or private at the option of the Superintendent. At such hearing, he/she may have legal counsel at his/her own expense.

15. DISPUTE RESOLUTION

In the event of a dispute between the parties relating to any provision of this Agreement, or a dispute concerning any of the parties' rights or obligations as defined pursuant to this Agreement, the parties hereby agree to submit such to binding arbitration. Such arbitration shall be conducted under the rules of, and administered by, the American Arbitration Association. The arbitrator's fee and the expense of the American Arbitration Association shall be shared equally by the parties. All parties are entitled to have representation of their own designation; however, each party shall be responsible for the costs of such respective representation.

16. BREACH

In the event of a breach on the part of either party to this agreement, nothing contained herein shall be construed to render the obligations of either party under this agreement null and void.

IN WITNESS WHEREOF the parties hereto have set their hands the day and year above written.

By _____ Board President

By _____ Superintendent

SAMPLE CONTRACT ADDITIONS

PROFESSIONAL GROWTH

The Board shall provide the Superintendent _____ week(s) paid study leave plus necessary expenses in order to visit schools, attend an indepth conference or research a specific topic or goal. The Superintendent shall submit a brief report on the study leave to the Board.

(OR)

The District shall reimburse the Superintendent for all reasonable expenses incurred for successfully completed academic university courses including tuition, textbooks, mileage, meals and other necessary costs.

(OR)

To encourage professional growth, the Superintendent shall receive additional per diem pay for attendance at conferences and other professional development activities outside the district, not to exceed ___ days per year.

ADDITIONAL EXPENSES

The Board shall provide to the Superintendent a stipend of $_____, in addition to wages, fringes, and other compensation. This stipend is to assist the Superintendent with expenses such as contributions made for School District employee dinners, receptions, and miscellaneous expenses; fund-raising solicitations; service club related costs; expenses for his/her spouse at school-related dinners, receptions, etc.; and other costs associated with performance of duties connected with state and national professional association(s) and community service functions. The stipend shall be paid annually at the beginning of each fiscal year.

PAYMENT OF FICA COSTS

The Superintendent's compensation shall be increased by an amount equal to the employee contribution required annually by FICA.

PAY FOR PERFORMANCE/MERIT

In addition to the aforementioned salary, the Superintendent shall be eligible for a salary adjustment based upon the successful completion of the goals and/or performance objectives to be agreed upon within ninety (90) days of the signing of this agreement and subsequently prior to each designated school year.

The amount awarded to the Superintendent as pay for performance compensation shall/shall not be a permanent adjustment to the base salary.

(OR)

Upon successful completion of the following goals, the Superintendent's salary shall be increased by the accompanying amounts stipulated below:

Goal 1 ($5,000)

Student achievement will increase by _____ percent as measured by performance of the district's students on the 4th and 8th grades (state assessment).

Goal 2 ($5,000)

The district's audit of its financial records will show an excess of current revenues over expenditures at the close of the fiscal year.

Goal 3 ($5,000)

The Superintendent and his/her staff shall develop a comprehensive professional development program for the instructional staff.

Goal 4 ($_____)

For each category in which the Board awards a mean score of eight or better, on a 10-point scale, on the annual evaluation of the Superintendent, the Superintendent shall receive an additional $_____.

PAYMENT OF RETIREMENT SYSTEM CONTRIBUTIONS

The Board recognizes that the Superintendent participates in the Member Investment Plan of the (state) Public School Employees Retirement System. The Superintendent's compensation will be increased by an amount equal to the contributions required by participation in the System.

ADVANCED DEGREE

The Superintendent shall annually receive an amount equal to _____ percent of his/her base salary in recognition of his/her advanced degree.

(OR)

The Superintendent shall annually receive $_____ in recognition of his/her advanced degree.

LONGEVITY

After ___ years of service, the Superintendent shall annually receive an amount equal to _____ percent of his/her base salary.

(OR)

After ___ years of service, the Superintendent shall annually receive an additional $_____ in compensation.

PURCHASE OF ADDITIONAL SERVICE CREDIT
Universal Credit (where applicable)

For each _____ year(s) of satisfactory service, the Board shall purchase one year of universal retirement service credit in the (state) Public School Employees Retirement System on behalf of the Superintendent. This shall be considered an employer pickup contribution on behalf of the employee in lieu of contributions by the employee within the meaning of IRS Code Section 414(h)(2).

Military Service Time

The Board shall contribute to the (state) Public School Retirement System Fund a sufficient sum to entitle the Superintendent to service credit for years of military active duty service by him/her from _____ to _____, said payment to be made prior to _____, 20___. This shall be considered an employer pickup contribution on behalf of the employee in lieu of contributions by the employee within the meaning of IRS Code Section 414(h)(2).

Service Outside of the State of _____

For the 20____–20____ contract year, the Board shall pay $_____ to the (state) Public School Retirement System Fund to purchase out-of-state service credit earned by the Superintendent between July 1, 20____, and June 30, 20____, said payment to be made prior to _____, 20___. This shall be considered an employer pickup contribution on behalf of the employee in lieu of contributions by the employee within the meaning of IRS Code Section 414(h)(2).

LIFE INSURANCE

The Board shall during the term of this contract purchase and maintain a whole life insurance policy on the life of said Superintendent in the face amount of $_____ with the Board as beneficiary and owner. Should the Superintendent's employment be terminated for any reason by the Board, other than for reasonable and just cause, or should the Superintendent elect to retire or elect not to re-enter into a renewal of the contract, the Board shall assign such life insurance policy to the Superintendent without cost to him/her. In the event of the Superintendent's death during the term of employment provided for herein, twenty percent (20%) of the proceeds of the policy shall be retained by the School District and the remainder of the proceeds shall be paid by the School District to such beneficiary as the Superintendent may designate in writing filed with the secretary of the Board or, if no beneficiary is designated, in accordance with the last will and testament of the Superintendent or to his/her estate if he/she dies intestate.

(OR)

The Board shall purchase and keep in effect a universal term life insurance policy in the amount of $300,000. This shall be a continuous policy, with premium paid in full by the Board.

The Board's premium expense liability would end should the Superintendent terminate employment with the District. The policy, including all balances, shall be assigned and transferred to the Superintendent upon his/her termination or retirement.

The Board, as policy beneficiary, will pay the Superintendent's spouse, or survivors, $100,000 upon his/her death ($200,000 going to the Board); after five (5) years of employment and up to ten (10) years of employment, the Board will pay the Superintendent's spouse, or survivors, $200,000 upon his/her death ($100,000 going to the Board); after ten (10) years of employment, the entire $300,000 would be paid to the Superintendent's spouse or survivors.

(OR)

During the term of this contract, the Superintendent shall be furnished a fully paid group-term life insurance policy in an amount four times the Superintendent's gross salary, to a maximum of $_____ prior to age 70 and to a maximum of $_____ after age 70, payable to the beneficiary of the Superintendent's choice. In the event this agreement terminates by Superintendent's voluntary retirement or is occasioned by medical disability, Superintendent shall be furnished a fully paid group-term life insurance policy in an amount two times the Superintendent's gross salary at termination, to a maximum of $_____ , until said Superintendent reaches the age of seventy-five years, and in the amount of the Superintendent's gross salary at termination, to a maximum of $_____ , from the age of seventy-five years until the age of eighty years.

PHASE-IN DEFERRED COMPENSATION

The school district agrees to contribute to a deferred compensation program in the name of the Superintendent in the amount of $_____ annually, beginning with the school year 20___. Ownership in the accumulated value of such program shall vest to the Superintendent at the rate of 20% annually.

In case employment as Superintendent of schools of the district should end, for any reason, this agreement shall terminate. The vested portion of the program, as of the date, will be paid to the administrator or his/her estate.

FRINGE BENEFITS (ELECTION NOT TO RECEIVE)

In the event the Superintendent elects not to receive health, dental, vision, life or disability insurance, he/she shall receive additional salary in an amount equal to the annual premium of that insurance.
(This clause should be used only if you are definitely *not* going to receive insurance benefits. If this clause is contained in your contract and you elect to receive insurance benefits, those benefits could be considered taxable by the IRS.)

APPENDIX D: THE STRATEGIC PLAN

VISION AND MISSION

The first step in a strategic planning process is the identification or creation of the organization's vision and mission. The vision states the reasons for the organization's existence and the ideal it sets out to achieve. The mission identifies major goals defined within the framework of the organization's philosophy. An organization must be very clear in both its vision and its mission or it will not steer a clear course.

ENVIRONMENTAL SCAN

The next step is the environmental scan. This consists of an examination of the context in which the organization doing the planning operates and of the probable changes that appear likely to occur in that context over the period of the plan (usually the next five to ten years). Closely related to the environmental scan is an examination of organizational resources and capabilities.

A principal function of the environmental scan is to identify significant external and internal factors that the planning process needs to take into account and decide how to respond to. In an education institution the scan involves examining the organization itself in order to identify its principal strengths (resources and capabilities) and weaknesses (challenges) that help define the opportunities for improvement.

GAP ANALYSIS

A gap analysis is the process by which organizations evaluate the difference between their current position and desired future. As a result of the comparison and analysis, an organization can develop specific strategies and allocate resources to close the gap and achieve its desired state.

BENCHMARKING

Benchmarking is the process used to measure and compare the organization's operations, practices, and performance against others for the purpose of identifying best practices. Through an ongoing systematic benchmarking process, organizations can determine reference points for setting their own goals and targets.

STRATEGIC PROGRAMMING

Strategic programming is the development of strategies for achieving the mission of the organization. This includes setting strategic goals, developing action plans, and determining tactics.

- Strategic goals are the milestones the organization desires to achieve as it addresses the various issues identified through the gap analysis. One process used to achieve goals is the SMART goals model. SMART goals are Specific, Measurable, Agreed upon, Realistic, and Time/cost bound.
- Action plans define the steps taken to reach the strategic goals. (See the action planning worksheet in appendix E.)
- Tactics are specific actions used to achieve the strategic goals and implement the strategic plan.

EVALUATION OF STRATEGY

Periodic evaluations of strategies, tactics, and action programs are important in determining the level of success of the strategic planning process based on the effect of specific actions on both results and the organization's vision and mission.

REVIEW OF THE STRATEGIC PLAN

Following evaluation of the progress of the strategic planning process, the organization needs to review the strategic plan, make necessary changes, and adjust its course based on these evaluations.

APPENDIX E: ACTION PLANNING WORKSHEET

Goal: _____

_____

_____

_____

_____

Objective: _____

_____

_____

_____

_____

Strategy/Tactic: _____

_____

_____

_____

_____

_____

Action Step	Responsibility	Time Line

REFERENCES

1988 Deskbook Encyclopedia of American School Law. Rosemont, MN: Data Research, 1988.

The AAUW Report: How Schools Shortchange Girls. Washington, DC: AAUW Educational Foundation, 1992.

"Administrators' Views on Women in Higher Education," *The Chronicle of Higher Education*, v. 40, n. 1 (Almanac Issue, August 25, 1993): 46.

Ah Nee-Benham, K. P. Maenette, and Joanne E. Cooper. *Let My Spirit Soar: Narratives of Diverse Women in School Leadership.* Thousand Oaks, CA: Corwin Press, 1998.

Aisenberg, Nadya, and Mona Harrington. *Women of Academe: Outsiders in the Sacred Grove.* Amherst: University of Massachusetts Press, 1988.

"American Workers under Pressure." Technical Report, St. Paul Fire and Marine Insurance Company. St. Paul, MN: St. Paul Fire and Marine Insurance Company, 1992.

Anderson, Mark. "Induction Programs for Beginning Principals." Project paper of the Oregon School Study Council. Eugene: University of Oregon College of Education, 1988.

Archer, Jeff. "Survey Studies Barriers to Women Leaders," *Education Week*, March 5, 2003, pp. 1, 14.

Ashe, James S., John R. Haubner, and Nicholas F. Troisi. "University Preparation of Principals: The New York Study," *NASSP Bulletin* (September 1991): 145–150.

Austin, Nancy K. "Now about This Female Management Style . . ." *Executive Female*, v. 15, n. 5 (September/October 1992): 48–51.

Bacharach, Samuel, and Byran L. Mundell. "Organizational Politics in Schools: Micro, Macro, and Logics of Action," *Educational Administration Quarterly*, v. 29, n. 4 (November 1993): 423–452.

Baldrige, Letitia. *Complete Guide to Executive Manners*. New York: Macmillan, 1985.

Baldrige, Letitia. *New Complete Guide to Executive Manners*. New York: Macmillan, 1993.

Baldrige, Letitia. *New Manners for New Times: A Complete Guide to Etiquette*. New York: Simon and Schuster, 2003.

Ball, Karen. "Old-Boy Network: Women Denied Top-Level Jobs," *The Patriot News* (Harrisburg, PA), August 26, 1991, p. A5.

Banner, James M., Jr. "On Transforming Teaching into a True Profession," *Education Week*, October 23, 1985, p. 20.

Bass, Bernard M. *Stogdill's Handbook of Leadership*. New York: Free Press, 1981.

Bass, Bernard M. *Bass and Stogdill's Handbook of Leadership*. New York: Free Press, 1990.

Beekley, Cynthia. "Dancing in Red Shoes (Why Women Leave the Superintendency)," in Brunner, C. Cryss. *Sacred Dreams: Women and the Superintendency*. Albany: State University of New York Press, 1999.

Beekley, Cynthia. "Gender, Expectations, and Job Satisfaction: Why Women Exit the Public School Superintendency." Paper presented at the annual meeting of the American Educational Research Association, New York, 1996.

Belenky, Mary Field, et al. *Women's Ways of Knowing*. New York: Basic Books, 1986.

Bell, Colleen S. "Review of *Women in Educational Administration* by Charol Shakeshaft," *Educational Administration Quarterly*, v. 25, n. 3 (August 1989): 315–318.

Bem, Sandra L., and Daryl J. Bem. "Training the Woman to Know Her Place: The Social Antecedents of Women in the World of Work." Pennsylvania Department of Education, 1975.

Bennis, Warren. "The Executive's Fat-Free Reading Diet," *Executive Female*, v. 16, n. 4 (July/August 1993): 45–47.

Bennis, Warren. "The Leadership Advantage," *Leader to Leader*, v. 12 (Spring 1999): 18–23.

Bennis, Warren. *On Becoming a Leader*. Reading, MA: Addison-Wesley, 1989.

Berkson, I. B. (Isaac Baer). *Ethics, Politics and Education*. Eugene: University of Oregon Books, 1968.

Bernard, Jessie. *The Female World*. New York: Free Press, 1981.

Berry, Jane, and Richard Kushner. "A Critical Look at the Queen Bee Syndrome," *Journal of the National Association for Women Deans, Administrators, and Counselors*, v. 38 (Summer 1985): 117.

Bland, Jed. "About Gender: Testosterone and Aggression." 2004. www .gender.org.uk/about/06encrn/63_aggrs.htm.

Blaum, Paul A. "Attitude Influences First Impressions with the Boss," *Penn State Intercom*, April 22, 1993, p. 11.

Blount, Jackie M. *Destined to Rule the Schools: Women and the Superintendency*. New York: New York University Press, 1998.

Bolman, Lee G., and Terrence E. Deal. "Leading and Managing: Effects of Context, Culture, and Gender," *Educational Leadership Quarterly*, v. 28, n. 3 (August 1992): 314–329.

Bovee, Tim. "Pay: Women Get 75% of Men at Start and Gap Grows," *Evening News* (Harrisburg, PA), November 14, 1991, n.p.

Bredeson, Paul V. "Letting Go of Outlived Professional Identities: A Study of Role Transition and Role Strain for Principals in Restructured Schools," *Educational Administration Quarterly*, v. 29, n. 1 (1993): 34–68.

Broudy, Harry S. "Conflicts in Values," in Ohm, Robert E., and William G. Monahan, eds. *Educational Administration—Philosophy in Action*. Norman: University of Oklahoma Press, 1965, pp. 42–54.

Broudy, Harry S. *Truth and Credibility: The Citizen's Dilemma*. New York: Longman, 1981.

Brownmiller, Susan. *Femininity*. New York: Linden Press / Simon and Schuster, 1984.

Bruce, Michael G. "Women in Leadership," *Phi Delta Kappan*, v. 72, n. 5 (May 1991): 723–724.

Brunner, C. Cryss. *Principles of Power: Women Superintendents and the Riddle of the Heart*. Albany: State University of New York Press, 2000.

Brunner, C. Cryss. *Sacred Dreams: Women and the Superintendency*. Albany: State University of New York Press, 1999.

Brunner, C. Cryss, Margaret Grogan, and Cynthia Prince. "The American Association of School Administrators' National Study of Women Superintendents and Central Office Administrators: Early Findings," reprinted in *The Leadership Challenge*, Women's Caucus of the Pennsylvania Association of School Administrators, Hershey, PA, May 5–7, 2004.

Burleson, Clyde W. *Effective Meetings: The Complete Guide*. Indianapolis, IN: John Wiley & Sons, 1990.

Cantor, Dorothy W., and Toni Bernay, with Jean Stoess. *Women in Power*. Boston: Houghton Mifflin, 1992.

Capell, Perri. "Women Find Untraditional Ways to Network for Advancement," *The Wall Street Journal* online, November 8, 2004. www.careerjournal.com.

Carlson, Kenneth. "Review of *Revolving Doors: Sex Segregation and Women's Careers* by Jerry Jacobs," *Educational Administration Quarterly*, v. 26, n. 2 (May 1990): 187–195.

Carter, Graydon. "Editor's Letter," *Vanity Fair*, v. 57, n. 4 (1994): 10.

Chalker, Don, and J. Casey Hurley. "Beastly People," *The Executive Educator*, v. 15, n. 1 (January 1993): 24–26.

Chamberlain, Marian, ed. *Women in Academe: Progress and Prospects*. New York: Russell Sage, 1988.

Chase, Susan E. *Ambiguous Empowerment: The Work Narratives of Women School Superintendents*. Amherst: University of Massachusetts Press, 1995.

Clamp, Peter G. "Professionalism in Education: A State of Mind," *Education Digest* (October 1990): 53–56. (Reprinted from *Education Canada*, v. 29, pp. 12–15.)

Conran, Patricia Cannon. *School Superintendent's Complete Handbook*. Upper Saddle River, NJ: Prentice Hall, 1989.

Covey, Stephen R. *Principle-Centered Leadership*. New York: Simon and Schuster, 1990.

Covey, Stephen R. *The 7 Habits of Highly Effective People*. New York: Simon and Schuster, 1989.

Cramer, Gary W. "What Do Women Business Travelers Really Want?" *Penn State Intercom*, v. 23, n. 23 (March 3, 1994): 11.

Curry, Barbara K. *Women in Power: Pathways to Leadership in Education*. New York: Teachers College Press, Columbia University, 2000.

Cushman, Kathleen. "'So Now What?' Managing the Change Process," *Horace* (Coalition of Essential Schools newsletter, Brown University) (January 1993): 1–11.

Dalton, Margaret R. "Leaders for Learning: A Collaborative Learning Process," *The AASA Journal of Scholarship and Practice*, v. 1, n. 1 (Spring 2004): 14–18.

Davis, Beverly Irby, and Genevieve Brown. "Your Interview Image," *The Executive Educator*, v. 14, n. 6 (June 1992): 22–23.

Davis, Stephen, Linda Darling-Hammond, Michelle LaPointe, and Debra Meyerson. *School Leadership Study: Developing Successful Principals*. Review of Research. Stanford Educational Leadership Institute, commissioned by the Wallace Foundation, August 2005.

Deal, Terrence, Cheryl Lison, and Linton Deck. "Exits and Entrances," *The Executive Educator*, v. 15, n. 5 (May 1993): 26–28.

Dee, Catherine, ed. *50/50 by 2000: The Woman's Guide to Political Power*. National Association of Female Executives. Berkeley, CA: EarthWorks Press, 1993.

Demmon-Berger, Debbie. *The Superintendent's First Day in the Office*. Lanham, MD: Scarecrow Education, 2003.

Desjardins, Carolyn. "Gender Issues and Community College Leadership," *AAWCJC Journal* (1989): 5–6.

Desmond, Cheryl. "Using Positive Power." Presentation, Summer Institute for Service Learning, Center for Service Learning, Cabrini College, August 4, 1993.

Diener, Marc. "How to Beef Up Your Negotiating Game," *Entrepreneur*, August 2004, pp. 72–73.

Dimock, Hedley G. *Groups: Leadership and Group Development*. San Diego: University Associates, 1987.

Dolnick, Edward. "Super Women," *Health* (July/August 1991): 42–48.

Dowling, Colette. *The Cinderella Complex*. New York: Summit Books, 1981.

Doyle, Ruth H., and Barbara Mueller. "Cognitive Differences of Male and Female Administrators," *AAWCJC Journal* (1989): 17–19.

D'Souza, Dinesh. "The Visigoths in Tweed," *Forbes*, April 1, 1991, pp. 81–86.

Durbin, Karen. "Testosterone Poisoning," *Mirabella* (reprint, n.d., n.p.).

Dyer, Timothy J. "Leaders: We've Never Needed Them So Much," *NASSP NewsLeader*, v. 38, n. 6 (February 1991): 2.

Eagly, Alice H., Steven J. Karau, and Blair T. Johnson. "Gender and Leadership Style Among School Principals: A Meta-Analysis," *Educational Administration Quarterly*, v. 28, n. 1 (February 1992): 76–102.

Eby, Douglas. "What Keeps a Smart Woman Down? Gifted Women: The Search for Actualization," *Mensa Bulletin*, v. 333 (January/February 1990): 20–21.

Edson, Sakre Kennington. *Pushing the Limits: The Female Administrative Aspirant*. Albany: State University of New York Press, 1988.

Elmore, R. F. *Building a New Structure for School Leadership*. Washington, DC: Albert Shanker Institute, 2000.

Emerson, Ralph Waldo. *Self-Reliance*. 1841. In Blair, Walter, Theodore Hornberger, and Randall Stewart, eds. *The Literature of the United States*. Chicago: Scott Foresman, 1957, pp. 250–264.

"Employee Burnout: Causes and Cures." Report from Northwestern National Life Insurance Company. Minneapolis, MN: Northwestern National Life Insurance Company, 1992.

Epstein, Cynthia Fuchs. *Woman's Place: Options and Limits in Professional Careers*. Berkeley: University of California Press, 1971.

Eskey, Kenneth. "The World's Smartest," Scripps-Howard, news clipping, 1991, pp. A1–A3.

Faber, Mary. "Women in Education: How Far Can They Go?" *NEA Today*, v. 10, n. 4 (November 1991): 6.

Farmanfarmaian, Roxane. "Career Goodbyes," *Executive Female*, v. 16, n. 3 (May/June 1993): 36–39.

Fast, Julius. *The Incompatibility of Men and Women*. New York: M. Evans, 1971.

Fausto-Sterling, Anne. *Myths of Gender*. New York: Basic Books, 1985.

Fausto-Sterling, Anne. *Myths of Gender, Biological Theories about Women and Men*. New York: Basic Books, 1992.

Ferguson, Tim W. "At Risk in the Marketplace Instead of the Streets," *The Wall Street Journal*, April 27, 1993, p. A21.

Fisher, Roger, and William Ury. *Getting to Yes: Negotiating Agreement Without Giving In*. Boston: Houghton Mifflin, 1992.

Fleming, Karen A. "Mentoring: Is It the Key to Opening Doors for Women in Educational Administration?" *Education Canada*, v. 31, n. 3 (Fall 1991): 27–33 (ERIC EJ433466).

"Foil the Time Grabbers," *Executive Female*, v. 15, n. 4 (July/August 1992): 9–10.

Follo, Eric J., and Michael A. Lonze. "Selected Websites to Support Mastery of ISLLC Standards," *AASA Journal of Scholarship and Practice*, v. 1, n. 3 (Fall 2004): 14–19.

Fray, Lionel L. *How to Develop the Strategic Plan*, 2nd ed. Boston: American Management Association, 1987.

Friedan, Betty. *The Feminine Mystique*. New York: Dell, 1963.

Friedan, Betty. "My Quest for the Fountain of Age," *Time*, September 6, 1993, pp. 61–64.

Fullan, Michael. *Leading in a Culture of Change*. San Francisco: Jossey-Bass, 2001.

Gabler, June E. "Leadership: A Woman's View," in *Leadership: Examining the Elusive*. ASCD Yearbook, 1987, pp. 64–77.

Gardiner, Mary E., Ernestine Enomoto, and Margaret Grogan. *Coloring Outside the Lines: Mentoring Women into School Leadership*. Albany: State University of New York Press, 2000.

Gardner, John W. *Attributes and Context*. Leadership Papers 6. Washington, DC: Independent Sector, 1987.

Gardner, John W. *Leadership Development*. Leadership Papers 7. Washington, DC: Independent Sector, 1987.

Gardner, John W. *The Heart of the Matter: Leader-Constituent Interaction*. Leadership Papers 3. Washington, DC: Independent Sector, 1986.

Gardner, John W. *The Tasks of Leadership*. Leadership Papers 2. Washington, DC: Independent Sector, 1986.

Getzels, Jacob W., and Egon G. Guba. "Social Behavior and the Administrative Process," *School Review*, v. 65 (1957): 423–441.

Gilligan, Carol. *In a Different Voice*. Cambridge, MA: Harvard University Press, 1982.

Gilligan, Carol, Nona P. Lyons, and Trudy J. Hanner, eds. *Making Connections*. Cambridge, MA: Harvard University Press, 1990.

Gilman, David Alan, and Barbara Lanman-Givens. "Where Have All the Principals Gone?" *Educational Leadership* (May 2001): 72–74.

Glass, Thomas E. "The Slighting of Administrator Preparation," *The School Administrator* (April 1991): 29–30.

Glass, Thomas E. "Where Are All the Women Superintendents?" *The School Administrator*, v. 57, n. 6 (June 2000): 28–32.

Glazer, Judith S. "Feminism and Professionalism in Teaching and Educational Administration," *Educational Administration Quarterly*, v. 27, n. 3 (August 1991): 321–342.

Godfrey, Joline. *Our Wildest Dreams: Women Entrepreneurs Making Money, Having Fun, Doing Good*. New York: HarperBusiness, 1992.

Goldberg, Clara. "A Study of the Career Paths of Administrators in Central Office Positions in New York State Public Schools." Research Report, 1991 (ERIC ED341145).

Goldman, William. *Boys and Girls Together*. New York: Bantam Books, 1967.

Gordon, Meryl. "Discrimination at the Top," *Working Woman* (September 1992): 68–70+.

Gotwald, Norma, and Kathryn Towns. "Rare As They Are, Women at the Top Can Teach Us All," *The Executive Educator*, v. 8, n. 12 (December 1986): 13–14, 29.

Greene, Maxine. *Landscapes of Learning*. New York: Teachers College Press, Columbia University, 1978.

Greer, Germaine. *The Female Eunuch*. New York: McGraw-Hill, 1970.

Grier, Terry B., and Louis Trenta. "Landing the Big One," *The Executive Educator*, v. 14, n. 6 (June 1992): 20–22.

Griffin, Betsy Q. "Perceptions of Managers: Effects of Leadership Style and Gender." Paper presented at the thirty-eighth annual meeting of the Southeastern Psychological Association, Knoxville, TN, March 1992.

Grogan, Margaret. "Laying the Groundwork for a Reconception of the Superintendency from Feminist Postmodern Perspectives," in Young, Michelle D., and Linda Skrla, eds. *Reconsidering: Feminist Research in Educational Leadership*. Albany: State University of New York Press, 2003.

Grogan, Margaret. *Voices of Women Aspiring to the Superintendency*. Albany: State University of New York Press, 1996.

Grogan, Margaret, with Mary Gardiner and Ernestine Enomoto. *Coloring Outside the Lines: Mentoring Women into Educational Leadership*. Albany: State University of New York Press, 2000.

Grumet, Madeleine R. *Bitter Milk*. Amherst: University of Massachusetts Press, 1988.

Gupton, Sandra Lee, and Gloria Appelt Slick. *Highly Successful Women Administrators*. Thousand Oaks, CA: Corwin Press, 1996.

Gursky, Daniel. "Business Principals," *Teacher Magazine* (April 1992): 14–15.

Hallinger, Philip, and Joseph Murphy. "Developing Leaders for Tomorrow's Schools," *Phi Delta Kappan*, v. 72, n. 7 (March 1991): 514–520.

Halpin, Andrew W. *Manual for the Leadership Behavior Description Questionnaire*. Fisher College of Business, Ohio State University, 1957.

Hanson, E. Mark. *Educational Administration and Organizational Behavior*. Newton, MA: Allyn & Bacon, 1985.

Harnischfeger, Eileen. "How Networking Makes Us Better Managers," *Female Executive* (January/February 1994): 56.

Harris, Janet. *The Prime of Ms. America*. New York: G. P. Putnam's Sons, 1975.

Hart, Amy Weaver. "Reflection: An Instructional Strategy in Educational Administration," *Educational Administration Quarterly*, v. 29, n. 3 (August 1993): 339–363.

Hearn, Jeff, Deborah L. Sheppard, Peta Tancred-Sheriff, and Gibson Burrell, eds. *The Sexuality of Organization*. Newbury Park, CA: Sage, 1990.

Helgesen, Sally. *The Female Advantage: Women's Ways of Leadership*. New York: Doubleday, 1990.

Herbst, Jurgen. *And Sadly Teach*. Madison: University of Wisconsin Press, 1989.

Herman, Jerry J. "Don't Do It Yourself," *The Executive Educator*, v. 14, n. 11 (November 1992): 26–27.

Herman, Joan, Pamela R. Aschbacher, and Lynn Winters. *A Practical Guide to Alternative Assessment*. Alexandria, VA: ASCD, 1992.

Hill, Linda A. "Why Won't They Do What I Ask?" *Executive Female*, v. 15, n. 5 (September/October 1992): 13–20.

Hitchens, Christopher. "Sensitive to a Fault," *Vanity Fair*, v. 57, n. 4 (April 1994): 48–54.

Hole, Carol. "The Feminization of the Public Library," *Education Digest* (February 1992): 21–24.

Holmes, Natalie Carter. "Wondering What You're Worth? Use Savvy in Aiming for Top," *AASA Leadership News*, November 16, 1999.

Horner, Matina S. "Fail: Bright Women," *Psychology Today*, v. 2, n. 62 (1969): 36–38.

Houston, Paul. "Be Your Own Spin Doctor," *The Executive Educator*, v. 15, n. 6 (June 1993): 14–17.

Huffman, Frances. "Gender Gap," *Entrepreneur*, v. 21, n. 10 (October 1993): 46–48.

Huffman, Frances. "Taking the Lead," *Entrepreneur*, v. 21, n. 11 (November 1993): 96–101.

Hunt, Morton M. *Her Infinite Variety: The American Woman as Lover, Mate and Rival*. New York: Harper and Row, 1962.

Ihle, Elizabeth L. "Historical Perspectives on Women's Advancement in Higher Educational Administration." Paper presented at the annual meeting of the American Educational Research Association, Chicago, IL, April 3–7, 1991 (ERIC ED331381).

Illingworth, Montieth. "Citizen Gates," *Mirabella*, n. 57 (February 1994): 96.

"Institutional Policies to Improve Doctoral Education." Policy statement. AGS Task Force on Institutional Education, 1990.

Janeway, Elizabeth. *Between Myth and Morning*. New York: William Morrow and Co., 1974.

Johnson, Janet R. "Networking: How to Permeate the Glass Ceiling—Some Highlights from Recent Studies of Networking and Women." Paper presented at the annual meeting of the American Educational Research Association, Chicago, IL, April 3–7, 1991 (ERIC ED332356).

Johnsrud, Linda K. "Administrative Promotion: The Power of Gender," *The Journal of Higher Education*, v. 62 (1991): 119–149.

Kahn-Hut, Rachel, Arlene Kaplan Daniels, and Richard Colvard. *Women and Work: Problems and Perspectives*. New York: Oxford University Press, 1982.

Kanter, Rosabeth Moss. *Men and Women of the Corporation*. New York: HarperCollins / Basic Books, 1977.

Kaplan, George. "Shotgun Wedding: Notes on Public Education's Encounter with the New Christian Right," *Phi Delta Kappan*, v. 75, n. 9 (May 1994): 697–705.

Kaplan, Sheila, and Adrian Tinsley. "Women in Administration of Higher Education," *Education Digest* (December 1989): 25–27.

Kaukas, Dick. "Single-Sex Classes Found to Cut Failure Rate," *The Courier-Journal* (Indiana), September 16, 2003, p. B3.

Keever, Wythe. "Math and Science Crisis," *Sunday Patriot-News* (Harrisburg, PA), March 17, 1991, pp. D1–D2.

Kessler-Harris, Alice. *A Woman's Wage: Historical Meanings and Social Consequences* (The Blazer Lectures for 1988). Lexington: University Press of Kentucky, 1990.

Kimbrough, Ralph B., and Michael Y. Nunnery. *Educational Administration*, 2nd ed. New York: Macmillan, 1983.

Kleiman, Carol (*Chicago Tribune*). "Federal Official Focuses on 'Glass Ceiling' Issues," *Sunday Patriot-News* (Harrisburg, PA), July 11, 1993, p. F3.

Kohlberg, Lawrence. *The Philosophy of Moral Development: Moral Stages and the Idea of Justice* (Essays on Moral Development, vol. 1). New York: HarperCollins, 1981.

Konrad, Alison M., and Jeffrey Pfeffer. "Understanding the Hiring of Women and Minorities in Educational Institutions," *Sociology of Education*, v. 64, n. 3 (July 1991): 141–157 (ERIC EJ438420).

Kowalski, Theodore J. *Contemporary School Administration*, 2nd ed. Boston: Allyn & Bacon, 2003.

Leatherman, Courtney. "Colleges Hire More Female Presidents, but Questions Linger about Their Clout," *The Chronicle of Higher Education*, v. 38, n. 11 (November 6, 1991): A19–21.

Leighninger, Matt. "Working with the Public on Big Decisions." *The School Administrator* online edition, November 2003. www.aasa.org/publications.

Levin, Michael. *Feminism and Freedom*. New Brunswick, NJ: Transaction Books, 1987.

Lopata, Helena Z. *Occupation: Housewife*. New York: Oxford University Press, 1971.

Mahoney, James. "Do You Have What It Takes to Be a Super Superintendent?" *The Executive Educator*, v. 12, n. 4 (April 1990): 26–28.

Marsh, Barbara. "Women-Owned Businesses Attract a Lot of Attention," *The Wall Street Journal*, May 13, 1993, p. B2.

Martin, Chuck. *Managing for the Short Term*. New York: Doubleday, 2002.

Maslow, Abraham H. *New Knowledge in Human Values*. Chicago: Henry Regnery, 1959.

McGrath, Sue Thrasher. "Here Come the Women," *Educational Leadership* (February 1992): 62–64.

"The Memo Every Woman Keeps in Her Desk," *Executive Female*, v. 16, n. 4 (July/August 1993). Reprinted from *Harvard Business Review* (March/April 1993) by Kathleen Reardon.

"Men Versus Women: It's Different at the Top" (editorial), *The Executive Educator* (clipping, n.d.): 4–6.

Mertz, Norma T., and Sonja R. McNeely. "Getting to Be a Professor of Educational Administration: A Study of How Females 'Got' the Job." Paper presented at the annual meeting of the American Educational Research Association, Boston, MA, April 16–20, 1990 (ERIC ED320298).

Mertz, Norma T., and Sonja R. McNeely. "Groundbreakers: Females Who 'Succeed' in Male-Dominated Line Administrative Positions." Paper presented at the annual meeting of the American Educational Research Association, Boston, MA, April 16–20, 1990 (ERIC ED320299).

Mertz, Norma T., and Sonja R. McNeely. "What's Happening to School Administration: Gender in Line Administration," *Planning and Changing*, v. 19, n. 3 (Fall 1988): 166–177.

Miller, Lyle H., and Alma Dell Smith. "Your Personal Stress Action Plan," *Executive Female*, v. 16, n. 3 (May/June 1993): 29–35.

Milstein, Mike M. "The Danforth Program for the Preparation of School Principals (DPPSP) Six Years Later: What We Have Learned." Paper presented at the annual meeting of the University Council for Educational Administration, Minneapolis, MN, October 30–November 1, 1992 (ERIC ED355659).

Mims, Nancy Griffin. "A Study of Women's Perceptions of Administrative Opportunities in the Advent of the 21st Century." Paper presented at the Annual Conference of Women in Administration, Lincoln, NE, September 27–28, 1992 (ERIC ED352733).

Moir, Anne, and David Jessel. *Brain Sex: The Real Difference between Men and Women*. New York: Carol Publishing Group, 1991.

Molloy, John. "Women Needs Iron Fist in Velvet Glove to Climb," *Patriot Evening News* (Harrisburg, PA), October 22, 1993, p. C2.

Moran, Mary. "Up Against the Glass Ceiling," *The American School Board Journal* (February 1992): 38–41.

Murphy, Jerome T. "Superintendents as Saviors: From the Terminator to Pogo," *Phi Delta Kappan*, v. 72, n. 5 (March 1991): 507–513.

Murphy, Joseph. "Reculturing Educational Leadership: The ISLLC Standards Ten Years Out." National Policy Board for Educational Administration, September 2003.

Murphy, Joseph, and Amanda Datnow. *Leadership Lessons from Comprehensive School Reforms*. Thousand Oaks, CA: Corwin Press, 2003.

Murphy, Joseph, and Karen Seashore Louis, eds. *Handbook of Educational Administration*, 2nd ed. (A publication of the American Educational Research Association.) San Francisco: Jossey-Bass, 1999.

Nelton, Sharon. "Men, Women and Leadership," *The Nation's Business* (May 1991): 15–22.

Newmann, Fred, Bruce King, and Peter Youngs. "Professional Development That Addresses School Capacity." Paper presented at the annual meeting of the American Educational Research Association, New Orleans, April 2000.

Nicholson, John. *Men and Women: How Different Are They?* New York: Oxford University Press, 1985.

Noddings, Nel. *Caring: A Feminine Approach to Ethics and Moral Education.* Berkeley: University of California Press, 1984.

"Notebook," *The Chronicle of Higher Education*, v. 40, n. 24 (February 16, 1994): A41.

"Older Workers: The Good, the Bad, and the Truth," *Money*, v. 22, n. 4 (April/May 1993): 10.

O'Rourke, Carolyn L., and Rosemary Papalewis. "Women and Their Stories: Nine Case Studies in Educational Administration." Paper presented at the annual meeting of the California Educational Research Association, Burlingame, CA, November 16–17, 1989 (ERIC ED327978).

Pajak, Edward F., and Joseph J. Blase. "Teachers in Bars: From Professional to Personal Self," reprint. Originally appearing in *Sociology of Education*, v. 57 (1984): 164–173.

Pancrazio, Sally Bulkley. "Alternative Collegial Model-Based Forms of Networking Among Women, or Networking in the Nineties for the Professional Woman." Paper presented at the annual meeting of the American Educational Research Association, Chicago, IL, April 3–7, 1991 (ERIC ED333556).

Pavan, Barbara, and Judith McCloud D'Angelo. "Gender Differences in the Career Paths of Aspiring and Incumbent Educational Administrators." Paper presented at the annual meeting of the American Educational Research Association, Boston, MA, April 16–20, 1990 (ERIC ED321393).

The Pennsylvania School Law Book. New Cumberland, PA: Pennsylvania School Boards Association, 2001.

Peters, Thomas J., and Robert H. Waterman, Jr. *In Search of Excellence.* New York: Harper and Row, 1982.

Phillips, Kathryn. "Why Can't a Man Be More Like a Woman . . . and Vice Versa?" *Omni* (October 1990): 42–48, 68.

Pierce, Milli, and Deborah Stapleton, eds. *The 21st Century Principal.* Cambridge, MA: Harvard Education Press, 2003.

Pogrebin, Letty Cottin. *Getting Yours.* New York: David McKay, 1975.

Porat, Karin A. "Women in Administration: The Difference Is Positive," *The Clearing House*, v. 64, n. 6 (July/August 1991): 412–414.

Powell, Gary N. *Women and Men in Management.* Newbury Park, CA: Sage, 1988.

"The Preparation of School Administrators—A Statement of Purpose by the National Policy Board for Educational Administration," March 1990.

Professional Development Inventory, York County Assessment Center Pilot. Pennsylvania Association of Elementary and Secondary School Principals, Dennis Baughman, York County Director, 1986.

Professional Standards for the Superintendency. American Association of School Administrators brochure, 1993.

"Racial Bias: Honest Review Is Essential," *You and the Law*, v. 21, n. 6 (March 25, 1991): 4.

Regan, Helen B. "Not for Women Only: School Administration as a Feminist Activity," *Teachers College Record*, v. 91, n. 4 (Summer 1990): 565–577.

Reimer, Joseph, Diana Pritchard Paolitto, and Richard H. Hersh. *Promoting Moral Growth.* New York: Longman, 1979.

Reiss, Karla. "Coaching for Leadership," *Leadership* (January/February 2004): 13–15.

Reiss, Karla, "Why Coaching Matters," *The School Administrator*, v. 60, n. 10 (November 2003): 16–18.

Restine, L. Nan. *Women in Administration: Facilitators for Change.* Newbury Park, CA: Corwin Press, 1993.

Ries, Paula, and Delores H. Thurgood. *Summary Report 1992: Doctorate Recipients from United States Universities.* Washington, DC: National Academy Press, 1992.

"The Right Moves," *Entrepreneur*, v. 21, n. 12 (December 1993): 160.

Rooney, Joanne. "Survival Skills for the New Principal," *Educational Leadership* (September 2000): 77–78.

Rosenblatt, Roger. "Sexual Bigotry," *Life* magazine, December 1991.

Rosener, Judy B. "Ways Women Lead," *Harvard Business Review* (November/December 1990): 119–125.

Rossi, Peter H., and Howard E. Freeman. *Evaluation: A Systematic Approach.* Newbury Park, CA: Sage, 1993.

Rudolph, Barbara. "Why Can't a Woman Manage More Like . . . a Woman?" *Time* (Special Issue, Fall 1990): 53.

Russell, Anne M. "How to Wing It at Golf," *Executive Female*, v. 15, n. 5 (September/October 1992): 62–63.

Sandroff, Ronni. "Between Lives," *Executive Female*, v. 16, n. 5 (September/October 1993): 36–39.

Saphier, Jon, Tom Bigda-Poyton, and Geoff Pierson. *How to Make Decisions That Stay Made.* Alexandria, VA: ASCD, 1989.

Schmuck, Patricia A. "Networking: A New Word, A Different Game," *Educational Leadership*, v. 43, n. 5 (February 1986): 60–61.

Schneider, Ann M. "Mentoring Women and Minorities into Positions of Educational Leadership: Gender Differences and Implications for Mentoring."

Paper presented at the annual conference of the National Council of States on In-service Education, Houston, TX, November 21–26, 1991 (ERIC ED344843).

Schneider, Gail T., and Lynn Wallich. "Assessment Centers as Avenues to Administrative Career Advancement," *Planning and Changing*, v. 21, n. 4 (Winter 1990): 225–238.

Schouten, Fredreka. "Superintendent/Board Relationships: An Interview with Anne Bryant." Monograph for the 2002 AASA Women Administrators Conference, Washington, DC, November 1–3, 2002.

Schuster, Daphne J., and Tom H. Foote. "Differences Abound Between Male and Female Superintendents," *The School Administrator*, v. 47, n. 2 (February 1990): 14–16, 18–19.

Scott, Jennifer. "The Linguistic Production of Genderlessness," in Young, Michelle D., and Linda Skrla, eds. *Reconsidering: Feminist Research in Educational Leadership*. Albany: State University of New York Press, 2003.

Scott, Jennifer. *The New Superintendency*. Greenwich, CT: JAI Press, 2001.

"The Secret Advantage," *Working Woman* (August 1993): 146.

Sergiovanni, Thomas J. "The Dark Side of Professionalism in Educational Administration," *Phi Delta Kappan*, v. 72, n. 5 (March 1991): 521–526.

Sergiovanni, Thomas J., Martin Burlingame, Fred S. Coombs, and Paul W Thurston. *Educational Governance and Administration*. Boston: Allyn & Bacon, 1992.

Settles, I. *Marketing Yourself: A Handbook for Educational Administration Applicants*. Olympia, WA: Washington Association of School Administrators, 1983.

Shakeshaft, Charol. "The Gender Gap in Research in Educational Administration," *Educational Administration Quarterly*, v. 25, n. 4 (November 1989): 324–337.

Shakeshaft, Charol. *Women in Educational Administration*. Newbury Park, CA: Sage, 1987.

Shakeshaft, Charol, Irene Nowell, and Andy Perry. "Gender and Supervision in School Personnel," from *Theory into Practice*, v. 30, n. 2 (February 1991): 134–139. Reprinted in *Education Digest* (February 1992): 14–17.

Sharp, Helen M., and William L. Sharp. "Ten Tips for Better Writing," *The Executive Educator*, v. 15, n. 8 (August 1993): 33–34.

Sheehy, Gail. "The Flaming Fifties," *Vanity Fair*, v. 56, n. 10 (October 1993): 270–273+.

Sheehy, Gail. *Passages*. New York: Bantam, 1977.

Short, Paula M., and James S. Rinehart. "Reflection as a Means of Developing Expertise," *Educational Administration Quarterly*, v. 29, n. 4 (November 1993): 501–521.

"Sidelines," *The Chronicle of Higher Education*, v. 40, n. 22 (February 2, 1994): A29.

Silver, Susan. *Organized to Be the Best!* 4th ed. Los Angeles: Adams-Hall, 2000.

Skrla, Linda. "Mourning Silence: Women Superintendents Rethink Speaking Up and Speaking Out," in Young, Michelle D., and Linda Skrla, eds. *Reconsidering: Feminist Research in Educational Leadership*. Albany: State University of New York Press, 2003.

Skrla, Linda. "Normalized Femininity: Reconsidering Research on Women in the Superintendency," in Young, Michelle D., and Linda Skrla, eds. *Reconsidering: Feminist Research in Educational Leadership*. Albany: State University of New York Press, 2003.

Smith, Leslie. "Don't Ignore Body Language," *Executive Female*, v. 16, n. 6 (November/December 1993): 57.

Smith, Leslie. "Learn the Crucial Difference Between Networking and Selling," *Executive Female*, v. 15, n. 5 (September/October 1992): 82.

Smith, Marguerite T. "How to Fight Age Bias and Come Out Ahead," *Money*, v. 22, n. 3 (March 1993): 22.

Smulyan, Lisa. *Balancing Acts: Women Principals at Work*. Albany: State University of New York Press, 2000.

Snowden, Lynn. "The Roots of Rejection," *Working Woman* (September 1992): 72–74+.

Sobehart, Helen C., and Kara L. Giron. "Athena as Mentor." Monograph for the 2002 AASA Women Administrators Conference, Washington, DC, November 1–3, 2002.

Splitt, David. "Should You Sue for Defamation?" *The Executive Educator*, v. 15, n. 6 (June 1993): 35, 37.

Staines, Graham, Carol Tavris, and Toby Epstein Jayaratne. "The Queen Bee Syndrome," *Psychology Today* (January 1974): 55–59.

Starratt, Robert J. "Building an Ethical School: A Theory for Practice in Educational Leadership," *Educational Administration Quarterly*, v. 27, n. 2 (May 1991): 185–202.

Stopp, Margaret T. "'Just Joking' or Sexual Harassment?" *Women in Higher Education*, v. 2, n. 6 (June 1993): 9.

Stover, Del. "Education Is Getting Serious About Administrator Preparation," *The Executive Educator*, v. 12, n. 4 (April 1990): 18–20.

Strengthening Support and Recruitment of Women and Minorities to Positions in Education Administration: A Resource Manual. U.S. Department of Education, Office of Educational Research and Improvement, 1992.

Strike, Kenneth A., Emil J. Haller, and Jonas F. Soltis. *The Ethics of School Administration*. New York: Teachers College Press, 1988.

Summary Report of American Association of School Administrators. Data on dissertations awarded. 1992.

Surrey, Janet. "Self-in-Relation: A Theory of Women's Development," Work in Progress n. 13, Stone Center for Developmental Services and Studies. Wellesley, MA: Wellesley College, 1985.

Swiss, Deborah J., and Judith P. Walker. "Fast Track Moms," *Executive Female*, v. 16, n. 6 (November/December 1993): 44–47+.

"Take It Like a Woman," *Entrepreneur*, v. 21, n. 4 (April 1993): 186.

Tallerico, Marilyn. *Accessing the Superintendency: The Unwritten Rules*. Newbury Park, CA: Sage, 1999.

Tallerico, Marilyn. "Women and the Superintendency," in Brunner, C. Cryss. *Sacred Dreams: Women and the Superintendency*. Albany: State University of New York Press, 1999.

Tallerico, Marilyn, Joan Burstyn, and Wendy Poole. "Gender and Politics at Work: Why Women Exit the Superintendency." Monograph. Fairfax, VA: The National Policy Board for Educational Administration, 1993.

Tallerico, Marilyn, et al. "Gender and Politics at Work: Why Women Exit the Superintendency." Research report sponsored by the Danforth Foundation. Fairfax, VA: National Policy Board for Educational Administration, August 1993 (ERIC ED361911).

Tannen, Deborah. *Talking from 9 to 5*. New York: William Morrow, 1994.

Tannen, Deborah. "Teachers' Classroom Strategies Should Recognize That Men and Women Use Language Differently," *The Chronicle of Higher Education*, v. 37, n. 40 (June 19, 1991): B2–3.

Tannen, Deborah. *You Just Don't Understand: Women and Men in Conversation*. New York: William Morrow, 1990.

Tanner, C. Kenneth, Carl J. Schnittjer, and Truman T. Atkins. "Effects of the Use of Management Strategies on Stress Levels of High School Principals in the United States," *Educational Administration Quarterly*, v. 27, n. 2 (May 1991): 203–224.

Thompson, Katherine P. Interview, Curwensville, PA, July 19, 1993.

Titus, Harold H., and Morris Keeton. *Ethics for Today*, 5th ed. New York: D. Van Nostrand, 1973.

Tomaszewski, Maciej. Abstract, Scientific Sessions 2003 of the American Heart Association, Orlando, FL, November 9–12, 2003.

Toufexis, Anastasia. "Coming from a Different Place," *Time* (Special Issue, Fall 1990): 64–66.

Tunick, George. "Continuing Confessions," *Executive Female*, v. 16, n. 2 (March/April 1993): 78.

Vail, Kathleen. "The Changing Face of Education," *Education Vital Signs*, a supplement to *American School Board Journal*, v. 188, n. 12 (December 2001): 39–42.

Villani, Susan. *Are You Sure You're the Principal? On Being an Authentic Leader*. Thousand Oaks, CA: Corwin Press, 1999.

Wall, Thomas J. "Working Smarter," *Executive Educator*, v. 16, n. 4 (April 1994): 48–51.

Wallace, Mike. "How to Handle Bad News," *The Rotarian*, v. 163, n. 6 (December 1993): 16–17.

Watkins, Michael. *The First 90 Days: Critical Success Strategies for New Leaders at All Levels*. Boston: Harvard Business School Press, 2003.

Wellner, Alison Stein. "Everyone's a Critic," *Inc. Magazine* (July 2004): 38.

Wentworth, Marylyn. "The Dynamics of Change: Understanding and Achieving Community," *Doubts and Certainties: Newsletter for the NBA Mastery in Learning Project*, v. 3, n. 8 (April 1989): 1–3.

"Where Are All the Women Superintendents?" *The American School Board Journal*, v. 177, n. 9 (September 1990): 8.

Whitaker, Kathryn S., and Kenneth Lane. "What Is 'a Woman's Place' in Educational Administration?" *The School Administrator*, February 1990. Reprinted in *Education Digest* (November 1990): 12–15.

Wilson, Meena. "The Search for Teacher Leaders," *Educational Leadership* (March 1993): 24–27.

Winkler, Karen. "Scholar Whose Ideas of Female Psychology Stir Debate Modifies Theories, Extends Studies to Young Girls," *The Chronicle of Higher Education*, v. 36, n. 36 (May 23, 1990): A6–A7.

Witmer, Judith T. "Alumni—Your Best Hidden Asset! Part One," *Connections*, v. 1, n. 1 (Fall 1993): 1–3+.

Witmer, Judith T. "Alumni—Your Best Hidden Asset! Part Two," *Connections*, v. 1, n. 2 (Spring 1994): 1–3.

Witmer, Judith T. "The Case for Training Educational Administrators in Making Ethical Decisions." EdD dissertation, Temple University, 1989.

Witmer, Judith T. "The Case for Training Educational Administrators in Making Ethical Decisions," in Landers, Thomas J., ed. *Education Leadership: German and American Perspectives*. Papers from the International Conference on Educational Leadership, Cologne, West Germany, June 27–30, 1989. Washington, DC: International Council on Educational Leadership, pp. 177–193.

Witmer, Judith T. "Gifted Girls, Wise Women: The Challenge to Educators," *Information Legislative Service Bulletin*, Pennsylvania School Boards Association, April 1992, pp. 11–13.

Witmer, Judith T. "Interviewing Know-How." Presentation to Women's Caucus, Southeastern Region of Pennsylvania School Administrators Association, Ft. Washington, PA, March 4, 1993.

Wolcott, Lisa. "Like Father, Like Son?" *Teacher Magazine* (January 1991): 22–23.

Wolfe, Warren (*Minneapolis–St. Paul Star Tribune*). "Older Workers Rated Much-Neglected Resource," *Sunday Patriot-News* (Harrisburg, PA), December 5, 1993, p. F3.

Wolter, Romanus. "Take No for an Answer: Don't Dismiss Naysayers—Ask for Advice and Turn It into a Tool for Success," *Entrepreneur* (October 2004): 128.

Women Administrators in New York State Public Schools, 1968–1991. Albany, NY: Information Center on Education, New York State Education Department, 1992.

"Women a Minority of Tenured Faculty and Administrators," Associated Press, February 17, 2004. www.cnn.com/2004/EDUCATION/02/17/women.on .campus.ap.

"Women in School Administration: Overcoming the Barriers to Advancement," *WEEA Digest* (Women's Educational Equity Act) sponsored by the Office of Educational Research and Improvement, Washington, DC. Newton, MA: Education Development Center, August 1990 (ERIC ED 360753).

Yeager, Neil, and Lee Hough. *Power Interviews*. New York: John Wiley & Sons, 1990.

Yeats, William Butler. "Among School Children." 1926. In G. B. Harrison, ed. *Major British Writers*. New York: Harcourt, Brace & World, 1967, p. 999.

Young, Michelle D., and Linda Skrla, eds. *Reconsidering: Feminist Research in Educational Leadership*. Albany: State University of New York Press, 2003.

Zirkel, Perry A., Sharon Nalbone Richardson, and Steven S. Goldberg. *A Digest of Supreme Court Decisions Affecting Education*, 4th ed. Bloomington, IN: Phi Delta Kappa International, 2001.